Lecture Notes in Computer Science　　8924

Commenced Publication in 1973
Founding and Former Series Editors:
Gerhard Goos, Juris Hartmanis, and Jan van Leeuwen

More information about this series at http://www.springer.com/series/7409

Javier Lopez · Indrajit Ray
Bruno Crispo (Eds.)

Risks and Security of Internet and Systems

9th International Conference, CRiSIS 2014
Trento, Italy, August 27–29, 2014
Revised Selected Papers

 Springer

Editors
Javier Lopez
University of Málaga
Málaga
Spain

Bruno Crispo
University of Trento
Trento
Italy

Indrajit Ray
Colorado State University
Fort Collins, CO
USA

ISSN 0302-9743   ISSN 1611-3349   (electronic)
Lecture Notes in Computer Science
ISBN 978-3-319-17126-5   ISBN 978-3-319-17127-2   (eBook)
DOI 10.1007/978-3-319-17127-2

Library of Congress Control Number: 2015937937

Springer Cham Heidelberg New York Dordrecht London

Printed on acid-free paper

Springer International Publishing AG Switzerland is part of Springer Science+Business Media
(www.springer.com)

Preface

These are the post-proceedings of the 9th International Conference on Risks and Security of Internet and Systems (CRiSIS 2014). The purpose of the conference is to bring together researchers to explore risks and security issues in Internet applications, networks, and systems. Each year papers are presented covering topics including trust, security risks and threats, intrusion detection and prevention, access control, and security modeling.

In response to the call for papers, 48 papers were submitted to the conference. These papers were evaluated on the basis of their significance, novelty, and technical quality. Each paper was reviewed by at least three members of the Program Committee. The Program Committee meeting was held electronically with intensive discussion over a period of ten days. Of the papers submitted, 13 full papers and 6 short papers were accepted for their inclusion in these post-proceedings.

The conference program also included an invited talk by Edgar Weippl (Director of SBA Research and Associate Professor at the Vienna University of Technology) and three tutorials, respectively, given by instructors Josep Domingo-Ferrer and Jordi Soria-Comas (University Rovira-Virgili, Spain), Esma Aïmeur (University of Montreal, Canada), and Yury Zhauniarovich (University of Trento, Italy). The tutorials are also included in these post-proceedings.

We are grateful to the many people who contributed to the success of the conference. First, to the members of the Program Committee and external reviewers, who performed an excellent job and contributed with long and interesting discussions. Our gratitude also goes to Seconomics and Tenace Research Projects, as well as to the University of Trento, for their support to the organization of the conference. Last, but not least, the conference would not be possible without the authors who submitted their papers, the presenters, and the attendees.

August 2014

Javier Lopez
Indrajit Ray
Bruno Crispo

CRiSIS 2014
9th International Conference on Risk and Security of Internet and Systems

Trento, Italy
August 27–29, 2014

Organized by
University of Trento
Italy

Program Committee Chairs

Javier Lopez   University of Málaga, Spain
Indrajit Ray   Colorado State University, USA

General Chair

Bruno Crispo   University of Trento, Italy

Publicity Chairs

Muhammad Rizwan Asghar   CREATE-NET, Italy
Joaquin Garcia-Alfaro   IIR – TELECOM Bretagne, France

Tutorial Chair

Nora Cuppens-Boulahia   TELECOM Bretagne, France

Program Committee

Marco Carvalho	Florida Institute of Technology, USA
Yu Chen	Binghamton University, SUNY, USA
Jorge Cuellar	Siemens AG, Germany
Rinku Dewri	University of Denver, USA
Frédéric Cuppens	TELECOM Bretagne, France
Nora Cuppens-Boulahia	TELECOM Bretagne, France
Sabrina De Capitani di Vimercati	Università degli Studi di Milano, Italy
Roberto Di Pietro	Università di Roma Tre, Italy
Juan M. Estevez-Tapiador	University Carlos III of Madrid, Spain
Jose M. Fernandez	École Polytechnique de Montréal, Canada

Simon Foley	University College Cork, Ireland
Rose Gamble	University of Tulsa, USA
Dimitris Gritzalis	Athens University of Economics & Business, Greece
Stefanos Gritzalis	University of the Aegean, Greece
Mina Guirguis	Texas State University, USA
Igor Kotenko	SPIIRAS, Russia
Sokratis Katsikas	University of Piraeus, Greece
Jean-Louis Lanet	University of Limoges, France
Jorge L. Hernandez-Ardieta	INDRA, Spain
Fabio Martinelli	CNR, Italy
Refik Molva	EURECOM, France
Martin Olivier	University of Pretoria, South Africa
Xinming Ou	Kansas State University, USA
Brajendra Panda	University of Arkansas, USA
Guenther Pernul	Universität Regensburg, Germany
Joachim Posegga	University of Passau, Germany
Kai Rannenberg	Goethe University Frankfurt, Germany
Kaliappa Ravindran	City University of New York, USA
Craig Rieger	Idaho National Laboratory, USA
Michael Rusinowitch	Inria, France
Pierangela Samarati	Università degli Studi di Milano, Italy
Sachin Shetty	Tennessee State University, USA
Sejun Song	University of Missouri–Kansas City, USA
Miguel Soriano	Polytechnic University of Catalonia, Spain
Alex Sprintson	Texas A&M University, USA
Ketil Stoelen	SINTEF, Norway
Jianying Zhou	I2R, Singapore

External Reviewers

Ashraf Al Sharah	Sascha Koschinat	Rolf Schillinger
Bastian Braun	Leanid Krautsevich	Fredrik Seehusen
Shaoying Cai	Olav Ligaarden	Bjørnar Solhaug
Andrey Chechulin	Manolis Maragoudakis	George Stergiopoulos
Elena Doynikova	Antony Martin	Santiago Reinhard Suppan
Gencer Erdogan	Weizhi Meng	Welderufael Tesfay
Jérôme François	Alexios Mylonas	Markus Tschersich
Ludwig Fuchs	Dimitrios	Nick Virvilis
Wolfram Gottschlich	Papamartzivanos	Fengguo Wei
Adrian Granados	Juan Parra	Shuzhe Yang
Abdessamad Imine	Henrich C. Pöhls	Artsiom Yautsiukhin
Vasanth Iyer	Andreas Reisser	Loai Zomlot
Christos Kalloniatis	Panagiotis Rizomiliotis	
Miltos Kandias	Igor Saenko	

Contents

Detecting Anomalies in Printed Intelligence Factory Network

Matti Mantere, Mirko Sailio, and Sami Noponen(✉)

VTT Technical Research Centre of Finland, Kaitoväylä 1, 90570 Oulu, Finland
matti.mantere@gmail.com,{mirko.sailio,sami.noponen}@vtt.fi
http://www.vtt.fi

Abstract. Network security monitoring in ICS, or SCADA, networks provides opportunities and corresponding challenges. Anomaly detection using machine learning has traditionally performed sub-optimally when brought out of the laboratory environments and into more open networks. We have proposed using machine learning for anomaly detection in ICS networks when certain prerequisites are met, e.g. predictability.

Results are reported for validation of a previously introduced ML module for Bro NSM using captures from an operational ICS network. The number of false positives and the detection capability are reported on. Parts of the used packet capture files include reconnaissance activity.

The results point to adequate initial capability. The system is functional, usable and ready for further development. Easily modified and configured module represents a proof-of-concept implementation of introduced event-driven machine learning based anomaly detection concept for single event and algorithm.

Keywords: Anomaly detection · Cybersecurity · Machine learning · Network security monitoring · SCADA network · ICS network

1 Introduction

Using machine learning algorithms for network anomaly detection systems has been under investigation for several years. The approach has faced challenges particularly when faced with open networks after development in e.g. laboratory environment [28]. We have proposed that while machine learning based anomaly detection might be infeasible in certain types of environments as claimed in [28], it could well be applicable in other environments. The basic underlying idea is that the approach should be feasible when used in restricted environments, such as industrial control system (ICS) networks [17,18].

Based on our previous investigations and the related work, e.g. [12,16,18], it seems that machine learning based anomaly detection should be a very feasible approach for ICS networks. Therefore it should be feasible for the network discussed in Sect. 3.4 that is used as a source for traces in this work. The network in question is a control network of a printed intelligence factory located in Oulu,

© Springer International Publishing Switzerland 2015
J. Lopez et al. (Eds.): CRiSIS 2014, LNCS 8924, pp. 1–16, 2015.
DOI: 10.1007/978-3-319-17127-2_1

Finland and is further discussed in Sect. 3.4. The test network is of limited size and complexity, but represents a real-world environment. It is explicitly not a laboratory setup just for anomaly detection development purposes.

When comparing our solution to related work reviewed in Sect. 2 and existing systems, our system is the first published extension module for Bro NSM implementing artificial neural network (ANN) algorithm and in particular self-organizing maps (SOM) algorithm [13]. ANN in general and also SOM algorithm have been investigated for anomaly detection purposes e.g. in [11,26] and the algorithm in itself has no novelty claim for use in this purpose besides being targeted for use in ICS environments. The SOM implementation for Bro NSM is a single-event and single-algorithm PoC implementation of a event-driven machine learning anomaly detection (EMLAD) concept, which is explicitly introduced in Sect. 3.7. Our implementation targets solely the restricted and ICS networks. The stateful nature of the underlying Bro NSM system [27] allows us to use network state information in a flexible manner and combine this with data for the individual events to obtain feature vectors for the learning. Additional information, such as information from individual packets and their payload can also be used, but these have not yet been implemented for the presented system.

In this paper we report on the performance and detection rates of the initial implementation and introduce the EMLAD concept.

The structure of this paper follows the standard model. After the introduction we provide a short Section on related work Sect. 2. Related work is followed by section on materials and methods Sect. 3 in which we present a summarization of our implementation and updates as well as test network, operation, learning phase and detection rates in their respective subsections. The EMLAD concept is presented in Sect. 3.7. After this there are the sections on results Sect. 4, discussion and conclusions in Sect. 5, followed by acknowledgements.

2   Related Work

This Sect. 2 discussing the related work contains much of the same information as in the authors previous papers [18,19].

Use of machine learning algorithms for network security monitoring and anomaly detection has been studied extensively. The self-organizing maps algorithm has also been researched and deployed for this purpose, such as in the work presented in the papers [11,25,26].

Work presented in [11] leverages hierarchical SOM using SOM-PAK [1] and uses Bro logs as input. The approach presented also uses some identical features as the initial implementation of the SOM module used in this paper. These features are connection duration and the data sent by the originator and responder of an terminated connection.

Work presented in paper [26] investigates a multilevel hierarchical approach and comparison to a single level approach, which is what we use here. The work presented in paper [14] investigates the training of neural network anomaly detectors for intrusion detection purposes and also brings up the challenge of the variability present in most networks. Work in [10] investigates the usage of fuzzy SOM's in place of the classical SOM implementation as presented in [13]. The issues related to the convergence of SOM algorithm are discussed in detail in [5].

In one of the papers that are most important for our work [28] Sommer *et al.* discuss the applicability of machine learning for network intrusion detection and the challenges faced by the system as it is transported out of the laboratory and into the open world. This work has been instrumental for our work in mapping the difficulties of using machine learning for intrusion or anomaly detection.

In paper [9] Hadeli *et al.* presents investigations for leveraging determinism in ICS network for anomaly detection, this stands in contrast to the challenge of diversity and variability for more open networks as stated in [14]. Linda *et al.* in paper [16] describe a neural network based method for detection intrusions in critical infrastructure settings with good test results. The paper by Yang *et al.* [34] also investigates the intrusion detection through anomaly -based approach presenting interesting work. Important previous work that we are building upon also includes other more generic seminal work done on intrusion and anomaly detection such as presented in the papers [3,30].

The work presented by Lin *et al.* in [15] describes a new protocol parser for Bro specifically meant for a protocol used in supervisory control and data acquisition (SCADA) systems, namely DNP3. The advancement of the Bro in the field of SCADA systems is very important for the continuation of the work presented in this paper and therefore of great interest. The ability to parse most SCADA protocols would enable a machine learning approach to use protocol specific information as a basis of additional features. Relevant information on Bro is available in [2,4,8,31,32].

Our previous research concerning this topic was lastly presented in the papers [18,19].

Usage of SOM or ANN for anomaly detection purposes carries no novelty claim in itself. The novelty claim of the work presented in this paper is tied to the application for a novel domain with a novel, configurable implementation which is not dependent on SOM_PAK [1]. The domain being the Printocent ICS network and the implementation being pure Bro NSM scripting language. The SOM represents early proof-of-concept implementation of an machine learning module for the Bro NSM framework. The system is to incorporate several machine learning algorithms and to handle several different Bro NSM events. This includes events particular to protocols such as DNP3 and Modbus. Modbus has also been accurately modeled for IDS use in SCADA networks [7], which would provide good feature candidates. The additional algorithms are still being implemented.

3   Materials and Methods

The SOM ANN module is implemented as a normal optional extension for Bro [23] using the scripting language implemented by the system. The system is not intended as a stand-alone solution for network security monitoring needs. The system seeks to complement other NSM's by providing an easily configurable system which adapts to the network environment semi-automatically.

For the SOM algorithm [13] a number of features were implemented. The feature set from which the user can select from includes a number of connection specific features, as well as a number of features derived from the current network state as reported by Bro's internal functions. The highly stateful nature of the Bro allows us to use the network state information it has stored as additional features. The user can select from a set connection specific information as well as the network state information for the subset of features he wishes to use when training the system and finally using for detection.

The system learns the normal connections and state of the network. It reports as anomaly any terminating connection, network state or combination of these which differs from previously seen input to an certain value. The difference is user configurable variable which represent the euclidean distance between input and SOM neuron feature vectors. User can configure a multitude of actions as a response to an anomaly using the Bro scripts. At the moment the possible anomaly is merely logged. It is important that the data used for teaching the system does not contain connections that should later on be classified as possible anomalies by the system.

It is also noteworthy that Bro handles UDP and ICMP message flows as connections based on internal logic [23]. This definition of ICMP and UDP flows is used when discussing UDP or ICMP connections in our work.

Other tools used for supporting the work include the applications used for packet capturing and analysis. Such as Tcpdump and Wireshark [29,33]. Anomalies were embedded using tools such as Nmap, Nikto and Nessus [20–22].

The network traffic used for the proof-of-concept implementation was derived from the MAXI [24]. It represents a pristine setup which is deterministic and cyclic with up-to-date architectural documentation available for reference. The network environment, captured data used and anomalies implanted into the network traces are described in Sect. 3.4.

3.1   Machine Learning Module Implementation

The current proof-of-concept level implementation is presented in the [19], and the SOM algorithm structure follows the standard SOM structure [13] with a number of configurable parameters. The implementation allows the envisioned end-user to tune the system to his or her needs by setting various attributes and variables defined in the configuration file. New functionality has also been implemented. These include alternative neighborhood function, ability to update SOM only for connections representing a selected transport protocol. The system has also been modified to allow user to configure what events will be handled by what machine learning algorithm. Currently only SOM functionality for the "connection_state_remove" Bro event is usable. Other functionality is still being designed and implemented.

The implementation of the module makes use of the core Bro functionality. In addition to the normal connection information, the SOM functionality uses

Bro's internal functions for retrieving the network state at the time of the logging of a terminating connection as well. The module currently requires no changes to the core Bro installation. This was a cleanup done to improve the ease of installation and use alongside other Bro functionality after the [19].

For general information on the SOM algorithm, it is advisable to refer to the Kohonen's book on the subject [13]. The following papers provide good insights into using SOM for anomaly detection: [11,25,26].

3.2 Features

The features used and their combination controls the efficacy of a machine learning based anomaly detection system [16]. The decision on features is therefore one of the important research topics as discussed earlier also by the authors of this paper in [18].

Currently the implementation exists for the features depicted in Table 1 with the ICMP connection feature added since the initial system depiction. The first four features are based on the network state information as reported by the Bro NSM. UDP and ICMP connection features represent the Bro NSM's opinion of UDP and ICMP flows handled as pseudo-connections [23]. The rest of the features are connection specific information based on individual terminated connections. Normalization is done using maximum previously seen values for features with corresponding transport protocol. These features have been used in other combinations by other authors as well, e.g. [11] in which the authors use connection duration and bytes sent as features for SOM.

Table 1. Implemented features for SOM extension

1	The number of live TCP connections at the moment of connection termination
2	The number of live UDP connections at the moment of connection termination
3	The number of live ICMP connections at the moment of connection termination
4	Overall network fragments pending reassembly by Bro
5	Duration of a connection that terminated
6	The amount of data (bytes) sent by connection responder
7	The amount of data (bytes) sent by connection originator
8	Number of packets sent by the connection responder
9	Number of packets sent by the connection originator

3.3 Operation

The system operates in two modes: learning mode and detection mode. After a long enough a learning phase, the map is assumed to have converged sufficiently and reached a stable enough state for testing. If testing reveals a sub-optimal but stable representation is reached, it is advisable to scrap the map and then initialize and teach a new one. SOM convergence is an open subject with no complete existing theoretical solution [5].

The detection mode requires that the learning mode has been run beforehand and the SOM model saved as a separate file, or the system is in automatic mode and the SOM lattice is in memory already. The SOM file also contains the features that were selected at the time of its initialization and all the other relevant parameters modified during learning phase. The SOM module retrieves this information from the file as well when instructed to use a ready SOM lattice. For the either of the modes several variables can be set to control the systems operation and sensitivity.

For the Bro logging framework additional alarm type has been defined for possible anomalies seen as deducted by the SOM algorithm. The new alarm type is accompanied by the additional information on which was the closest neuron in the SOM lattice for which the euclidean distance was greater than pre-set alert distance `delta`.

3.4   Test Network and Packet Capture Data

The packet captures used for testing the system were recorded from the network of the MAXI printing line of the Printocent pilot factory for printed electronics. The system represents a state-of-the-art installation of its kind and was deployed during 2012 [24]. It is the world's first printed intelligence pilot factory that is capable of mass production.

The target network consists of Siemens Simatics S7 and Rexroth industrial controllers, 10 Human-Machine interface (HMI) panels, maintenance laptop, and our monitoring setup. All of the devices are in the same subnetwork. HMI-panels communicate constantly to the S7 controller with regular intervals.

We have placed a network tap in the environment for recording the network traffic. The traffic is recorded with a standard Ubuntu laptop with two separate network interfaces that are both connected to the tap. Both sides of the traffic capture are merged into a single daily capture and archived to the hard drive. TCPdump [29] is used for recording of the traffic, and mergecap is used for merging the files. The unique protocol count found from the captures is low. Only two application layer protocols are used for messaging between the panels and controllers: Siemens S7 proprietary communications protocol and PROFINET. Standard network protocols such as ARP, LLDP, and DHCP was also detected.

Table 2. Network attributes

1	Relatively fresh environment
2	Limited number of protocols
3	Stable when operational
4	Deterministic to a degree
5	Cyclic with roughly one day cycle

The network represents a limited size and deterministic environment to test an anomaly detection aimed at ICS networks using Internet protocol (IP) based communication schemes. The system is also undergoing a degradation of its initial clean installation base, showing the iterative process of adding and removing equipment and tuning various functionalities. Table 2 lists the attributes important for leveraging our anomaly detection approach for this specific network.

3.5   SOM Learning

For teaching the SOM we used packet captures beginning from the fourth of January 2013 to 27th of June 2013 and the feature vector of **tcp_connections, udp_connections, icmp_connections, duration, orig_data_sent, resp_data_sent, orig_packets_sent, resp_packets_sent, fragments**. The individual full day packet captures were merged to form a single packet capture file. The packet capture file encompassed 103 daily capture files with a total size of 32GB. The average size of a single daily capture file therefore being roughly 314MB. The accurate statistics are displayed in Table 3. It is noteworthy that number of connections in Table 3 is the number of connections as reported by Bro NSM according to its interpretation of ICMP and UDP flows as connections for this purpose. Average rates of units per time unit had to be derived from individual packets and averages derived from these values due to the merged capture file duration including the empty periods. These empty periods were days when the system was non-operational or night-time when it is also shut down.

The average daily packet rates and sizes for the period used for teaching the SOM are depicted also in the Fig. 1. The information shows that there is little daily variance. On the average these attributes see little fluctuation between different days. This also supports the usage of the type of anomaly detection we are using, pointing to at least some level of determinism in the network.

While teaching the system, we had to initialize several maps, before coming up with one that produced an suitable lattice. The system suffers from a tendency to converge divergent traffic to the same neurons, due to them still representing the closest one. Initializing multiple instances might be necessary to initially come up with a viable SOM representation of the network environment. Using different neighborhood functions and sizes was also required. Currently there are two neighborhood functions based on modified Gaussian distribution and Ricker wavelet functions that can be used.

3.6   Detection Rates

For testing the system we used packet captures for one day. Five captures without any embedded anomalies were used with out any further action, to test the rate of false positives.

In the second batch, capture files were first tested without any changes and then with the changes and additions. The anomalous events were embedded manually to the captures off-line to avoid causing any issues with the operations of the printed intelligence factory. This was done by merging the two packet captures, MAXI and the scans. For our monitoring approach, this manner of merging anomaly traffic with the clean traffic should cause no bias to the detection rates.

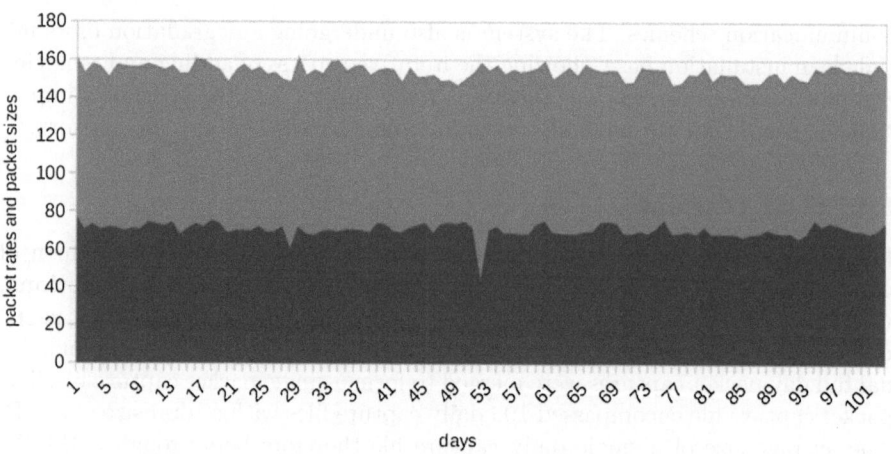

Fig. 1. Average daily packet rates and sizes for the selected SOM teaching range

Table 3. Statistics of captures used for teaching SOM. Time range: 1/4/2013 to 6/27/2013

Number of individual connections	184100
Number of daily captures	103
Number of packets in captures	199440667
Size of the merged capture file	33927 MB
Average daily captured data	298 MB
Average packet size in merged file	154 B
Average packet rate in captures	70.738 packets/s
Average byte rate in captures	10914.7 B/s
Average duration of capture files in range	27364.9 s

The injected anomalies represent reconnaissance events. Namely scans by Nmap [22], Nessus [20] and Nikto [21]. These represent port scans and vulnerability scans. For the first dirty packet capture, three nmap scans were embedded by running scan against the monitoring device itself. For the latter four dirty traces, a clean trace of single day was used, and different types of anomalous same day scans were merged to the file to create several files with anomalies embedded. The information on the type of capture files and embedded reconnaissance anomalies are itemized in Table 5. The packet captures used for testing were not part of the captures used for teaching the SOM in the earlier phase.

As we can see from the Table 6 there were a number of false positives in all of the traces used for testing. This false positive value fluctuated, ranging from a single false positive to 28, occurring at the end of the day when the TCP connections terminated to several of the TCP connections in addition to UDP connections during the day.

Table 4. Statistics as averages of dirty test captures with anomalies: Dx_d and without embedded anomalies Dx_c

Capture	Byte rate	Pkt. rate	Packets	Pkt. size
$D1_c$	10751 B/s	70.98 p/s	2005 K	151.47 B
$D1_d$	10762 B/s	71.12 p/s	2009 K	151.33 B
$D2_c$	11130 B/s	71.93 p/s	2193 K	154.87 B
$D2_d$	11352 B/s	73.86 p/s	2251 K	153.69 B
$D3_d$	13086 B/s	81.22 p/s	2480 K	161.12 B
$D4_d$	11144 B/s	72.02 p/s	2195 K	154.75 B
$D5_d$	11143 B/s	72.00 p/s	2194 K	154.78 B

The detection statistics for the dirty as well as clean captures listed in Table 5 are itemized in the Table 6. In the Table 6 F_p denotes false positives and A_p all positives whether true or false. Statistics of the dirty traces and their clean counterparts are presented in the Table 4. It is noteworthy that the statistics of the clean versions of D2,D3,D4 and D5 are all identical to $D2_c$ as the same day capture was used for embedding different anomalies in.

For test trace 1D with three embedded Nmap scans the detection of an anomaly was clear. The system reported over 1 K of possible anomalous connections, or an anomalous combination of connection and network context. The number of anomalous connections in relation to the false positives in the clean file was considerable.

For the test trace 2D and for the embedded Nikto scan, the results were also clear, the system reported over 10 K of potential anomalies, compared to the two false positives in the clean file. Nikto was not used with any stealth attributes enabled in this case.

For the test trace 3D there was a Nessus scan embedded. The scan was not exactly silent, and our system reported a very significant increase in the number of connections when compared to the normal situation of around 2–3 K of connections per day. Nessus is not an actual reconnaissance tool, but it can used as such if detection is not an issue.

For the test trace 4D we embedded an Nmap scan with just UDP port scan. This attack was less obvious compared to the others, but still caused an increase of 47 new anomalous connections reports compared to the two false positives normally present in the particular trace files clean version.

For the test trace 5D a Nmap scan with operating system detection was used. This again resulted in an obvious anomalous situation reported by the system, with over 1 K of anomalous connections logged.

3.7   Event-Driven Machine Learning Anomaly Detection Concept

The Event-driven machine learning anomaly detection (EMLAD) core concept is the usage of network events, such as produced by systems like Bro NSM,

Table 5. Captures used for training and testing

Training capture:	A merged clean capture file including 103 full day traffic captures in the range of 1/4/2013 to 6/27/2013
Test capture 1C:	7/16/2013: Clean packet capture file
Test capture 2C:	7/17/2013: Clean packet capture file
Test capture 3C:	7/18/2013: Clean packet capture file
Test capture 4C:	9/12/2013: Clean packet capture file
Test capture 5C:	9/30/2013: Clean packet capture file
Test capture 6C:	10/07/2013: Clean packet capture file
Test capture 1D:	9/11/2013: Dirty packet capture file. Three Nmap scans, one basic scan directed at our own machine responsible for monitoring and two more scans with -A flag (Enable OS detection, version detection, script scanning, and traceroute)
Test capture 2D:	10/10/2013: Dirty packet capture file. Nikto scan against a web server host set up for this purpose. Dirty trace created by merging recorded scan and clean traffic
Test capture 3D:	10/10/2013: Dirty packet capture file. Nessus scan against a web server host set up for this purpose. Dirty trace created by merging recorded scan and clean traffic
Test capture 4D:	10/10/2013: Dirty packet capture file. Nmap UDP port scan on a host set up for this purpose. Dirty trace created by merging recorded scan and clean traffic
Test capture 5D:	10/10/2013: Dirty packet capture file. Nmap operating system detection routine against a host set up for this purpose. Dirty trace created by merging recorded scan and clean traffic

to produce machine learning models specific to that single event. The events can be of a higher or lower abstraction level, thus modeling network activity on that same such level of abstraction. The event data can also be enriched by network context data, such as is stored by Bro NSM and shared between possible cluster nodes [27]. The EMLAD concept core is depicted in the Fig. 2. The events produced by the Bro NSM core are handled by different machine learning algorithms. Each machine learning algorithm instance is specific to the Bro core event it is handling. Multiple instances of the same algorithm can be in use, but each use their own stored model. Multiple algorithms can also be used to handle the same algorithm.

The network events produced by Bro represent different level of specificity. The are more general events, such as an event for termination of a connection, including ICMP and UDP pseudo-connections and more specific ones, such as generated for a modbus write single register response.

As an example, given that specific Modbus/TCP event that the Bro is capable of producing:

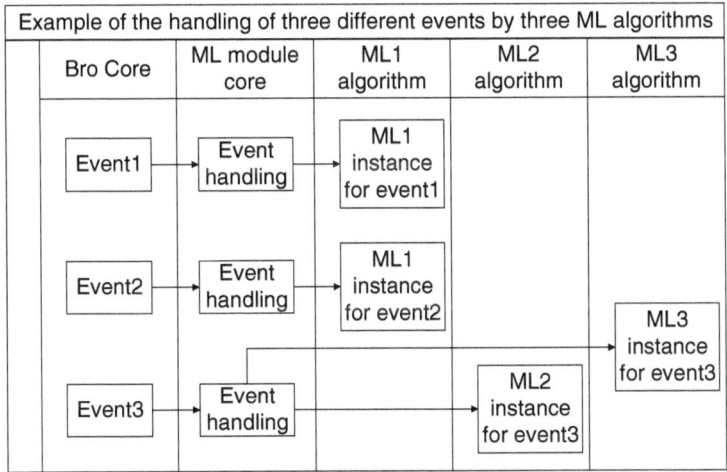

Example of the handling of three different events by three ML algorithms				
Bro Core	ML module core	ML1 algorithm	ML2 algorithm	ML3 algorithm
Event1	Event handling	ML1 instance for event1		
Event2	Event handling	ML1 instance for event2		ML3 instance for event3
Event3	Event handling		ML2 instance for event3	

Fig. 2. Event-driven machine learning approach (EMLAD) concept

modbus_write_single_register_response which has the following type: event (c: connection, headers: ModbusHeaders, address: count, value: count, an algorithm could be instructed to handle only these particular events. Depending on the environment this could be a very resource expensive action to perform. However, a visibility on the actual value transmitted using the modbus protocol could be accessed and the algorithm could learn the way it varies. This would allow for a very fine grained protocol-specific detection of anomalies.

On the other hand, handling the network termination connection as was implemented in the PoC [19]. Allows for a higher-level representation to be modeled by the system. Different attributes and anomalies would be visible by interpreting the information provided by the different network events produced by the Bro. Combining a selected set of these events, algorithms and features, henceforth called the **detection set** would allow for monitoring the network on multiple different levels simultaneously. The output produced by the constituencies of a specific detection set could also be correlated to further screen for possible anomalies causing changes across different events.

Network state information stored by the NSM system can also be used to provide context features for the event handlers. This was accomplished in the PoC by using information of live TCP, UDP and ICMP connections as features with the connection termination event. Bro NSM interprets UDP and ICMP as types connections for certain purposes [23].

4 Results

Due to the system using context information as well, even normal terminating connections can be reported as anomalous, due to the fact that the context has changed so much that the feature vectors with the connection information are too different from any of the previously seen traffic. For this reason the system

Table 6. Detection statistics: F_p for false positives and A_p for all positives

Capture	F_p	A_p	Whether anomalies were detected, not counting false positives
1C:	1	1	NA
2C:	1	1	NA
3C:	1	1	NA
4C:	3	3	NA
5C:	28	28	NA
6C:	11	11	NA
1D:	13	>1 K	Yes, over 1 K anomalous connections reported
2D:	2	>10 K	Yes, over 10 K anomalous connections reported
3D:	2	>150 K	Yes, over 150 K anomalous connections reported
4D:	2	58	Yes, but with a more subtle number of reported possible anomalies
5D:	2	>1 K	Yes, over 1 K anomalous connections reported

is prone to producing extensive amount of possible anomaly notifications in the case of actual anomalies in the network for the duration of the anomaly. For anomalies with longer durations this enables the user to easily verify that there is some sort of an anomaly ongoing, but also hinders the usability of the system log files due to their large size.

It is notable, that most if not all of the false positives are triggered by the same group of connections. The false positives in 5 C are suspect to be caused by an unspecified maintenance or upgrade activity in the environment, the nature of which we are still investigating. This change did not persist, and for the capture 6 C we still see less false positives. The false positives we see are the same ones occurring for 1D as well. The false positives in trace 1D were caused by a group of TCP connections, most of which could have been weeded out by raising the detection threshold by a value of 0.02 and the current threshold being 0.05.

Also the network environment used had a variable operational period each day, starting in the morning and being shutdown sometime during the afternoon. The duration of the TCP connections reflected this, as did the transmitted data and packets. Therefore, using the duration and data transmission statistics as features is troublesome. As the printed intelligence factory reaches maturity, this element of reduced determinism should be eliminated.

Expanding the implemented Bro NSM module to include more of the EMLAD concept is also deemed feasible based on the experiences with the single-event single-algorithm approach tested.

5   Discussion and Conclusions

It is likely that the system would have yielded improved performance should the used packet captures been very close to the ones used for testing. Currently there were several months between the latest capture used for learning, and the last packet capture file used for testing. However, as no major changes were reported by researchers handling the environment, this was not seen as a major issue. In operational environments, it is necessary to fall back to the learning phase after changes are made in to the system. It is also acknowledged that Nikto and Nessus are rather noisy tools for actual covert reconnaissance operations in the mode they were used while the Nmap might present a more realistic approach.

More features, algorithms and event handlers are needed for the EMLAD approach. Especially events specific to the industrial control system protocols present. Protocol parser for Bro for the Siemens proprietary protocol would enable us to develop much more accurate and specific features. Work such as presented in the paper [15] is very beneficial for the improvement of our approach as well using Bro as the core system.

Optimization of the learning phase and providing mechanisms to prevent the SOM algorithm from converging to sub-optimal states is required. Currently the learning phase requires manual tuning of the parameters to produce a viable SOM lattice. Also, in an operational situation the monitoring setting in the test network should be adjusted so that more of the network traffic would be available to the monitoring device.

The system was capable of detecting the types of reconnaissance and vulnerability scanning methods used for testing. The number of false positives remains an issue, even while it can be argued that they were constantly similar in nature due to the environments lack of determinism in the particular feature of operational time each day. This resulted in fluctuating duration and total data transmission amounts for the TCP connections which were open for the entire duration of the day.

Even while the system is currently capable of detecting that something is going on in the test cases, finding the actual cause might be difficult at first. Due to the context features, even normal network traffic will be reported as anomalous due to the shifting context values in their input feature vectors. This creates a situation where the output available in anomalous situation might not be as helpful as desired. This is something that needs to be addressed in the future. However, even the functionality of reporting that something is wrong and that there is an anomaly present, corresponds to our expectations of the system at this phase of its development and underlying research.

Further work into providing support for optimization of the system, implementing new features and fine tuning is under way. The system is also being rewritten to incorporate handling of different Bro events. The user is intended to be able to select what machine learning algorithm to use, the feature set used for that algorithm and the events handled. For example: A Modbus/TCP protocol specific event `modbus_write_single_register_response` could be handled by a Restricted Boltzmann Machine (RBM) with a feature vector of $(X)^1$ whereas a `connection_state_remove` could be handled by a SOM with a feature vector of $(X)^2$. RBM algorithm is currently being implemented, but is still unfinished for testing. The RBM algorithm is investigated for anomaly detection purposes in Paper [6] and is reported as usable for the purpose.

This manner of handling separate network events generated by the Bro NSM by separate instances of machine learning algorithms is presented as an example of the EMLAD concept. This concept is a subject of further study. Further implementation, testing in new environments and with more sophisticated attacks and anomalies is required to further evaluate the performance of the MBM and the EMLAD concept.

Acknowledgments. The research presented in this paper was mainly done as a collaborative effort in two research projects at VTT: VTT funded project called INCYSE or Industrial Cyber Security Endeavour and SASER, which is a Celtic+ project funded by TEKES in Finland.

References

1. The Self-Organizing Map Program Package. http://www.cis.hut.fi/research/som_pak/. (Accessed July 2 2013)
2. Bro NSM. http://www.bro.org/. (Accessed February 12 2013)
3. Denning, D.: An intrusion-detection model. IEEE Trans. Softw. Eng. **SE-13**(2), 222–232 (1987)
4. Dreger, H., Feldmann, A., Paxson, V., Sommer, R.: Predicting the resource consumption of network intrusion detection systems. In: Lippmann, R., Kirda, E., Trachtenberg, A. (eds.) RAID 2008. LNCS, vol. 5230, pp. 135–154. Springer, Heidelberg (2008). http://www.dx.doi.org/10.1007/978-3-540-87403-4_8
5. Erwin, E., Obermayer, K., Schulten, K.: Self-organizing maps: Ordering, convergence properties and energy functions. Biol. Cybern. **67**, 47–55 (1992)
6. Fiore, U., Palmieri, F., Castiglione, A., Santis, A.D.: Network anomaly detection with the restricted boltzmann machine. Neurocomputing Adv. Cogn. Ubiquitous Comput. **122**, 13–23 (2013). http://www.sciencedirect.com/science/article/pii/S0925231213005547. Advances in cognitive and ubiquitous computing
7. Goldenberg, N., Wool, A.: Accurate modeling of modbus/tcp for intrusion detection in SCADA systems. Int. J. Crit. Infrastruct. Prot. **6**(2), 63–75 (2013). http://www.sciencedirect.com/science/article/pii/S1874548213000243
8. Gonzalez, J.M., Paxson, V.: Enhancing network intrusion detection with integrated sampling and filtering. In: Zamboni, D., Kruegel, C. (eds.) RAID 2006. LNCS, vol. 4219, pp. 272–289. Springer, Heidelberg (2006). doi:10.1007/11856214_14. http://dx.doi.org/10.1007/11856214_14
9. Hadeli, H., Schierholz, R., Braendle, M., Tuduce, C.: Leveraging determinism in industrial control systems for advanced anomaly detection and reliable security configuration. In: IEEE Conference on Emerging Technologies Factory Automation, ETFA 2009, pp. 1–8 (2009)
10. Hu, W., Xie, D., Tan, T., Maybank, S.: Learning activity patterns using fuzzy self-organizing neural network. IEEE Trans. Syst. Man Cybern. Part B Cybern. **34**(3), 1618–1626 (2004)
11. Kayacik, H., Zincir-Heywood, A., Heywood, M.: A hierarchical som-based intrusion detection system. Eng. Appl. Artif. Intell **20**(4), 439–451 (2007). http://dx.doi.org/10.1016/j.engappai.2006.09.005
12. Knapp, E.: Industrial network security: securing critical infrastructure networks for smart grid, SCADA, and other industrial control systems. Elsevier Science (2011). http://books.google.fi/books?id=Et9u-mxq0B4C

13. Kohonen, T., Schroeder, M.R., Huang, T.S. (eds.): Self-Organizing Maps. Springer, New York (2001)
14. Lee, S., Heinbuch, D.: Training a neural-network based intrusion detector to recognize novel attacks. IEEE Trans. Syst. Man Cybern. Part A Syst. Hum. **31**(4), 294–299 (2001)
15. Lin, H., Slagell, A., Di Martino, C., Kalbarczyk, Z., Iyer, R.K.: Adapting bro into scada: building a specification-based intrusion detection system for the dnp3 protocol. In: Proceedings of the Eighth Annual Cyber Security and Information Intelligence Research Workshop, CSIIRW 2013, pp. 5:1–5:4. ACM, New York (2013). http://doi.acm.org/10.1145/2459976.2459982
16. Linda, O., Vollmer, T., Manic, M.: Neural network based intrusion detection system for critical infrastructures. In: Proceedings of the 2009 International Joint Conference on Neural Networks, IJCNN 2009, pp. 102–109. IEEE Press, Piscataway (2009). http://dl.acm.org/citation.cfm?id=1704175.1704190
17. Mantere, M., Uusitalo, I., Sailio, M., Noponen, S.: Challenges of machine learning based monitoring for industrial control system networks. In: 2012 26th International Conference on Advanced Information Networking and Applications Workshops, March 2012
18. Mantere, M., Sailio, M., Noponen, S.: Network traffic features for anomaly detection in specific industrial control system network. Future Internet **5**(4), 460–473 (2013). http://www.mdpi.com/1999-5903/5/4/460
19. Mantere, M., Sailio, M., Noponen, S.: A module for anomaly detection in ics networks. In: Proceedings of the 3rd International Conference on High Confidence Networked Systems, HiCoNS 2014, pp. 49–56. ACM, New York (2014). http://doi.acm.org/10.1145/2566468.2566478
20. Nessus Vulnerability Scanner. http://www.tenable.com/products/nessus/. Accessed 2 January 2014
21. Nikto2 Web Server Scanner. https://www.cirt.net/nikto2/. Accessed 3 February 2014
22. Nmap Network Security Scanner. http://www.nmap.org/. Accessed 2 July 2013
23. Paxson, V.: Bro: a system for detecting network intruders in real-time. Comput. Netw. **31**(23–24), 2435–2463 (1999). http://www.sciencedirect.com/science/article/pii/S1389128699001127
24. PrintoCent. http://www.printocent.net. (Accessed 6 January 2013)
25. Ramadas, M., Ostermann, S., Tjaden, B.C.: Detecting anomalous network traffic with self-organizing maps. In: Vigna, G., Kruegel, C., Jonsson, E. (eds.) RAID 2003. LNCS, vol. 2820, pp. 36–54. Springer, Heidelberg (2003)
26. Sarasamma, S., Zhu, Q., Huff, J.: Hierarchical kohonen net for anomaly detection in network security. IEEE Trans. Syst. Man Cybern. Part B: Cybern. **35**(2), 302–312 (2005)
27. Sommer, R., Paxson, V.: Exploiting independent state for network intrusion detection. In: Proceedings of the 21st Annual Computer Security Applications Conference, ACSAC 2005, pp. 59–71. IEEE Computer Society, Washington, DC (2005). http://dx.doi.org/10.1109/CSAC.2005.24
28. Sommer, R., Paxson, V.: Outside the closed world: On using machine learning for network intrusion detection. In: 2010 IEEE Symposium on Security and Privacy (SP), pp. 305–316, May 2010
29. Tcpdump. http://www.tcpdump.org/. (Accessed 6 July 2013)
30. Thottan, M., Ji, C.: Anomaly detection in ip networks. IEEE Trans. Sig. Process. **51**(8), 2191–2204 (2003)

31. Vallentin, M., Sommer, R., Lee, J., Leres, C., Paxson, V., Tierney, B.: The NIDS cluster: scalable, stateful network intrusion detection on commodity hardware. In: Kruegel, C., Lippmann, R., Clark, A. (eds.) RAID 2007. LNCS, vol. 4637, pp. 107–126. Springer, Heidelberg (2007)
32. Weaver, N., Paxson, V., Sommer, R.: Work in progress: Bro-lan pervasive network inspection and control for lan traffic. In: Securecomm and Workshops, pp. 1–2 August 28–September 1 2006 (2006)
33. Wireshark. http://www.wireshark.org/. (Accessed 5 February 2013)
34. Yang, D., Usynin, A., Hines, J.: Anomaly-based intrusion detection for scada systems. In: Proceedings of the 5th International Topical Meeting on Nuclear Plant Instrumentation, Control and Human Machine Interface Technologies. NPIC&HMIT 05 (2006)

Context-Awareness Using Anomaly-Based Detectors for Smart Grid Domains

Cristina Alcaraz$^{(\boxtimes)}$, Lorena Cazorla, and Gerardo Fernandez

Computer Science Department, University of Malaga,
Campus de Teatinos S/n, 29071 Malaga, Spain
{alcaraz,lorena,gerardo}@lcc.uma.es

Abstract. Anomaly-based detection applied in strongly interdependent systems, like Smart Grids, has become one of the most challenging research areas in recent years. Early detection of anomalies so as to detect and prevent unexpected faults or stealthy threats is attracting a great deal of attention from the scientific community because it offers potential solutions for context-awareness. These solutions can also help explain the conditions leading up to a given situation and help determine the degree of its severity. However, not all the existing approaches within the literature are equally effective in covering the needs of a particular scenario. It is necessary to explore the control requirements of the domains that comprise a Smart Grid, identify, and even select, those approaches according to these requirements and the intrinsic conditions related to the application context, such as technological heterogeneity and complexity. Therefore, this paper analyses the functional features of existing anomaly-based approaches so as to adapt them, according to the aforementioned conditions. The result of this investigation is a guideline for the construction of preventive solutions that will help improve the context-awareness in the control of Smart Grid domains in the near future.

Keywords: Smart Grid · Control systems · Context-awareness · Prevention

1 Introduction

Anomaly-based detection has become one of the most challenging research areas within critical infrastructure protection in recent years, despite its extended application in intrusion and fault detection in conventional systems. There are a multitude of anomaly-based techniques for prevention available [1–3], but not all of them are equally feasible for critical contexts where the networks are extremely complex, dynamic and strongly-interconnected. Any perturbation in the functional requirements of these systems can seriously affect not only the underlying infrastructures but also those interdependent networks themselves. This is the case of Smart Grid systems, which are based on seven chief domains: control systems, energy (production, transmission and distribution) substations, providers,

© Springer International Publishing Switzerland 2015
J. Lopez et al. (Eds.): CRiSIS 2014, LNCS 8924, pp. 17–34, 2015.
DOI: 10.1007/978-3-319-17127-2_2

market and end-users. In this context, the operational tasks related to monitoring, supervision and data acquisition become fundamental to the correct use of the power grid. This also means that any inaccuracy in the detection processes of anomalies, computational overhead or a misunderstanding of the situation can trigger a (slight or serious) change in the control of the entire grid, and therefore cause an undesirable or contrary effect in its stability.

We therefore explore in this paper those anomaly-based approaches that can be found in the current literature, so as to evaluate their functionalities and applicability in the context of Smart Grids, paying particular attention to those conditions that entail a degradation in control. These conditions are related to a set of requirements associated with the monitoring and security of the entire Smart Grid, and the natural conditions of the communication infrastructures. The result of this investigation is a guideline to which approaches are most suitable for each section of the grid related to the control, such as substations. Thus, we contribute with the means necessary to help those responsible members for the control of the grid, such as human operators/engineers or network designers, and even researchers, define and implement future effective solutions for context-awareness. The paper is organized as follows: we briefly review in Sect. 2 the control technologies and communication infrastructures in order to then decide in Sect. 3.1 what requirements have to be fulfilled by the existing anomaly-based approaches. The functionalities and functional features of these approaches are discussed in Sect. 3.2 to later look at their suitability in control contexts (in Sect. 4) before concluding with a discussion of our findings and on-going work in Sect. 5.

2   General Architecture and Technologies

An introduction to the communication infrastructures and technologies that comprise a Smart Grid is given in this section [4]. The central architecture of these systems corresponds to a decentralized control network capable of remotely communicating with the rest of the sub-domains of the Smart Grid, e.g., substations. At this point, smart meters, gateways, Remote Terminal Units (RTUs), sensors and a set of control objects interact with each other through large and small communication infrastructures such as backhaul, Wide Area, Field Area, Neighbourhood Area, and Local Area Networks (WANs, FANs, NANs and LANs, respectively). All these infrastructures base their communications on wired and wireless systems such as mobile cellular technology, satellite, WiMAX, power line communications, microwaves systems, optical fiber, Bluetooth, Wi-Fi, Wireless Sensor Networks (WSNs), Ethernet, and so on. These infrastructures are in charge of distributing monitored evidence (e.g., commands, measurements or alarms) occurring at any point of the Smart Grid system, where backhaul and the Internet are the chief infrastructures that connect the different sub-domains with the rest of the networks, including Advanced Metering Infrastructures (AMIs). An AMI is a bidirectional interface with the capability to manage and interact with smart meters and utility business systems, thus substituting the traditional one-way advanced meters.

This interconnection map primarily focuses on the secure monitoring of services and the effectiveness of energy production according to the real demand. These services mainly addresses the means of notifying electricity pricing at any time and provide the end-users with customizable services to efficiently manage energy consumption. Continuing with the topic of monitoring services, the control transactions between the control system and substations are led by communication interfaces (e.g., RTUs, gateways, servers, etc.) which serve as intermediary nodes between the remote substation and the Master Terminal Units (MTUs) of the central system. An RTU is a device working at ∼22 MHz–200 MHz with 256 bytes–64 MB RAM, 8 KB–32 MB flash memory and 16 KB–256 KB EEPROM. These hardware and software capabilities are enough to compute data streams, operate mathematical formulations and identify those sensors or actuators in charge of executing a specific action in the field. These interfaces are also able to establish connections with other substations, allowing an inter-RTU communication with the ability to ensure store-and-forward using one of the two existing communication modes, serial (e.g., IEC-101) or TCP/IP (e.g., Modbus-TCP).

Control objects can be classified according to the type of micro-controller (weak, normal, and heavy-duty), the type of radio transceiver (wideband and narrowband radios) and the type of communication (synchronous/asynchronous) [5]. Within the category weak, we find those limited devices such as home-appliances and sensors with extremely constrained capabilities such as ∼4 MHz, 1 KB RAM and 4 KB–16 KB ROM, but with sufficient capacity to execute simple applications. Conversely, those classed as normal are those nodes that are able to comply with any kind of collaborative network. A node belonging to this category usually has a micro-controller of ∼4 MHz–8 MHz, 4 KB–16 KB RAM and 48 KB–256 KB ROM. Finally nodes belonging to the heavy-duty category are expensive devices (e.g., handled devices) that are able to execute any simple or complex critical application. Their microprocessors are quite powerful working at around 13 MHz–180 MHz, 256 KB–512 KB RAM and 4 MB–32 MB ROM. With respect to transceivers, most of the sensory devices follow the IEEE-802.15.4 standard working with wideband radios (e.g., CC2420) at frequencies of 2.4 GHz with certain demand restrictions in power. The narrowband radio-based transceivers (e.g., CC1000/C1020), to the contrary, work at lower frequencies and are more susceptible to noise, but they have less power consumption and faster wake up times.

Within the heavy-duty class, we highlight the industrial WSNs which are normally deployed close to critical systems (e.g., generators, transformers, pylons, etc.). Their capabilities are slightly greater than the conventional ones equipped with a ∼4 MHz–32 MHz micro-processor, 8 KB–128 KB RAM, 128 KB–192 KB ROM, and specific sensors to measure physical events associated with the industrial context such as temperature, voltage load, etc. They have the possibility to be directly linked to energy suppliers or industrial equipment in order to maximize their lifetime with self-capacity for processing and transmitting measurements to a base station (e.g., a gateway or an RTU). With similar features, smart meters can become heavy-duty devices working at ~8–50 MHz, 4 KB–32 KB RAM and 32–512 KB flash memory. An electrical meter is a device capable of logging the consumption values in synchronous and frequent intervals, sending this information back to the control utility for monitoring and billing purposes. Depending on the type of network, the communication can also vary [4]. For example, in power generation, transmission and distribution substations the communication can depend on specific or property protocols such as IEC-61850, Modbus, Zigbee, WirelessHART, ISA100.11a, and so on. Many of these offer technical solutions for customizing and optimizing the conditions of the application context in order to improve its quality of service, or avoid, for example, industrial noise, interferences or obstacles.

3   Detectors: Requirements and Common Approaches

Given that the great majority of the control objects (e.g., sensors, smart meters, etc.) are distributed over large-scale distributions where the control generally relies on only a few (or perhaps none) human operators in the field, topics related to dynamic and reliable context-awareness solutions should therefore be considered. Specifically, we explore a set of existing anomaly-based techniques as a support to these solutions. But as the number of techniques is significant within the current literature, we also stress here primary requirements and conditions that such techniques should comply with so as to ensure a better prevention in critical systems contained within a Smart Grid.

3.1   Requirements for Anomaly-Based Detection

The concept of 'context' was introduced by A. Dey in [6] as *"any information that can be used to characterize the situation of an entity"*, where entity can be a person, place or object. This characterization is widely used by dynamic context-aware computing systems to detect, prevent and alert to unforeseen changes in the normal behaviour of the system being observed [7]. An example of these detection systems are the Intrusion Detection Systems (IDSes), the configurations of which should respect the intrinsic requirements of the control not to perturb the normal behaviour of the entire grid. These requirements are as follows:

- *Operational performance* (**[R1]**) is part of the control of a Smart Grid. This includes the availability in-real time of assets and data from anywhere, at any time and in anyway; in addition to ensuring a fast supervision, data acquisition and response, avoiding communication and computational delays as much as possible.
- *Reliability and integrity* in the control (**[R2]**). Any change in the system can cause serious deviations in the power production and distribution, putting the stability of the power grid at risk.

- *Resilience* ([**R3**]) to address anomalies or unexpected incidents, which might also come from intrusive actions. Likewise, aspects related to *security* ([**R4**]) at the different levels of the communication and architecture must therefore also be considered as primary requirements for resilience.
- As part of the security, data confidentiality and anonymity are requirements required to guarantee *privacy* ([**R5**]) of both users and utilities.

Working within these requirements, anomaly-based detectors need to ensure a set of conditions to guarantee a fast, integral and reliable monitoring of evidence. That is to say, detectors need to show their potential to quickly find pattern sequences that prove the existence of a deviation within a set of data instances; i.e.:

- Low computational complexity through optimized algorithms and handling of parameters, in addition to guaranteeing a speedy classification, learning and comprehensibility of the data instances. In this way, it is possible to meet the operational requirement ([**R1**]).
- Reliability through accurate detection with a low false positive/negative rate, comprehensibility of the results obtained, easiness to handle parameters, and tolerance to highly interdependent data, noise, missing values or redundancy. The idea is to offer the best way of understanding a situation so as to act accordingly ([**R2**]).
- Capacities for incremental learning to update the knowledge of the system with new (discrete/continuous) values, states, threat patterns or parameters. This will permit the underlying infrastructures to provide an updated protection layer for survivability (security and resilience against future threats, [**R3, R4, R5**]).
- Ability to control drastic or persisting changes in the normal behaviour of the system, as these deviations can mean the proximity or existence of intrusive actions, affecting [**R3, R4, R5**].

Taking all this into account, we explore and analyse the functional features of the existing anomaly-based approaches to evaluate their functionalities according to the fulfilment of the requirements given for the application context.

3.2   Context Awareness Through Anomaly-Based Detection

Given that there are so many techniques available in the literature, and we are interested in detecting single anomalies that can cause significant damage to critical systems, we concentrate all our attention on the surveys carried out by M. V. Chandola et al. in [1] and S Kotsiantis et al. in [2], and on the taxonomy given by Gyanchandani et al. in [3]. Examining these three papers, we explore functional features to later discuss the suitability of the existing techniques in the Smart Grid context.

Data Mining-Based: this classification defines a type of analysis which is carried out on a set of data to find the behaviour pattern sequences, such as:

- **Classification-based** techniques: these correspond to classifiers in charge of assigning data instances to (normal or anomalous) classes [1]. Within this category, the **decision trees** (e.g., ID3, C4.5) are the most representative structures which deal with mapping observations into conclusions using hierarchical rules under the assumption of 'divide and conquer'. This assumption consists of recursively breaking down a problem into sub-problems until these become atomic units. There are two types of decision trees: *classification* and *regression* trees, the results of which depend on the type of data managed and the desired outputs of the models. These tree-like structures are capable of providing fast computations and decisions since each data instance (in the testing phase) is compared against a precomputed model. Their advantages are the speed of classification and the comprehensibility degree of their outputs to humans. Nonetheless, their shortcomings are the tolerance to redundant or highly interdependent data, as well as, their reliance on predefined models primarily based on labels [2,3].

- **Association rule learning-based** techniques: unsupervised schemes which try to identify the relationships between categorical variables, using strong rules and thresholds to prune. As part of this classification, we highlight the *Apriori* algorithm and the *FP-growth* algorithm. The former is an influential algorithm for mining frequent patterns, which tries to find rules in large datasets to predict the occurrence of an item based on the occurrences of others. In fact, its main property is: "any subset of a frequent pattern must be frequent"; and its pruning principle is "if there is a pattern which is infrequent, its superset should not be generated". Similarly, FP-growth has the same goals, but uses a compact frequent-pattern tree (FP-tree) structure under the assumption of 'divide-and-conquer'. This assumption consists of finding frequent rules/patterns to decompose mining tasks into smaller ones, the aim of which is to recursively delete all the data items that are not frequent; instead of generating candidates for each study. As mentioned, the technique itself has to make use of pruning approaches to reduce the sets of rules. Hence, the effectiveness of the learning process depends heavily on the parameters that configure the pruning operations and their algorithms, and on the number of rules that have to be launched, where the processing time may increase exponentially regarding the number of attributes [3]. Nonetheless, the comprehensibility of the results is an advantage.

- **Clustering-based** techniques: these aim to classify data instances in clusters through an unsupervised or semi-supervised method; i.e., no knowledge of threats, attacks or anomalies are needed in advance during training. This feature helps the testing phase process the evidence quickly, where the unsupervised models only compare the instances with a small number of clusters. To do this, the technique needs an evaluation function (e.g., a distance function, density, etc.) to compute the distances between data points, where each instance is evaluated according to its entire cluster. Although there are several clustering algorithms (e.g., hierarchical, centroid-based, distribution-based, density-based, etc.), the most popular approach is the *k-means*. Clustering-based techniques are quite dependent on the algorithm's parameters, which consequently have associated computational costs, which are mainly influenced by the type of dataset and the parameters selected [1,8]. Most approaches follow a quadratic order, except those based on heuristics (e.g., k-means), which take a linear complexity. In addition, the tolerance of the algorithms to different constraints in the data are quite dependent on the configuration of the parameters selected [1].

Statistical-Based: this class defines those statistical techniques that compute statistical models to apply interference tests so as to verify whether or not a specific instance belongs to a statistical model. Within these techniques, it is possible to find:

- **Parametric and nonparametric-based** methods: these refer to inference engines with a strong dependence on the data observed and which are composed of well-known statistical models, such as Gaussian or histograms [1,8]. These statistical models are in general accurate and tolerant to noise and missing values. Additionally, the statistical analysis provides additional information to the detection systems, such as the confidence interval associated with the anomaly. However, depending on the dataset, these methods can be sensitive to subtle changes and the output results are difficult for humans to understand. Moreover, depending on the dynamics of the problem, the efficiency of the model can be reduced, and in some cases, these techniques can potentially have quadratic complexity if dealing with large databases [1]. In contrast, the chief disadvantage here is that these techniques assume that the production of the data follows a particular distribution, which in real life scenarios is not true [1], consequently there are difficulties in determining the best distribution to fix such data. This category also includes the **operational models**, the observations of which are evaluated according to counters, bounded by predefined (upper and lower) thresholds. If these boundaries are not efficiently computed, the approach itself can then hamper the dynamic detection of anomalous events. In general, operational models may not be suitable for those dynamic scenarios that regularly change their normal behaviour [3].
- **Time series-based** techniques: these, can be both non-parametric and parametric [9], basically aim to provide behaviour forecasting using times series, which are sequences of data points, measured at successive and uniformly distributed time intervals. These methods are generally suitable for detecting those threats launched in series form with subtle perturbations (e.g., stealth attacks), but its effectiveness decays when there are drastic changes [3]. There are several methods of time series analysis; one of the most useful for detection are the *smoothing techniques*, which provide weighted data instances. The smoothing mechanisms provide accurate observations and their approaches are tolerant to insignificant changes and missing values, in addition they help

optimize parameters. Unfortunately, as in the case of the rest of the statistical methods, they tend to be difficult to understand for humans and have great difficulty handling parameters. The smoothing techniques also produce weak models for medium or long-range forecasting, which heavily rely on past history and on the smoothing factor to predict the future; the variant *exponential smoothing models*, in particular, cannot easily forecast future events in the presence of fluctuations in recent data [10].

– **Markov models**: are mathematical representations with quantitative values that help predict the future behaviour of a system according to the current evidence. There are many types of Markov models, and all them have functionalities and features in common, such as operations based on successive data and dependence on a state transition (probabilistic) matrix to illustrate activity transactions without having knowledge of the problem in hand. However, and unfortunately, the Markov models are highly complicated when addressing complex situations with multiple dimensions, the complexity of which increases when leaving the most simple (first order) Markov chains, in favour of more precise and complicated models [11] (e.g., the Hidden Markov Models (HMMs)). In addition, abrupt changes in the normal activity sequence within a system becomes unmanageable, so that this feature may become undesirable in critical contexts [3].

Knowledge Detection-Based: this technique consists of progressively acquiring knowledge about specific attacks or vulnerabilities, guaranteeing accuracy of the technique with a low false positive rate, and flexibility and scalability for adding new knowledge. The result is a system potentially capable of ensuring resilience against threats, but this security also depends on the update frequency of this knowledge and the degree of granularity to specify the threat patterns. According to M. Gyanchandani et al. in [3], there are a few types of knowledge detection-based approaches, such as state transition, expert systems and Petri nets. **State transactions** aim to define threat models through state transaction diagrams illustrating the activity sequences and operandi mode; similarly, **Petri nets** represents state transactions using directed bipartite graphs to show events and conditions. Conversely, **expert systems** are composed of intelligence engines based on simple rules which define different models capable of reasoning about the provided knowledge like a human expert. Expert system models can be provided with varied knowledge; e.g., different types of threats or vulnerabilities, or even conditions given by the security policies.

Information and Spectral Theory-Based: both theories are based on statistical approaches. Particularly, the information-based techniques focus on analysing the data itself and its order to observe whether there are irregularities (related to meaning, features or properties) within it [1]. Through concepts of entropy, their approaches are in general efficient, but this feature depends on the size of the dataset to be compared; and they are also tolerant to insignificant changes in the data and redundancy [14]. As for spectral theory methods, these work with approximations of the data (or signals) to observe whether there are differences, more visible in other dimensions of the data. Spectral analysis is an approach fairly linked to time series analysis and the characteristics of the communication channels. It performs dimensionality reduction to handle high dimensional data; however, its efficiency varies according to the mathematical method used to translate the model into other dimensions, e.g., Fourier, and these techniques usually have a high computational complexity [1].

Other Machine Learning-Based: in this group, we stress the rest of machine-learning-based approaches [15] such as artificial neural network or Bayesian networks, amongst others. Note that the vast majority of these techniques overlap with other aforementioned ones, such statistical or mining data.

- **Artificial neural networks** (ANNs): these, in the artificial intelligence field, can be applied for anomaly detection using a multi-class or one-class configuration for training and learning. The models essentially consist of the computation of the sum of weighted inputs to produce weighted outputs [2]. Thus, the performance of ANNs depends on three main aspects: input and activation functions, network architecture and the weight of each connection. ANNs are generally accurate and fast classifiers, capable of tolerating highly interdependent data, whose learners can need of back propagation algorithms where the output models may not be comprehensible to humans and produce over-fitted models. These drawbacks make it difficult to ensure real-time in the operational processes since most ANN approaches need extra processing-time.
- **Bayesian networks** (BNs): these networks are composed of directed acyclic graphs, where the nodes represent states that have associated probabilities, and parameters encoded in tables. The BN first learns from structures of the (either unknown or known) networks, and then computes the parameters of the model. This category can be well-applied in intrusion detection models as powerful and versatile solutions, but may become computationally complex if the networks are unknown a priori [2], or present too many features (large BNs). Despite its ideal accuracy, this technique is too expensive in terms of time and storage, and tends to be infeasible for constrained scenarios. An extension of BNs are the **Naïve Bayes networks**, where their digraphs only hold one parent for each node and the probabilistic parameters of the network are calculated using conditional probabilities. These types of probabilities in the form of a product can be transformed into a sum through the use of logarithms, allowing the decision system to be computationally efficient and fast [2]. Other benefits, given the simplification of the model, are the diminished computational overhead for training, understandability of their networks, and the possibilities for handling parameters and introducing incremental learning. However, a disadvantage of this model is that it is not as accurate as a BN due to the existing independence between the child nodes, which imposes strong constraints on its behaviour [2].
- **Support vector machines** (SVMs): this method is a supervised learning model based on a non-probabilistic binary linear classifier under a one-class

configuration to recognize data patterns or outliers in datasets [12]. Given that SVMs work with linear combination of (data) points, the computational cost follows a quadratic order and the number of vectors selected is usually small. Thus the complexity of an SVM is not affected by the number of features in the training data so SVMs are suitable for addressing large numbers of features. The main weaknesses found is that most real-world problems involve inseparable data for which no hyperplane exists that successfully separates the positive from negative instances in the training set; and in optimization problems, the presence of local minimums and maximums affects the accuracy and speed. Even so, SVMs are, in general terms, accurate and fast classifiers, and tolerant to irrelevant and redundant data. However, the method itself usually presents problems with the speed of learning, the comprehensibility and the ability to handle the model and incrementally learn [2].

- **Rule-based techniques**: these focus on learning rules that interpret the normal behaviour of the system with the capability of multi-class and one-class settings. Their main strengths are the accuracy, comprehensibility, handling of simple parameters and low complexity. In contrast, they are weak in incremental learning, dependence on expert knowledge, tolerance to noise and are unsuitable for anomaly detection. Within this class, we highlight the **rule learners** (e.g., Ripper). These algorithms use rules from trained data to construct a rule-based decision engine under the assumption 'separate and conquer' by looking at one class at a time and producing rules that match the class. This procedure, apparently simple, requires exploring the whole dataset where their learners become slow and inaccurate with low tolerance to missing irrelevant and redundant data. Nonetheless, they provide speedy classifiers with comprehensible results, and allow easiness to manage system parameters.

- **Nearest neighbour-based**: this corresponds to those methods based on the distance measures of the data, such as the kth *nearest neighbour* or on the *density*. These approaches are characterized by their speedy learning with respect to the number of attributes and the number of instances present in the dataset. In addition, they are suitable for incremental learning and their parameters can be modified with fairly easily. Despite these benefits, these approaches are quite sensitive to the selection of the similarity function [8], do not provide a deterministic way of choosing the parameter k, and require storage. The size of the instance sets are also dependent on k whose value affects the time required to classify an instance; in addition to exhibiting an extensive testing phase in which their methods can reach a low tolerance to noise and a low stability depending on the parameters adjusted.

- **Fuzzy logic** and **genetic algorithms**. Fuzzy logic consists of simple rule-based structures that define reasoning [3]. The approaches are in general simple, flexible and fast in the processing of rules and in the determination of anomalies, in which their approaches are able to establish the normality boundaries and manage large databases. The technique is also able to model complex systems and situations without requiring precision or complete databases; however, its conclusions may not reflect the confidence degree of a problem. Regarding genetic algorithms, these deal with optimization and search heuristics where their implementations can require a large number of iterations to reduce a problem, and according to a fitness function. This also means that the detection rate depends on the accuracy of this function, where the approach itself has proven be unable to detect unknown or new threats, as well as, multi-interactive attacks [13].

Table 1. Work related with approaches applied in Smart Grid environments

Reference	Technique	Application	Application area
[16]	ANNs	Fault diagnosis	Substations
[17]	Decision trees	Intrusion detection	Control and substations
[18]		Fault detection	Substations
[19]	BNs	Intrusion detection	HANs
[20]	Naïve Bayes net	Islanding detection	Power systems
[21]	SVMs	Fault detection and classification	Transmission lines
[22]		Intrusion detection	HANs, NANs, WANs
[23]	Rules	Intrusion detection	WANs, NANs and HANs
[24]	Statistical	False-data injection detection (Markov graph-based)	Control and substations
[25]		Load/Price Forecasting, Demand (time series)	HANs, Control and substations
[26]	Fuzzy logic	Diagnosis and maintenance	Substations
[27]		Optimization for power storage	Microgrid networks
[28]	Petri Nets	Fault diagnosis	Distribution substations
Examples of combined solutions			
[29]	ANNs and rules	Fault diagnosis	Control and substations
[30]	BNs on an expert system	Fault diagnosis	Substations (distribution feeder)
[31]	Fuzzy logic and decision tree	Islanding detection	Substations

To ensure these techniques are effective, they can be integrated inside intrusion detection systems to monitor and analyse events following one of the three detection modes: **anomaly-based** (to detect unexpected deviations regarding the normal behaviour of a system), **signature-based** (to detect changes according to an updated database containing threat models) and **specification-based** (to detect abnormal behaviours taking into account the legitimate specifications of a system). According to P. Jokar in [19], anomaly-based IDSes have a tendency towards high false positive rates, complex training and tuning time, but they do have the ability to detect unknown attacks. Signature-based IDSes present low false positive rate but they are not able to detect unknown threats; whereas specification-based IDSes ensure low false positive rates and have the capability to detect new attacks. Nonetheless, specification-based IDS presents great disadvantages related to the computational cost required implementing the threat/vulnerability models, which are very dependent on the functional features of the devices (legitimate specification). Table 1 summarizes some related work so as to show the extensive application field of these techniques: monitoring, detection, optimization and maintenance.

4   Suitability of Detection Approaches for Smart Grid Domains

In this section, we explore several ways to select anomaly-based techniques. To do this, Table 2, summarizes the functional benefits of each scheme analysed in Sect. 3.1, but compared against the control and security conditions stated in Sect. 3.1 and the characteristics of the communication systems (dimension, traffic and capabilities of the network devices).

4.1   Utilities: Control Centres and Corporate Networks

Control and corporate networks of a Smart Grid may range from large distributions with potentially thousands of nodes (e.g., servers) with connections to backhauls, WANs or NANs, to small and local networks. Depending on the type of domain and utility, they may have different kinds of protocols and topologies to connect different networks (e.g., control and AMI, providers and AMI). However, this interconnection mode and its relation to public networks, like the Internet, forces us to consider heavy-duty IDSes that help detect potential (anonymous, unknown, concurrent or stealthy) threats, and thereby comply with the minimum security requirements [**R3, R4, R5**]. As part of this information belongs to users or the business itself, and the other part corresponds with control transactions for the protection and stability of the entire power grid, topics related to reliability of the data itself [**R2**] should also be considered. Therefore, and observing Table 2, the most suitable techniques for this section of the grid could be:

– **Knowledge-based**: the dynamic features of the knowledge-based approaches, such as expert systems, make them be one of the most attractive approaches to be applied in complex and dynamic contexts. However, this protection will highly depend on the degree of granularity of their knowledge and the frequency to with which this knowledge is updated; two conditions that should be well-specified in the security policies.
– **Statistics**: statistical-based techniques, as described in Sect. 3.2 are powerful methods that can be adapted to different scenarios, from simple to complex and dynamic contexts, and serve as anomaly-detection engines in multiple IDSes in the literature [1,8]. Statistical methods could be useful for detection at any level of a communication network because of their great accuracy

(except the operational models) despite being computationally complex. Note that the **Markov models** may also be considered due to their inherent characteristics, but their transaction matrices should be well-fixed to control drastic changes. Specifically, HMMs are useful tools for detecting hidden dynamics and extracting knowledge when there are gaps in the information received. Thus in the presence of encrypted traffic, the use of Markov models would be useful to detect certain hidden evidence (**[R3, R4]**).

As mentioned, there are other methods that could equally be applicable to theses types of networks, e.g., rule learners, SVMs, Markov models or clustering techniques. However they could be more difficult to adapt to the scenario, or present more challenges and inconveniences than benefits due to their inherent characteristics. For example, these methods tend to produce over-fitting, a characteristic that makes them inappropriate when the environment is continuously adapting new dynamics and new constraints (e.g., frequent upgrades and maintenances). As for the detection modes, the use of a **signature-based IDS** seems to be a good option since utility networks might apply existing and complex databases with diverse types of signatures defining threat patterns or known undesirable dynamics related to the network. The main problem found in this detection mode is the need to keep the threat databases up-to-date.

4.2   Substations: Production, Transmission and Distribution

The communication between the control centre and the remote nodes (i.e., RTU/gateway) is done through MTU, where the data traffic between the MTU-RTU/gateway is generally regular and standardized, and operational performance (**[R1]**), reliability in the control transactions (**[R2]**) and security (**[R3, R4]**) are all required. As mentioned in Sect. 2, RTUs are powerful enough to be able to execute a set of operations or instructions, as well as, advanced algorithms such as machine learning ones. Their hardware capacities also allows them to run specialized detection techniques capable of detecting sophisticated threats in an environment that has a regular behaviour with a monotonous activity (note that this consideration is dependent on the security policies). Assuming that the communications are configured to be synchronous with regular traffic, the most suitable techniques for this section of the grid would be those related to **knowledge**. However, and as described above, the implementation of knowledge-based systems also depends on the functional features of the interfaces and the maintenance of these intelligent systems. As an alternative, it is also possible to choose those approaches that do not infringe, at least, **[R1, R2]** to ensure control at all times, such as:

– **Rule-based techniques**: this method is characterized by its simplicity (**[R1]**) and accuracy (**[R2]**), which should not degrade the main conditions for control. For the effectiveness of the approach and its use for protection, it is necessary to specify in detail, the rules, exposing all the possible threat scenarios that can arise in the connectivities between the MTU and the substations.

Table 2. Requirements of Smart Grids vs. anomaly-based approaches

	Complexity	Speed of classification	Speed of learning	Handle parameters	Comprehensibility	Accuracy	Learning from observation	Control - interdep. data	Control - missing data	Control - redundancy	Control - noise	Control - subtle changes	Control - drastic changes	Incremental learning	Unlimited networks	Limited networks	R1	R2	R3	R4	R5	Control - Corporative net.	Control - RTU/Gateway (Subst.)	RTU/Gateway - sensors (Subst.)	Gateway - embedded dev. (NAN)	Embedded devices (HAN)
	⊤ᵃ	⊤	⊤	⊤*	*	*	*	*	*	*	*	o	o	o	*		*o	⊤*o	⊤*o	o	⊤	*o	⊤*o	⊤*o	o	⊤
Classification trees	-	✓	✓	✓	✓	✓	-	-	✗	-	✗	-	-	-	✓	•ᵇ	✓	✗	-	-	-	•	-	-	-	✓
Regression trees	-	-	-	✓	-	-	✓	✗	✓	✗	-	-	-	✓	✓	•	✗	✗	✓	✓	✓	•	-	-	-	-
Association rule learners	✗	-	✓	✗	✓	-	✓	✓	-	✓	✗	-	-	✗	✓	✗	✗	✗	✗	✗	✗	•	•	-	-	-
Clustering	✓	✗	✗	✗	✗	✗	✓	✗	✓	✓	✓	✗	-	✓	✓	•	•	✗	✓	✓	✓	•	-	-	•	•
Parametric and non-parametric	✓	-	✗	✗	✗	✓	-	-	✓	-	✓	✗	-	✓	✓	•	•	✓	•	•	•	✓	✓	•	•	•
Operational models	✓	-	-	✗	✗	✗	-	-	-	-	-	-	✗	-	✓	✓	✓	✗	✗	✗	✗	-	-	-	-	•
Smoothing	✗	-	-	✗	✗	✓	-	✓	-	✓	✓	✗	-	-	✓	✗	✓	•	•	•	•	✓	•	-	•	-
Markov chains	✗	-	✗	✗	✗	✓	✓	-	-	-	✗	-	✗	-	✓	✗	✗	✓	✗	✗	✗	•	-	-	-	-
Artificial neural networks	✗	✓	✗	✗	✗	✓	✓	✓	✓	✗	✗	✗	-	-	✓	✗	✗	✓	-	-	-	•	•	-	-	-
Bayesian networks	✗	✓	-	✓	✓	-	✓	-	✓	✗	✓	-	-	-	✓	✗	✗	•	-	-	-	•	•	-	-	-
Naïve Bayes networks	-	✓	✓	✓	✓	✗	✓	✗	✓	✗	✓	-	-	-	✓	✗	✓	✗	•	•	-	•	•	-	•	-
Support vector machines	✓	✓	✗	✗	✗	✓	✓	✓	✓	-	✓	✗	-	✗	✓	•	✓	•	✗	✗	✗	•	✓	✓	-	•
Rule-based techniques	✓	-	-	✓	✓	✓	-	-	-	-	✗	-	-	✗	✓	✓	✓	✓	✗	✗	✗	•	✓	✓	-	✓
Rule learners	-	✓	✗	✓	✓	✓	✗	✓	✗	✗	✗	✗	-	✗	✓	-	•	✗	✗	✗	✗	•	-	-	-	-
Nearest neighbour	-	✗	✓	✗	✗	✓	✗	✓	✗	✗	✗	✗		✓	✓	-	✗	✗	•	•	•	-	-	-	•	-
Fuzzy logic	✓	✓	✓	✓	✓	✗	-	-	✓	-	✓	-	-	-	✓	✓	✓	✗	-	-	-	•	-	-	-	✓
Genetic algorithm	✗	-	-	✓	-	✗	-	-	-	-	-	-	-	-	✓	✗	✗	✗	✗	✗	✗	•	-	-	-	-
Knowledge-based	✓	-	-	✓	-	✓	-	-	-	-	-	-	-	✓	✓	•	•	✓	•	•	•	✓	✓	•	✓	-
Information-spectral theory	-	-	-	✗	✗	-	-	-	-	-	✓	✗	✓	-	✓	-	✗	✗	-	-	-	•	-	-	-	-
Anomaly-based IDS															✓	✗	✗	✗	✓	✓	✓	•	-	-	-	-
Signature-based IDS															✓	•	-	✓	✗	✗	✗	✓	•	•	•	•
Specification-based IDS															✓	•	-	✓	✓	✓	✓	•	✓	✓	✓	✓

ᵃ ⊤ means that the property complies with [R1]; * with [R2]; and o with [R3, R4, R5].

ᵇ • states the benefits for the network device but with 'dependence' on the functional features of the approach (e.g., data structure, abilities to control noise, changes, etc.) regarding the hardware or software constraints.

- **Support vector machines**: this method is powerful and well-suited to dealing with large numbers of features. SVMs are accurate ([R2]) and they have low complexity models ([R1]) [2]. However they present problems in the speed of the learning process, a handicap that makes SVMs difficult to implement in networks with constrained resources, and particularly in the presence of dynamic scenarios. Nevertheless, this can be easily overcome in networks with sufficiently powerful nodes (e.g., gateways) deployed in rather static scenarios, where the set of representative training instances is small.
- **Statistics**: optimized parametric or non-parametric solutions can become effective approaches for these sections of the Smart Grid, but without considering those related to operational models, since these do not guarantee the fulfilment with [R2].

In addition, the detection methods that have problems in addressing over-fitting do not have as big an impact as the corporate networks, because the stability and periodicity of the scenario makes the classification instances very similar to the training datasets. However, signature-based IDSes configured inside RTUs can become complex since these IDSes requires big databases with known threat patterns to be kept, forcing the RTU to depend on external databases. However, **specification-based** IDS could be a good candidate since legitimate specifications of the interfaces are well known, and sometimes limited in terms of specification, favouring the definition of threat patterns according to the technical characteristics of the devices. This criteria is also applicable for constrained devices such as sensors or smart meters [19].

Another important part of a substation is the communication between RTU/ gateways working in ISA100.11a/ WirelessHART (or coordinators in ZigBee) and the industrial sensor nodes. These sensors are heavy-duty devices with restrictions on executing complex operations and algorithms, and these generally maintain a regular and static traffic where their functions consist of constantly monitoring an object or an infrastructure, and sending this information to the gateway. Assuming that the communications are completely synchronous, our goal is now to find those lightweight solutions that ensure, at least, [**R1, R2**]; and in this way, do not degrade the operational activities in the field, such as:

- **Rule-based** techniques: this method, described above, is a simple approach that can be computed by constrained devices, but its effectiveness will depend on how the rules and threat scenarios are defined.
- **Support vector machines**: SVM methods, as we discussed, have good qualities to be used as detection engines for the IDSes deployed in constrained networks (favouring [**R1, R2**]). But to apply the method, it is necessary that these networks need to ensure regular and static traffic patterns to avoid triggering the learning processes with frequency.
- Optimized **statistic-based** solutions: as mentioned, these can also become quite effective for [**R1, R2**], since their approaches present a moderate complexity and a high efficiency. However, the feasibility also depends on the optimization degree to avoid overhead costs.

The communication between industrial sensors is thoroughly analysed in the next section because home appliances and smart meters present similar behaviours.

4.3   Neighbourhood and House Areas: Metering and Control

The type of data managed in the hierarchical communications (NANs) between data aggregation point and metering devices (smart meters) and its relation to the end-users, makes the topics related to security and privacy prevail over questions of control; but this control must exist as well. Depending on the characteristics of the interfaces and assuming a constant communication, **knowledge-based** approaches can be good candidates to ensure [**R3, R4, R5**] together with those related to the **statistics** (e.g., smoothing approaches). As regards HAN networks, the communication between embedded devices ((weak, normal or heavy-duty) sensors, smart meters and home appliances) becomes the most predominant infrastructure for the constant monitoring and reporting of consumption evidence to smart meters. Their efficiency, however, depends on the type of energy consumption of these activities (many of these devices are very dependent on batteries), software and hardware capabilities, and even, on the type of configuration of their networks, overwhelmingly ad-hoc in nature. Therefore, the selection of techniques should primarily be focused on complying with [**R1**], such as:

– **Decision trees, Fuzzy logic, rule-based** techniques: these three approaches are in general fast and efficient learners and classifiers ([**R1**]); a set of functional features for those application scenarios built on strong restrictions and constrained devices [18]. Nonetheless, we could also consider the **operational models** for their simplicity, but always keeping in mind the need to define appropriate normality thresholds.
– Optimized **statistic** and **clustering** techniques: a well-configured simple approaches could result in a lightweight detection tool ([**R1**]). In the case of clustering, this solution would be more valid and useful in a scenario where the patterns of behaviour suffer few variations, and the learning and testing mechanisms are seldom triggered.

On the other hand, ad-hoc networks could be used by human operators for local control, acquisition and management of controllers, sensors, actuators, smart meters and other related devices for control. In this regard, the control establishes a collaborative environment where human operators can directly operate in the field or in populated areas (e.g., to locally check neighbourhood areas, status values of energy charging spots) without going through the control centre; thereby facilitating the execution of actions in real-time and the mobility within the area. This collaboration is generally based on very diverse kinds of technologies (e.g., PDA, cellular devices) with similar capacities to the technical specifications defined for the heavy-duty devices in Sect. 2, and hence, they can adopt similar approaches to those described for sensors. But due to their relativity to control ([**R2, R3, R4**]), their lightweight IDS solutions should also consider supplementary mechanisms, such as secure aggregation and reputation methods, to provide extra layer of protection and improve the detection procedures in the face of sophisticated threats. At this point, we also conclude that methods with costly training processes are less appropriate for dynamic networks regardless of the computational power of their nodes. This is because the constant changes and new dynamics constantly appearing in those networks make the IDSes trigger the learning mechanisms more frequently, and in this case they are computationally costly. However, in networks with regular and constant traffic, the training procedures are triggered only a few times, thus the use of these methods does not produce overhead excess in the system.

5   Conclusions

A set of anomaly-based techniques have been analysed in this paper so as to explore and exploit functionalities for context-awareness in Smart Grid environments. The result is a comparative study in the form of a guideline that helps in the selection of most suitable schemes and detection modes according to the restrictions of the context and functional characteristics of the technologies and communication systems (see Table 2). Taking into account this guideline, our future work will consist of investigating lightweight solutions that aim to detect stealth attacks in the different control domains that comprise a Smart Grid.

Acknowledgment. The results of this research have received funding from the Marie-Curie COFUND programme U-Mobility, co-financed by the University of Málaga, the EC FP7 under GA No. 246550 and the Ministerio de Economía y Competitividad (COFUND2013-40259). The second author has been funded by a FPI fellowship from the Junta de Andalucía through the project FISICCO (P11-TIC-07223). Additionally, this work has been partially supported by the research project ARES (CSD2007-00004) and the EU FP7 project FACIES (HOME/2011/CIPS/AG/4000002115).

References

1. Chandola, V., Banerjee, A., Kumar, V.: Anomaly detection: a survey. ACM Comput. Surv. **41**(3), 15–58 (2009). 15
2. Kotsiantis, S., Zaharakis, I., Pintelas, P.: Supervised machine learning: a review of classification techniques. In: Frontiers in Artificial Intelligence and Applications, pp. 249–268 (2007)
3. Gyanchandani, M., Rana, J., Yadav, R.: Taxonomy of anomaly based intrusion detection system: a review. Neural Netw. **2**(43), 1–14 (2012)
4. Yan, Y., Qian, Y., Sharif, H., Tipper, D.: A survey on smart grid communication infrastructures: motivations, requirements and challenges. IEEE Commun. Surv. Tutor. **15**(1), 5–20 (2013)
5. Roman, R., Alcaraz, C., Lopez, J.: A survey of cryptographic primitives and implementations for hardware-constrained sensor network nodes. Mob. Netw. Appl. **12**(4), 231–244 (2007)
6. Abowd, G.D., Dey, A.K.: Towards a better understanding of context and context-awareness. In: Gellersen, H.-W. (ed.) HUC 1999. LNCS, vol. 1707, p. 304. Springer, Heidelberg (1999)
7. Alcaraz, C., Lopez, J.: Wide-area situational awareness for critical infrastructure protection. IEEE Comput. **46**(4), 30–37 (2013). IEEE Computer Society
8. Bhuyan, M., Bhattacharyya, D., Kalita, J.: Network anomaly detection: methods, systems and tools. IEEE Commun. Surv. Tutor. **99**, 1–34 (2013)
9. Fan, J.: Nonlinear Time Series: Non-parametric And Parametric Methods. Springer, Handbook (2003)
10. Demand Planning, Exponential Smoothing (SCM-APO-FCS), SAP. http://help.sap.com/. Accessed May 2014
11. Friedman, N., Geiger, D., Goldszmidt, M.: Bayesian network classifiers. Mach. Learn. **29**(2–3), 131–163 (1997)

12. Jyothsna, V., Prasad, R.V.V.: A review of anomaly based intrusion detection systems. Int. J. Comput. Appl. **28**(7), 26–35 (2011)
13. Shanmugam, B., Idris, N.: Hybrid intrusion detection systems (HIDS) using Fuzzy logic. In: Skrobanek, P. (ed.) Intrusion Detection Systems, pp. 135–155, Chap. 8. InTech (2011)
14. Mackay, D.: Information Theory, Inference and Learning Algorithms. Cambridge University Press, Cambridge (2003)
15. Cazorla, L., Alcaraz, C., Lopez, J.: Towards automatic critical infrastructure protection through machine learning. In: Luiijf, E., Hartel, P. (eds.) CRITIS 2013. LNCS, vol. 8328, pp. 197–203. Springer, Heidelberg (2013)
16. Chow, M., Yee, S., Taylor, L.: Recognizing animal-caused faults in power distribution systems using artificial neural networks. IEEE Trans. Power Delivery **8**(3), 1268–1274 (1993)
17. Choi, K., Chen, X., Li, S., Kim, M., Chae, K., Na, J.: Intrusion detection of NSM based DoS attacks using data mining in Smart Grid. Energies **5**, 4091–4109 (2012)
18. Kher, S., Nutt, V., Dasgupta, D., Ali, H., Mixon, P.: A detection model for anomalies in smart grid with sensor network. In: Future Instrumentation International Workshop (FIIW), pp. 1–4 (2012)
19. Jokar, P.: Model-based intrusion detection for Home Area Networks in Smart Grids, pp. 1–19. University of Bristol, Bristol (2012)
20. Najy, W., Zeineldin, H., Alaboudy, A., Woon, W.: A bayesian passive islanding detection method for inverter-based distributed generation using ESPRIT. IEEE Trans. Power Delivery **26**, 2687–2696 (2011)
21. Shahid, N., Aleem, S., Naqvi, I., Zaffar, N.: Support vector machine based fault detection & classification in smart grids, pp. 1526–1531. Globecom, IEEE (2012)
22. Zhang, Y., Wang, L., Sun, W., Green, R., Alam, M.: Distributed intrusion detection system in a multi-layer network architecture of smart grids. IEEE Trans. Smart Grid **2**(4), 796–808 (2011)
23. Mitchell, R., Chen, I.R.: Behavior rule based intrusion detection systems for safety critical smart grid applications. IEEE Trans. Smart Grid **4**, 1254–1263 (2013)
24. Sedghi, H., Jonckheere, E.: Statistical structure learning: towards a tobust Smart Grid, arXiv, pp. 1–16 (2014)
25. Chan, S., Tsui, K., Wu, H., Hou, Y., Wu, Y., Wu, F.: Load/price forecasting and managing demand response for smart grids. IEEE Signal Process. Mag. **29**, 68–85 (2012)
26. Chang, C., Wang, Z., Yang, F., Tan, W.: Hierarchical fuzzy logic system for implementing maintenance schedules of offshore power systems. IEEE Trans. Smart Grid **3**(1), 3–11 (2012)
27. Manjili, Y., Rajaee, A., Jamshidi, M., Kelley, B.: Fuzzy control of electricity storage unit for energy management of Micro-Grids. In: World Automation Congress, pp. 1–6. IEEE (2012)
28. Calderaro, V., Piccolo, A., Siano, P.: Failure identification in smart grids based on petri net modeling. IEEE Trans. Industr. Electron. **58**(10), 4613–4623 (2011)
29. Syafaruddin, S., Karatepe, E., Hiyama, T.: Controlling of artificial neural network for fault diagnosis of photovoltaic array. In: The 16th International Conference on Intelligent System Application to Power Systems, pp. 1–6. IEEE (2011)
30. Chien, C., Chen, S., Lin, Y.: Using bayesian network for fault location on distribution feeder. IEEE Trans. Power Del. **17**(3), 785–793 (2002)
31. Samantaray, S., El-Arroudi, K., Joos, G., Kamwa, I.: A Fuzzy rule-based approach for islanding detection in distributed generation. IEEE Trans. Power Delivery **25**(3), 1427–1433 (2010)

Automated Detection of Logical Errors in Programs

George Stergiopoulos[1], Panagiotis Katsaros[2(✉)],
and Dimitris Gritzalis[1]

[1] Information Security and Critical Infrastructure Protection Laboratory,
Department of Informatics, Athens University of Economics
and Business (AUEB), Athens, Greece
{geostergiop,dgrit}@aueb.gr
[2] Department of Informatics, Aristotle University of Thessaloniki,
Thessaloniki, Greece
katsaros@csd.auth.gr

Abstract. Static and dynamic program analysis tools mostly focus on the detection of a priori defined defect patterns and security vulnerabilities. Automated detection of logical errors, due to a faulty implementation of applications' functionality is a relatively uncharted territory. Automation can be based on profiling the intended behavior behind the source code. In this paper, we present a new code profiling method that combines the crosschecking of dynamic program invariants with symbolic execution, an information flow analysis, and the use of fuzzy logic. Our goal is to detect logical errors and exploitable vulnerabilities. The theoretical underpinnings and the practical implementation of our approach are discussed. We test the APP_LogGIC tool that implements the proposed analysis on two real-world applications. The results show that profiling the intended program behavior is feasible in diverse applications. We discuss the heuristics used to overcome the problem of state space explosion and of the large data sets. Code metrics and test results are provided to demonstrate the effectiveness of the approach.

Keywords: Risk · Logical errors · Source code profiling · Static analysis · Dynamic analysis · Input vectors · Fuzzy logic

1 Introduction

In software development we aim to derive an executable program description from a set of given requirements that reflect the intended program behavior, i.e. what the programmer wants his code to do and what not to do. In essence, software development is an intellectual activity that translates intended functionality - in the form of requirements - into source code.

The logical errors introduced in the source code are due to erroneous translation of software requirements, and they cause unintended program behavior, due to execution flow deviations. Modern techniques for static and dynamic program analysis have been proven effective in detecting a priori defined program flaws, but they do not go far enough into the detection of logical errors.

© Springer International Publishing Switzerland 2015
J. Lopez et al. (Eds.): CRiSIS 2014, LNCS 8924, pp. 35–51, 2015.
DOI: 10.1007/978-3-319-17127-2_3

As an example of a logical error, we consider the following [5]: "a web store application allows, using coupons, to obtain a one-time-discount-per-coupon on certain items; a faulty implementation can lead to using the same coupon multiple times, thus eventually zeroing the price". Automated detection of such program behavior is a relatively uncharted territory.

We address this problem by extracting the programmed behavior of the Applications Under Test (AUTs) based on code profiling techniques. Potential logical errors are then detected and classified by applying heuristics on the gathered data. The method consists of the following steps:

1. For an AUT, a representation of its programmed behavior is generated in the form of *dynamic invariants*, i.e. source code rules expressed as assert statements. Invariants are collected by dynamic analysis of the AUT with the MIT Daikon tool [12].
2. A preliminary analysis with the JPF tool from NASA and custom-made methods gathers the following data: (i) a set of execution paths and program states along these paths and (ii) input data vectors and a map of all program points, in which execution can follow different paths (execution flow branching points).
3. Logical errors are then detected by crosschecking information gathered with the dynamic invariants collected, during the steps (1) and (2). Invariants are checked upon multiple execution paths and their accessed program states.
4. Logical errors due to faulty input data manipulation are also detected by a tainted object propagation analysis. "Tainted" input data are traced throughout the source code and the applied sanitization checks are verified.

The main contributions of this paper are summarized as follows:

– We formally define the notion of logical error and lay the foundations of the method.
– We show how the programmed behavior of an AUT can be used as a map for logical error detection. Our approach is based on previous research [5–7]. In this paper we augment and reconstruct the method, in order to be able to apply it to complex, real-world applications. We change the static analysis, from scripted execution of possible paths to symbolic execution with various types of data listeners for the source code variables. Also, we use a new parser for dynamic invariants, in order to present test results using diverse, complex AUTs; in this way, we show that our method can be utilized to detect many different kinds of errors.
– We introduce fuzzy logic membership sets used to classify logical errors: (i) *Severity*, with values from a scale quantifying the impact of a logical error, with respect to how it affects the AUT's execution flow and (ii) *Vulnerability*, with values from a scale quantifying the likelihood of a logical error and how dangerous it is. The proposed fuzzy sets aim to automate reasoning based on the analysis findings, similarly to a code audit process.
– We analyze two real-world, open source applications with diverse characteristics: the *Reaction Jet Control (RJC)* application from NASA's Apollo Lunar Lander and an SSH framework called *JSCH* from the JCraft company [18]. Tests involve the injection of logically malformed data based on code metrics [15], which divert the AUT's execution paths to non-intended states.

In Sect. 2, we review previous work on the used techniques. Section 3 provides the background terminology and some definitions needed to describe our approach. In Sect. 4, we present the method implementation in the APP_LogGIC tool and we discuss the problems faced and the proposed solutions. Section 5 focuses on the results of our experiments with the two AUTs. Finally, we conclude with a review of the main aspects of our approach and a discussion on possible future research directions.

2 Related Work

In [5], the authors describe how they used the Daikon tool [13] to dynamically infer a set of likely invariants encoding various behavioral properties during the execution of web applets. They use NASA's Java Pathfinder (JPF) [8, 9] for model checking the application behavior over symbolic input, in order to validate whether the Daikon results are satisfied or violated. The analysis yields execution paths that, under specific conditions, can indicate the presence of certain types of logical errors that are encountered in web applications. The described method is applicable only to single-execution web applets. Also, it is not shown that the approach can scale to larger, standalone applications.

We used a variant of the same method in [6, 7], where we first presented a first implementation of the APP_LogGIC tool. In [6], we specifically targeted logical errors in GUI applications. We proposed a preliminary version of a Fuzzy Logic ranking system to address the problem of false positives, a common problem in static program analysis [31]. We applied our method on lab test-beds. In [7], the Fuzzy Logic ranking system was formally defined and further developed.

The research work presented in [10], focuses exclusively on specific flaws found in web applications. In [11], the authors combine various analysis techniques to identify multi-module vulnerabilities in web applications, but they do not address the problem of profiling source code behavior or logical errors per se.

In our current work, the method that we first proposed in [6, 7] is evolved into a more complete and effective approach with the capacity to be tested on real-world complex applications, instead of test-beds and simple GUI AUT. Also, we move towards eliminating false positives through classification and various heuristics.

3 Profiling the Behavior Behind the Source Code

Judging from experiments, requirements analysis [17] and previous research [5–7] on profiling the logic behind an AUT, we need: (i) a set of parsable logical rules (dynamic invariants) referring to the intended program functionality, (ii) a set of finite execution paths and variable valuations with adequate coverage of the AUT functionality, (iii) the Boolean valuation of the logical rules over the set of execution paths to allow detection of logical errors and (iv) a classification system for source code instructions to filter variables in branch conditions and data input vectors.

3.1   Extracting Intended Program Functionality as Rules (Dynamic Invariants)

The functionality of an AUT is captured in the form of dynamic invariants generated by the Daikon tool from MIT. Invariants represent the programmed behavior in the form of logical rules for variables, such as `p!=null` or `var=="string"` that hold true at certain program point(s) in all monitored executions. If the monitored executions are representative use-case scenarios of the AUT, then the generated dynamic invariants refer to the AUT's intended functionality. Intuitively, if an execution path is found that violates a (combination of) dynamic invariant(s), this means that a possible logical error exists, which affects the variable(s) referred in the invariant.

3.2   Program States and Their Variables

In order to verify Daikon invariants we need to crosscheck them with a set of finite execution paths and variable valuations, with adequate coverage of the AUT functionality. In this section, we introduce formal definitions for the used data sets.

An imperative program $P = (X, L, \ell_0, T)$ defines a set X of typed variables, a set L of control locations, an initial location $\ell_0 \in L$, and a set T of transitions. Each transition $\tau \in T$ is a tuple (ℓ, ρ, ℓ'), where $\ell, \ell' \in L$ are control locations, and ρ is a constraint over free variables from $X \cup X'$, where X denotes the variables at control location ℓ and X' denotes the same variables at control location ℓ'. For verification purposes, the set L of control locations comprises the source code points, which control the execution flow of a program, i.e. conditional statements such as branches and loops.

State of a program P is a valuation of the variables in X. The set of all possible states is denoted as $u.X$. We shall represent sets of states using constraints. For a constraint ρ over $X \cup X'$ and a valuation $(s, s') \in u.X \times u.X'$, we write $(s, s') \models \rho$ if the valuation satisfies the constraint ρ. We focus on AUTs with an explicitly provided *initial state* that assigns specific values to all variables in X. Finite computation of the program P is any sequence $(\ell_0, s_0), (\ell_1, s_1), ..., (\ell_k, s_k) \in (L \times u.X)$, where ℓ_0 is the initial location, s_0 is an initial state, and for each $i \in \{0, ..., k-1\}$, there is a transition $(\ell_i, \rho, \ell_{i+1}) \in T$ such that $(s_i, s_{i+1}) \models \rho$. A location ℓ is reachable if there exists some state s such that (ℓ, s) appears in some computation. An *execution path* or, simply, *path* of the program P is any sequence $\pi = (\ell_0, \rho_0, \ell_1), (\ell_1, \rho_1, \ell_2), ..., (\ell_{k-1}, \rho_{k-1}, \ell_k)$ of transitions, where ℓ_0 is the initial location.

3.3   Source Code Profiling for Logical Error Detection

According to NIST [21], the impact that a source code point has in a program may be captured by the program's Input Vectors (entry points and variables with user data) and *Branch Conditions* (e.g. *conditional statements* like if-statements). These characteristics determine the program's execution flow. Our approach studies how the AUT's execution is affected by crosschecking the truth values of the extracted dynamic invariants. A logical error is defined as follows:

Definition 1. A *logical error* manifests if there are execution paths π_i and π_j with the same prefix, such that for some $k \geq 0$ the transition $(\ell_k, \rho_k, \ell_{k+1})$ results in states (ℓ_{k+1}, s_i), (ℓ_{k+1}, s_j) with $s_i \neq s_j$ and for the dynamic invariant r_k, $(s_{i-1}, s_i) \models r_k$ in π_i and $(s_{j-1}, s_j) \not\models r_k$ in π_j, i.e. r_k is satisfied in π_i and is violated in π_j.

If a program error located in some transition does not cause unstable execution in the analyzed paths, it does not manifest as a logical error according to Definition 1. For this reason, our framework adopts a notion of risk for logical error detection. Risk is quantified by means of a fuzzy logic classification system based on two measuring functions, namely Severity and Vulnerability. These functions complement invariant verification and act as source code filters for logical error detection.

Our fuzzy logic approach also aims to confront two inherent problems in automated detection of code defects: the large data sets of the processed AUT execution paths and the possible false positives. Regarding the first mentioned problem, APP_LogGIC helps the code auditor to focus only to those transitions in the code that appear having high ratings in our classification system. Regarding false positives, due to the absence of predefined error patterns, APP_LogGIC's ratings implement criteria that take into account the possibility of a logical error in some transition.

Severity (Critical Source Code Points). Depending on the logic realized by some transition $(\ell_k, \rho_k, \ell_{k+1})$, $k \geq 0$ a logical error might be of high severity or not. We assume that all program transitions have a severity measurement and we define the measuring function Severity for quantifying the relative impact of a logical error in the execution of the AUT, if it were to manifest with the transition $(\ell_k, \rho_k, \ell_{k+1})$. *Severity*$(\ell_k, \rho_k, \ell_{k+1})$ measures the membership degree of the transition in a fuzzy logic set. Variables from states (ℓ_k, s_k) and (ℓ_{k+1}, s_{k+1}) that are used in the transition are weighted based on how they affect the execution flow. Those variables that directly affect the control-flow (e.g. they are part of the AUT's input vectors and are used in branch conditions) are considered dangerous: if a logical error were to manifest because of them, it causes an unintended behavior.

Definition 2. Given a transition $\tau \in T$ enabled at a source code point, we define Severity as

$$\text{Severity}(\tau) = v \in [0, 5]$$

measuring the severity of τ over a Likert-type scale [28] from 1 to 5. If a logical error were to manifest at a source code point, the scale-range captures the intensity of its impact in the AUT's execution flow. A fuzzy logic method evaluates transitions as being of high Severity (4 or 5), medium (3) or low (1 or 2). Technical details about the criteria used in severity assignments are presented in Sect. 4.5.

Vulnerability (Logical Error Likelihood and Danger Based on its Type). Vulnerability is a measuring function quantifying the likelihood of a logical error in a given transition based on its type and how dangerous it is. Vulnerability memberships are evaluated by taking into account: (i) the violations of dynamic invariants by the reached program states and (ii) input from an information flow analysis revealing the extent to which variable values are sanitized by conditional checks [21].

Definition 3. Given a tuple (τ, s, r), where r is a dynamic invariant, τ = (ℓ, ρ, ℓ′) and (ℓ′, s) ∈ (L × u.X), we define Vulnerability as

$$\text{Vulnerability } (\tau, s, r) = v \in [0, 5]$$

Ratings here also use a Likert scale [28] from 1 to 5. Similarly to Severity(τ), our fuzzy logic method evaluates transitions as being of "high" Vulnerability, "medium" or "low".

Tables 1 and 2 in Sect. 4.5 show the considered severity and vulnerability levels, while a more detailed presentation of the fuzzy logic system is given in [7].

Table 1. App_LogGIC's severity ranks in the Likert scale

Linguistic Value	Condition	Severity Level
Low	Random variable Severity	1
Low	Random variable Severity	2
Medium	Severity for variables used as data sinks (i.e. data originated from user input)	3
Medium	Severity for variables used in a conditional branch once on an "IF" branch	3
High	Severity for variables used in a conditional branch twice or more on an "IF" branch and/or a "SWITCH" branch	4
High	Severity for variables used as a data sink and in a conditional branch on an "IF" branch and/or a "SWITCH" branch	5

Table 2. APP_LogGIC vulnerability levels in the Likert scale

Linguistic value	Condition	Vulnerability level
Low	No invariant incoherencies / No improper checks of variables.	0
Medium	Multiple propagation of input data using only general, insufficient checks on variable content. (**Input Vector Method**)	2
Medium	Sound checks in variable contents but multiple propagation to method variables with relatively improper checks (**Input Vector Method**)	3
High	Improper/insufficient checks on variables holding input data – Variables also used in branch conditions (**Input Vector Method**)	4
High	Invariant enforcement AND invariant violation in alternate versions of same execution path (**Invariant-Based Method**)	5

Quantifying the Risk Associated with Program Transitions. According to OWASP, *the standard risk formulation is an operation over the likelihood and the impact of a finding* [25]:

$$\text{Risk} = \text{Likelihood} * \text{Impact}$$

We adopt this notion of risk into our framework for logical error detection. In our approach, Severity(τ) reflects the relative *Impact* of the transition τ at some source code point, whereas Vulnerability(τ, s, r) encompasses the *Likelihood* of a logical error in τ. Given the dynamic invariant r for τ, an estimate of the risk associated with τ can be computed by combining Severity(τ) and Vulnerability(τ, s, r) into a single value called Risk. There may be many different options for combining the values of the two measuring functions. We opt for an aggregation operation on the fuzzy sets, which allows to combining the fuzzy sets in a desirable way to produce a single fuzzy set. In this way, we take into account the two membership degrees in our Fuzzy Logic system [16]:

Definition 4. Given an AUT and a set of paths with $s \in u.X$ representing an accessed state and $\tau \in T$ an executed transition associated with the dynamic invariants r, function *Risk(τ, s, r)* is the aggregation

$$\text{Risk}(\tau, \text{ s, r}) = aggreg(\text{Severity}(\tau), \text{Vulnerability}(\tau, \text{ s, r}))$$

with a fuzzy set valuation

$$\text{Risk}(\tau, \text{ s, r}) = \{\text{Severity}(\tau)\} \cap \{\text{Vulnerability}(\tau, \text{ s, r})\}$$

APP_LogGIC applies defuzzification [20] on the resulting set, using the Center of Gravity technique. Defuzzification is the computation of a single value from two given fuzzy sets and their corresponding membership degrees, i.e. the involvedness of each fuzzy set presented in Likert values.

Risk ratings have the following interpretation: for two tuples $vs_1 = (\tau_1, s_1, r_1)$ and $vs_2 = (\tau_2, s_2, r_2)$, if Risk($vs_1$) > Risk($vs_2$), then vs_1 is more dangerous than vs_2, in terms of how τ_1 and τ_2 affect the execution of the AUT and if the analysis detects a manifested logical error. In the next section, we provide technical details for the techniques used to implement the presented analysis.

4   Design and Implementation of the APP_LogGIC Tool

4.1   APP_LogGIC's Architecture

APP_LogGIC flags possible logical errors based on information for their impact on the program's behavior and their location in code. The more suspicious a source code point is, the higher it scores in the Fuzzy Logic system. Figure 1 depicts how the applied analysis methods are combined in our tool:

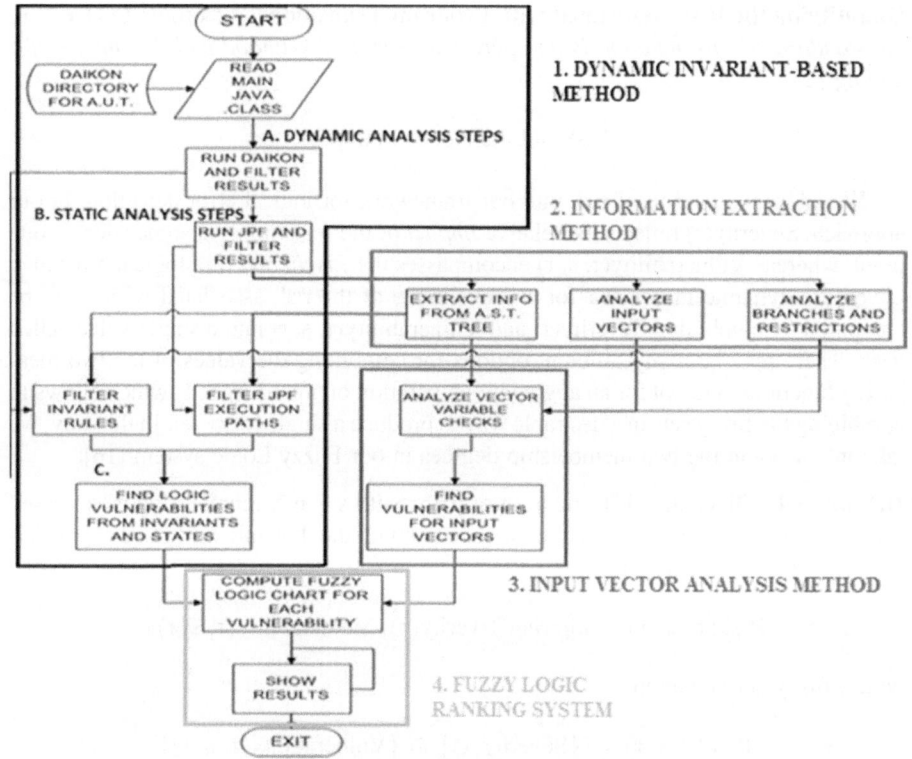

Fig. 1. The APP_LogGIC architecture

1. The *Dynamic Invariant-Based Method* extracts dynamic invariants and verifies them against tuples (ℓ, s) of program states at specific code locations gathered from AUT executions. For every checked state s and dynamic invariant r a vulnerability rating is then applied using the function Vulnerability(τ, s, r).
2. The *Information Extraction Method* analyzes branches in the source code and rates them using the function Severity(τ).
3. The *Input Vector Analysis Method* analyzes input vectors and applies a Vulnerability rating on variables of program states that hold input data, as in (1).
4. *Fuzzy Logic ranking system*: APP_LogGIC combines all information gathered from (1), (2) and (3), and assesses the Risk of source code points and states based on their position and the analysis findings.

4.2 Dynamic Invariant-Based Method

To automate the verification of dynamic invariants for logical error detection we need: (i) a set of parsable dynamic invariants for the AUT, (ii) a set of execution paths and information for the contents of the state variables and (iii) a complete analysis of the AUT's source code to gather input vectors and map all possible points, in which execution flow can be diverted.

A. Extracting the Programmed Behavior – Dynamic Analysis Step. Daikon performs dynamic analysis and produces *dynamic invariants* which describe the AUT's programmed behavior. If the tool runs for a sufficient set of use-cases with adequate coverage of the AUT's functionality, then the extracted programmed behavior matches the programmer's intended behavior. An example dynamic invariant generated from our tests is:

Daikon runs the program, observes the values that the program computes, and then reports, as in Fig. 2, assertions about source code variables that hold true throughout all AUT executions (much like "laws of conduct" for correct execution [12, 13]). The dynamic invariant of Fig. 2 shows that, upon invocation of method `Wait_for_stable_rate_exec()`, the value of the variable `TopLevel_Chart_count` is equal to '2'.

```
rjc.Chart.Wait_for_stable_rate_100000203_exec():::ENTER
this.TopLevel_Chart_count == 2.0
[...]
```

Fig. 2. Dynamic invariants produced by Daikon Dynamic Analysis

Invariant rules are filtered and only those that refer to control flow points and input vector points of the source code are kept. APP_LogGIC has a built-in Daikon parser that creates method objects with invariant objects based on the tokens of the parsed invariants. Thus, we have a fast way to parse invariants by method type, variable or class type.

B. Gathering Execution Paths and Program States – Static Analysis Step. Execution paths and program states are gathered using the Java Pathfinder tool (JPF) from NASA Ames Research Center [9]. The JPF core is a Virtual Machine (VM) for Java bytecode [9]. The default instruction set makes use of execution choices. JPF identifies points in programs from where execution flow can follow different paths and then systematically explores all of them [9].

Compared to our previous work in [6, 7], we have changed the static analysis from scripted execution of possible paths to symbolic execution (as in [5]). Symbolic Path-Finder (SPF) [8] combines symbolic execution with model checking and constraint solving for test case generation. This provides us a large number of execution paths along with program states (Fig. 3 depicts an example execution instruction record), while at the same time helps us avoid the error-prone process of manually configuring multiple application runs.

```
[rjc/Chart.java:342] :
if (execute_at_initialization_464 == 1) {
VARIABLE: execute_at_initialization_464 -> 1
```

Fig. 3. SPF output: instruction executed and variable content

SPF's results are then used to check if Daikon's dynamic invariants hold true along the executions paths or not. If APP_LogGIC detects two different versions of an execution path that according to Definition 1 differ in some state, such that one path satisfies a Daikon invariant while the other violates it, then a logical error is flagged and the membership in the Vulnerability Fuzzy Logic set is increased.

In order to gather the sets of execution paths and states for given inputs of the AUT (store, access, update of data), we had to re-code SPF's basic listener, namely the Java class named: gov.nasa.jpf.symbc.SymbolicListener. Since SPF's model checking is based on listener objects, we extended the @override executeInstruction() and instructionExecuted() methods implemented to watch for and collect data during instruction invocation.

C. Verifying Dynamic Invariants - Logical Error Detection. Let us consider the invariant shown in Fig. 2: APP_LogGIC checks if there are execution paths with the same prefix and some differing program state corresponding to the shown dynamic invariant. In this case, APP_LogGIC tries to find a path/state combination that violates that assertion upon entering the exec() method (variable's value is not '2.0') and, simultaneously, a second combination that satisfies it. This contradiction, if present, is a clear sign of a possible logical error inside exec() and variable TopLevel_Chart_count.

APP_LogGIC uses Severity ranks and focuses on dynamic invariants that refer to variables used in conditional statements (branch conditions), which are responsible for execution path deviations; if there is a possibility for a logical error manifestation, then this may happen in a branch condition since conditional branching is a decision-making point in the control flow [5]. Information for the Vulnerability rating methods is provided in Sect. 4.5 below.

4.3   Information Extraction Method

In order to gather input vectors and all source code points where execution flow can follow different paths we are based on the JavaC compiler and an appropriate abstract syntax tree (AST) representation. The JavaC Treescanner methods (visitIf(), visitMethodInvocation() etc.) were overridden, in order to detect and analyze sanitization checks of input data, i.e. source code points in which the data context of variables is checked.

4.4   Input Vector Analysis Method

A tainted object propagation analysis complements the dynamic invariant method for logical error detection. All variables that hold input data (input vectors) and the checks enforced upon them are analyzed for their role in conditional statements (as in Sect. 3.3) and for the following correctness criterion: all input data should be sanitized before their use [21]. This analysis shows: (i) whether a *tainted variable* (i.e. a variable that contains potentially dangerous input data) is accessed in a conditional statement without having previously checked its initial values, (ii) if data from a tainted variable is passed along in methods and other variables and (iii) instances of user input that are never checked or sanitized in any way.

APP_LogGIC checks tainted variables by analyzing the conditions enforced on their content. For example, if an input vector variable is used only in the conditional statement `if(a != null)` and then variable a is used in a command without further sanitization of its contents, then this check is flagged as ineffective and APP_ LogGIC gives a high rating on the Vulnerability scale for that variable. More information for how rank values are assigned is provided in the tables of Sect. 4.5.

4.5   The Fuzzy Logic Ranking System

As explained in Sect. 3, a Fuzzy Logic system add-on [19] is used in APP_LogGIC to rank possible logical errors. In order to aid the APP_LogGIC end-user, Severity and Vulnerability values are grouped into 3 sets (Low, Medium, High), with an approximate width of each group of $(5/3) = 1,66 \sim 1,5$ (final ranges: Low in [0...2], Medium in (2...3,5] and High in (3,5...5]).

Severity (Impact of a Source Code Point on Execution Flow). As a program transition we consider any instruction at a source code point that accesses variable values of the program's state. By measuring the Severity of a transition, we also assign the given Severity rating to the accessed variables; e.g., the IF-statement `if (isAdmin == true) {...}` represents a check on `isAdmin`: This conditional branch is a source code point where unintended execution deviations may occur [5]. Thus, the involved transition is classified as important (rating 3-5 on the scale). The variable isAdmin and its transition are rated as **Medium (3)**. A variable is assigned only one rating, depending on how the variable is used in transitions throughout the AUT. Table 1 below depicts the Likert ratings for Severity. For example, if two transitions exist, an if-statement and a data input transition, then a variable used in both transition will get an overall Severity value of five (5) as it can be shown on the last line of Table 1. For formal presentations on the ranking system and its conditions the reader is referred to [7], due to lack of space.

Vulnerability. By measuring the Vulnerability of a tuple (τ, s, r) as seen in Sect. 3.3, we also assign the given Vulnerability rating to the accessed variables used in transition τ and the corresponding program state. Similar to Severity, a variable is assigned only one overall Vulnerability rating, depending on how the variable is used in transitions throughout the AUT. Rating conditions are presented in Table 2 below.

Risk. Risk represents a calculated value assigned to each tuple (τ, s, r) and its corresponding variables, by aggregating the aforementioned Severity and Vulnerability ratings. Our tool produces a set of graphs where the combined risk factor is drawn, which is calculated using Fuzzy Set Theory: Fuzzy Logic's linguistic variables in the form of IF-THEN rules (Fig. 4). For clarity, all scales (Severity, Vulnerability and Risk) share the same linguistic characterization: *"Low"*, *"Medium"* and *"High"*.

Figure 4 shows how Risk is calculated. The complete analysis of how formal Fuzzy Logic rules are calculated and defined is provided in [7]. Table 3 depicts the fuzzy logic output for Risk, based on the aggregation of Severity and Vulnerability.

IF Severity IS low AND Vulnerability IS low THEN Risk IS low

Fig. 4. Example of a Fuzzy Logic rule

Table 3. Risk for each variable = Severity x Vulnerability

Vulnerability \ Severity	Low	Medium	High
Low	Low	Low	Medium
Medium	Low	Medium	High
High	Medium	High	High

5 Experiments and Test Results

To the best of our knowledge, there is no commercial test-bed or open-source revision of an application with a reported set of existing logical errors. For this reason, our experiments were based exclusively on formal fault injection into two different open-source applications: (i) The *Apollo Lunar Lander Reaction Jet Controller* (RJC) provided along with SPF by the Java Pathfinder team in NASA Ames Research Center [9] and (ii) an SSH framework called *JSCH* from the JCraft company [18].

To cope with the inherent analysis scalability problems, we switched to method invocation paths instead of entire execution paths. This is consistent with the Daikon analysis, since Daikon dynamic invariants only describe a program's execution during entry and exit of a method invocation. As a consequence, the size of the data set for the RJC AUT was reduced from 155 MB to 73 MB and the execution of the APP_LogGIC analysis was speed up by ~ 5 min, an improvement of up to 80 %.

5.1 Invariant Tests: RJC Application

To validate APP_LogGIC's effectiveness, we injected two faults into NASA's RJC application. A malformed Java object was created that was initialized with an invalid value. The result of injecting the object in the code was a change in the AUT execution flow from its intended path to an erroneous one, thus causing a logical error.

Our approach was based on recent results from research on fault injection, which show that the key issue when injecting software faults is *fault representativeness* [15]: there is a strong relationship between fault representativeness and fault locations, rather than between fault representativeness and the various types of faults injected. To pinpoint source code methods into RJC with relatively high representativeness we used common software engineering metrics. According to [15], fault-load representativeness can be achieved by looking at the following metrics: *Lines of Code* and *Cyclomatic Complexity* which represent respectively the number of statements and the number of paths in a component [15, 23]. *The Average methods per Class* counts the number of methods defined per type in all Class objects. If this metric scores high, it benefits these experiments since method invocation paths will be more complex and, therefore, likely more error-prone. This metric synergizes well with Cyclomatic Complexity in the RJC experiments. With the above mentioned metrics, we detected methods in RJC that have high representativeness and then we injected logic errors in them. For our analysis, we used the tool CodePro Analytix from Google. More specifically, we evaluated the system behavior when one of its components is faulty and not the behavior of the faulty component itself. We did not consider additional metrics, as metrics tend to correlate with each other. On the other hand, the used metrics suffice in order to detect key points in the source code for fault injection [15].

As we can see in Table 4, these five classes have the highest ratings in RJC source code. `Reaction_Jet_Control` classes have the highest Lines of Code and Complexity values. Yet, their average methods per type are significantly low. Also, they have no execution-defining branch statements inside their code able to diverge the execution of RJC. To this end, we decided to inject the faulty values in the `rjc.Chart.Wait_for_stable_rate_100000203_exec()` method within Chart.java. JPF provided the needed method invocation paths that were used by APP_LogGIC to check the Daikon-generated dynamic invariants. **8063** method invocation paths were satisfying the invariant "`TopLevel_Chart_count == 2`" and three injected paths were violating it. APP_LogGIC detected the dynamic invariant violation for both of the two fault injections. Variable `TopLevel_Chart_count` held injected data and was also used in an if-statement: APP_LogGIC's Fuzzy Logic system classified the logical error with the following ratings (Tables 5, 6, 7 and 8):

Table 4. Highest metric scores for NASA's RJC

	Lines of Code	Cyclomatic Complexity	Average methods per Type
Rjc.Chart.java	10,48	3,31	29
Rjc.Chart_1.java	13,68	3,31	29
Rjc.Chart_2.java	13,68	3,31	29
Rjc.Reaction_Jet_Control0.java	99,50	7,50	2
Rjc.Reaction_Jet_Control1.java	85,50	7,50	2

Table 5. Severity **rank** for RJC injection by APP_LogGIC

Medium	Severity for variables used in a CB **ONCE** on: o An "IF" branch o A 'SWITCH' branch	3

Table 6. Vulnerability **rank** for RJC injection by APP_LogGIC

High	Invariant enforcement AND invariant violation in alternate versions of same execution path (**Invariant-Based analysis**)	5

Table 7. Severity **rank** for JSCH input vectors by APP_LogGIC

Medium	Severity for variables used as data sinks (i.e. data originated from user input)	3

Table 8. Vulnerability **rank** for JSCH input vectors by APP_LogGIC

High	No check or improper checks in variables depended on input data and used in branch conditions	4

A total of 6,240 control flow locations (such as if-statements) were gathered and analyzed from symbolic execution. Also, 515,854 method invocations and variable Store and Invoke instructions were processed. The injected paths had 8,064 comparisons. Before injection, all 8,064 paths were found satisfying the invariant. As mentioned earlier, after injection, three paths were found having different states (variable TopLevel_Chart_count had different values while entering and exiting method exec()). Both injected faults were discovered and all possible deviated execution paths were detected. Data sets can be downloaded via the link at the end of this work.

5.2   Tainted Object Propagation Tests: JSCH Framework

JSCH [18] is an SSH2 framework licensed under a BSD-style open-source license. Here, we tested APP_LogGIC's capability to detect logical errors manifesting from input data. We didn't have to inject any logical errors in JSCH since, to some extent, some were already present in examples provided along with the framework's code. JSCH uses SSH connections and built-in encryption for security. Yet, the examples provided with their source code have improper sanitization of user input.

Using Tainted Object analysis, AST trees and the Java compiler, APP_LogGIC created a map of the AUT (variable assignments, declarations, method invocations etc.). The analysis traced the tainted input and gathered the variables were input data could reside (a.k.a. *sinks*) to detect whether sanitization checks had been enforced or not. APP_LogGIC detected variables without proper sanitization and ranked these input vectors accordingly:

APP_LogGIC found out that sanitization checks in JSCH were only comparing *initialization data to actual variable data*. This is a common logical error [21], since such checks can only show that variable data is updated compared to their initial value, but lack further content checks.

The tool detected eleven (11) sinks where data was stored without proper sanitization. Its Fuzzy Logic system calculated which of these points are dangerous based on their position and utilization inside the source code; it then detected and ranked four of them as potentially dangerous. Indeed, out of the eleven aforementioned variables used in sinks, those four variables where the ones that did not have proper sanitization checks enforced on their data.

Method Applicability Issues. Even though APP_LogGIC's result had a 100 % success rate in flagging dangerous and injected points of logical errors, yet, the sample upon which APP_LogGIC was tested still remains very small, if we would like to claim a high average detection rate. The applicability of the presented method depends on how thoroughly the input vectors and dynamic invariants are analyzed. At the moment, APP_LogGIC can only analyze simple invariants and two types of input vectors. Yet, judging from the parsable syntax of dynamic invariants, one can safely deduct that, with the right parser, most dynamic invariants can be verified. This program could evolve into a potentially valuable tool: program tests created by developers using APP_LogGIC in various stages of the development cycle, could help detect logical errors and reduce the costly process of backtracking to fix them.

State explosion remains a major issue, since it is a problem inherited by the used analysis techniques. Yet, state explosion is manageable using source code classification. Both Daikon and JPF can be configured to target specific source code methods of interest rather than analyze the entire source code of an AUT. Severity ranking helps in this. The use of method invocation paths downsized the initial data set for RJC from 155 MB to 73 MB and speeded up execution almost 80 % in comparison with experiments using the entire execution paths, as shown in Table 9.

Table 9. Execution times for APP_LogGIC experiments

	Execution – Full paths and states	Execution – Method invocation paths and states
Size	155 MB	73 MB
Time elapsed	~8 min (RJC) ~6 min (JSCH)	~4 min (RJC) ~6 min (JSCH)
Errors detected	2 out of 2 injections (RJC)	2 out of 2 (RJC)

Both of the analyzed applications are relatively small in comparison to other AUT (on the order of many GB). The AUT size will be considered in future research. APP_LogGIC ran on an Intel Core 2 Duo E6550 PC (2.33 GHz, 4 GB RAM).

6 Conclusions

Preliminary results show that profiling the intended behavior of applications is feasible (up to a certain complexity level) even in real-world applications. Logic profiling with the use of Fuzzy Logic provides the following advantages: (i) the data to be analyzed is reduced by focusing on high impact (dangerous) source code points (Severity ranking) and (ii) it is a way to treat false positives by assessing logical errors and ignoring irrelevant dynamic invariants (Vulnerability ranking). Thus, invariant violations referring to source code points that do not somehow affect any conditional branches (such as if-statements) during execution can be discarded.

The method suffers by a number of limitations. Complex invariant rules generated by Daikon need deep semantic analysis in order to be usable. Also, Daikon does not support analysis of loops ("While" and "For"). On top of that, Daikon's dynamic execution must cover as much AUT functionality as possible, if a logical error is to be discovered. Otherwise, dynamic invariants generated will not correctly describe the AUT behavior intended by its programmer. We plan to explore different approaches using design artifacts provided by developers for a more efficient reasoning of the source code [24] such as XBRL or OWL, in order to describe programming logic.

Another research venue is to test this method on control systems used in critical infrastructures (CI) or manufacturing facilities. Widely used programmable logic controllers control functions in critical infrastructures such as water, power, gas pipelines, and nuclear facilities [26]. Logic errors might lead to weaknesses that make it possible to execute commands not intended by their programmer. The effect of this attack might lead to cascading effects amongst numerous interconnected CI, or can have an impact on a number of other infrastructures, including mobile systems, etc. [27–30].

Method path files, AST tree mappings along with execution snapshots for RJC and JSCH can be found at: www.cis.aueb.gr/Publications/APP_LogGIC-2014.zip

Acknowledgment. This research has been co-financed by the European Union (European Social Fund ESF) and Greek national funds through the Operational Program "Education and Lifelong Learning" of the National Strategic Reference Framework (NSRF) - Research Funding Program: Thalis Athens University of Economics and Business - Software Engineering Research Platform.

References

1. Dobbins, J.: Inspections as an Up-Front Quality Technique. In: Handbook of Software Quality Assurance, pp. 217–252. Prentice Hall, New York (1998)
2. McLaughlin, B.: Building Java Enterprise Applications. Architecture, vol. 1. O' Reilly, Sebastopol (2002)
3. Peng, W. Wallace, D.: Software Error Analysis. In: NIST Special Publication 500-209. NIST, Gaithersburg, pp. 7–10 (1993)
4. Kimura, M.: Software vulnerability, definition, modeling, and practical evaluation for e-mail transfer software. Int. J. Pressure Vessels Pip. **83**(4), 256–261 (2006)
5. Felmetsger, V., Cavedon, L., Kruegel, C., Vigna, J.: Toward automated detection of logic vulnerabilities in web applications. In: Proceedings of the 19th USENIX Symposium, USA, p. 10 (2010)
6. Stergiopoulos, G., Tsoumas, B., Gritzalis, D.: Hunting application-level logical errors. In: Barthe, G., Livshits, B., Scandariato, R. (eds.) ESSoS 2012. LNCS, vol. 7159, pp. 135–142. Springer, Heidelberg (2012)
7. Stergiopoulos, G., Tsoumas, B., Gritzalis, D.: On business logic vulnerabilities hunting: the APP_LogGIC framework. In: Lopez, J., Huang, X., Sandhu, R. (eds.) NSS 2013. LNCS, vol. 7873, pp. 236–249. Springer, Heidelberg (2013)
8. Păsăreanu, C.S., Visser, W.: Verification of Java programs using symbolic execution and invariant generation. In: Graf, S., Mounier, L. (eds.) SPIN 2004. LNCS, vol. 2989, pp. 164–181. Springer, Heidelberg (2004)
9. The Java PathFinder tool, NASA Ames Research Center, US. http://babelfish.arc.nasa.gov/trac/jpf/

10. Doupe, A., Boe, B., Vigna, G.: Fear the EAR: discovering and mitigating execution after redirect vulnerabilities. In: Proceedings of the 18th ACM Conference on Computer and Communications Security, pp. 251–262. ACM (2011)
11. Balzarotti, D., Cova, M., Felmetsger, V., Vigna, G.: Multi-module vulnerability analysis of web-based applications. In: Proceedings of the 14th ACM Conference on Computer and Communications Security, pp. 25–35. ACM (2007)
12. Ernst, M., Perkins, J., Guo, P., McCamant, S., Pacheco, C., Tschantz, M., Xiao, C.: The Daikon system for dynamic detection of likely invariants. Sci. Comput. Program. **69**, 35–45 (2007)
13. The Daikon Invariant Detector Manual. http://groups.csail.mit.edu/pag/daikon/
14. Brumley, D., Newsome, J., Song, D., Wang, H., Jha, S.: Towards automatic generation of vulnerability-based signatures. In: IEEE Symposium on Security and Privacy (2006)
15. Natella, R., Cotronneo, D., Duraes, J., Madeira, H.: On fault representativeness of software fault injection. IEEE Trans. Softw. Eng. **39**(1), 80–96 (2013)
16. Foundations of Fuzzy Logic, Fuzzy Operators, Mathworks. http://www.mathworks.com/help/toolbox/fuzzy/bp78l6_-1.html
17. Systems Engineering Fundamentals: Supplementary text prepared by the Defense Acquisition University Press, Defense Acquisition University, USA (2001)
18. JSCH SSH framework, JCraft. http://www.jcraft.com/jsch/
19. Cingolani, P., Alcala-Fdez, J.: jFuzzyLogic: a robust and flexible fuzzy-logic inference system language implementation. In: Proceedings of the IEEE International Conference on Fuzzy Systems, pp. 1–8. IEEE (2012)
20. Leekwijck, W., Kerre, E.: Defuzzification: criteria and classification. Fuzzy Sets Syst. **108** (2), 159–178 (1999)
21. Stoneburner G., Goguen, A.: SP 800-30. Risk management guide for information technology systems. Technical report. NIST, USA (2002)
22. Burns, A., Burns, R.: Basic Marketing Research. Pearson Education, p. 245 (2008)
23. Fenton, N., Pfleeger, S.: Software Metrics: A Rigorous and Practical Approach. PWS, Boston (1998)
24. Giannakopoulou, D., Pasareanu, C., Cobleigh, J.: Assume-guarantee verification of source code with design-level assumptions. In: Proceedings of the 26th International Conference on Software Engineering, pp. 211–220. IEEE (2004)
25. The OWASP Risk Rating Methodology, www.owasp.org/index.php/OWASP_Risk_Rating_Methodology
26. Theoharidou, M., Kotzanikolaou, P., Gritzalis, D.: Risk assessment methodology for interdependent critical infrastructures. Int. J. Risk Assess. Manage. **15**(2/3), 128–148 (2011)
27. Kandias M., Mitrou L., Stavrou V., Gritzalis, D.: Which side are you on? A new Panopticon vs. privacy. In: Proceedings of 10th International Conference on Security and Cryptography, pp. 98–110. SciTePress (2013)
28. Albaum, G.: The Likert scale revisited. J. Market res. soc. **39**, 331–348 (1997)
29. Mylonas A., Dritsas, S., Tsoumas V., Gritzalis, D.: Smartphone security evaluation - the malware attack case. In: Proceedings of the 8th International Conference on Security and Cryptography, pp. 25–36. SciTepress, (2011)
30. Theoharidou, M., Mylonas, A., Gritzalis, D.: A risk assessment method for smartphones. In: Gritzalis, D., Furnell, S., Theoharidou, M. (eds.) SEC 2012. IFIP AICT, vol. 376, pp. 443–456. Springer, Heidelberg (2012)
31. Chatzieleftheriou, G., Katsaros, P.: Test driving static analysis tools in search of C code vulnerabilities. In: Proceedings of the 35th IEEE Computer Software and Applications Conference on Workshops (COMPSACW), Munich, Germany, pp. 96–103. IEEE Computer Society (2011)

Evaluation of Dynamic Instantiation in CPRM-Based Systems

Ana Nieto$^{(\boxtimes)}$

Computer Science Department, University of Málaga, Málaga, Spain
nieto@lcc.uma.es

Abstract. Context-based Parametric Relationship Models (CPRMs) reduce the complexity of working with various numbers of parameters and dependencies, by adding particular contexts to the final scheme when it is required, dynamically. In this paper the cost of including new information in CPRM is properly analysed, considering the information in the parametric trees defined for the parameters in the CPRM-based system. Some strategies for mitigating the cost of the instantiation process are proposed.

Keywords: CPRM · Security · QoS

1 Introduction

Security and Quality of Service (QoS) mechanisms are fundamental to providing a total network convergence. The convergence of networks poses several challenges regarding QoS and security. Most of these are inherited from the traditional tradeoffs in isolated networks, but the *Internet of Things* (IoT) and the *Future Internet* (FI) open the door to new challenges to be met.

For example, the user's participation in these networks, requires providing multimedia capabilities that, in many cases, may be provided through limited-resource devices, such as sensors acting as relays. Moreover, the user's participation requires taking into account misbehaviour issues, and security mechanisms should be applied. The problem is that security mechanisms require network and local resources that the QoS mechanisms handle to guarantee the performance of services. Moreover, in future networks, multipurpose devices may have to coexist. That means that, on the one hand, different capabilities can be provided regarding the local resources and functionality of the devices. On the other hand, some devices in the network have different purposes and therefore are not available for providing security or QoS requirements.

Consequently, in the IoT and FI, security and QoS tradeoffs cannot be considered, only taking into account specific scenarios, but also have to consider abstract issues or generic composition of *things*. Diverse models for measuring the security and QoS tradeoff have emerged [1–3]. In particular, from our point of view, the *generic models for the analysis of Security and QoS tradeoff* are well suited to be used in heterogeneous networks of dynamic composition, in where

© Springer International Publishing Switzerland 2015
J. Lopez et al. (Eds.): CRiSIS 2014, LNCS 8924, pp. 52–66, 2015.
DOI: 10.1007/978-3-319-17127-2_4

it is very difficult to predict, with any great accuracy, the devices that will form the network. An example of these types of models are *Context-based Parametric Relationship Models* (CPRM).

The main objective of this paper is to evaluate, the impact of the instantiation of parameters in CPRM-based systems. That is, provides a discussion about the complexity of the models based on the number of dependencies, and the location of the instantiated parameters in the general tree, and draw conclusions about how the effect on performance may be mitigated in order to enhance the implementation of the instantiation process carried out in CPRM-based systems.

The paper is structured as follows. Section 2 presents the state of the art in generic models for the analysis of the security and QoS tradeoff. Section 3 provides an overview of the CPRM model. Section 4 defines the impact of the instantiation in CPRM-based systems, according with the definitions provided by the model. Finally, Sect. 5 proposes some new directions that could be taken to mitigate the impact on performance.

2 Background

Generic models for assesing the Security and QoS tradeoff are those capable of analyzing the security and QoS requirements and characteristics of a set of elements and components in a network, being able to change the composition of said elements and characteristics for other ones and still be useful. Therefore, the idea behind these models is that a part of the model has to remain abstract prior to knowing or receiving the new components in the information system.

Related work that focus on security and QoS tradeoff consider the composition of services based, for example, on the selection of a set of security goals that may be analysed based on their interdependencies [2], or the definition of ontologies where security is taken as a static metric for the QoS [4], whereas, our perception, is that security can be very dynamic, based on the context, and, moreover, it is not always possible to predict the final mechanisms that will be available in the network.

Moreover, there are additional approaches that have provided interesting results but cannot be easily integrated in static approaches. For example, security and QoS are analysed as separate issues in [5,6]. In [5] an analysis of QoS and *Quality of Experience* (QoE) is provided, while in [6] authentication protocols for mobile devices are analysed. Despite the fact that both of them focus on next generation networks, the possibility of comparing them and drawing conclusions is very difficult without using generic models for the analysis. Furthermore, security and QoS analysed as separate issues is useful for providing rich information to be added to the former, and, then, use rule-based parametrization techniques for defining different compositions, at service layer [7]. However, these approaches focus on services, and do not consider the composition of *things* (e.g. combination of anti-tampering mechanisms and high-layer services).

Generic approaches for analyzing complex decisions such as *Analytic Hierarchy Process* (AHP) [8], or *Potentially All PaiRwIse ranKings of possible Alternatives*

(PAPRIKA) [9] are fixed and do not define contextual parameters as CPRM does. Moreover, the purpose of CPRM is the analysis of security and QoS tradeoff based on the composition of mechanisms, and for this reason CPRM defines the set of relationships required to perform this type of analysis and to vary the subjective value of the parameters based on the context.

3   Contex-Based Parametric Relationship Models

The structure of a CPRM-based system, defined in [10], is based on a set of parameters and the relationships between them, a set of operations (*op*) which define the effects on the dependent parameters, and a set of weights which define the relevant subjective and non-subjective components in the model. To do that, the model defines three types of structures, depending on the type of context integrated:

- *Parametric Relationship Model* (PRM) structure. If only general parameters and their relationships are defined. The default relationships are defined for Security and QoS parameters.
- *Context-based PRM* (CPRM) structure. If there is a general context integrated.
- *Instance of CPRM/CPRM$_i$* (*CPRM$_i$*) structure. If there are one or more particular contexts integrated. The definition of this structure is recursive, and defines the dynamic behaviour of CPRM-based systems.

Therefore, a CPRM-based system is defined based on the parameters and relationships, using one structure of type CPRM or *CPRM$_i$*. The particularity of these systems is that we can change the context dynamically to evaluate the new mechanisms which operate in these systems.

With this objective in mind, there are two structures (scripts) for defining the contexts:

- *General Contexts* (GC), which define the weights for the elements in a PRM or a CPRM (parameters, types, layers, operations, relationships).
- *Particular Contexts*(PC), which define new parameters (instances) that instantiate to existing parameters in the model structure (CPRM/*CPRM$_i$*). The existing parameters are targeted with the type *instantiated* when the instantiation process concludes.

Contexts can be integrated into schemes to define the behaviour of the CPRM-based systems. Figure 1 illustrates the dynamic generation of CPRM-based systems according the description provided in [10], that should be implemented by any handler of CPRM-based systems. First, using a PRM the generic relationships between parameters are provided. In our case, the model is defined to be used for assessing the security and QoS tradeoff, so the set of parameters that is the result of diverse security and QoS analyses is used. The set of parameters chosen are general properties (e.g. authentication) or parameters that can

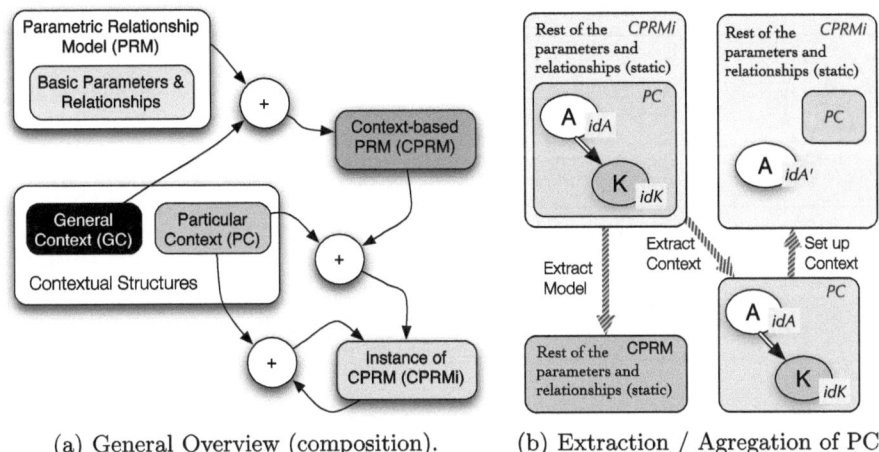

(a) General Overview (composition).   (b) Extraction / Agregation of PC.

Fig. 1. Dynamic Generation of CPRM-based Systems.

be expresed using mathematical formulation (e.g. delay). So, using these parameters, it is very easy to understand the concept of *instantiation*: the goal is
to replace the parameters with the specific mechanisms which implement them,
when this information becomes available.

In consequence, the composition of a CPRM-based system is dynamic, and
the objective is the evaluation of the mechanisms for implementing new properties as soon as they are known. Note that this is an approach for measuring the
security and QoS tradeoff that respects the uncertainly in the composition of
dynamic networks, where it is very difficult to predict the mechanisms provided
by the heterogeneous devices which compose the network.

Moreover, the model defines a set of action rules for adding dependencies
between the parameters once the instantiation process has been initated. Figure 2
shows an example of instantiation of parameters. For example, the parameters
A, B, and C were defined in the initial PRM, as well as the dependency $d(A, B)$.
However, the parameters a1, b1, and c1 are instances, defined in the PC, and
instantiate to the parameters A, B and C, respectively.

As a PRM is considered to be the most general structure, and, therefore,
provides all general information, the relationship $d(a1, c1)$, defined in the PC,
generates an inconsistency in the model, because information $d(A, C)$ was not
previously defined. So, the action rules are defined to consider these cases and
add these kinds of relationships between instantiated parameters.

Furthermore, any instance inherits the relationships of the instantiated parameter. Then, as $d(A, B)$ has been previously defined in the general behaviour,
$d(a1, b1)$ inherits this behaviour with the same weight as defined in the general
relationship. In fact, the relationship $d(A, C)$ was added with weight 0 to avoid
the effect of this last action rule.

In addition, during the instantiation process, the system checks the identifier
of the parameters to prevent different parameters from being considered as the

Weights: parameters (Wp), operations (Wo), types (Wt), layers (Wl), dependence between parameters (Wd)

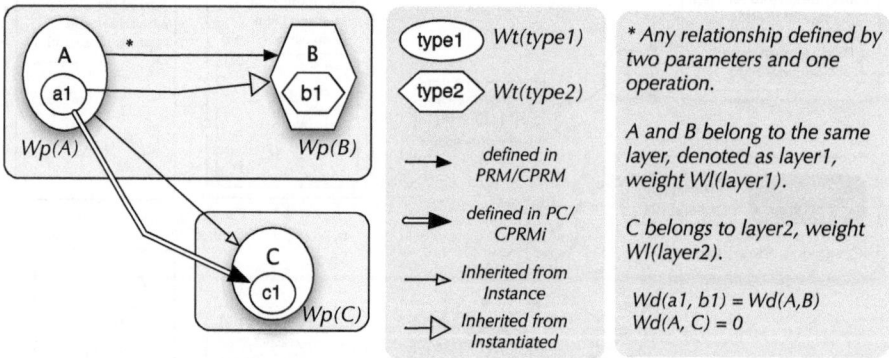

Fig. 2. Weight-based Relationship and instantiation.

same parameter, or to identify when a parameter in a PC extracted from a model has a different identifier in another contextual model where the PC has to be integrated. This latter case is shown in Fig. 1(b).

After the integration process, the model defines a set of operations that can be performed on the information to analyse the security and QoS tradeoff. Specifically, the set of operations are defined in Table 1. These operations are responsible for the final parametric tree for a parameter. For example, if the parameter A defines the relationship $A \xrightarrow{+} B$, and A is increased, then, the effect on B according to the dependence and Exp. 1 is an increase in B. To the contrary, if A is decreased, then, there is nothing to do, if the only information available is that $A \xrightarrow{+} B$, because in this case, only the effect when A is increased, is defined.

Therefore, a parametric tree is a tree that shows all the parameters affected by an increase or (exclusive) decrease of a parameter. The initial dependencies are set as a graph, so the cycles are avoided by creating branchs when loops are found. Moreover, the rest of the leaves of the model are generated when the operation defined for the relationship does not show an effect on the parameter in the consequent.

Finally, consider that the cost of this dynamic behaviour is memory and computational. This is inevitable when considering the integration of new information in a cross-layered dependencies model. Measuring the cost based on the new

Table 1. Operations in a CPRM.

Basic Formulation Set (BFS)	Complex Formulation Set (CFS)
$D^+ :: aD^+b \Rightarrow (\Delta a \rightarrow \Delta b)$ (1)	$D^c :: (\Delta a \rightarrow \Delta b) \wedge (\nabla a \rightarrow \nabla b) \equiv aD^+b \wedge aD^{\neg+}b$ (5)
$D^- :: aD^-b \Rightarrow (\Delta a \rightarrow \nabla b)$ (2)	$D^t :: aD^cb \wedge bD^ca$ (6)
$D^{\neg+} :: aD^{\neg+}b \Rightarrow (\nabla a \rightarrow \nabla b)$ (3)	$D^{\neg c} :: (\Delta a \rightarrow \nabla b) \wedge (\nabla a \rightarrow \Delta b) \equiv aD^-b \wedge aD^{\neg-}b$ (7)
$D^{\neg-} :: aD^{\neg-}b \Rightarrow (\nabla a \rightarrow \Delta b)$ (4)	$D^{i+} :: (\Delta a \rightarrow \Delta b) \wedge (\nabla a \rightarrow \Delta b) \equiv aD^+b \wedge aD^{\neg-}b$ (8)
	$D^{i-} :: (\Delta a \rightarrow \nabla b) \wedge (\nabla a \rightarrow \nabla b) \equiv aD^-b \wedge aD^{\neg+}b$ (9)

infomation provided is vital in order to evaluate the suitability of the model for different purposes.

4   Impact of a Particular Context

The aim in this section is raise awareness of the impact of a PC based on the location of the instantiated parameters in the dependencies graph. When the PC defines a type of sensor or device, it is usual that the parameters involved will be leaves or parameters with low accumulative dependence. In this case, the parameters in the consequent are instantiated parameters whose impact on the rest of parameters is null. Hence, the impact of the relationships defined for these parameters, when they are set up in our model do not provide much information as regards from where there are extracted. So, the impact of a new PC is greater, as the new parameters defined (instances) affect parameters far away from the leaf nodes, and with a high number of relationships.

Table 2. Set-based definitions in a CPRM-based system [10].

Acumulative Influence (ι) and Acumulative Dependence (δ)	
$\iota(a) = \lvert I_a \rvert, I_a = \{x \mid x \to a \lor xRa, x \neq a, x \in P\}$	(10)
$\delta(a) = \lvert D_a \rvert, D_a = \{y \mid a \to y \lor aRy, y \neq a, y \in P\}$	(11)
$xRy \iff x \to y \lor \exists k \mid k \in D_x \land k \in I_y$	(12)

This conclusion can be analysed using the formulation in Table 2. Considering N parameters in a CPRM, and Y the parameter that will be instantiated by K number of instances, which means that there are k parameters which satisfy that Y is their parent: $K = \lvert \{x \mid Y \in P(x)\} \rvert$. This set is known as the set of instances of a parameter Y, and is denoted as H in Exp. 14. Moreover, P defines the set of parents of a parameter, which is the information provided by the PC. Whether Y is a leaf node, that is, $\delta(Y) == 0$, and the accumulative influence on Y preceeding the instantiation of the CPRM is $\iota(Y) = M$, then the new accumulative influence on Y after the instantiation is $\iota(Y) = K * M$, considering that Y is the only instantiated parameter.

Moreover, if the instantiated parameter Y is not a leaf node, it impacts on other parameters in the PRM ($\delta(Y) > 0$). So, in case that prior the instantiation the accumulative dependence on Y was $\delta(Y)$, and that $\delta(Y)^t$ defines the dependence degree of Y once the instances 1 to $t <= K$ have been added, and therefore $\delta(Y)^0 = \delta(Y)$, after the instantiation the accumulative dependence on Y is given by Exp. 13 (δ'):

$$\delta(Y)' = \delta(Y) + \sum_{i=1}^{K} (\delta(y_i) - \delta(Y)^{i-1}) \tag{13}$$

$$H = \{x \mid Y \in P(x)\}, K = \lvert H \rvert \tag{14}$$

Therefore, the new accumulative dependence is calculated based on the new dependencies that are included because the instances can define new relationships, so new parameters can be affected. Therefore, the complexity when a new PC is added depends on the number of parameters and relationships but also the location of the instantiated parameters in the general parametric tree.

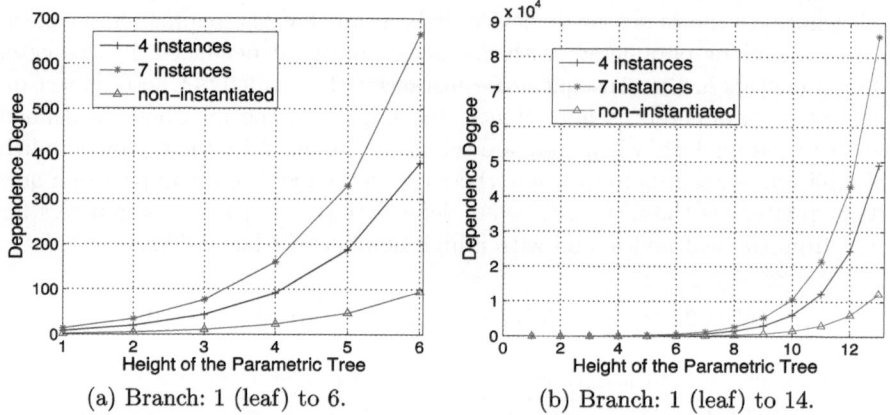

(a) Branch: 1 (leaf) to 6.   (b) Branch: 1 (leaf) to 14.

Fig. 3. Instantiation of one Parameter

Figure 3 shows the increasing number of dependencies (dependence degree) for a parameter regarding the length of the branch, considering 6 as the length of the longest branch in Fig. 3(a) and 13 in 3(b). The problem is simplified considering that the new instances only inherit the relationships defined by their parents, and do not define new relationships, and that the number of dependencies per parameter is fixet at 2.

Considering these restrictions, note that, although the instances do not define new dependencies, the number of dependencies for the parameters at upper layers increases. According to Table 2, the accumulative dependence is higher in those parameters far away from the leaves. Specifically, it depends on the position of the parameter and the number of dependencies behind it. When the parameter is instantiated, the accumulative dependence increases if new parameters appear in the parametric tree as a result of the new information provided in the instantiation.

Furthermore, the values chosen to show the previous results have been chosen only for testing purposes. Indeed, in a PRM, the number of dependencies, parameters and instances is free. For example, Fig. 4, shows the length of the parametric trees in a PRM with real parameters used for testing, where the longest branch may vary considerably, depending on the parameter, precisely because there is no fixed limit for the number of relationships. Moreover, in Fig. 4, two types of results are shown: the results for the increasing and decreasing parameters may generate different parametric trees according to the formulation in Table 1 and the weights. If a dependence is weighted 0, then the effect of the parameter that is in the antecedent of the dependence is not propagated by the tree.

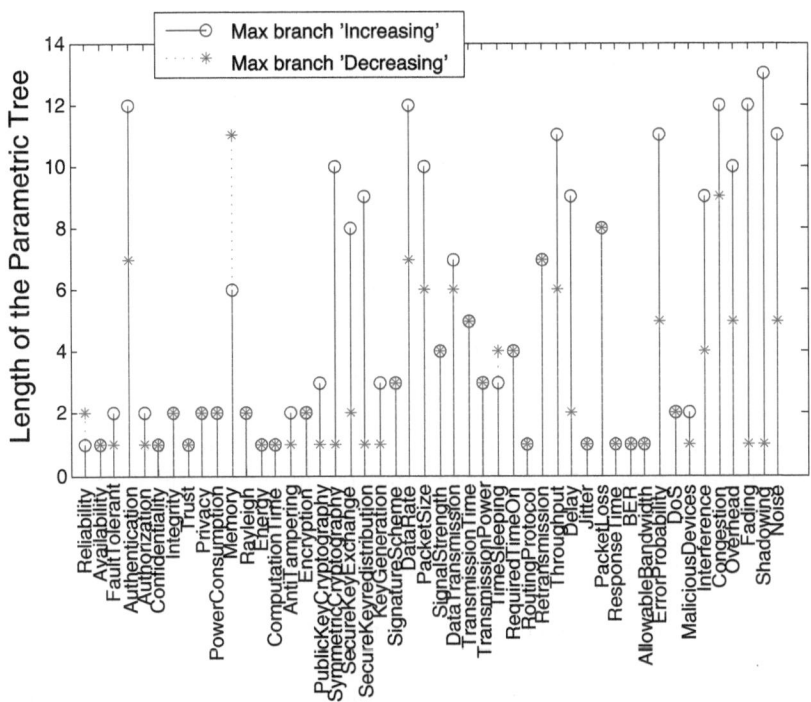

Fig. 4. Example: Length of Parametric Trees in a CPRM-based system.

Finally, the accumulative dependence degree depends on the number of dependencies defined for the system, and the instantiation may add new dependencies not defined by the parents. It must be remembered that Fig. 3 has been built, taking into account that the instances do not define new relationships. When new relationships are defined in the PC, which is generally the case, the impact on the final accumulative dependence increases. Moreover, it must be appreciated that, even if the instances only inherit the behaviour of their parents and do not include new dependencies, the calculation of the impact on the model of the instantiated parameters takes more time, because the process is repeated per instance.

For example, when the accumulative dependence increases, the complexity of the integration of parameters carried out by a handler of CPRM-based systems, is higher. An intuitive conclusion is that a possible way to reduce the time of integration of PCs, is to select the PCs which describe the physical layer components from the very beginning, because, in general, the physical description of components has a low dependency degree, when it concentrates on, for example, the characteristics of the battery. These components are usually instantiated with instances that are affected by other components (appear as consequents in the formulation).

However, given the nature of our model, this is not always the best choice, because new relationships, that is, new behaviour, defined in PCs may completely change the behaviour of the final $CPRM_i$.

In other words, if the instances with new relationships, not defined in the model for the instantiated parameter, are not integrated at the begining, and the instantiated parameter has a large number of instances, then, the new relationships have to be added to all the instances. The cost for this is very high, because it implies triggering action rules to maintain the coherence in the model, so, the whole parametric system is checked again when some incoherence is found. If the instances with new relationships are added at the begining of the instantiation process, then, this new behaviour is taken by the parents which transfer the sum of the whole behaviour learned (the parent's behaviour and the new relationships) to the instances. Note that this criteria concerns the order in which the instances in the PC are to be set up in the model, so it can be done independently from the order in the selection of PCs or parameters to be instantiated in the CPRM.

As a result, the instantiation process may be enhanced to mitigate the adverse effects which impact on performance, considering:

R1. Dependency degree and accumulative dependence of parameters to be instantiated.
R2. The effect of the changes on the rest of the system (length of the max. parametric tree).
R3. The order of the new instances and relationships defined in PCs, because the new behaviour may totally change the final $CPRMi$.

5   Classifications and Mitigations

In this section, the focus is to provide a classification based on the information in the CPRM-based system and the type of the PC that will be integrated in order to adapt the integration process, to mitigate the effect on the performance because of the dynamic instantiation. Some conclusions that are drawn from this analysis are sumarized in Table 3, where order means the priority in the instantiation process.

In order to test these conclusions, the CPRM-based system described in Table 4 is processed taking into account Table 3, to mitigate the effect in the integration of the PC, that is also structured according to the recommendations in Table 3[1]. Note that the only relationships that are marked with a weight are those defined by the instances to make changes in the behaviour of the model.

---

[1] Information about default weights omited for sake of clearness. It is assumed that the relationships that are completely new have weight 1.

Table 3. Recommendations in the Integration process.

Component	Characteristic	Order
CPRM	Parameters with shortest branch first (SBF)	1
CPRM	Parameters with max numer of instances	2
PC	Parameters that define new behaviour: new relationships to be added that maximizes max δ'	1
PC	Parameters that maximizes the final longest branch (if available)	2

Table 4. CPRM and PC definitions.

Parameter	Direct relationships	Branch	Instances	New relationships
A	3: B,C,E	6	A1, A2	-
B	0	1	B1, B2, B3	$B3 \to F1$
C	0	1	C1, C2, C3, C4	$C4 \to F1$
D	3: B,C,E	8	D1	-
E	2: F,I	7	E1, E2	$E1 \to C3$, $E1 \to B2$
F	1: H	3	F1	-
G	1: H	2	G1, G2, G3	$G1 \xrightarrow{w=0} H1, G1 \xrightarrow{w=3} H2$
H	0 -	1	H1, H2	-
I	2: J,K	9	I1	$I1 \xrightarrow{w=2} J1, I1 \xrightarrow{w=0} K2$
J	1: L	8	J1,J2	-
K	0 1	1	K1,K2,K3,K4	-
L	1: M	7	L1,L2	$L2 \xrightarrow{w=4} M2$
M	2: J,A	6	M1,M2	$M1 \xrightarrow{w=2} J1$
N	1: B	2	N1	$N1 \to A, N1 \xrightarrow{w=2} B3$

For example, I is related to J and K according to Table 4. Then, the instances of I inherit the relationships of I, which means that they will be related to J and K, and, therefore, with their instances. However, the relationship $I1 \xrightarrow{w=0} K2$ redefines the weight in the relationship inherited to avoid the relationship between the instances I1 and K2. These relationships do not add additional relationships to the model, because the parents of the instances are already related with each other, so it is unnecessary to apply action rules. Therefore, the relationships that add new information in the model are $B3 \to F1$, $C4 \to F1$, $E1 \to C3$, $E1 \to B2$, and $N1 \to A$. These requires, respectively, to include the relationships $B \to F$, $C \to F$, $E \to C, B$ and $N \to A$ to be included.

Consider that the order $A - N$ corresponds to the unsorted or default distribution where letters describe non-instantiated parameters and the instances for each parameter are described using the letter of the parent and a number. Note that one of the recommendations in Table 3 suggest the *Shortest Branch*

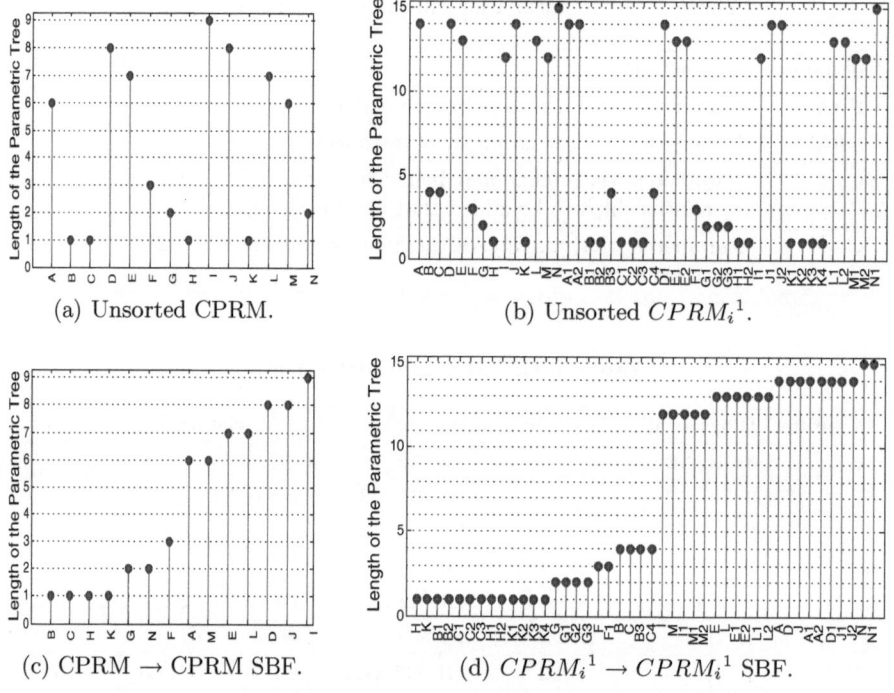

(a) Unsorted CPRM.   (b) Unsorted $CPRM_i^1$.

(c) CPRM → CPRM SBF.   (d) $CPRM_i^1 → CPRM_i^1$ SBF.

Fig. 5. Changes in the Parametric Trees after the Instantiation

First (SBF) criterion, that is the opposite to the *Longest Branch First* (LBF) criterion. Using the CPRM and the PC, 9 $CPRM_i$ are generated:

– $CPRM_i^1$: Unsorted CPRM. Unsorted PC.
– $CPRM_i^2$: Unsorted CPRM, PC SBF.
– $CPRM_i^3$: Unsorted CPRM, PC LBF.
– $CPRM_i^4$: CPRM LBF, Unsorted PC.
– $CPRM_i^5$: CPRM LBF, PC SBF.
– $CPRM_i^6$: CPRM LBF, PC LBF.
– $CPRM_i^7$: CPRM SBF, Unsorted PC.
– $CPRM_i^8$: CPRM SBF, PC SBF.
– $CPRM_i^9$: CPRM SBF, PC LBF.

Figure 5 shows the length of the branches of the original CPRM (before the instantiation process) and $CPRM_i^1$, before and after the instantiation. Note that a simple ordering in the CPRM before the instantiation is not sufficient, because the PC adds changes in the behaviour of the model that have to be considered. Indeed, the order of the parents (parameters of type *instantiated*) before and after the instantiation is not the same. For example, in Fig. 5(c), in a CPRM SBF it is recommended C before G. However, as can be seen in

Fig. 5(d), the instance $C4$ introduces more changes than the instances of G. So, this information cannot be considered if only the parameters in the CPRM are taken into account. Specifically, Fig. 5(d) has been built from Fig. 5(b), but this order is different from the final order that can be generated following the recommendations in Table 3, thay may vary depending on the recommendations.

In order to check the different alternatives and the suitability of the recommendations, the instantiation process (add CPRM to PC to generate $CPRM_i$) is repeated 60 times per $CPRM_i$, and the average execution times for these processes are shown in Fig. 6[2]. Note that the CPRM and PC chosen as seeds, integrate diverse relationships, defined only in order to force the maximum number of operations to action rules.

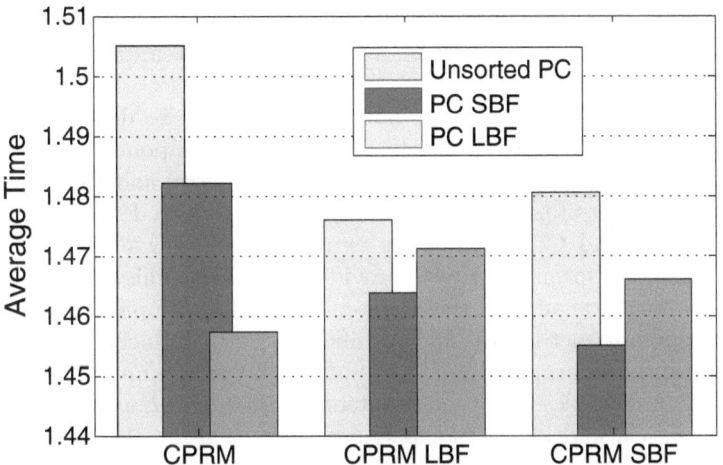

Fig. 6. Average Times in $CPRM_i{}^{1-9}$ Calculation.

Considering the results, when restrictions in Table 3 are applied to the CPRM before the instantiation, the performance (measured in terms of computation time) is improved with respect to the case where the CPRM is not sorted, or is sorted acording to LBF. Moreover, in this case, the PC does not integrate a high number of relationships. Despite this, given the results, it is possible to appreciate that the advantages for sorting the parameters in the PC are conditioned by the max branch of the parameter that will be instantiated and the number of new relationships that the parameter introduces in the CPRM, and, therefore, the length of the new branches that have been added as a consequence of the

---

[2] Results calculated using MATLAB and our handler of CPRM systems for Security and QoS Tradeoffs (SQT). During the process, the handler plots different graphs and information for testing. Note that this additional funcionality increases the overall time in all the integrations.

instantiation process. Moreover, as Figs. 5(c) and (d) show, the order in CPRM LBF and PC LBF or CPRM SBF and PC SBF is not the same, because the order in the PC is generated considering the new information that will be integrated in the model. It is the reason because CPRM LBF + PC LBF is not optimal, instead CPRM LBF + PC SBF. Note that, in the absence of informacin (case CPRM), the integration of the PC LBF is the best option, in this case.

It can be observed that the effect when sorting the parameters (instances) in the PC is higher than the effect in sorting the parameters in the CPRM. This is precisely because the integration process is costly, and, especially so, when the instances and relationships define a behaviour that is very different from the behaviour defined by the parents. It is expected that new instances inherit most of the behaviour of their parents, so in these cases maybe a better definition of the properties of the system to be instantiated, or a new classification in different layers of the parametes would be very helpful in mitigating the effect of the instantiation process. The knowledge of the system can be very helpful in order to identify the order of the parameters in a PC, because, when the environment is very dynamic, it is not always possible to define the adequate order in the integration of PCs or the order of their componets.

Finally, CPRM schemes are used to identify security and QoS tradeoffs. In previous work, a set of parameters and relationships which define general behaviour of security and QoS parameters extracted from a wide range of studies and mathematical formulation was provided [10]. With this purpose, the original scheme used to compose these systems, classifies the parameters based on their type and abstract layers. The classification of types includes: security (e.g. authentication), performance (e.g. delay), QoS (e.g. streamming), resources (e.g. battery), characteristics (e.g. type of antenna), *Quality of Experience* (e.g. mechanisms for measuring the user's experience), etc.

The objective then, is to have different PCs and instantiate the CPRM when the information about the final composition of the system becomes available. Given the previous results, and our classification, the integration of PCs should be performed as follows, based on the dynamisms of the parameters and our focus[3]:

1. High-layer relationships. Security and QoS requirements are described at this layer. So, given the nature of our analysis, the parameters in this layer should be instantiated at the end of the process, because, probably, they change frequently.
2. Local properties. At this layer there are described the resources in the devices of the network and the characteristics. For example, this layer describes physical characteristics of the components. So, at this layer there are several parameters that are leafs in many parametric trees.
3. Communication and Measurements layers. The most of the parameters defined at these layers are of type performance. These parameters are the most of

---

[3] These are conceptual/abstract layers, not physical layers.

them defined based on mathematical formulation, and are influenced by other parameters at the same layer or from other layers. It is expected that the instances for the parameters at this layer do not include additional relationships that affect to the behaviour of the model. It is expected that the new changes redefine the weight to some parameters and relationships.

4. Environmental conditions. The effect of the environment in the system is described at this layer. As these are restrictions given by the environment, some of these parameters may not vary during a long time (e.g. the probability for wireless eavesdropping in a wired system; average of devices in an office, etc.). These parameters depend on the dynamism of the system.

Moreover, the preferences in the selection/integration of PCs, should be adapted based on the whole information about the system where this mechanism will be used. In general, this solution may be useful when the system provides a rich variety of information that is stored in data bases and may be defined using parametric relationships. Then, the integration/extraction of contexts may help to understand the different problems in the integration of security and QoS mechanisms in the environment, before their deployment.

6   Conclusions and Future Work

The Context-based Parametric Relationship Model (CPRM) enables the composition of parameters that may be instantiated based on the context. The instantiation consists in providing mechanisms for general parameters, which are defined in the model. It is a fact that when the number of parameters increases, so does the complexity of the CPRM-based system. In these models, the complexity can be analised, using the size of the parametric tree defined for the parameters to be instantiated. In this paper, the impact on the influence and the dependence degree based on the position of the instantiated parameter in the dependencies tree has been discussed, and alternatives to mitigate this impact are proposed and analysed.

In addition, a problem beyond the scope of this paper is that the dependence degree affects the visualization of the data handled by these models, because the number of relationships increases the complexity of the final diagram. Therefore, despite the problems of having a large number of dependencies, the benefit is that, the more dependencies and parameters there are, the more information there is available to extract useful information about the security and QoS trade-off. For this reason future work will aim to provide a recommendation system for extracting information from CPRM-based models where large numbers of parameters coexist.

Acknowledgments. This work has been partially supported by the Spanish Ministry of Economy and Competitiveness through the project ARES (CSD2007-00004). Additionally, it has been funded by Junta de Andalucia through the projects PISCIS (TIC-6334) and FISICCO (TIC-07223). The author has been funded by the Spanish FPI Research Programme.

References

1. Alia, M., Lacoste, M., He, R., Eliassen, F.: Putting together qos and security in autonomic pervasive systems. In: Proceedings of the 6th ACM Workshop on QoS and Security for Wireless and Mobile Networks, pp. 19–28. ACM (2010)
2. Karatas, F., Kesdogan, D.: A flexible approach for considering interdependent security objectives in service composition. In: Proceedings of the 28th Annual ACM Symposium on Applied Computing, pp. 1919–1926. ACM (2013)
3. Yu, F.R., Tang, H., Bu, S., Zheng, D.: Security and quality of service (qos) co-design in cooperative mobile ad hoc networks. EURASIP J. Wirel. Commun. Netw. **2013**(1), 1–14 (2013)
4. Carapinha, J., Bless, R., Werle, C., Miller, K., Dobrota, V., Rus, A.B., Grob-Lipski, H., Roessler, H.: Quality of service in the future internet. In: Kaleidoscope: Beyond the Internet?-Innovations for Future Networks and Services, 2010 ITU-T, pp. 1–8. IEEE (2010)
5. Ernst, J.B., Kremer, S.C., Rodrigues, J.J.P.C.: A survey of qos/qoe mechanisms in heterogeneous wireless networks. Phys. Commun. **13**, 61–72 (2014)
6. Aiash, M., Loo, J.: An integrated authentication and authorization approach for the network of information architecture. J. Netw. Comput Appl. **50**, 73–79 (2015). http://dx.doi.org/10.1016/j.jnca.2014.06.004
7. Yen, I.-L., Ma, H., Bastani, F.B., Mei, H., et al.: Qos-reconfigurable web services and compositions for high-assurance systems (2008)
8. Golden, B.L., Wasil, E.A., Harker, P.T.: Analytic Hierarchy Process. Springer, Heidelberg (2003)
9. Hansen, P., Ombler, F.: A new method for scoring additive multi-attribute value models using pairwise rankings of alternatives. J. Multi-Criteria Decis. Anal. **15**(3–4), 87–107 (2008)
10. Nieto, A., Lopez, J.: A context-based parametric relationship model (cprm) to measure the security and qos tradeoff in configurable environments. In: IEEE International Conference on Communications (ICC), pp. 755–760. IEEE (2014)

Privacy Issues in Geosocial Networks

Zakaria Sahnoune$^{(\boxtimes)}$, Cheu Yien Yep, and Esma Aïmeur

Département d'Informatique et de Recherche Opérationnelle (DIRO),
Université de Montréal, Montreal, Canada
{sahnounz,yepcheuy,aimeur}@iro.umontreal.ca

Abstract. A GeoSocial Network (GSN) is a social network enhanced with the capability to associate user data and content with location. This content-location link is getting stronger due to the swift development of GSNs and mobile technologies. Indeed, the gathered location information generates a huge amount of publicly-available location data, information that was always considered private or at least known only by friends or family. Hence, a serious privacy threat is revealed: being tracked in real time, or having location history disclosed to everyone, is a privacy invasion that needs addressing before too much control is lost. In this paper we are interested in several questions such as: How much are we at risk? Are we vigilant enough to face this risk? Are existing privacy-protection techniques sufficient to let us relax? And if so, which technique is more efficient? Are we legally protected? This paper explores these and other related questions.

Keywords: Geolocation · Privacy · Traceability · Geosocial network · Privacy protection

1 Introduction

In the fiction movie "Minority Report" [1], the character played by Tom Cruise walks into a GAP store and an interactive billboard, through an eye scanner, knew his name, his personal interests, his visits and purchase records. Today, with mobile phones and their applications, we are not so far from this reality. We already live in a world where the biggest companies may know more about us than we do ourselves.

Driven by the proliferation of smartphones and their Internet and positioning capabilities, geo-location is becoming more and more popular among users. Nearly every social network has incorporated a location-based service that allows users to know and see on a map where their friends are located in real-time. These are the so-called locative social media services or location-based social networking sites [2]. For instance, Foursquare [3], WhosHere [4] allow users to see the location of their friends, while Google Maps [5], AroundTheWay [6], GyPSii [7] and iPling [8] allow individuals to access and upload their location information, getting not only other users' addresses and telephone numbers but also the instructions on how to get there. Yelp [9] is another online community service that offers reviews of restaurants, bars or stores in your vicinity, written by other people.

These features are attractive, and they have become easily reachable by a smartphone user, but do we really know who has access to our information? It is safe to

© Springer International Publishing Switzerland 2015
J. Lopez et al. (Eds.): CRiSIS 2014, LNCS 8924, pp. 67–82, 2015.
DOI: 10.1007/978-3-319-17127-2_5

publish it online? Is our information well protected? These simple questions lead us to take privacy issues seriously.

We must know that, although this technology is useful for many aspects of everyday life, the information gathered may also fall into the hands of malicious users, and practically anyone can exploit it. We take as an example the mobile application "Girls around me", which uses Foursquare data to tell users where they can find girls nearby. It then connects them to the Facebook profiles of spotted ones so they can learn more about their lives before meeting them. Foursquare banned this application from using its data [10]. However, there are many other applications of this type; they cannot all be banned. A malicious person can review a user's data and analyze and create intelligent information that could be used to generate behavioral patterns of the places he visits and his undertaken activities. For instance, what if some serial killer wants to locate potential victims around. *Paul Bernardo*, the well-known Canadian serial killer, would have an easier time to find them than in the 90's. What we want to say is, if exposing our information already presents a serious privacy issue, the problem is even more serious when location data is added. Since adopting such technologies demands more awareness and vigilance, it is not hard to imagine privacy-related dangers in GSNs. Also, being able to locate people easily implies that we can be located too. For example, the website "Please Rob Me" [11] can fetch all the locations related to a Twitter account, showing the danger of publicly shared location data.

In this non-technical paper, we highlight the privacy issues in GSNs and related work. Section 2 classifies currently deployed GSNs. In Sect. 3, we focus on the collection and usage of user location data in GSNs. Section 4 deals with the main privacy issues and consequences. Section 5 discusses the main privacy-related work and models in the literature. In Sect. 6, we compare models and protocols of privacy protections in GSNs to determine their efficiency and performance. Finally we examine some legal issues about the protection of users' privacy in GSNs.

2 Geosocial Networks

2.1 What Is a Geosocial Network?

According to the definition given by Gambs *et al.* [12], a GSN is: "a web-based or mobile-based service that allows users to construct a profile containing some of their geo-located data (along with additional information), connect with other users of the system to share their geo-located data and interact with the content provided by other users (for instance by commenting, replying or rating)" [12].

Users by building a profile with geo-located data become geo-identified and thus establish a direct link between real and virtual worlds.

To better understand this notion, a more precise definition is given by Zheng where "a Location-Based Social Network (LBSN) does not only mean adding a location to an existing social network so that people in the social structure can share location-embedded information, but also consists of the new social structure made up of individuals connected by the interdependency derived from their locations in the physical world as well as their location-tagged media content, such as photos, video, and texts" [13].

Zheng also explains that this kind of location-embedded and location-driven social structure helps bridge the gap between the physical and virtual worlds and enables a deep understanding of user preferences, behaviors and activities.

2.2 Classification

There are many GSN sites throughout the web. Each one serves a different purpose and may be categorized according to its target users or the kind of contents it publishes. In order to understand this new social reality, we must learn more about the different types of GSN operating in the Web.

Since GSNs are a relatively new concept, a well-defined classification does not exist yet. So, scholars try to classify them according to their own criteria. For instance, based on the studies and the growing popularity of GSN, Zheng defined three major ways to group them [14].

Geotagged-media-based: These services enable users to add location labels and comments on media contents such as text, photos, videos or others. Examples include Flickr, Panoramio and Geo-twitter.

Point-location-driven: These services encourage people to share their current locations by checking-in into the places they visit and adding "tips" to venues. Foursquare is an example of this type.

Trajectory-centric: These services provide not only a point location but also the detailed path by connecting the locations of several points. Users do not only receive the basic information (distance, duration and velocity) for a trajectory, but also the user experiences (tips, tags and photos). Examples include Bikely and SportsDo.

We choose this classification since it covers the more well-known GSNs. Practically, every mentioned GSN in this paper falls into one of this classification's groups.

The addition of location-awareness capabilities to computing and communication devices will surely have profound privacy implications. In order to properly provide the safeguards necessary to protect the rights of individuals, it is necessary to carefully understand from where and how our data is collected.

3 Information Collected

Location data is often related to other information that was originally stored on a social network; it is not a visible connection between location and personal data.

The strength of this relation is GSN type-dependent. Some GSNs are useless without location information; they focus on both user location and some other basic information. Foursquare is a known GSN of this category. Others don't even require it; they already have too much information. The location in this case will be combined to get more detailed user information. In all cases, GSNs assume using this location data will "improve" the user experience.

In other words, if the user decides to use a GSN, we cannot stop him; the only thing that can be done is to show him how and where his geo-location data is collected, and why sharing it might be harmful.

User location data can be gathered from any connected device, from a smartphone to a work station. The means of connection includes all types, including data and cellular connections. Figure 1 shows techniques used to collect location data from a smartphone.

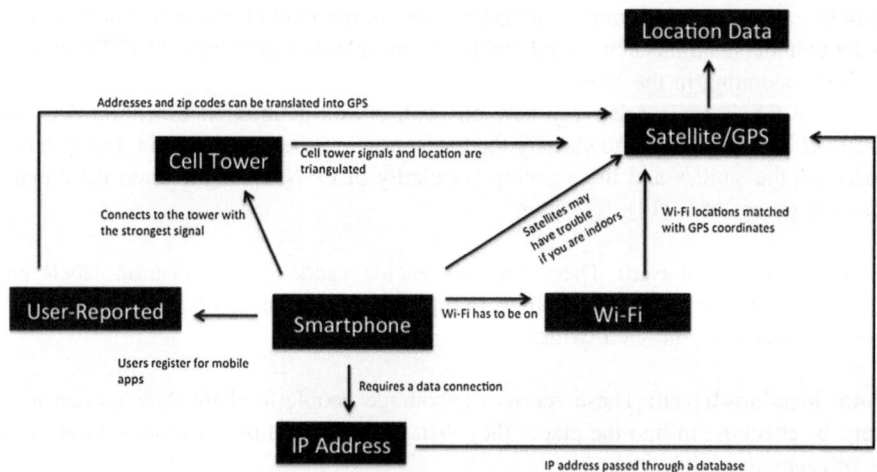

Fig. 1. Techniques used to get location data from smartphone (Data from [15])

Location data can be gathered from smartphone devices either by the system or with third party applications.

Location data collection can be classified into two main categories: system collection and third party application collection; those categories are platform-independent.

3.1 System Collection

In this type, the users' location data are collected and revealed directly through a system interface. The most recent example is Facebook and its Graph Search engine, which can reveal all the publicly available results just by asking a question, like "Photos taken in Montreal, Quebec, of friends of my friends who went to Tim Hortons" [16] (Tim Hortons is a popular casual restaurant in Canada). In most cases, the compilation is explicitly declared in privacy policies. The system's owners assume that location data is never collected without the consent of their users.

3.2 Third-Party Application Collection

In this case, users' location are collected by a third party application most often a mobile one. According to *Pew Research Center* [17], from May 2011 to February 2012, the proportion of smartphone owners who shared their location on geosocial services increased from 12 % to 18 %. These applications gather users' information from different sources to build a complete profile that includes personal content and location data. "Analyzing social networks and micro-blogging websites such as Facebook, Google+, Myspace, LinkedIn, Twitter or Tumblr can offer even better insights than monitoring online searches" [18].

This category is the most intrusive to the user. As an example, mobile application "Highlight" requires a connection to Facebook or Twitter accounts, as well as access to a mobile's location features. However, unlike, Facebook, this application collects and shares information continuously unless users manually disable it. Moreover, it has the ability to log user's location data and activities on its backend servers, and link them to their Facebook or Twitter accounts [19].

The ease of collection of a user's location data and its linking with other information show the severity of the privacy threat in GSNs.

In the next section we discuss the privacy issues in GSNs in more detail, and the consequences of recklessness in their use.

4 Privacy Issues and Consequences

Nowadays, transmitting automatically our information via mobile applications is a simple matter of clicking on the option "location" or having the cell phone' GPS enabled. Some market strategies even reward consumers who share their location. Yet despite all this, users still hesitate sharing their exact location. An increasing number of users want to benefit from this technology, but without the high cost of disclosing sensitive information such as their private data.

We now discuss some privacy issues and consequences when sharing location information in GSNs.

4.1 Privacy Issues

The issue of online privacy has been a main problem for a long time. However, due to technological breakthroughs, it has grown exponentially in the last few years.

According to some studies [20], users do not think or are not aware of the risks of sharing their information online. For them, the decision of sharing something online is "made at the moment". Similarly, a study conducted by Acquisti *et al.* [21] found that "people's ideas about privacy are malleable depending on the context of interaction". Their research suggested that people are more willing to divulge sensitive personal information on a social network website than on other sites. They also observed that people disclose information when they see others do it. This trend, in their opinion, may explain why so many people are ready to share personal information online [22].

Statistically, a study titled *Young Canadians in a Wired World* conducted by *MediaSmarts* in 2013 [23] reveals that 68 % of young people wrongly believe that if a website has a privacy policy, it will not share their personal information with others. Similarly, 39 % of them think that companies are not interested in what they do online. Based on these results, we can conclude that young people need to be better informed about the corporate uses of their personal data.

Moreover, the high penetration of mobile devices equipped with geo-location capabilities exposes users to a new set of privacy concerns. With these features, it is feasible to track a user's past, present or even predicted future location and thus facilitate unfortunate situations like being the victim of stalking or even worse.

Research carried out by Alrayes and Abdelmoty [24], identified four aspects of location privacy issues:

Location Data Collection: the gathering and storage of location information as well as its quality.

Location Information Accessibility: it is closely related to the disclosure of the user's data; that is, the accessibility and visibility of this information by other users and third parties of the service.

Location Data Exploitation: how the user's location information is used and for what purposes, either by the application itself or any third parties.

Location Data Security: the level of protection of the user's data against the risk of loss or unauthorized access.

Although, the privacy issues raised in collecting location information are relatively minor compared with other aspects (since there is a low risk of abuse until that information is used, disclosed or exploited in some way), it is important to consider the same questions when dealing with privacy-related discussions: What information is stored? Where will it be stored? Could we know who controls the information, how it can later be used or disclosed, and how long will it be stored? How securely will it be stored? Some of these questions will be addressed in the legal issues section.

These days, not knowing what companies do with users' information, the irresponsible treatment of their data, or the violation of their privacy settings, is an issue of major concern among users nowadays.

4.2   Examples of Consequences

As with any technology, geo-location can be a double-edged sword. Below we will mention several examples of its positive effects or how it could endangers our lives.

Advantages (Positive Effects). Some capabilities empower social networks to aid in law enforcement and provide protection against unwarranted surveillance of individual activities, or to improve medical research, it also allows the identification of the exact location of an injured mountaineer in the middle of an inaccessible geographic point, or the location of stolen vehicles.

Another example that could illustrate the use of these tools in law enforcement occurred in 2012, when Higinio O. Ochoa III, a 30-year-old Galveston programmer and a member of "CabinCr3w", an offshoot of the hacking collective Anonymous, hacked into official websites and released the names, home addresses, home telephone numbers and mobile phone numbers of several police officers, while leaving a taunting message along with a photo of his girlfriend's barely-clad breasts. Thanks to this photo, FBI agents were able to identify the exact location where his girlfriend lived and later arrested him [25].

Geo-location and the ability to assign coordinate information to exploit it from a computer can be, and is being, used in many different domains. An example of success in institutional communication is *Harvard University*, the first American university to use Foursquare to help students explore their campus and surrounding places of interest. In 2010, they announced a new location-based mobile social networking application where students can create and update reviews and rating guides of stores, restaurants, businesses and other venues on campus; they can also earn points and acquire Foursquare "badges" for it [26].

In the case of the 'anti-social network' trend, an application for Apple's iPhone, called "Cloak", was launched to help people avoid unwanted friends nearby, using data from other GSNs (Instagram and Foursquare) to pinpoint the location of your contacts based on their latest check-ins and photographs. Users can track their friends and acquaintances in order to steer clear of those who are unwanted [27].

Disadvantage (Negative Consequences). While online disclosures can have positive results, negative consequences that facilitate criminal acts are also a possible outcome of GSNs and information sharing.

Information from GPS and geo-location tags, in combination with other personal information, can be used by criminals to identify an individual's present or predicted future location, thus facilitating the ability to cause harm others and their property. This ranges from burglary and theft to stalking, kidnapping and domestic violence.

Cybercriminals, ex-lovers and/or jealous friends are the main authors of computer crimes that threaten the integrity, morality, self-esteem and safety of persons. The lack of caution when posting photos, comments and stories, along with their physical location, can become the best tools for kidnapping, robbery, rape, dismissal from work, divorce or separation of the couple, and so on.

A survey made by "Credit Sesame" in 2011, revealed that 78 % of ex-burglars had used Facebook, Twitter, Grupo and Foursquare to track people's locations for robbery, and 74 % of criminals had used Google maps and Street View to review and locate an empty residence prior to stealing in it [28].

Unfortunately, there is little concrete information about the actual consequences of online disclosure. Most of what is available are anecdotal reports in popular media. An example is the case of a husband who wanted to know if his wife was cheating on him with someone else, and decided to install a geo-location application (Google latitude) on her phone without her knowledge to track all her movements.

Nowadays, location information is among the most sensitive and highly-valued data being collected. It contains the historical record of the individual whereabouts and can be used to reconstruct their movements across space and time. To have a clear idea of how location data could be sensitive, researchers [29] demonstrated that, by using inference attacks, it is possible to discover user Points Of Interests (POIs) such as where someone lives, where he works, places where he practices sports, his usual itineraries, etc. Additionally, other studies proved that only four spatiotemporal points are enough to uniquely identify 95 % of the individuals [30].

From our point of view, one of the major problem is that we simply don't know how people perceive the risks of using GSNs. Further research is necessary in order to understand the relationship between the behavior of people regarding personal information disclosure on GSNs and their perception of the associated risks. In next section, we review the main work done in the area of privacy threats on GSNs.

5   Related Work

Prior work on geo-privacy can be divided into two main categories: work on privacy in general location-based systems, and work dedicated to geosocial systems. We note that GSNs are a type of geosocial systems, which is a subtype of location-based systems.

5.1   Work on Privacy in General Location-Based Systems

According to the above classification, the work on the privacy aspects of location-based systems can be easily adapted to GSN. We can distinguish two main research directions, including those that focus on spatial and temporal cloaking, and those that focus on location transformation.

Spatial and Temporal Cloaking. The main idea behind spatial and temporal cloaking is to send approximate location and time coordinates instead of the real values. Several approaches are used to perform the cloaking. *K-anonymity*, one of those approaches, assumes that we cannot distinguish a user among k other users [31, 32], this approach negatively influences the server response accuracy and timeliness [33]. Another approach is using Pseudonyms and silent times [34], to anonymize user data by changing device identifiers periodically and preventing data transmission for long periods at regular intervals.

Location Transformation. This technique assumes that the user location privacy can be guaranteed by transforming location coordinates [33]. The new coordinates are generated from the originals using a secret key. This ensures data security as the transformed coordinates cannot be reversed without using the same secret key for the transformation. The main issue with this technique is that processing nearest-neighbor queries on the transformed location can reveal the real-world neighbors' location [33].

5.2   Work on Privacy in Geosocial Networks

This is work dedicated to geosocial systems. In most cases, they are adaptations of work already done on general location-based systems.

Some papers present a full system architecture or model that respects the privacy concerns; others deal with the privacy issue as a security problem, dealing with each attack independently.

SmokeScreen [35]: Appeared in 2007, SmokeScreen is one of the first works on privacy in geosocial networks; it attempts to preserve user presence privacy by revealing location information only to trusted users. It splits location requests into friend requests and stranger requests.

Longitude [36]: The Longitude working group has developed since 2009 a privacy-aware centralized solution based on a secure computation protocol, which generalizes and transforms the users' location before sending it to the service provider. The latter computes the transformed location proximity and shares it with other users, only authorized ones being able to reverse transformation and determine the original location.

C-Hide&Seek and C-Hide&Hash [37]: Introduced in 2011, these are two protocols for preserving privacy by encrypting location information in order to prevent other users and service providers from gaining knowledge about user-related geographic information.

Mobishare [38]: This was developed in 2012. The fact that Mobishare distinguishes two locations, strangers' and friends' requests, makes it an extension of Smokescreen. It assumes that users are able to share their location information with third party applications and other users while preserving the privacy of their location data. It uses two separate servers and cellular towers. The first server is the social network server and does not have access to location information. The second server contains the location data but does not know the users' identities, dealing only with fake ones. The cellular tower is assumed to be unidentified by the social network server in order to protect the user's IP address. In other words, this mechanism separates location data from identification data to ensure the user's location privacy.

N-Mobishare [39]: Presented in 2013, this system can be seen as the architectural evolution of Mobishare. N-Mobishare drops the cellular tower and has the location encryption performed on the mobile device itself, for the same privacy protection level with fewer resources required.

LocX [33]: Unveiled in 2014, it uses two separated servers and a proxy. The servers, named index server and data server, are used respectively to store an encrypted location index and the associated data index. The proxy is used to secure connections between the index server and the users. The key idea is that location is revealed only to specified trusted users, by revealing a secret key to them. This key is used to generate/unlock the encrypted location indexes for the trusted users.

Adding to those papers, other researchers focused on treating specific attacks or privacy problems; we mention the following.

Ruiz Vicente *et al.* [40] suggest a method to protect co-location and identity privacy, in which privacy preservation concepts are complemented by an extension of spatial and temporal scopes in such a way that the number of persons within a certain area and time span is large enough to prevent others from identifying possible co-located users. Similarly, Camilli [41] and Freni *et al.* [42] have developed an algorithm for preserving co-location privacy in GSNs.

Gambs *et al.* [43], extensively studied inference attacks and proposed sanitization techniques to preserve the privacy of individuals with a trail of traces present among the datasets. They also introduce the software GEPETO (GEoPrivacy-Enhancing Toolkit), a toolkit for evaluating various sanitization techniques and inference attacks as well as visualizing the results and evaluating the resulting trade-off between privacy and utility on geo-located data [43].

The previous papers and others focused on protecting user privacy in GSNs, but the question about their effectiveness arises. The next section will compare the technics mentioned earlier.

6   Comparison

In this section, we compare the GSN privacy work presented in Sect. 5 according to the used technology and some key properties.

6.1   Technology-Based Comparison

As preserving privacy techniques in GNS are adaptations of ones found in general location-based systems, we define two main categories: spatial and temporal cloaking-based work and location transformation-based work as shown in Table 1.

Table 1. Categorization of GSNs privacy-preserving works

Techniques	Spatial and temporal cloaking-based	Location transformation-based
SmokeScreen	■	
Longitude		■
C-Hide&Seek and C-Hide&Hash		■
Mobishare	■	
N-Mobishare	■	
LocX		■

6.2   Key Properties-Based Comparison

We compare the systems according to the following properties:

Centralization: Is the server responsible of location updates between users? Unlike a decentralized one, where the user is who have to contact their friends whenever he/she needs to know their locations. Which often causes a high communication cost comparing to a centralized one.

Implementation Complexity: The level of complexity of the technique by approximating the required time and cost to implement it.

Communication Cost: Since GSNs are highly used in smartphones, evaluate the volume of communication required for each technique to properly operate is essential. We estimate this cost according to the number of total emitted and received requests.

Time Cost: This property is about how much time the technique needs to perform adequately. In most cases, and even when the technique does a great job, taking too long can downgrade it. The estimation is based on the number of encryption operations and computation costs.

Hardware Cost: An approximate cost of the required hardware.

User Pre-settings: Is user's interaction required for the proper operation of the technique. This interaction usually provides the user's sharing preferences.

After identifying the key properties, each technique is ranked according to a value from Low (L), Fair (F) to High (H) if it is present in the technique. Where Low relates to the cost. If the property is used or not in the technique: yes (Yes) or no (No). Table 2 shows each technique and the given value of each property.

Table 2. A comparison between different GSNs privacy-preserving works

Techniques	Centralization	Implementation complexity	Communication cost	Time cost	Hardware cost	User pre-settings
SmokeScreen	Yes	F	F	H	F	Yes
Longitude	Yes	L	F	F	F	Yes
C-Hide&Seek	Yes	F	F	L	F	No
C-Hide&Hash	Yes	F	F	H	F	No
Mobishare	No	H	L	H	H	Yes
N-Mobishare	No	F	L	H	F	Yes
LocX	No	H	L/H	L/H	F	No

As shown on Table 2, works on privacy preserving in GSNs are clearly different. We have used each technique's own analysis to fill the table cells.

Starting with SmokeScreen [35], we note that its main disadvantage is the time cost. According to its authors, transforming an opaque identifier to a real identity takes 10 seconds in best cases [35].

Another analyzed technique, Longitude [36], a protocol which performs encryptions and computations faster than other techniques have been criticized about being an effective privacy protection technique [33].

C-Hide&Seek and C-Hide&Hash are other protocols that help to prevent privacy in GSNs. According to their evaluation results [37], C-Hide&Hash provides a higher level of privacy than C-Hide&Seek do, but at the cost of higher communication and computation costs.

The next technique called Mobishare, requires a complexes implementation and an additional hardware to adequately perform [39]. Even when hardware inconvenience was dropped in its new version named N-Mobishare, this technique still immature in terms of privacy preserving according to some critics [34].

The last analyzed technique, named LocX [33], although it is more complicated to implement than other techniques, it seems to be the most efficient one in pointing queries. Its main weakness is the nearest-neighbor queries, in which it needs too much time and data to properly perform.

From this comparison, to our point of view, each privacy preserving technique has its pros and cons. Some of them provide a very high privacy-protection efficiency at cost of running time, others compute faster but protect weaker. However, we consider that newest one (LocX) is more adapted to the actual constraints of GSNs.

Finally, despite the fact that this comparison was not very detailed, we can still conclude that choosing one technique over another depends on the extent to which a GSN is willing to protect the privacy of its users. In other words, preferring one technique over the others depends on our available resources on one hand, and what we expect as results on the other hand.

The next section discusses the main legal issues around privacy in GSNs.

7   Legal Issues

As mentioned earlier in this paper, sharing our location can reveal far more than just a latitude and longitude; it implies also the disclosure of personal and intimate aspects of our life, information that is rightfully considered private.

In the current technological era, where online social life is taking a great portion of our time, it is more important than ever to protect our online identity. Under this reality, people are starting to worry about location privacy and wonder about what kind of information is stored, where it is stored, how securely it is stored and, most importantly, what is the purpose for the information collected? Furthermore, they wonder if we are legally protected and if we can trust that our sensitive location information will remain private. Unfortunately, the laws and legal protection are not keeping pace with the current technological advancements.

During the past years, personal privacy policymakers and lawmakers have proposed and approved significant new regulations with the intent to protect users.

However, location privacy has not received equal attention in the legal system due to the newness of this concept.

These issues affect all governments. In The United States, the *Cable Act* (47 USC § 551) and the *Electronic Communications Privacy Act* (ECPA) (47 USC § 551) prohibit operators and telecommunication providers from disclosing a customer's location information to a third party without their consent and restrict the use of a tracking device to monitor an individual's movement without warrant by federal agencies. However, these acts do not provide any standards about the collection and use of location information.

According to Kar *et al.*, although the United States legislation differs from state to state, it does not exist currently a codified or coherent case law that protects personal privacy, especially location privacy [44].

Nonetheless, a draft of the *Online Communications and Geolocation Protection Act* was presented in March 2013, with the highest impact thus far. The reasons lie in its good definition of measures and safeguards, rightly referring to the protection of all kinds of information, especially location. It includes not only GPS data, but also log data, traceability of people and goods, and geo-location technology.

The rule that inspired this new legislation is that location data may only be disclosed by legal requirement or court order. Among the new measures proposed, carriers have to publicly publish an annual "transparency report" in which they report their location information requirements and what kind of information they reveal [45].

On May 2013, the *Office of the Privacy Commissioner of Canada*, an Officer of Parliament who reports directly to the House of Commons and the Senate and is responsible for investigating complaints under the Privacy Act of Canada, released a position paper calling for substantial changes to the *Personal Information Protection and Electronic Documents Act (PIPEDA)*. It argued that PIPEDA is currently insufficient to meet the challenges posed by the advent of technology that allows organizations to collect, use, and disclose an unprecedented amount of data that includes personal information [46].

While the gap between new technologies and the legal system is recognized, the privacy policies of companies that provide geo-location services play an important role in the market.

Other research [47] considers that the goal of all laws is to provide people with a set of rights, so they can have control over the collection, use and disclosure of their own personal information and decide how to manage their privacy. In other words, an individual can determine by himself how to weigh costs and benefits of sharing his information with the companies. These rights consist basically of rights to notice, access and consent regarding the collection, use and disclosure of personal data. This is known as "privacy self-management".

It also states that several cognitive problems exist that prevent people from having full control over their data. These can be summarized as follows: (1) people do not read privacy policies; (2) if they read them, they do not understand the content; (3) if they read and understand them, usually the lack of knowledge and necessary expertise do not allow them to make an informed decision; and (4) if they read, understand and can make an informed choice, their decision could be slanted by several difficulties that may arise in the decision-making process.

Similar studies [48] affirm that the existence of a privacy policy only protects company interests and not the consumer. They argue that the privacy protection of GSN users is often inadequate or uncertain.

In our opinion, legal reform is needed in order to match today's new online and mobile world and provide proper safeguards for individual privacy rights. Until then, the responsibility of ensuring privacy protection falls primarily upon the shoulders of the designers of GSNs, who should take the necessary measures to eliminate users' privacy concerns and thus motivate them to use such applications.

8 Conclusion

Thanks to technological advances, life is much easier nowadays, but there are side effects that can affect us in indirect ways. Applications that are mostly constructed to depend on geo-location services are slowly invading and colonizing our daily life. Due to the huge number of exploitations and uses they can have access to our addresses and locate the residences of our friends, family and acquaintances. As was seen in this review, there's nothing wrong with the use of this type of service as long as the consumers are fully conscious and totally aware of what is happening with their personal information and understand the meaning of disclosing location in terms of security.

Firstly, to simplify the matter at hand, which concerns the safe use of these new technologies, we have shown how and where our location data is being collected. In addition, we provided an overview of numerous privacy scenarios regarding the latter, and the direct consequences that might possibly harm our physical safety. Secondly, we have also described the privacy issues in the geo-location context. We have analyzed and compared several techniques of privacy-protection in GSNs, and we have seen that choosing a technique over another one depends on what extend a GSN is willing to protect the privacy of its users.

Finally, we discussed and analyzed legal issues and, to sum up, we concluded that many users are unaware of the scope of geo-location technology and this is why they need to be better informed and less complacent. Hence, they can be more circumspect when it comes to sharing data with others. Above all, it is time for all categories of concerned people, policymakers, enterprises and consumers to work together to ensure that sensitive personal information is under control.

References

1. De Bont, J., Courtis, B., Molen, G., Parkes, W.F., Spielberg, S.: Minority report [Motion Picture]. United States: Amblin Entertainment, Cruise/Wagner Productions (2002)
2. Thielmann, T.: Locative media and mediated localities. Aether: J. Media Geogr. 5(1), 1–17 (2010)
3. http://foursquare.com/. Accessed 19 July 2014
4. http://web.whoshere.net/. Accessed 19 July 2014
5. http://maps.google.com/. Accessed 19 July 2014

6. http://aroundthewayapp.com/. Accessed 19 July 2014
7. http://www.gypsii.com.cn/. Accessed 19 July 2014
8. http://www.ipling.com/. Accessed 19 July 2014
9. http://www.yelp.com/yelpmobile. Accessed 19 July 2014
10. http://mashable.com/2012/04/02/girls-around-me-defense/. Accessed 27 March 2014
11. http://pleaserobme.com/. Accessed 02 April 2014
12. Gambs, S., Heen, O., Potin, C.: A comparative privacy analysis of geosocial networks. In: Proceedings of the 4th ACM SIGSPATIAL International Workshop on Security and Privacy, GIS and LBS, pp. 33–40. ACM (2011)
13. Zheng, Y.: Tutorial on location-based social networks. In: Proceedings of the 21st International Conference on World Wide Web, WWW, vol. 12 (2012)
14. Zheng, Y.: Location-based social networks: users. In: Zheng, Y., Zhou, X. (eds.) Computing with Spatial Trajectories, pp. 243–276. Springer, New York (2011)
15. http://www.businessinsider.com/how-mobile-location-data-is-collected-2013-7. Accessed 28 March 2014
16. https://www.facebook.com/about/graphsearch. Accessed 28 March 2014
17. http://www.pewinternet.org/2012/05/11/three-quarters-of-smartphone-owners-use-location-based-services/. Accessed 27 March 2014
18. Aïmeur, E., Lafond, M.: The scourge of internet personal data collection. In: 2013 Eighth International Conference on Availability, Reliability And Security (ARES), pp. 821–828 (2013)
19. http://www.nbcnews.com/technology/trendy-iphone-app-highlight-privacy-nightmare-386931. Accessed 27 March 2014
20. Das, B., Sahoo, J.S.: Social networking sites – a critical analysis of its impact on personal and social life. Int. J. Bus. Soc. Sci. 2(14), 222–228 (2011)
21. http://www.ted.com/talks/alessandro_acquisti_why_privacy_matters. Accessed 27 March 2014
22. Gross, R., Acquisti, A.: Information revelation and privacy in online social networks. In Proceedings of the 2005 ACM Workshop on Privacy in the Electronic Society, pp. 71–80 (2005)
23. http://mediasmarts.ca/sites/default/files/pdfs/publication-report/full/YCWWIII_Online_Privacy_Online_Publicity_FullReport.pdf. Accessed 27 March 2014
24. Alrayes, F., Abdelmoty, A.: Privacy concerns in location-based social networks. In: Geoprocessing 2014, The Sixth International Conference on Advanced Geographic Information Systems, Applications, and Services, pp. 105–114 (2014)
25. http://www.smh.com.au/technology/technology-news/hacking-cases-body-of-evidence-20120411-1wsbh.html. Accessed 27 March 2014
26. http://foursquare.com/Harvard. Accessed 27 March 2014
27. http://www.bbc.com/news/technology-25554192. Accessed 27 March 2014
28. http://smallbusiness.yahoo.com/advisor/being-too-social-crime-200544050.html. Accessed 27 March 2014
29. Gambs, S., Killijian, M.O., Del Prado Cortez, M.N.: Show me how you move and i will tell you who you are. In: Proceedings of the 3rd ACM SIGSPATIAL International Workshop on Security and Privacy in GIS and LBS, pp. 34–41 (2010)
30. De Montjoye, Y.A., Hidalgo, C.A., Verleysen, M., Blondel, V.D.: Unique in the crowd: The Privacy Bounds of Human Mobility. Scientific reports, 3 (2013)
31. Gruteser, M., Grunwald, D.: Anonymous usage of location-based services through spatial and temporal cloaking. In: Proceedings of the 1st International Conference on Mobile Systems, Applications and Services, pp. 31–42 (2003)

32. Mokbel, M.F., Chow, C.Y., Aref, W.G.: The new casper: a privacy-aware location-based database server. In: IEEE 23rd International Conference on Data Engineering, 2007, ICDE 2007, pp. 1499–1500 (2007)

33. Puttaswamy, K.P., Wang, S., Steinbauer, T., Agrawal, D., El Abbadi, A., Kruegel, C., Zhao, B.Y.: Preserving location privacy in geosocial applications. IEEE Trans. Mob. Comput. **13** (1), 159–173 (2014)

34. Jiang, T., Wang, H.J., Hu, Y.C.: Preserving location privacy in wireless LANs. In: Proceedings of the 5th International Conference on Mobile Systems, Applications and Services, pp. 246–257 (2007)

35. Cox, L.P., Dalton, A., Marupadi, V.: Smokescreen: flexible privacy controls for presence-sharing. In: Proceedings of the 5th International Conference on Mobile Systems, Applications and Services, pp. 233–245 (2007)

36. Mascetti, S., Bettini, C., Freni, D.: Longitude: centralized privacy-preserving computation of users' proximity. In: Jonker, W., Petković, M. (eds.) SDM 2009. LNCS, vol. 5776, pp. 142–157. Springer, Heidelberg (2009)

37. Mascetti, S., Freni, D., Bettini, C., Wang, X.S., Jajodia, S.: Privacy in geosocial networks: proximity notification with untrusted service providers and curious buddies. VLDB J. Int. J. Very Large Data Bases **20**(4), 541–566 (2011)

38. Wei, W., Xu, F., Li, Q.: Mobishare: flexible privacy-preserving location sharing in mobile online social networks. In: INFOCOM, 2012 Proceedings IEEE, pp. 2616–2620 (2012)

39. Liu, Z., Li, J., Chen, X., Li, J., Jia, C.: New privacy-preserving location sharing system for mobile online social networks. In: 2013 8th International Conference on P2P, Parallel, Grid, Cloud and Internet Computing (3PGCIC), pp. 214–218 (2013)

40. Vicente, C.R., Freni, D., Bettini, C., Jensen, C.S.: Location-related privacy in geosocial networks. IEEE Internet Comput. **15**(3), 20–27 (2011)

41. Camilli, M.: Preserving Co-location Privacy in Geosocial Networks. Arxiv preprint arxiv:1203.3946 (2012)

42. Freni, D., Ruiz Vicente, C., Mascetti, S., Bettini, C., Jensen, C.S.: Preserving location and absence privacy in geosocial networks. In: Proceedings of the 19th ACM International Conference on Information and Knowledge Management, pp. 309–318 (2010)

43. Gambs, S., Killijian, M.O., Del Prado Cortez, M.N.: Gepeto: a geoprivacy-enhancing toolkit. In: 2010 IEEE 24th International Conference on Advanced Information Networking and Applications Workshops (WAINA), pp. 1071–1076 (2010)

44. Kar, B., Crowsey, R.C., Zale, J.J.: The myth of location privacy in the United States: surveyed attitude versus current practices. Prof. Geogr. **65**(1), 47–64 (2013)

45. http://beta.congress.gov/bill/113th-congress/house-bill/983/text. Accessed 27 March 2014

46. http://www.priv.gc.ca/parl/2013/pipeda_r_201305_e.asp. Accessed 27 March 2014

47. Solove, D.J.: Privacy self-management and the consent paradox. Harvard Law Rev. **126**, 1880–1903 (2013)

48. Ozer, N., Conley, C., O'Connell, D.H., Gubins, T.R., Ginsburg, E.: Location-Based Services: Time For a Privacy Check-In. ACLU Of Northern California, San Francisco (2010)

SocialSpy: Browsing (Supposedly) Hidden Information in Online Social Networks

Andrea Burattin[1], Giuseppe Cascavilla[2,3]([✉]), and Mauro Conti[1]

[1] University of Padova, Padua, Italy
{burattin,conti}@math.unipd.it
[2] University of L'Aquila, L'Aquila, Italy
g.cascavilla@student.vu.nl
[3] VU University, Amsterdam, The Netherlands

Abstract. Online Social Networks are becoming the most important "places" where people share information about their lives. With the increasing concern that users have about privacy, most social networks offer ways to control the privacy of the user. Unfortunately, we believe that current privacy settings are not as effective as users might think.

In this paper, we highlight this problem focusing on one of the most popular social networks, Facebook. In particular, we show how easy it is to retrieve information that a user might have set as (and hence thought as) "private". As a case study, we focus on retrieving the list of friends for users that did set this information as "hidden" (to non-friends). We propose four different strategies to achieve this goal, and we evaluate them. The results of our thorough experiments show the feasibility of our strategies as well as their effectiveness: our approach is able to retrieve a significant percentage of the names of the "hidden" friends: i.e., some 25 % on average, and more than 70 % for some users.

1 Introduction

Online Social Networks (OSNs) are web applications that allow users to build connections and establish relationships to other Internet users. Social networking can be used to stay in touch with friends, make new contacts and find people with similar interests and ideas. These online services have grown in popularity since they were first adopted on a large scale in the late 1990s. Geocities was among the first social networking sites on the Internet, launching its website in 1994 [1]. Currently, one of the most famous and used OSNs is Facebook. On October 4th, 2012, Facebook reached one billion users [2]. All these users generate, share, and link a huge amount of data. According to statistics as of August 2012 [3], 300 million photos were uploaded daily, 2.7 billion likes were made daily, and an average of 500 terabytes of new data were stored on a daily basis. Looking at the recent growth rate of Facebook, it is possible to assert that its only limit is given by two factors: the world population and government policies. Specifically, as reported in [4–6], Facebook is still not available for all the users around the world. Facebook, in order to handle such growth, went through a lot of improvements, many of them

© Springer International Publishing Switzerland 2015
J. Lopez et al. (Eds.): CRiSIS 2014, LNCS 8924, pp. 83–99, 2015.
DOI: 10.1007/978-3-319-17127-2_6

closely related to privacy and security issues [7]. However, as reported for example in [8,9], the platform is still affected by data leakages.

We argue that one of the biggest challenges of OSNs is to ensure privacy and security for the data of their users. In [10], authors give a generic idea about methods and reasons that push a user to launch an attack against OSNs. In particular, the authors claim that the basic motivation behind such attacks is an economical reward, and most of the users just use "horse sense" to protect themselves. Moreover, the same study pinpoints the OSNs as being responsible of warning users against the risk of attacks, enhancing their spam filters, and taking care of application bugs. For these reasons, OSNs privacy and security are well studied issues.

To ensure the privacy of the data, OSNs give to their users tools to set up rules for the visibility of their data. In Facebook, for example, there is the possibility to divide friends in *"Folders"*, and set different privacy rules for each folder. In Google Plus there are *"Circles"* to define different privacy rules for the different group of friends. LinkedIn and Twitter do not have custom privacy rules for specific set of contacts. The main problem with privacy settings is to learn how to properly use and tune them. Several guides, today, are available on Internet, with the explicit goal to help people in such configuration. However, even when the user configures his profile in a proper way, problems may arise with the privacy settings of third-party applications. For example, the current Graphical User Interface (GUI) of Facebook does not help inexperienced users in understanding what kind of permissions are better to give to an application to keep a good level of privacy [11]. Using this Facebook GUI, a user simply authorizes the application to have access to (all) his data. Once the application is authorized, the data from the user could become publicly available. Almost 13 million users said they had never set, or did not know about Facebook's privacy tools. Furthermore, 28 % share all, or almost all, their wall posts with an audience wider than just their friends [12]. According to our studies and experiments, we hardly believe that users are completely aware of actual privacy that OSNs provide them. On the other hand, whenever users know that their profiles have some information leakages, they are often too lazy (or inexperienced) to properly modify the privacy options and make the profile private [13].

The approach we propose in this paper can be considered as Open Source INTelligence (OSINT) techniques. In the intelligence community, the term "open" refers to overt, publicly available sources (as opposed to covert or clandestine sources). OSINT approaches aim at extracting knowledge from publicly available sources [14,15]. In fact, our study, uses only information publicly available on Facebook. In particular, the tools we use in our strategies are: *(i)* Graph APIs [16], i.e., set of APIs which allows developers to build applications capable of reading and writing user data; *(ii)* Mutual Content Page [17], i.e., a page that displays which content two users have in common; *(iii)* FacePile plugin [18], i.e., a web page that displays a portion of the people who liked a given page. The FacePile plugin is usually used in a website to show who liked the related Facebook fan page.

We underline that all these tools are freely available to any Facebook user.

The contribution of this paper is threefold. We first underline the problem that Open Source Intelligence (OSINT) [19,20] applied to Online Social Network allows to retrieve a significant amount of information that the user consider, set, and think as remaining private. Then, we propose four different practical OSINT strategies to retrieve the Friends List from a popular OSN (i.e., Facebook). Finally, we prototype our strategies, and run a set of experiments. Our implementation demonstrates the feasibility of our approaches, while the results of the experiments show their effectiveness: our approach is able to retrieve a significant percentage of Facebook identifiers (IDs) of the "hidden" friends: i.e., some 25 % on average, and more than 70 % for some users.

The remaining part of the paper is organized as follows. In Sect. 2 we review the state of the art. In Sect. 3 we give a formalization of Facebook and of our framework. In Sect. 4 we present the weakest part of Facebook. In Sect. 5 we describe our strategies to retrieve data. In Sect. 6 we present our experimental settings and we discuss the results. Finally, Sect. 7 draws some conclusions.

2   Related Work

In the literature, there are several studies about privacy in Online Social Network. These works revealed the lack of privacy and security in OSNs and how simple it is to get private information about users. The literature is split between studies on OSNs privacy issues on one hand, and possible data protection solutions on the other side. We can then divide this related work section in three parts: "Attacks", "Solutions" and "Motivations". Under the "Attacks" section we are going to present all those studies that try to retrieve information, considered private, from OSNs. Instead, in "Solutions", we analyze the proposed way to protect users data in OSNs. Lastly, in "Motivations", we discuss some issues that make user profiles in OSNs lacking of privacy.

Attacks. As part of "Attacks" studies we have the work described in [9]. It aims at retrieving user age by crawling through Facebook [21]. The study shows how to retrieve the victim's age using "reverse friend lookup technique". Indeed, exploiting the lack of privacy of victim's friends it is possible to retrieve personal information from the profile of the victim itself. Similarly to the study above mentioned is [22]. The study uses a crawling technique to retrieve names of users from Facebook. Cong Tang et al. use for the experiment only public profiles from Facebook and citizens of New York City. The study processed all the properties of the retrieved names and compared them with a popular name list obtained via offline mechanisms. Having the names of users with a public profile in Facebook [22] tries to infer the gender of the retrieved users. Another experiment based on crawling is presented in [23] where Kurt et al. show the failure of privacy options provided by Facebook to protect users from personal content leakage by friends. An interesting study, that tries to discover hidden information about a victim user is reported in [24]. In this work, authors use public information available from a social network. Collecting the information retrieved from the social network, they build queries for search engines. With the queries and the corresponding results they try to discover new information about the victim. Costantino et al. [25] proposes Phook, a Facebook application. Once the user authorizes Phook to have access to his data, the application is able to retrieve, from the profile of the user, photos based on keywords. Using Facebook Query Language (FQL), Phook makes queries on the Facebook user profile and retrieves all the photos related to the keywords. However, Phook does not discover hidden information from users on Facebook. Phook retrieves information from the profile of the user that is connected to the Phook application.

Solutions. If above we have a handful of attacks, the literature proposes also some solutions to mitigate the lack of privacy in OSNs. An approach is presented in [26], where Luo et al. propose a solution for the disclosure of information based on the architecture "FaceCloak", where information from a user are hidden to the non authorized profiles. The study described in [27] proposes a system which is able to enforce privacy protection in Facebook. With a Firefox plugin, called FaceVPSN, Conti et al. try to mitigate the problem of lack of privacy in Facebook. FaceVPSN is completely distributed, Facebook independent, and hides information from users outside the Virtual Private Social Network (VPSN). This plugin hides public information "covering" them with fakes. Then, only those users that are part of the VPSN network can retrieve the real information of a user. Solutions such as FaceVPSN provides user anonymity via registering a fake identity in Facebook. However, de-anonymization solution have also been proposed [28]. Hence, solutions as FaceVPSN should be used in conjunction with mechanisms that make the de-anonymization of networks more hard [29,30]. Buchegger et al. propose PeerSoN [31]: a tool to address privacy concerns over Online Social Networks (OSNs). This tool is based on a peer-to-peer architecture and provides users with privacy protection in OSN. This system is decentralized and independent from any OSN: it is able to encrypt the communication with the OSN. When a peer wants to connect to another peer, it first queries the look-up service in order to get all required information. Then, peers are able to directly connect each other. Once the peers exchanged a message or file, they immediately disconnect. This architecture, however, is still a prototype. An approach to mitigate the problem of Fake Profile Attack in OSNs is showed in [32]. The aim of this work is to understand, from the behavior of a user in OSNs, if a Facebook profile is real or fake. In [32], the authors made their experiments looking at some different variables as *"Evolution over time of the number of friends"*, *"Real life social network based verification"*, and *"OSN graph structure for fake profile detection"*.

Motivations. Lastly, as part of motivation part, we try to understand how it is possible this lack of information in OSNs. One of the many reason for the disclosure of information in OSNs is reported in [33]. Through a simple experiment, Nagle and Singh show how easily people accept a request of friendship on Facebook from a stranger. The percentage of people that add an unknown user on Facebook increases if there is a common friend between the user and the unknown new friend. This is also due to the lack of attention from the user that does not care too much about the problem that someone can steal his information. Beyond the reasons that lead users disclosure information, it is necessary to state that, in recent years, profiles in OSNs are becoming more private. The experiment, concerning privacy in OSNs reported in [34], shows the raising of awareness from users concerning the lack of privacy in OSNs. Ratan et al. ran the same experiment twice; the first one in 2010 and the second one in 2011 and compared the results. Crawling some profiles, that are part of the NYC subnetwork, they discovered that in 2010 the amount of hidden profile was close to 17 %. Ratan et al. restarted the crawler on the same subnetwork in 2011 and the percentage of hidden profiles has been increased up to 52 %. Therefore, according to this paper, users had a growth of awareness and started to take care of their online data and on the OSNs as well.

The work we present in this paper aims at understanding how easily and how much supposedly hidden information can be retrieved from a Facebook profile. In fact, all the above-mentioned studies are related to discover some simple information of a given user or to try to protect the information itself. Instead, we propose an approach to retrieve information, set as private, from a user Facebook profile. The first part of our study can be classified under the "Attacks" field. On the other hand, the study aims to create awareness in OSN users. Through our attacks we show how a user can protect his information using privacy options provided by OSNs. Moreover, we show what privacy options the OSNs require an update in order to better protect its users information. These last part can be classified as "Solutions". Our strategies, differ from the above mentioned studies on several aspects: *(i)* we do not need any type of authorization from the user to have access to his data (our strategies are not based on a Facebook application); *(ii)* we keep the victim user completely unaware of the attack; *(iii)* we are able to rebuild the friends list of a user that is not a friend of the attacker (they do not have to share any information); *(iv)* we are able to retrieve the friends list set as *"private"*; *(v)* we work on random profiles from Facebook, on which we do not have any type of information, except the username; *(vi)* neither information nor friends are shared between our experimental profiles and the victim profiles.

3   System Model

Facebook is composed of different entities. All these entities, together, give the possibility to the final user to perform different actions into such "ecosystem". The entities we consider are: *pages*, *users*, *groups* and *pictures*. *Users* are allowed to perform some actions: become "friend" of another user; "like" a *page* (and revoke the "like"), "join" a *group* (and leave the group), and "like" or "comment" pictures (and revoke the "like" or delete the "comment"). Instead, *pages*, *groups* and *pictures* are "passive" entities (i.e., they are managed by *users*). *Pages* are always public. The set of pages a user likes can be interpreted as the *tastes* of that user. Usually *pages* enable public figures (such as companies, organizations, or celebrities) to create a presence on Facebook [35]. *Groups* on Facebook are "places" where people can share and discuss their common interests and express their opinion around common causes, issues or activities to organize [35]. A group is not always public: tuning its privacy rules, it is possible to set it as public (accessible and searchable to all users in Facebook), private (accessible only if invited; searchable) or hidden (accessible only if invited; not searchable). *Pictures* are usually uploaded by users. On Facebook, it is really difficult to take under control the privacy settings of pictures. There are pictures directly uploaded by a user, pictures where users are tagged, cover photos (that are always public) and profile pictures.

More formally, the portion of Facebook that we are going to use in the rest of this paper can be formalized as the tuple: $Facebook = (\mathbb{P}, \mathbb{U}, \mathbb{G}, \mathbb{I})$. Specifically, in this notation, we have that:

- $\mathbb{P}$ is the set of pages. A page $p \in \mathbb{P}$ is something related to the tastes of a user, i.e., what a user might like.
- $\mathbb{U}$ is the set of users. A user $u \in \mathbb{U}$ represents a person. Each person can "like" a page p, join a group g, leave comments into a page, request friendships to other users (accept friendship from other users), upload pictures into his own profile pages.
- $\mathbb{G} = (G', n)$ is the multiset that represents groups, where $G' \subseteq \mathcal{P}(\mathbb{U})$ (given a set A, $\mathcal{P}(A)$ is the power set of A, i.e., the set of all subsets of A) and $n : G' \to \mathbb{N}_{\geq 1}$ is the multiplicity function. $\mathbb{G}$ represents all the groups on Facebook (please note the same set of users may appears several times). A group, from the "application" point of view, is a place where a user can promote, share and discuss relevant topics.
- $\mathbb{I}$ is the set of pictures. Every picture $i \in \mathbb{I}$ can receive one or more "likes" and one or more "comments" from a user $u \in \mathbb{U}$. Therefore, it is possible to consider a picture as the pair $i = (U_i^l, U_i^c)$. Where $U_i^l \subseteq \mathcal{P}(\mathbb{U})$ is the set of users that liked i, and $U_i^c \subseteq \mathcal{P}(\mathbb{U})$ is the set of users that commented on i.

Within our model, a user u is defined as the tuple $u = (Personal, U, P, G, I)$, where: *Personal* is the set of "personal" information (such as the name, the family name, the age), $U \subseteq \mathbb{U}$ is the set of friends of u; $P \subseteq \mathbb{P}$ is set of pages u likes; $G \subseteq \mathbb{G}$ is the set of groups u belongs to; and $I \subseteq \mathbb{I}$ is the set of personal pictures (pictures that u uploaded into the social network).

Due to all these interacting entities, and their complex set of privacy settings, it is very easy to observe information leakages out of Facebook.

4   Retrieving Hidden Information

The aim of this work is to retrieve the lists of friends of a victim. We decided to have as target the friends list because we believe this is one of the most important information on Facebook. In fact, this list might be interesting as a starting point to find even more information. Specifically, from these friends, it is possible to retrieve pictures or comments where the victim user is tagged, or information posted directly from him. It is also possible to consider the revealing of friends list as the *foundation stone* of the process of rebuilding an entire victim profile.

To retrieve the friends list, we start looking at which information can be exploited from the profile of the victim. Specifically, it is possible to categorize the information to exploit in:

- Personal Info: general information about the user, which exist independently from Facebook. Examples of this type of information are the gender, the address, the job, the hometown, and the phone number.
- Facebook Related Info: information which exist because of the profile page on Facebook. We can categorize this information in three groups: the *pages* a user likes (P), the *groups* (G), and *pictures* (I).
- Application Related Info: information connected to the Facebook applications that the victim uses. For example, applications like TripAdvisor [36] could publish data, such as the visited places. Other applications may publish tastes information, such as Spotify [37].

The easiest retrievable information, from the profile of user, are the Facebook Related Info: groups, pictures and pages a user likes. After some studies we figured out that this information is frequently left public, either on purpose by the users, or by the lack of a proper Facebook privacy settings configuration. Let us briefly analyze how we are going to exploit this Facebook Related Info:

- Groups (G). Using the group pages that belong to the victim user v, we find user IDs that are friends of v. To do this, we apply two different strategies:
  1. Using the Graph API, we retrieve all the groups from the profile of v. We sort the groups from the smallest to the largest (w.r.t. their number of subscribers). For each group we retrieve all the user profiles and validate the friendship with v, using Mutual Content Page. This verification is made using the text "Are friends since (date)". If the Mutual Content Page shows "Are friends since (date)", then we are sure that v and the retrieved user are friends. There is no need to have the friendship with the victim, because the Mutual Content Page is publicly accessible.
  2. Using the Graph API, we retrieve all the groups from the profile of v. We sort the groups from the largest to the smallest. Group by group we retrieve all the user IDs and we validate the friendship with v using Mutual Content Page.

  We did not implement the strategies above illustrated because of the huge number of subscribers that usually are part of a group, and also because not all groups are publicly available. As previously outlined, groups have settings to make them "private" and "hidden". With the "private" setting, the group is not accessible. With the "hidden" setting it is not possible to find the group on Facebook.
- Public pictures of victim user v (I). Very often it is possible to find public pictures on a Facebook *wall* (the profile main page). After some studies, we figured out that among all the pictures, cover photos are always publicly available and it is not possible to set them private. The strategy exploits the likes and the comments that each picture receives. In particular, given a picture belonging to the victim v, we can retrieve all the user IDs that liked or

commented the picture. Each of them, using Mutual Content Page, is checked
for his friendship with v.

– Liked pages (P). When a victim user v clicks on the "Like button" of a page
p, he becomes fan of p. These information are usually left public on the wall
of v. With our strategy we retrieve the user IDs that clicked the Like button of
the page p. All the user IDs of this set are checked for their friendship with v,
using the Mutual Content Page.

5   Strategies

We are now going to analyze in detail our strategies. The first three strategies are
based on liked pages. We decided to use liked pages, for our strategies, because
of the meaning of page itself in Facebook. Pages are made to aggregate people
around a common interest. The page could be related to an interest really big,
like a page of famous actor. Moreover, a fan page could be related to something
really small like a little household music group. Statistics say that Facebook
Like or Share buttons are viewed more than 22 billion times a day. Furthermore,
7.5 million is the number of sites that contain Facebook Like or Share button [38].
From this information, we believe it is really common that users are attracted
from friend's interests and attract friends sharing and liking pages. Therefore, we
think that the possibility to find friends of a victim, between users that liked a
page, is really high. The fourth strategy works on likes and comments of pictures
of a victim.

5.1   Strategy 1 ($S1$): Likes Random Order

Working on like pages, $S1$ is able to target and retrieve the likes from a victim v.
Once the strategy has a list of likes, there is a high probability to find a handful
of friends. The list of user IDs from like pages, sharing the same interest of our
victim, is only the starting point to retrieve the friends list of v. Algorithm 1
illustrates $S1$.

As mentioned in Sect. 3, this strategy uses P to build U. Using the public
Facebook page of v, $S1$ retrieves the liked pages P left public from the profile of v
(line 1 of Algorithm 1). The strategy then retrieves the list of fans (the procedure
is wrapped on the "FanOf" procedure, mentioned in line 4). To perform this
retrieval we use FacePile plugin. Starting from the list of fans, $S1$ checks, for
each fan if he is a friend of v (line 7). To understand if two users are friends we
use the Mutual Content Page that shows mutual content between two users. If $S1$
finds a friend of v it adds the ID of friend in a list called $FriendsFound$ (line 8).
$S1$ repeats this procedure until there are no more candidate friends (friends that
like the same pages of v).

5.2   Strategy 2 ($S2$): Likes Ascending Order

The second strategy is similar to the previous one: once all liked pages from the
victim v are retrieved, $S2$ sorts them from the one with the smallest number

---

Algorithm 1. Strategy 1 ($S1$), Likes Random Order.

Data: Victim user v
Result: Set of friends U of v

1 $P \leftarrow$ set of pages v likes
2 $CandidateFriends \leftarrow \emptyset$
3 **foreach** $p \in P$ **do**
       /* Find page fans with FacePile   */
4      $CandidateFriends \leftarrow CandidateFriends \cup \text{FanOf}(p)$

5 $FriendsFound \leftarrow \emptyset$
6 **foreach** $c \in CandidateFriends$ **do**
       /* Check friendship with Mutual Content Page   */
7   **if** $AreFriends(c, v)$ **then**
8          $FriendsFound \leftarrow FriendsFound \cup \{c\}$

9 **return** $FriendsFound$

---

of fans to the one with the largest. This strategy is designed to start from the page with the smallest number of fans because we assume that these pages are closely related to the interests of our victim v, and therefore the probability to find user IDs of friends of v is higher. Once we have some user IDs of friends of v, we can retrieve the list of common friends using the Mutual Content Page itself. Algorithm 2 illustrates $S2$.

According to Sect. 3, $S2$ uses P to build U. Using the public Facebook page of v, $S2$ retrieves the liked pages P from the profile of v (line 1 of Algorithm 2). Since $S2$ has the set P, it organizes them in a priority queue and retrieves the list of fans U from the page using FacePile plugin (line 4). The liked pages are organized according to a priority min-to-max (line 6), it means that Algorithm 2 tries to find user IDs of friends starting from the page with the less number of fans till the one with the major number of fans. After that, $S2$ iterates over the list of fan $CandidateFriends$ and checks, for each user ID, if it is a friend of v (line 10). If this is the case, it adds the user ID in a list called $FriendsFound$ (line 11). $S2$ repeats this procedure since there are no more candidate friends.

5.3 Strategy 3 ($S3$): Likes Descending Order

This strategy is very similar to $S2$: we organize the pages starting from the one with the highest number of fans to the smallest (Set priority max-to-min). The main idea behind this strategy is that, fetching like pages from max-to-min, we have the biggest datasets at the beginning of our research where we could find, at least one user ID of friends of v. Having one user ID of a friend of v we can use the Mutual Content Page to discover if they have other friends in common and then add the user ID of them to our list of "Friends Found".

The Algorithm of $S3$ differs from $S2$ only at line 6: the priority, in the case of $S3$, is set as "max-to-min".

Algorithm 2. Strategy 2 ($S2$), Likes Ascending Order.

Data: Victim user v
Result: Set of friends U of v

1 $P \leftarrow$ set of pages v likes
2 *CandidateFriends* $\leftarrow$ empty priority queue
3 **foreach** $p \in P$ **do**
4 | *Fans* $\leftarrow$ FanOf(p)   /* Find fans with FacePile */
5 | Insert(*CandidateFriends*, *Fans*, TotalFansOf(p)) /* Inserts the set *Fans* into the *CandidateFriends* queue, with the total number of fans as priority */

6 Set priority of *CandidateFriends* as min-to-max

7 *FriendsFound* $\leftarrow \emptyset$
8 **repeat**
9 | $c \leftarrow$ ExtractFirst(*CandidateFriends*)   /* Returns (and removes) the first element of the queue */
   | /* Check friendship with Mutual Content Page   */
10 | **if** *AreFriends*(c, v) **then**
11 | | *FriendsFound* $\leftarrow$ *FriendsFound* $\cup$ $\{u\}$
12 **until** *CandidateFriends* **is** *empty*
13 **return** *FriendsFound*

5.4 Strategy 4 ($S4$): Likes and Comments from Pictures

$S4$ does not work with liked pages as Strategies 1, 2 or 3. Instead, it tries to take advantages from pictures of victim profile. The main idea is to use pictures that are left public from victim v or are not settable as private. There are images like "cover photos" that the user cannot hide, and are always publicly available. From public images and cover photos, $S4$, retrieves the user IDs of people that pressed the "Like" button or commented them. Once $S4$ obtains the list of user IDs, checks the friendship between them and v using the Mutual Content Page. Algorithm 3 illustrates $S4$.

According to Sect. 3, $S4$ uses I to build U. $S4$ starts fetching the pictures of victim v (line 1 of Algorithm 3). From these images the strategy collects all the candidate user IDs that liked or commented the picture itself (line 4). Once that $S4$ obtains this list of user IDs, it checks the friendship with v (line 7) using the Mutual Content Page. If $S4$ finds a user ID of a friend, it adds it in the *FriendsFound* set (line 8).

6 Evaluation

To evaluate our approaches, we conducted some experiments on different datasets. The datasets contain real profiles from Facebook users.

To perform our tests, we logged into Facebook using nine different accounts. These accounts do not have any friends, therefore they are as far away as possible

---

Algorithm 3. Strategy 4 ($S4$), Likes and Comments.

Data: Victim user v
Result: Set of friends of v

1 $I \leftarrow$ set of public images of v
2 $CandidateFriends \leftarrow \emptyset$
3 **foreach** $i \in I$ **do**
   /* Add candidate friends set all users that liked or commented
   the image   */
4     $CandidateFriends \leftarrow CandidateFriends \cup U_i^l \cup U_i^c$

5 $FriendsFound \leftarrow \emptyset$
6 **foreach** $c \in CandidateFriends$ **do**
   /* Check friendship with Mutual Content Page   */
7   **if** $AreFriends(c, v)$ **then**
8        $FriendsFound \leftarrow FriendsFound \cup \{c\}$

9 **return** $FriendsFound$

---

from victims (in terms of "*hops*" on the graphs that connects users according to their friendships). The only activity of these accounts consists in liking few pages. In order not to show an anomalous behavior, that could be detected as malicious by Facebook, we decided to split the load of our requests on nine different accounts. With nine accounts we appear like nine different users that make requests to the Facebook servers, each making requests with a lower frequency than the original one. After logging in Facebook with these accounts, we ran our tests to fetch data of victims.

For our experiments we decided to use two types of Facebook datasets: Mixed Dataset and Public Dataset.

Mixed Dataset. Using Firefox, we downloaded user IDs from public group pages. The groups we used are: Universitá degli Studi di Padova[1], Roma Giurisprudenza La Sapienza[2], Studenti dell' Universitá degli Studi di Milano - Unimi[3], Programmers in Padua[4], F.I.U.P[5], Pensionati della Polizia di Stato[6], Flowers[7], New York Italians[8], Team Ferrari Challange "Black Jack Café" & Friends[9], The Real Housewives of New York City[10]. Most of group pages allow to see their members and

---

[1] http://www.facebook.com/groups/unipd.
[2] http://www.facebook.com/groups/7795542586.
[3] http://www.facebook.com/groups/2310323055.
[4] http://www.facebook.com/groups/programmersinpadua.
[5] http://www.facebook.com/groups/fiupd.
[6] http://www.facebook.com/groups/58159395664.
[7] http://www.facebook.com/groups/246910381993344.
[8] http://www.facebook.com/groups/159253824092728.
[9] http://www.facebook.com/groups/WWW.BLACKJACKCAFE.
[10] http://www.facebook.com/groups/rhonyc.

therefore it is easy to download their user IDs. This dataset contains public pro-files and private profiles, therefore we call it *Mixed Dataset*. Public profiles are com-posed by those users that decided to have all the content, from their profile, pub-licly available. There are then private profiles composed by those users that care about their privacy. In this second case the content of their profile is in part or not accessible at all. This dataset contains 115 users.

Public Dataset. This dataset is public and generated "around July 15, 2010, by Ron Bowes". This set of user IDs is publicly available[11]. Bownes simply generated a tool to download all the Facebook user IDs that are public at the page https://www.facebook.com/directory/. This page points to all those user IDs that decided to have a public profile on Facebook or that have answered to the privacy options *"Who can see my stuff?"*, *"Who can contact me?"* and *"Who can look me up?"* with *"Public"* and *"Everyone"*. This public dataset contains 1000 public user names.

6.1   Experimental Results on Mixed Dataset

For this and the next paragraph, for readability purpose, all graphs do report a subset of the nodes for which we run experiments.

Let's first analyze the data coming from the Mixed Dataset. The graph in Fig. 1(a) shows the average of our four strategies by requests on 115 victims. The x-axis shows number of HTTP requests that every strategy requires to retrieve information from Facebook pages. On the y-axis, instead, we have the number of user IDs of friends, found by the specific strategy.

Figure 1(a) demonstrates that $S4$ works faster and finds the highest number of friends' user IDs. This is due to the fact that $S4$ works on victim's pictures. Since that $S4$ uses victim's images, we can assert that most of the comments and likes are from friends of the victim user. It is also possible that non-friend users like or comment victim's pictures. This is due to the fact that public pictures can be available to all the users in Facebook that could decide to like or leave a comment. To recognize who is a friend and who is not, we use the Mutual Content Page given directly by Facebook.

Going deeper into the graph it is possible to note that the four strategies work in a similar way: all the four curves start growing fast at the beginning going to be flat at the end (i.e., they have the same coarse-grained shape). This is due to the fact that all the friends' user IDs are almost found at the beginning and when the strategies do not have more chances to discover friends, the curve becomes flat. In Fig. 1(b) we draw the graph considering the time (in seconds) to process each request. From the graph below, on the x-axis, it is possible to see how long each strategy worked to find friends' IDs. On the y-axis, instead, how many user IDs of friends every strategy found. $S4$ fetches the major number of user IDs of friends.

---

[11] http://www.skullsecurity.org.

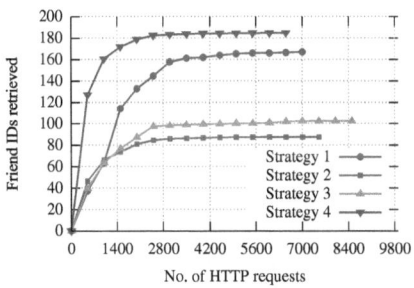

(a) Average number of user IDs of friends found with respect to the number of HTTP

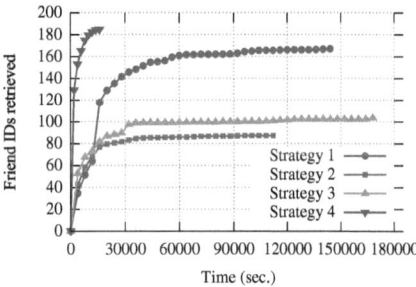

(b) Average number of user IDs of friends found against the time, on Mixed Dataset.

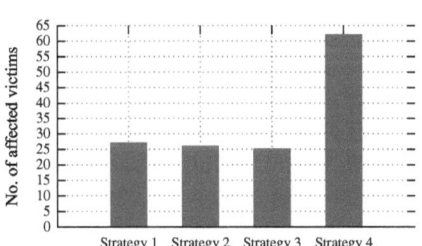

(c) Impact of each strategy in terms of number of user IDs that we succeeded to retrieve data from (on Mixed Dataset.

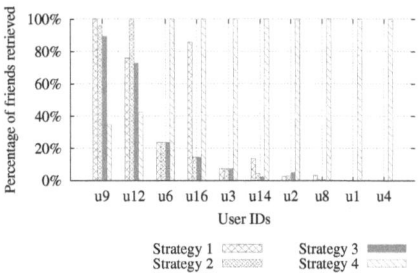

(d) Percentages of user IDs of friends found by each strategy for some users from our Mixed Dataset.

Fig. 1. Performance on the Mixed Dataset.

The graph in Fig. 1(c) shows how many victims our strategies succeeded to retrieve user IDs of friends from their supposed hidden data. Let us consider *S4* as an illustrative example: in the graph in Fig. 1(c), *S4* retrieved user IDs from about 65 users out of a dataset of 115. Figure 1(d) shows which strategy works better on some randomly selected victims of the Mixed Dataset. This figure does not show all the victims with the related best strategy, instead it reports just a small view of the performance on few elements of our dataset. Since we are not able to know how many friends our victims have, we decided to consider the strategy that fetched the highest number of user IDs of friends as 100 %. Then we draw all the other strategies around the highest one calculating the percentage as the ratio between: the number of friends found from strategy and the highest number of friends found. Using this graph, we have the possibility to analyze, for every single user, which strategy is the best in retrieving user IDs of friends and the percentage of friends found from the other strategies compared to the best one. Due to the results, we can state that the *S4* obtains better results for most of the users. There are two users, i.e., *u9* and *u12*, where *S1* and *S2* work better than others. From this graph we can assert that *S4* is not always the best one. This is due to the fact that there are some victims, that do not have "open" (publicly accessible) pictures but they have accessible liked pages. In this case *S1* or *S2* or *S3* are strongly suggested.

6.2 Experimental Results on Public Dataset

The Public Dataset is composed by Facebook profiles that have a public profile. The graphs in Fig. 2(a) and (b) present how our strategies become faster and more accurate on this dataset. As we expect, all the strategies work much better and find more user IDs of friends. These results are perfectly in line with our assumption: people with a public profile have much more information available. Therefore, our strategies have more possibilities to find their friends. It is possible to compare the curves reported in Fig. 2(a) and (b) with those in Fig. 1(a) and (b). Experiment reported in Fig. 2(a) requires, on average, more "HTTP requests" than strategies applied to the dataset of Fig. 1(a). This is due to the fact that more information is available from the victim profile. This means that strategies applied to Public Dataset need more requests to retrieve more information than strategies on Mixed Dataset. Also, the values of "Friends IDs retrieved" are higher, on average, in Fig. 2(a). It means that the strategies applied to the Public Dataset (Fig. 2(a)) found more user IDs of friends compared to the same strategies on the Mixed Dataset (Fig. 1(a)).

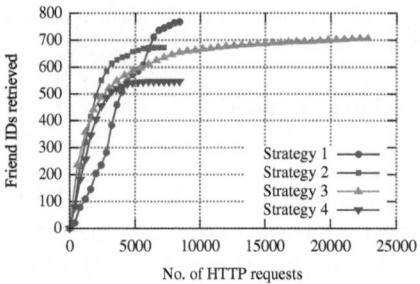
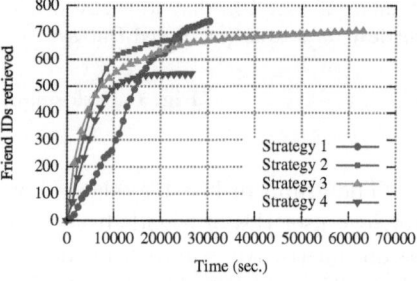

(a) Average number of user IDs of friends found with respect to the number of HTTP requests, on Public Dataset.

(b) Average number of user IDs of friends found against the time, on Public Dataset.

Fig. 2. Performance on the Public Dataset.

Generally speaking, the main difference between Mixed and Public Dataset is in terms of number of user IDs of friends found, which is much higher in the latter case. Although it seems meaningless to look for friends in the Public Dataset, we proposed these measures to prove the actual correctness of our approaches.

6.3 Discussion

We tested our approaches on a Mixed Dataset, composed by IDs of users that use privacy setting and IDs of users that have the Facebook profile publicly available. On the Mixed Dataset composed from those user IDs that use privacy settings, the fastest strategy is *S4*. It uses public pictures of a victim to retrieve IDs of friends. Strategies 1, 2 and 3 are slower than *S4*, but when pictures are not publicly available, Strategies 1, 2 and 3 are the best alternative. In some cases we noticed that the strategies are able to retrieve up to 70 % of user IDs of friends of a victim. On a Public Dataset all the strategies work better than on a Mixed Dataset: the number of IDs of friends found increases greatly. In this case, all four strategies retrieve a big amount of user IDs of friends. These results are in line with our thought. Figure 1(a) and (b), from the Mixed Dataset, give us the main information. The biggest leakage of privacy is due to the public pictures. The percentage of user IDs of friends found from *S4*, that exploits pictures, is 37.12 % with peaks of 70 %. Cover photos are always publicly available and it is not possible to make them private by Facebook privacy settings. This is the main reason that makes *S4* to work better than the others and retrieves more user IDs of friends compared to *S1* with 17.5 %, *S2* with 17.4 % and *S3* with 20.8 % of friends found.

On the other hand, we have to clarify the differences of percentages between *S1*, 2 and 3. All these strategies work almost in the same way. The main motivation of these three different percentages is due to the FacePile plugin. For the same victim and the same like page, among the three strategies, the plugin shows a page with different set of candidate friends. This is motivated by the fact that our profiles are completely empty of information and do not have friends. Therefore, the Facebook engine, is not able to assign different "distances" among all the users, and thus it randomly shows candidate friends.

7   Conclusion

The final aim of this work was to present a proof-of-concept approach that demonstrates a significant privacy issue on Facebook. Specifically, we exploited only tools publicly available in order to reveal information that the victim declared private. The presented technique consists of four strategies, that rely on the above-mentioned tools, with the final aim of rebuilding the list of friends of a victim user (in the event that the victim declared such list private). For our experiments we used two datasets of Facebook profiles, the Mixed Dataset and the Public Dataset. The first contains user IDs composed of profiles with different types of privacy settings and usually with information not publicly available; the latter contains user IDs profiles that are publicly available. Since we used only public tools our evaluation shows how easy is to overcome the willingness of privacy of the users. With our four strategies we can retrieve the friend list of every user with every type of privacy settings. Our percentages demonstrate a real lack of privacy in Facebook. We are now able to raise a real concern against Facebook. On the other hand, from our experiments, we hope to create awareness on Facebook users.

As a future work we want to analyze the possibility to rebuild not only a friend list, but the whole Facebook profile of a victim user.

Acknowledgments. Mauro Conti is supported by a Marie Curie Fellowship funded by the European Commission under the agreement n. PCIG11-GA-2012-321980. This work has been partially supported by the TENACE PRIN Project 20103P34XC funded by the Italian MIUR, and by the Project "Tackling Mobile Malware with Innovative Machine Learning Techniques" funded by the University of Padua.

References

1. Walker, M.: The history of Social Networking (2011). http://www.webmasterview. com/2011/08/social-networking-history
2. Money, C.: Facebook reaches one billion users (2012). http://money.cnn.com/2012/ 10/04/technology/facebook-billion-users
3. CNET: Facebook processes more than 500TB of data daily (2012). http://news.cnet.com/8301-10233-57498531-93/facebook-processes-more-than-500-tb-of-data-daily
4. Bass, S.: China's Facebook status: Blocked (2009). http://abcnews.go.com/blogs/ headlines/2009/07/chinas-facebook-status-blocked
5. Dehghan, S.K.: Iran clamps down on Internet use (2012). http://www.guardian. co.uk/world/2012/jan/05/iran-clamps-down-internet-use
6. Desk, N.: Bangladesh sets precondition for unblocking YouTube (2012). http:// www.weeklyblitz.net/2615/bangladesh-sets-precondition-for-unblocking
7. Groves, C.: Facebook changes through the years: Social Media Revolution (2011). http://blog.mad4flash.com/2011/10/facebook-changes-through-the-years-social-media-revolution
8. Facebook: Important message from Facebook's White Hat Program. https://www.facebook.com/notes/facebook-security/important-message-from-facebooks-white-hat-program/10151437074840766
9. Ratan, D., Cong, T., Keith, R., Nitesh, S.: Estimating age privacy leakage in online social networks. In: IEEE INFOCOM, pp. 2836–2840 (2012)
10. Luo, W., Liu, J., Liu, J., Fan, C.: An analysis of security in social networks. In: IEEE DASC, pp. 648–651 (2009)
11. Chaney, P.: Facebook Changes Layout of Mobile App (2013). http://www. practicalecommerce.com/articles/4000-Facebook-Changes-Layout-of-Mobile-App
12. Consumer Reports Magazine: Facebook & your privacy (2012). http://www. consumerreports.org/cro/magazine/2012/06/facebook-your-privacy
13. Madejski, M., Johnson, M., Bellovin, S.M.: A study of privacy settings errors in an online social network. In: IEEE PERCOM Workshops, pp. 340–345 (2012)
14. osint.it: OSINT, one important kind of intelligence. http://www.osint.it/english/ open-source-intelligence-osint.asp
15. Steele, R.D.: Open source intelligence. In: Johnson, L. (ed.) Handbook of Intelligence Studies. Routledge, New York (2007)
16. Facebook: Facebook developers page - Graph API. https://developers.facebook. com/docs/reference/apis
17. Constine, J.: Facebook Announces Friendship Pages That Show Friends' Mutual Content. http://www.insidefacebook.com/2010/10/28/friendship-pages-mutual-content
18. Facebook: Facebook Social Plugins. https://developers.facebook.com/docs/ plugins
19. Kandias, M., Mitrou, L., Stavrou, V., Gritzalis, D.: Which side are you on? - a new panopticon vs. privacy. In: SECRYPT, pp. 98–110 (2013)

20. Kosinski, M., Stillwell, D., Graepel, T.: Private traits and attributes are predictable from digital records of human behavior. Proc. Natl. Acad. Sci. **110**, 5802–5805 (2013)
21. Wisegeek: What is a web Crawler? http://www.wisegeek.org/what-is-a-web-crawler.htm
22. Tang, C., Ross, K., Saxena, N., Chen, R.: What's in a name: a study of names, gender inference, and gender behavior in facebook. In: Xu, J., Yu, G., Zhou, S., Unland, R. (eds.) DASFAA Workshops 2011. LNCS, vol. 6637, pp. 344–356. Springer, Heidelberg (2011)
23. Thomas, K., Grier, C., Nicol, D.M.: unFriendly: multi-party privacy risks in social networks. In: Atallah, M.J., Hopper, N.J. (eds.) PETS 2010. LNCS, vol. 6205, pp. 236–252. Springer, Heidelberg (2010)
24. Zhang, L., Zhang, W.: An information extraction attack against on-line social networks. In: SocialInformatics, pp. 49–55 (2012)
25. Costantino, G., Martinelli, F., Sgandurra, D.: Are photos on social networks really private? In: CTS, pp.162–165 (2013)
26. Luo, W., Xie, Q., Hengartner, U.: FaceCloak: an architecture for user privacy on social networking sites. In: IEEE CSE, pp. 26–33 (2009)
27. Conti, M., Hasani, A., Crispo, B.: Virtual private social networks and a facebook implementation. ACM Trans. Web **7**(3), 14:1–14:31 (2013)
28. Narayanan, A., Shmatikov, V.: De-anonymizing social networks. In: IEEE Symposium on Security and Privacy, pp. 173–187 (2009)
29. Beato, F., Conti, M., Preneel, B.: Friend in the Middle (FiM): tackling de-anonymization in social networks. In: IEEE PERCOM Workshops, pp. 279–284 (2013)
30. Beato, F., Conti, M., Preneel, B., Vettore, D.: VirtualFriendship: hiding interactions on online social networks. In: IEEE CNS (2014)
31. Buchegger, S., Schiöberg, D., Vu, L.H., Datta, A.: PeerSoN: P2P social networking: early experiences and insights. In: ACM Workshop, pp. 46–52 (2009)
32. Conti, M., Poovendran, R., Secchiero, M.: FakeBook: detecting fake profiles in on-line social networks. In: ASONAM, pp. 1071–1078 (2012)
33. Nagle, F., Singh, L.: Can friends be trusted? Exploring privacy in online social networks. In: ASONAM, pp. 312–315 (2009)
34. Dey, R., Jelveh, Z., Ross, K.W.: Facebook users have become much more private: a large-scale study. In: IEEE PERCOM Workshops, pp. 346–352 (2012)
35. Pineda, N.: Facebook tips: What's the difference between a Facebook Page and Group? (2010). https://www.facebook.com/blog/blog.php?post=324706977130
36. TripAdvisor: Tripadvisor. http://www.facebook/TripAdvisor
37. Get-Spotify: Spotify. http://www.facebook/get-spotify
38. He, R.C.: Facebook developers page - Introducing new Like and Share buttons. https://developers.facebook.com/blog/post/2013/11/06/introducing-new-like-and-share-buttons

Latent Semantic Analysis for Privacy Preserving Peer Feedback

Mouna Selmi[1](✉), Hicham Hage[2], and Esma Aïmeur[1]

[1] Département d'informatique et de recherche opérationnelle,
Université de Montréal, Montreal, Canada
{selmimou, aimeur}@iro.umontreal.ca
[2] Computer Science Department, Faculty of Natural and Applied Sciences,
Notre Dame University, Zouk Mosbeh, Lebanon
hhage@ndu.edu.lb

Abstract. Today's e-learning systems enable students to communicate with peers (or co-learners) to ask or provide feedback, leading to more efficient learning. Unfortunately, this new option comes with significantly increased risks to the privacy of the feedback requester as well as the peers involved in the feedback process. In fact, peers may unintentionally disclose personal information which may cause great threats to them like cyber-bullying, which in turn may create an *unfavorable* learning environment leading individuals to abandon learning. In this paper, we propose an approach to minimize data self-disclosure and privacy risks in e-learning contexts. It consists first of mining peers' feedback to remove negative comments (reducing bullying and harassment) based on machine learning classifier and natural language processing techniques. Second, it consists of striping sentences that potentially reveal personal information in order to protect learners from self-disclosure risks, based on *Latent Semantic Analysis* (LSA).

Keywords: Privacy risks · Self-disclosure · Latent Semantic Analysis · Sentiment analysis · Naïve Bayes · Singular Value Decomposition

1 Introduction

Since the advent of social networks, students are more actively and interactively involved in learning process [1]; this applies especially to distant learners who do not benefit from face-to-face interactions with their co-learners. In these situations, it is quite common to adopt collaborative strategies or techniques to foster interaction and communication between learners. One of these collaborative activities is allowing one learner to ask for feedback and receive several feedback or comments from their peers. Peers providing feedback and advice to those needing support, generally learn from their own experiences. Consequently, by participating in this process, learners, unwillingly, disclose and share a piece of themselves with others. This often leads to various forms of privacy threats, where a user's personal data are viewed, exposed, or misused by abusive users. This may cause financial and/or psychological damage to individuals [2].

© Springer International Publishing Switzerland 2015
J. Lopez et al. (Eds.): CRiSIS 2014, LNCS 8924, pp. 100–115, 2015.
DOI: 10.1007/978-3-319-17127-2_7

A recent study conducted by [3], shows that users often reveal sensitive personal information, ranging from personal characteristics such as age, gender, and address to health information in some cases.

To explain the potential threats to privacy caused by self-disclosed personal data, let us take an example in which private data should not be revealed.

Example: Bob wants to improve his English speaking skills in order to be able to talk to his new American girlfriend. He decided to find a partner among his classmates. He posted a message on his class forum in response to a peer request looking for a partner with whom he can practice English.

Bob wrote: "*I am **22 years old**, **engineering student** from **India** and my family cannot speak English and i am feeling bad to speak with **my American girlfriend** because i could be wrong...*"

From posting this message, Bob is expecting to receive positive feedback, and counted on for finding a partner. Nonetheless, while exposing his problem Bob is disclosing different personal information about himself (demographic information: age: 22, origin: Indian, education qualification: student engineer, and relationship status: American girlfriend). Reading his feedback, abusive users may misuse that information: identity theft, impersonation, or simply bully or ridicule him, which disappointed Bob.

The scenario above, while fictitious, is not far from reality. It highlights how sensitive personal information could be self-disclosed from such peers' interaction out of ignorance or indifference. Indeed, the divulgation of personal information particularly sensitive information that would otherwise remain private might expose users to many vulnerabilities such as *cyber-bullying* [3]. This is a serious challenge that infringes on the rights of learners to interact and collaborate free from fear in a safe e-learning environment. This phenomenon causes great harm to individuals, especially in educational contexts, and may lead to abandon learning. Therefore, in order to create a favorable learning environment and protect users from such threats, interaction observer (or an adversary in privacy context) should not be able to gain knowledge of the profile characteristics or identity of the user who asks or provides feedback based on some disclosed information in their interactions. This prevents the observer from re-identifying, at least partially, the users involved in the interaction process even in pseudonymous context.

To the best of our knowledge, only few works have addressed specificities of privacy protection from self-disclosure risks in peer feedback within an educational context. For instance, the work of Selmi *et al.* [4] proposed a framework to protect the privacy of learners involved in peer feedback process from cyber-bullying. Helou *et al.* [5], analyzed the risks of self-disclosure on users privacy in social networks and then suggested personalized recommendations to mitigate these risks. Other work such as [6], have tried to protect users from self-disclosure risks by restricting the access to the user disclosed information. While they focus on restricting the access and visibility of disclosed information to guarantee a privacy preserving environment, our study advocates a different approach for privacy protection, tailored for the peer feedback context, in order to create a favorable learning environment. The proposed privacy preserving approach relies on machine learning techniques and Latent Semantic Analysis (LSA) to ensure a favorable learning environment by preserving the privacy of peers involved in the feedback process from self-disclosure risks. It consists of first eliminating negative peer feedback (to reduce bullying or demeaning comments especially reactions to personal information disclosed), and second to strip sentences that potentially reveal personal information in order to prevent self-disclosure risks.

This paper is organized as follows: the next section provides an overview of the related work in regard to self-disclosure in peers' interactions and proposed solutions to protect privacy. This is followed by our approach of peer feedback mining and composition in Sect. 3. The data collection, experiments setup, and findings are presented in Sect. 4 together with a discussion of our results. Section 5 concludes the paper and provides an overview of future work.

2   Related Work

Two kinds of related work are relevant to this paper: self-disclosure in peers interaction and privacy solutions proposed to prevent or minimize the threats of self-disclosure.

2.1   Self-disclosure in Peers' Interactions

Privacy is generally seen by users as the control over their personal information in order to preserve anonymity while interacting with others [7]. Therefore, users who perceive higher threats or risks on privacy are likely to disclose less information about themselves while users who perceived a higher control over their personal information are found to disclose more about themselves [7].

Some of the earliest works on privacy in online interactions identified a conflicting relationship between users' privacy concerns and their self-disclosures online [8]. Berendt *et al.* [9] reported that users revealed significantly more information online than they were willing to share, according to a survey they have conducted to investigate the users privacy related information disclosure on the net. More recent research has tried to explain this relationship and have suggested that privacy and disclosure are closely related. In fact, according to [8], privacy concerns may serve as a barrier to some disclosures, especially if the request is more emotional in nature (such as a person requesting emotional support following an emotional distress). However, other research suggests that anonymity reinforces self-disclosure [10]. This idea was endorsed by a number of studies [11] which argued that anonymity decrease the risk perception and motivates the users to disclose more personal information. In [12], authors have investigated the factors motivating self-disclosure and have found that in addition to the negative influence of perceived risk, the desire for self-presentation and relationship building were other important factors. These findings explain the need for self-disclosure especially in distant learning where learners lack face to face interaction and try to create connections with distant co-learners in order to complete their learning.

In this context, with people publishing a lot of personal, and potentially damaging, data privacy requirements are hard to satisfy. Let us review the proposed solutions in the literature to protect users' privacy from self-disclosure risks.

2.2   Privacy Protection Solutions to Self-disclosure

Previous works in the literature have been interested in preventing potential data disclosure risks. These risks vary from inferring sensitive data with a reasonable accuracy (which is called attribute disclosure) to re-identifying an individual from the disclosed data (identity disclosure) [13]. Several solutions are proposed to preserve users' privacy for example the work of [14] who proposed an identity management system to preserve users from identity disclosure in forum discussion by relating the visibility of some identity characteristics to the trust level in the current context. Similarly, in [15], authors have proposed a multiparty access model as solution to control the access to disclosed data. Their solution preserves the users' privacy by restricting the parameter of the divulgation to trusted users. Unfortunately, these solutions do not protect the users' privacy from disclosing sensitive personal data, they only reduce the risks by restricting the visibility of disclosed data and including trust.

On the other hand, there exists few works that addressed the specificities of privacy protection in peer feedback such as the work of [4] who proposed a framework to protect the privacy of learners involved in peer feedback process from cyber-bullying. In their framework, the authors propose to anonymize the learners' data and select trustworthy learners to provide peer feedback. While the proposed feedback prevents from data disclosure, it does not protect the users' privacy from self-disclosing their personal data in their interactions with others.

Indeed, many studies in literature, especially in social networks, measure self-disclosure by investigating the identifiable characteristics exposed in profiles, such as name, age, education qualifications and interests [16]. Although this approach of measurement is reasonable, it does not include the amount of information disclosed by the users themselves in their interactions with others [1]. In this context, the research in [5], analyzes the risks of self-disclosure on users' privacy in social networks and then suggests personalized recommendations in order to decrease these risks. This approach is interesting in terms of self-disclosure quantification but it does not resolve the problem since it only recommend some suggestions to the user on how he decreases the risks.

While these works focus on restricting the access and visibility of disclosed information, some researchers have proposed methods to automatically remove or modify self-disclosed personal data from textual documents. For instance, Sánchez *et al.* [17] presented a sanitization approach that detects and hides sensitive textual information while preserving its semantics. Similarly, Abril *et al.* [18] recognize personal data in text documents. They predefined personal information categories and automatically recognized textual entities belonging to these categories. They used a Naive Bayes classifier for data classification. Although the use of machine learning classifiers to automatically recognize self-disclosed data is an interesting approach, it hasn't been used for privacy protection in the context of peers' interactions. In this paper, we attempted to use an approach based on machine learning techniques to preserve users' privacy while interacting. This approach is described in the next section.

3 LSA-Based Method for Privacy Preserving Peer Feedback

In this work, we are particularly interested in peers' interaction in an e-learning context, where a learner can ask for peer feedback. In response to such request, several peers can provide their feedback without revealing their real identities. Although anonymity has a positive impact in such a scenario (it enables users to express themselves freely), it may however elicit inappropriate behaviors, and permits people to express unpopular and demeaning comments. Additionally, anonymity increases the degree of self-disclosure in shy people, which raises privacy concerns. Consequently, this may create a non-favorable learning environment where learners have to face many threats like bullying, or privacy threats due to self-disclosed personal information. While researchers focus on who can use what information, our study aims to minimize data disclosure and privacy risks in peer feedback context by mining and composing peers' feedback in order to eliminate negative and self-disclosing feedback.

Our approach is composed of two steps: the *mining step* based on machine learning classifiers and the *composition step* performed using LSA- see Fig. 1. The first step removes and discards negative (demeaning, bullying, etc.) feedback messages that may be sent by some abusive peers, such that to guarantee a favorable learning environment. While the second step eliminates any self-disclosing sentences from mined feedback and then uses the remaining sentences to reconstruct a new feedback to be sent to the learner who asked for it. Specifically, the composition step removes any self-disclosure of personal data made by some peers, whether by ignorance or indifference, consequently preserving their privacy. Our approach, in contrast to other privacy preserving approaches, removes willingly self-disclosed data. Even though removing self-disclosing sentences goes against the learner's willingness to disclose his data, the goal from the composition is to minimize data disclosure and self-disclosure risks in order to preserve the learner's privacy.

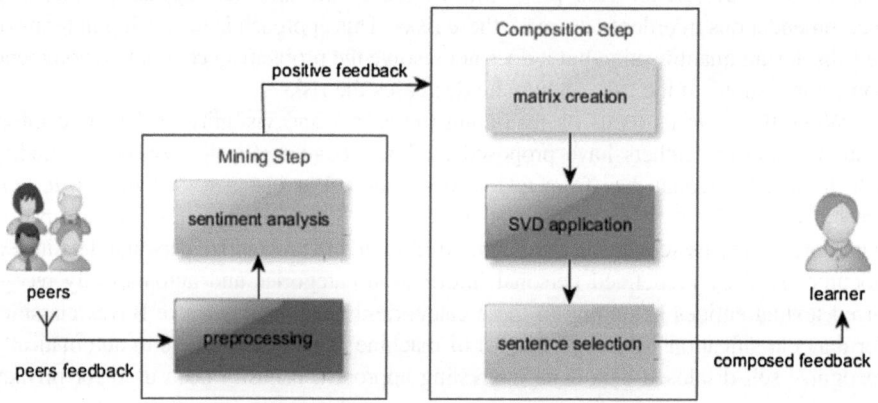

Fig. 1. Architecture of our approach

Each peer feedback is treated in our approach as a short text document. Hence, the output of our composition approach is to generate only one text document that contains the most relevant sentences in peers' feedback but do not contain any personal information self-disclosed by a peer. An example will be provided in the next section.

Figure 1 highlights the overall architecture of the proposed approach.

3.1 Mining Step

In this step, we apply a sentiment analysis to all given feedback to classify them as positive or negative in order to strip negative feedbacks that may negatively affect the learners and the learning process. We consider as negative each feedback containing bullying, demeaning, or other negative comments. Although this step is not in the scope of this paper, it is important to understand it, since it helps determine the quality of feedbacks used in the next step. In order to determine whether a feedback is positive or not, we rely on machine learning algorithms [19]. Hence, we first consider the representation of a given peer feedback as an input to our classifier. We use natural language processing techniques to automatically represent each peer feedback as a vector of text attribute values. This step, called preprocessing, computes the frequencies of the different words of the feedback and uses the result vector as a representation of the feedback. This representation considers the feedback as a set of words with stop words and non-content bearing words removed without taking into account any structural characteristics that discourse grammaticality, or positional information of the words.

In our work, the sentiment analysis task is performed using the Naïve Bayes classifier. It is a probabilistic classifier based on applying Bayes' theorem with independence assumptions on words position in the text [20]. For a given set of classes, it estimates the probability of a class as follows:

$$P(c|d) = P(c)\Pi_{1 \leq k \leq n_d} P(t_k|c) \tag{1}$$

Where:

- c is the target class
- d is the current document
- t is the current term
- n is the number of terms in the current document

The classifier then returns the class with the highest probability given the feedback. In practice, the log probability is estimated, given by:

$$\arg\max_{c} \log(\hat{P}(c)) + \sum_{1 \leq k \leq n_d} \log(\hat{P}(t_k|c)) \tag{2}$$

The prior class probability is given by the frequency of that given class in the training dataset. Since, we are using bag of words as the linguistic model, the probability of a term given the class is given by the empirical counts of that term in feedbacks in the same class.

Once the classification is done, only positive feedback will be retained to the composition step. By eliminating negative feedbacks, a learner is presented with only useful, motivating and encouraging feedback while protecting the learner from negative (for instance demeaning or bullying) feedback.

3.2   Composition Step

The role of the composition step is to remove any self-disclosure of personal data revealed by some peers in the feedback that they provide in order to preserve their privacy from potential threats.

The primary threat is that a malicious observer of the peer feedback may gain knowledge of peers involved in the feedback process or their identities based on some disclosed information.

Against such an adversary, our approach ensures that the feedback observer is not able to accurately gain knowledge of personal information of the peer who provided feedback. This prevents the observer from re-identifying peers involved in the feedback process even in pseudonymous context. Here the protection will be achieved in this context because the sentences that potentially reveal personal information will be removed to prevent disclosure of personal information.

To achieve that, we rely on Latent Semantic Analysis (LSA), which is generally used in text summarization, to compose peers' feedback. LSA captures information about which words are used in a sentence, while preserving information of common words between sentences [21]. It is based on Singular Value Decomposition (SVD) for finding out semantically similar words and sentences, which is important to extract significant sentences of each concept. Since sentences are composed of terms, we assume that the most representative sentences of the current concept would include the terms that best represent that concept. Similarly, we assume that any personal information disclosure will not be selected by SVD, since the enclosed personal information relates to that user and is not representative of that concept (for more details about SVD please refer to [21]). Hence this sentence will not be included in the composed feedback which will preserve the user privacy.

The first step in LSA is to create the input matrix A which represents the input text of the peers' provided feedback. The columns of the matrix represent the sentences of the input feedback and the rows represent the terms that appear in the feedback and extracted using preprocessing tools. In the second step, SVD is used on this matrix to derive the latent semantic structure. SVD captures the relationships among terms and sentences provided as inputs to the composition task. It decomposes the input matrix into three other matrices in order to extract the latent semantics of the sentences [21] as follows:

$$A = U \sum V^T \tag{3}$$

Where:

- A is the input matrix with dimensions $m \times n$
- U is an $m \times n$ matrix which represents the description of the original rows of the input matrix as a vector of extracted topics or concepts
- Σ is an $n \times n$ diagonal matrix containing scaling values sorted in descending order
- V is an $m \times n$ matrix which represents the description of the original columns of the input matrix as a vector of the extracted concepts from the provided feedback.

The next step in the LSA task is to select sentences from the input feedback text for the composed feedback. The method first creates a term-sentence matrix, where each column represents the weighted term-frequency vector of a sentence in the set of peers' feedback. Then, SVD is applied on this matrix in order to extract the latent semantic relationships between sentences and terms. The sentences with the greatest combined weights across all the given sentences are included in the composed feedback. The compression rate, i.e. how much shorter the composed feedback is in comparison to the original feedback, can be predefined before the composition step by defining the number of the significant sentences per terms and concepts to extract from peer feedbacks. Consequently, the number of significant sentences that will be included in the composed feedback is also predefined because it is related to the number of significant terms and concepts to extract.

Note that the LSA task is executed only once to extract the most important topics and sentences given by peers while excluding self-disclosing ones.

As for the weighting approach, binary representation of number of occurrence is the most appropriate weighting approach for our work. In fact, if the word is seen in the sentence, the cell is filled with 1; otherwise it is filled with 0.

To illustrate, let us consider the following example. Table 1 shows the list of feedback extracted from one of the peers' interactions on discussion forum for English learning composed of 3 feedbacks. These feedbacks are automatically decomposed into sentences (5 in the case of this example highlighted by the braces). The feedback sentences extraction is performed using linguistic preprocessing tools, particularly n-gram model. In fact, other models can be used such as bag of words. However, n-gram is the most suited in our context because it considers the correlations between words which is the main task of SVD. As it is shown, the first sentence in the feedback F2, which represents the sentence s2 in the feedback example, contains self-disclosure of the age, education and origin of the user providing feedback. Once the extraction and composition step is done, this information must be eliminated and not included in the composed feedback in order to preserve that user's privacy.

Table 1. Sample of peers' feedback

Feedback	Notation
{It is necessary to be determined, patient and hardworking when learning English}	**F1**
{I am 22 years old, engineering student from India} and{my family cannot speak English} and {i feel bad to speak with my American girlfriend because i think I could be wrong}	**F2**
{I think that we fail in learning and conversing efficiently because we are just feel shy to speak to someone}	**F3**

We regard the sentences as observations, the extracted terms as variables, and the value of variables as the number of occurrence of terms in each sentence (which is their cumulative frequency in the feedback). We disregard the terms that occur just once since they are not considered to be representative terms.

In our sample feedback, terms are extracted for the candidates for the most representative ones as shown in Table 2. In fact, 4 terms are extracted in order to select the significant sentences and all of these terms have occurrence at least twice in all given feedback. Additionally, during the preprocessing step, stop words and non-content bearing words (which are automatically determined) are removed such as the term "*English*". This term appears in almost every post (English learning forum), so it "*looses*" its contextual value.

Table 2. Sentence-term matrix

Sen\term	X_1 = feel	X_2 = learn	X_3 = speak	X_4 = think
1	0	1	0	0
2	0	0	0	0
3	0	0	1	0
4	1	0	1	1
5	1	1	0	1

The sample peers feedback has 3 peers' feedback originally, but there are 5 different sentences in sentence-term matrix, as shown in Table 2, since each feedback may contain more than one sentence. Then, the sentences which did not include the 4 extracted terms at all will be omitted logically since they cannot be considered as representative.

The column under the term X_1 shows the frequency of the term "*feel*" in the different sentences composing the given feedback.

Once the matrix sentence-term is created, it is time to apply SVD. Computing the SVD of this matrix, as shown in Table 2, decomposes this matrix into three matrices U, Σ and V (as described in Eq. 3). The sentence-concentrated matrix U and the term concentrated matrix V can be represented only by 4-dimensional vectors according to the 4 extracted terms as shown in Table 3.

Table 3. Matrix U

Sen\SVD	SVD_1	SVD_2	SVD_3	SVD_4
1	−0.145	−0.899	−0.413	0
2	0	0	0	0
3	−0.160	0.084	−0.071	0
4	−0.565	0.406	−0.696	0
5	−0.796	−0.142	0.583	0.577

At this step, the Euclidean distance between the significant term vectors and the sentence vectors (see Tables 2 and 4 respectively) can be computed by the above matrices V and U to extract the significant sentences. These sentences must be included in the composed feedback and they do not include self-disclosed information. The significant sentences SVD vectors are in our example, as illustrated in Table 4, the first, third and the fifth sentences after distance computing.

Table 4. Matrix V

Term\SVD	SVD1	SVD2	SVD3	SVD4	SVD5
X_1	−0.420	0.116	−0.060	0.00	0.191
X_2	−0.290	−0.458	0.090	−0.00	0.040
X_3	−0.420	0.116	−0.071	0.00	0.191
X_4	−0.469	0.153	−0.696	−0.00	−0.552

For instance, the significant sentences by the term X_1 are the third and fifth sentence in the given feedback represented respectively by the topic SVD Vector 3 and SVD Vector 4 because the Euclidean distance between the SVD vector of the term X_1 and the SVD vector of these two sentences are the most two shortest distances among the five sentences.

As illustrated in the previous example, the application of LSA on the peers' feedback preserves the privacy by eliminating self-disclosing sentences from given feedback. In fact, SVD selects the most representative terms and sentences in order to include them in the composed feedback. We argue that any personal information disclosing sentence (as in Table 1) will not be selected by SVD since it cannot be the most representative sentence of a concept in peer feedback. Hence, it will not be included in the composed feedback. This fact is also proven by the non-selection of terms appearing in the self-disclosing demographic information sentence s2 (Line 2 in Table 3 where the 4 selected SVD terms are null which means that this sentence has no semantic relationship with the selected significant terms. It is also proven by the non-selection of the sentence s4, which discloses another type of personal data: a relationship status. Even though this sentence contains two of the selected significant terms X_1 and X_3, it is not selected by SVD as significant sentence to be included in the composed feedback. This guarantees that these sentences will be removed and consequently will not be observed by others.

In this illustrative example, the composition task excludes first this sentence *{i am 22 years old, engineering student from India}* and second this sentence *{i feel bad to speak with my American girlfriend because i think I could be wrong}* because the distance computed between all SVD vectors excludes them from being selected as significant sentences. This implies that the information disclosed in these sentences will not be observed by others since they will not be included in the output feedback.

4   Testing and Validation

Note that the real scenario takes place in an e-learning environment where all peers' feedback is collected at the same time after a feedback request. The mining and composition steps are executed once for each feedback request.

Nonetheless, to test our approach, we collected and compiled 300 peers' feedback from various English learning forums. For each feedback request, an average of five peer's feedback is collected. Before using the collected data in the testing, we pre-processed the data to reduce its dimensionality. We also excluded any feedback with less than three words because they are considered too short to meet the learner's needs. These feedbacks will be removed when applying LSA because they are not considered significant. We first applied sentiment analysis using Naïve Bayes classifier to remove negative feedback. Second, we performed feedback composition on the positive feedback using LSA to exclude self-disclosing sentences.

We used Rapid Miner and Weka [22] which allows us to experiment numerous configuration of our classification model with valuable features and preprocessing tools for the training data. The confusion matrix of this algorithm, illustrated in Table 5, shows the mining results.

Table 5. Feedback classification applying Naïve Bayes

Predicted class	Actual class		
	Positive	Negative	Class precision
Positive	132	22	85.71
Negative	17	110	86.61

The obtained accuracy is a good result with respect to the sentiment analysis literature. Typical works in the literature have achieved results between 80–87 % when classifying movie reviews, such as [20, 23] with an accuracy of 82.90 % and 86.84, respectively, using SVM. As highlighted in the table above, the accuracy we achieved is good and satisfying considering the context of peer feedback and the training data collected from discussion forums. Feedback exchanged between peers is generally informal and contain many mistakes, *emoticons*, and symbols. This characteristic of these environments makes the data preprocessing and the sentiment analysis not an easy task.

Naïve-Bayes classifies 86.11 % of examples correctly at the cost of a loss of 4.56 % of good corrections. Only retained positive feedbacks will be used in the composition step.

Feedback Composition. From the learner, perspective, removing personal information that he may have disclosed could possibly alter the entire meaning of his feedback. Consequently, for the learner, the more similar a composed feedback is to the original feedback, the better. However, from a privacy perspective, the focus is on minimizing data disclosure and risks in order to preserve the learners' privacy. A possible solution would be to consider the learner privacy preferences in displaying his entire feedback even in case of self-disclosure which will be addressed in future work.

For demonstrating the effectiveness of composition in removing self-disclosing sentences from feedback, we compute the similarity of the composed feedback with the original ones to get the least similarity. We rely on the approach used by Wang and Ma [21] which measures the cosine similarity between a matrix U derived from the SVD on the input feedback and a matrix U' derived from the SVD on the composed feedback. For two related feedbacks, the cosine similarity is close to 1, which indicates a strong relation between them.

We first illustrate our testing procedure on the example used previously (see Table 1). We investigate the relationships between all sentences of peer's feedback to explain the effectiveness of using SVD to select significant sentences while excluding self-disclosing ones. To do that, we use cosine similarity between the SVD vectors of the different sentences in the feedback sample illustrated in Table 1. We consider SVD pairs (v1, v2) and (v2, v1) as a single match.

As illustrated in Fig. 2, the similarity between the SVD vectors of the three significant sentences selected for the composed feedback (illustrated with circles in the Fig. 2) is close to 0 which means that even though these sentences are not related semantically they are the most representative of the different concepts mentioned in the peers' feedback. On the other hand, although the similarity between the self-disclosing sentence s2 represented by the SVD vector v2 and all the sentences of peers' feedback is higher than 0, it is not selected as representative sentence. This means that even

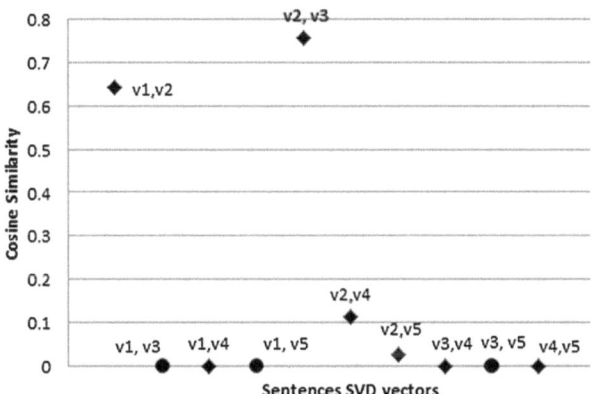

Fig. 2. Cosine similarity distance between sentences

though s2 is strongly semantically related to others sentences; it is carrying a different concept since SVD captures the latent relationship between sentences and concepts.

From a privacy point of view, Fig. 2 shows the effectiveness of using SVD to eliminate self-disclosing sentences s2 and s4. As it can be seen from Fig. 2, the cosine similarity between the SVD vectors of these two sentences is higher than 0 which means that they are semantically related according to SVD even if it is not apparent. This can be explained by the fact that they are *latently* carrying the same concept which is personal information. These two sentences are removed and are not observed by others. Hence, the composed feedback is comprised of the three sentences s1, s3, and s5 represented respectively by their SVD vectors v1, v3, and v5. The composed feedback is sent to the learner in form of bullet as follow:

- "It is necessary to be determined, patient and hardworking when learning English"
- "My family cannot speak English"
- "I think that we fail in learning and conversing efficiently because we are just feel shy to speak to someone".

Although the composed feedback may lack some semantic coherence, due to its reconstruction from different given feedback, it is still understandable. Moreover, the most important contribution of LSA is that it composes a privacy preserving feedback from peers' feedback, where the composed feedback does not contain identifying data, and cannot be used to recompose the original feedback.

To test our approach, we used 100 positive feedbacks requests selected after removing short feedback (shorter than three words) and applying sentiment analysis (see Table 5). For each feedback request, an average of 3 feedbacks is retained after applying data cleansing and sentiment analysis. In order to demonstrate the effectiveness of LSA, we first applied LSA on each feedback request to get the composed feedback. Then we computed the cosine similarity between each pair of original feedbacks and the composed feedback for each feedback request. As shown in the Fig. 3, most pairs are close to 0 indicating that the composed feedback and the original feedback are not highly similar in words composition. From a semantic perspective, this can be explained by the fact that these sentences are unrelated. But as LSA usually captures the latent semantic relationship between sentences, we suggest another explanation for this dissimilarity: peers' feedback contains sentences that are carrying different concept from those significant in peer's feedback. These sentences could be self-disclosing sentences and consequently they were removed by SVD.

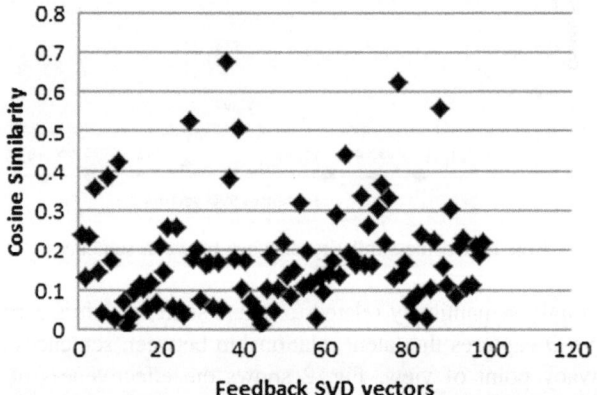

Fig. 3. Cosine similarity distance between original feedbacks and composed feedbacks

This indicates that there is practically no threat when using SVD that a self-disclosing feedback could be included in the composed feedback, even if it is semantically related to others significant sentences included in the composed feedback. This ensures the privacy protection from the primary threat in our context which is that an observer of the composed feedback may gain knowledge of peers involved in the feedback process or their identity based on some disclosed information since the disclosing feedback will not be included in the final composed feedback.

5   Conclusion

Although the interaction between learners in a learning context has many advantages, it comes with significant threats and challenges when privacy is concerned. In fact, peers may unintentionally disclose personal information which can ultimately cause great threats to them. These threats could be psychological, affecting negatively the learning process (like cyber-bullying), as well as privacy related threats (such as identity theft). In order to create a favorable learning environment and protect the learners' privacy, we took a different direction from existing works to address these issues. We proposed a two-step based approach; the first step is mining the peers' feedback to eliminate any negative messages that may cause psychological harm to the learner. Specifically, we used natural language processing techniques and Naïve Bayes classifier, and our evaluations show that this approach performs well, correctly classifying 86 % of the examples.

The second step in the proposed approach was to apply LSA on positively classified feedback, and create a composed feedback that can be visible to all learners without causing privacy threats to peers involved in the feedback process. In fact, the goal of this step is to preserve privacy by preventing an observer of the composed feedback from gaining knowledge of the peer who provided feedback or their identity based on some disclosed information. Towards this aim, we proceeded to automatically extract the most representative sentences and topics in peers' feedback using SVD to be included in the composed feedback.

The selection of the significant sentences is based on the extraction of the most representative term in given feedback. This process strips the sentences that do not contain these terms and are not semantically related to all the selected concepts using Euclidean distance calculus between all the SVD vectors. As self-disclosing sentences are generally not representative of all provided feedback, they will be implicitly removed and not included in the composed feedback.

Experiments demonstrate the effectiveness of the proposed approach in preserving the learner privacy by selecting, for the composed feedback, the most important sentences while eliminating self-disclosing ones. This prevents an observer from re-identifying peers involved in the feedback process even in pseudonymous context. The privacy protection is achieved in this context because the disclosed data cannot be observed by others.

On the other hand, privacy protection involves individual and social dimensions such as individual privacy preferences and trust. Indeed, individual's privacy perceptions are dependent upon context, i.e., voluntarily disclosing sensitive data to a trusted peer, even if risky in terms of quantification, doesn't seem harmful to the learners' privacy, from their point of view. Hence, the inclusion of these factors will adapt the privacy protection to peers' privacy preferences and context. Specifically, the system will request the user feedback before removing self-disclosing sentences, and will adapt accordingly. In future work, we will investigate the impact of these factors on privacy preservation and peers' interaction. Moreover, we will investigate the inclusion of advanced NLP techniques to enhance the coherence of the composed feedback. In fact, stripping away some sentences, even self-disclosing personal information, may affect the structure and the meaning of the feedback, resulting in a loss of information that might have been pertinent.

References

1. Thoms, B., Eryilmaz, E.: How media choice affects learner interactions in distance learning classes. Comput. Educ. **75**, 112–126 (2014)
2. Pridmore, J., Overocker, J.: Privacy in virtual worlds: a US perspective. J. Virtual Worlds Res. **7**(1), 1–14 (2014)
3. Lee, U., Yi, E., Ko, M.: Mobile Q&A: beyond text-only Q&A and privacy concerns. In: Proceedings of CHI 2013, pp. 1–4. ACM (2013)
4. Selmi, M., Aimeur, E., Hage, H.: Privacy framework for peer affective feedback. In: 2013 International Conference on Signal-Image Technology & Internet-Based Systems (SITIS), pp. 1049–1056. IEEE (2013)
5. Helou, C., Guandouz, A., Aïmeur, E.: A privacy awareness system for facebook users. J. Inf. Secur. Res. **31**, 15–29 (2012)
6. Squicciarini, A., Karumanchi, S., Lin, D., DeSisto, N.: Identifying hidden social circles for advanced privacy configuration. Comput. Secur. **41**, 40–51 (2014)
7. Weber, R.H.: Internet of things-new security and privacy challenges. Comput. Law Secur. Rev. **26**(1), 23–30 (2010)
8. Stutzman, F., Vitak, J., Ellison, N.B., Gray, R., Lampe, C.: Privacy in interaction: exploring disclosure and social capital in facebook. In: ICWSM (2012)
9. Berendt, B., Günther, O., Spiekermann, S.: Privacy in e-commerce: stated preferences vs. actual behavior. Commun. ACM **48**(4), 101–106 (2005)
10. Buckel, T., Thiesse, F.: Predicting the disclosure of personal information on social networks: an empirical investigation. In: Wirtschaftsinformatik, p. 101 (2013)
11. Zhao, C., Hinds, P., Gao, G.: How and to whom people share: the role of culture in self-disclosure in online communities. In: Proceedings of the ACM 2012 Conference on Computer Supported Cooperative Work, pp. 67–76. ACM (2012)
12. Krasnova, H., Spiekermann, S., Koroleva, K., Hildebrand, T.: Online social networks: why we disclose. J. Inf. Technol. **25**(2), 109–125 (2010)
13. Li, N., Li, T., Venkatasubramanian, M.: t-closeness: privacy beyond k-anonymity and l-diversity. In: IEEE 23rd International Conference on Data Engineering (ICDE 2007), pp. 106–115. IEEE (2007)
14. Anwar, M., Greer, J.: Facilitating trust in privacy-preserving e-learning environments. IEEE Trans. Learn. Technol. **5**(1), 62–73 (2012)
15. Pisey, M.S.H., Ramteke, P.L., Deshmukh, P., Burghate, B.R.: Privacy access control mechanism for online social network. Int. J. Comput. Sci. Appl. **6**(2), 172–179 (2013)
16. Mesch, G.S., Beker, G.: Are norms of disclosure of online and offline personal information associated with the disclosure of personal information online? Hum. Commun. Res. **36**(4), 570–592 (2010)
17. Sánchez, D., Batet, M., Viejo, A.: Automatic general-purpose sanitization of textual documents. IEEE Trans. Inf. Forensics Secur. **8**, 853–862 (2013)
18. Abril, D., Navarro-Arribas, G., Torra, V.: On the declassification of confidential documents. In: Torra, V., Narakawa, Y., Yin, J., Long, J. (eds.) MDAI 2011. LNCS, vol. 6820, pp. 235–246. Springer, Heidelberg (2011)
19. Ortigosa, A., Martín, J.M., Carro, R.M.: Sentiment analysis in Facebook and its application to e-learning. Comput. Hum. Behav. **31**, 527–541 (2014)
20. Pang, B., Lee, L., Vaithyanathan, S.: Thumbs up? Sentiment classification using machine learning techniques. In: Proceedings of the ACL 2002 Conference on Empirical Methods in Natural Language Processing, vol. 10. Association for Computational Linguistics, pp. 79–86 (2002)

21. Wang, Y., Ma, J.: A comprehensive method for text summarization based on latent semantic analysis. In: Zhou, G., Li, J., Zhao, D., Feng, Y. (eds.) NLPCC 2013. CCIS, vol. 400, pp. 394–401. Springer, Heidelberg (2013)

22. Bouckaert, R.R., Frank, E., Hall, M.A., Holmes, G., Pfahringer, B., Reutemann, P., Witten, I.H.: WEKA—experiences with a Java open-source project. J. Mach. Learn. Res. **11**, 2533–2541 (2010)

23. Martínez-Cámara, E., Martín-Valdivia, M.T., Ureña-López, L.A.: Opinion classification techniques applied to a Spanish corpus. In: Muñoz, R., Montoyo, A., Métais, E. (eds.) NLDB 2011. LNCS, vol. 6716, pp. 169–176. Springer, Heidelberg (2011)

Attacking Suggest Boxes in Web Applications Over HTTPS Using Side-Channel Stochastic Algorithms

Alexander Schaub[1], Emmanuel Schneider[1], Alexandros Hollender[1],
Vinicius Calasans[1], Laurent Jolie[1], Robin Touillon[1], Annelie Heuser[2],
Sylvain Guilley[2,3], and Olivier Rioul[1,2(✉)]

[1] Ecole Polytechnique, CMAP, Palaiseau, France
{alexander.schaub,emmanuel.schneider,alexandros.hollender,
vinicius.calasans,laurent.jolie,robin.touillon,
olivier.rioul}@polytechnique.edu
[2] Department Comelec, Télécom ParisTech, CNRS LTCI, Paris, France
{annelie.heuser,sylvain.guilley,olivier.rioul}@telecom-paristech.fr
[3] Secure-IC S.A.S., Rennes, France

Abstract. Web applications are subject to several types of attacks. In particular, side-channel attacks consist in performing a statistical analysis of the web traffic to gain sensitive information about a client. In this paper, we investigate how side-channel leaks can be used on search engines such as *Google* or *Bing* to retrieve the client's search query. In contrast to previous works, due to payload randomization and compression, it is not always possible to uniquely map a search query to a web traffic signature and hence stochastic algorithms must be used. They yield, for the French language, an exact recovery of search word in more than 30 % of the cases. Finally, we present some methods to mitigate such side-channel leaks.

Keywords: Side-channel leak · Web application · Suggest box · Stochastic algorithms · HTTPS

1 Introduction

Recent revelations by Edward Snowden have shown that there is no more privacy over the Internet. While it should perhaps not come as a surprise that governments worldwide are able to spy on their citizens, it has been widely believed that today's technology can at least protect our sensitive data from our neighbors or competitors. Actually, this is not so sure.

Search histories can be considered as sensitive data. As shown in the 2006 New York Times article [1], using a leakage in AOL search data, it is possible

---

The online demo of the attack (presented at the CRiSIS 2014 conference) is available on YouTube, at address: http://youtu.be/ynG6tuqeIuM.

Annelie Heuser is Google European fellow in the field of privacy and is partially founded by this fellowship.

© Springer International Publishing Switzerland 2015
J. Lopez et al. (Eds.): CRiSIS 2014, LNCS 8924, pp. 116–130, 2015.
DOI: 10.1007/978-3-319-17127-2_8

to identify a person only from his search history. At company scale, a look at the search history of competitors can be used to predict their future actions in order to gain a strategical advantage over them. *Google* recognized the necessity to protect this sensitive data during the fall of 2011, when they announced that they enabled SSL for all of their signed-in users [2]. Later they forced the use of SSL for every search query, by automatically redirecting every user to the HTTPS version of their website [3]. Unfortunately, this is not enough to hide search queries completely because some information still leaks through side-channels.

Side-channel leaks appear each time an interaction between a user and a website requires transmission of information packets containing relevant data. Assuming that the connection between the client and the server is encrypted (using a protocol such as HTTPS), three parameters of the packet flow can be observed:

- *lengths* of individual packets;
- *directions* of packet flow (client to server or server to client);
- *times* of packets' departure and arrival [4].

By analyzing the packet flow associated with the suggest boxes[1] from *Google* (or any other search engine), it is observed that for every character typed in the search box, several packets are exchanged between the server and the client. One of these packets contains relevant data that depends on the list of suggestions from the search engine. In particular, by analyzing packet lengths associated to different characters, it is possible to guess the most likely word that the user typed in, and thus uncover sensitive information about his search history.

The remainder of this paper is organized as follows. First, Sect. 2 gives a current state of the art and Sect. 3 describes the structure of relevant information packets for today's *Google* and *Bing* (Microsoft) search engines. Then, Sect. 4 investigates novel algorithms to carry out side-channel attacks, that use data structures such as trees and stacks. The corresponding test results and some implementation issues are given in Sect. 5. Finally, Sect. 6 concludes by giving some perspectives on this work and methods for mitigating side-channel leaks.

2   Previous Work

Numerous studies on the detection and analysis of side-channel data leaks in web applications can be found in the literature. The general approach is to examine the properties of packet sequences sent between a client and a server, in order to infer a relationship between these properties and the exchanged information.

The authors of [5] used a deterministic model of web applications that allowed them to deduce recorded diseases and types of physician of users of some medical advice application, or to obtain details on the annual income and expenses of

---

[1] See description of *Google Instant*: http://goo.gl/WI9Zu and *Google Autocomplete*: http://goo.gl/jv3fQ.

a family in a tax return software used in the USA. These results were obtained through a simple analysis of packet sizes exchanged between the client and the server. Most of the time, one could map each input mouse selection or typed word to a single sequence of packet lengths. Therefore, the user input can be retrieved simply by comparing the sequence to a database of precomputed sequences.

In [6], the authors attempt to find the sources of a certain user connection by comparing the received data to a list of predetermined website profiles. Effective methods carry out the comparison on packet sizes, using either a similarity metric (Jaccard coefficient) or a Bayesian classification. Under certain assumptions, the origin of the data can be traced in more than 6 cases out of 10. The effectivity of this fingerprinting attack is improved in [7] using a multinomial Naïve-Bayes classifier.

An interesting information theoretic approach is investigated in [8] to describe the interaction between server and client. A web application is modeled as a finite-state machine, where state changes produce "traces" (specifically, the exchanged packets). Since these do not follow a deterministic law, a stochastic analysis is performed using mutual information to estimate the average reduction of uncertainty on the input when the attacker intercepts the packets. The method is tested on a simple yes/no questionnaire that redirects to two different sites depending on the answer.

In [9], side-channel attacks are carried out on search engines such as *Google*. The search box operates using AJAX to display suggestions to the client as he types search terms, and the attack again consists of intercepting the exchanged packets in order to infer the user's query. The authors have assumed a *deterministic* relationship between input letters and exchanged packet lengths[2]. The query can therefore be deduced by pre-computing every possible query and then comparing the captured packets using this information. While there may be several possible results for a same sequence of packet sizes, words that are not in some dictionary are unlikely to have been typed in. Therefore, it is only necessary to compute and store the sequences of packet sizes corresponding to legitimate words in the chosen dictionary.

We found that their method does not work any longer on *Google* since the suggestion list sent to the user has been changed in summer 2012 in such a way that there are now many possible sequences of packet lengths corresponding to a given search query.

3 Packet Structure

Exchanged packets between a client and server can be observed using an internet packet sniffer such as *Wireshark*. In order to determine which packet contains the relevant information, we simply decrypted the packet flow using Fiddler[3]

---

[2] More precisely, the sizes of the packets sent by the user are fixed for a given number of letters, and the sizes of received packets containing suggestions depend only on the word typed by the user (it may only change if *Google* changes the suggested search queries).

[3] http://www.telerik.com/fiddler.

and determined the size of the packet we were supposed to observe. After these initial tries, we were able, whenever a character was typed in, to filter out the only packet with a reasonable size. It is then easy to isolate the important packet containing the suggest-box data, as shown in Fig. 1.

We observed that packet sizes fluctuate for identical requests. To understand how, we have decrypted and unzipped the packets to study their structure. Even if the attacker will eventually not access the content of the encrypted packets, this structure helps understand how packet sizes and search queries are related.

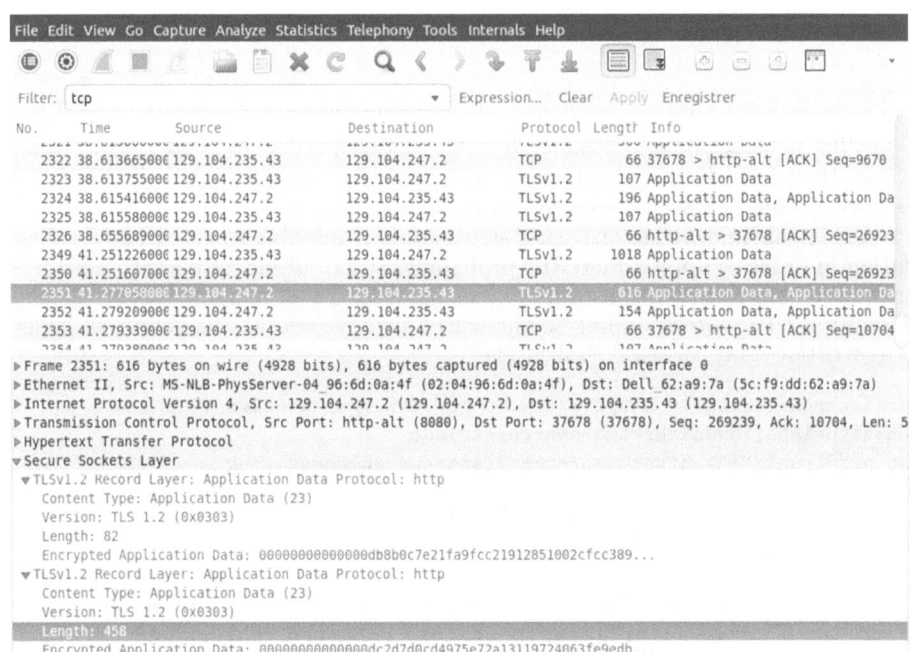

Fig. 1. A captured packet containing the suggest box data.

3.1 Google Packets

Previous works implementing side-channel attacks on suggest boxes did not analyze the structure of the exchanged packets. In [9], the only information needed is the link giving access to the packet related to a given search string. This is because, prior to summer 2012, there was no randomness in the packets that *Google* sent. Typing in an "a" for example, would always yield the same packet, and therefore the same packet length.

But at present, *Google* packets contain some kind of token (the value of which appears random to us), a milli-timestamp, and other numbers (which also appear random for an observer not aware of Google's protocols semantic). Figure 2 shows

```
{"e":"Ok6DU5HUDfD50gW6_oCADg","c":0,"u":"https://www.google.fr/s
?gs_rn=45&gs_ri=psy-ab&pq=a&cp=1&gs_id=ds&xhr=t&q=a&
es_nrs=true&pf=p&output=search&sclient=psy-ab&oq=&gs_l=&
pbx=1&bav=on.2,or.r_qf.&bvm=bv.67720277,d.d2k&fp=
1811953923e3f22&biw=1855&bih=718&tch=1&ech=2&psi=
xk6DU-joOsaHOAXH-4HYAw.1401114308196.3","p":true,"d":"[["a",[["a
<b>mazon</b>",0],["a<b>llocine</b>",0],["a<b>meli</b
>",0],["a<b>ir france</b>",0]],{"t":{"bpc":false,"tlw":
false},"q":"LZt_R7tHgjpU3Eask82JbvHZEY","j":"ds"}]"}/*""*/
```

Fig. 2. A packet sent by *Google* to a French user that hit an "a".

boxed elements that are random and change between two requests, even if the same list of suggestions is sent to the client. Since packets are compressed using *GZip*, the packet length also becomes random. For example, typing in "a" twice will yield different packet lengths.

Using this knowledge of packet structure it is possible to carry out a calculation in order to approximate the probability distributions of packet sizes for a given search string. First, as in [9], by using *Firefox*'s development tools we can identify a URL corresponding to the list of suggestions. At the time this paper was written (May 2014), it looked like:

```
url(search-string) = https://www.google.fr/s?gs_rn=45&gs_ri=psy-ab&
pq=a&cp=1&gs_id=ds&xhr=t&q=search-string&
es_nrs=true&pf=p&output=search&sclient=psy-ab&oq=&gs_l=&
pbx=1&bav=on.2,or.r_qf.&bvm=bv.67720277,d.d2k&fp=
1811953923e3f22&biw=1855&bih=718&tch=1&ech=2&psi=
xk6DU-joOsaHOAXH-4HYAw.1401114308196.3
```

From this we can approximate the required probability distribution as follows. First, the file given by url(search-string) is fetched. This is done only once for a given search string. Then, the identified random parts are replaced with randomly generated strings or numbers. Finally, the file is compressed using *GZip*, and the size of the compressed file is recorded. Repeating the last two steps (replace & compress) enables one to reliably estimate the distribution of the packet sizes, such as the one shown in Fig. 3. For our test purposes, we fetched every relevant file once, and replaced the random parts 1000 times in order to compute these probability laws.

3.2 Bing

Bing does not encrypt its traffic, but it is still interesting to analyze its auto-suggest feature. For example, side-channel attacks can also work on WPA-protected wireless traffic.

Before May 2014, the packets sent by Bing for the auto-suggest feature were neither compressed nor did they contain any random element. It was then very easy to find the search string by analyzing a sequence of packets: the same

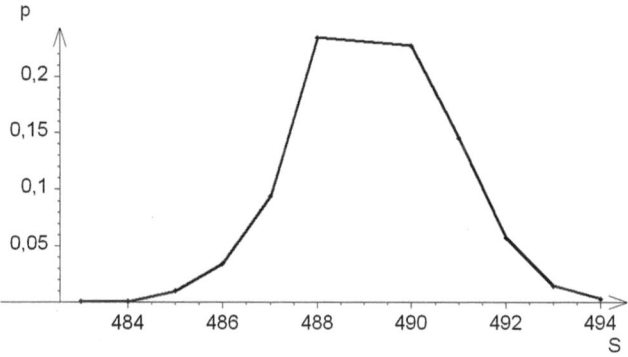

Fig. 3. Distribution of packet sizes (in bytes) for the letter "p", on the French version of *Google*.

method used for *Google* in [9] did work out very well. But now the situation has just changed: the packets are compressed and do contain some random elements. The corresponding file can be fetched at the following addresses:

```
url(search-string) = http://www.bing.com/AS/Suggestions?
pt=Page.Home&qry=search-string&cp=1&o=hs&css=1&
cvid=fbeb395a6a9b4f15bac899892c09b6a1
```

or

```
url(search-string) = http://www.bing.com/AS/Suggestions?
pt=Page.Home&qry=search-string&cp=1&o=hs&
cvid=fbeb395a6a9b4f15bac899892c09b6a1
```

There is an important difference between these two links: by specifying `css=1`, the whole CSS-code used for formatting the results will be sent. This happens when the first letter is typed in after having reloaded the web page. As a result, for some search strings, in particular those of length 1 (i.e., "a", "b", etc.), two different distributions must be computed by the attacker. However by looking at the file size it is easy to differentiate between a packet containing the CSS and a packet without CSS code (typically $\leq 3\,\mathrm{KB}$ for the CSS-free uncompressed version, $\geq 5\,\mathrm{KB}$ for the uncompressed file containing the CSS code).

4   Stochastic Algorithms

In this section, we describe the algorithms and data structures that we have used to solve the following problem.

Let l be the number of characters of a given word typed in by the user and let I be an interception vector containing the lengths of the l intercepted packets corresponding to the prefixes of length i of the given word for $i = 1$ to l. Using pre-computed probability distributions of packets lengths, determined as explained in the previous section, the goal is to find the most probable word (or list of words) that is most likely to have been typed by the user.

4.1   Restricting Possibilities

To simplify the problem, we make the plausible assumption that the user does not type a random sequence of letters but rather a sequence that makes sense. Therefore, we restrict the set of possible words to a certain "language" or dictionary, i.e., some predefined set of valid words. In our studies, we have chosen a simple French dictionary.

Restricting the set of possibilities has two main advantages. First, the algorithms will always return a valid word (or a list of valid words). Second, they will not waste computation time and memory space on words that do not even exist. As an example, there are about 11 million 5-letter sequences, for only 6812 valid French 5-letter words.

4.2   Data Structure

Once the dictionary is chosen, an adequate data structure representation of it should be implemented. Because a packet is intercepted for each prefix of the typed word, we choose to represent the set of all possible words of a given length l as a *prefix tree*. This tree has the empty word " " at its root, and contains each valid word of length l as a leaf. Going from the root to a certain word, one passes through the nodes representing all increasing prefixes of the word. This is called a *Trie* structure [10].

4.3   A Stack Algorithm

Recall from the previous section that at our disposal we have an algorithm, that we call LAW, that estimates the probability law of the packet length associated with a certain word prefix. Thus as an example, $LAW(\text{"plage"}, 435, \epsilon)$ returns an estimate of the probability that the packet sent by the server after the user has typed the last character of "plage", has a length in the interval $[\![435 - \epsilon, 435 + \epsilon]\!]$. Here ϵ is a tolerance parameter that is necessary for practical reasons. Because of the way the information is encapsulated during a packet exchange between a client and a server, it is not always possible to precisely determine the size of the relevant information that is hidden in the captured packets. An error of one or two bytes is not uncommon, and this is what ϵ represents.

Our first algorithm computes the likelihood f as the product of the estimated probabilities. For example, to measure how likely the prefix "pla" would be, we compute:

$$f(\text{"pla"}, I, \epsilon) := LAW(\text{"p"}, I[1], \epsilon) \times LAW(\text{"pl"}, I[2], \epsilon) \times LAW(\text{"pla"}, I[3], \epsilon)$$

where $I[i]$ is the size if the i-th intercepted packet. We have also tried other measures of likelihood f: sum of the prefix probabilities; or weighted sum (e.g., to emphasize the first letters of the word).

The detailed "stack" algorithm works as follows in the case $l = 5$ (`p.children` is the list of all children of prefix p in the prefix tree):

```
partial_solutions = {""}  # contains the empty word
amount_stored = {10, 20, 30, 20, 15} # example

for i = 1 to 5:
    new_solutions = {} # empty list
    for each prefix p in partial_solutions
        for each prefix r in p.children
            add r in new_solutions
    sort prefixes pr in new_solutions by value of f(pr, I, epsilon)
    put amount_stored[i] first prefixes from new_solutions into partial_solutions

return partial_solutions
```

At each step the algorithm keeps the best prefixes in a stack. It then goes deeper in the tree to find the best possible ways to extend those prefixes. The output is a list of words sorted by value of f, which are deemed most likely by the algorithm. Results obtained with this algorithm are presented in the next section.

4.4   Threshold Variant

A slightly modified version of the stack algorithm uses a different criterion to decide whether to keep or discard a prefix in the stack. Instead of selecting a fixed amount of prefixes in each step, all prefixes **pr** for which the value $LAW(\mathbf{pr}, I, \epsilon)$ is greater than a given threshold are kept. The value T of this threshold varies from one step to another. Only the "local" probability $LAW(\mathbf{pr}, I, \epsilon)$ is taken into account in each step, not the global $f(\mathbf{pr}, I, \epsilon)$, resulting in a more efficient computation. Results obtained with this variant are also presented next.

5   Test Results

This section presents the results of our algorithms tested on *Google*, by simulating an interception over Ethernet or Wifi. To simplify we assume a fixed value $l = 5$, i.e., a 5-letter French word is typed by the user.

5.1   Results Using the Stack Algorithm

The number of stored prefixes in each step from $i = 1$ to 5 were chosen as $\{20, 30, 50, 30, 15\}$. The final list will thus contain 15 possible words, ranked from the most to the least probable. Ten different target words were chosen, with ten retries per target, yielding 100 result samples. Table 1 shows the rank $\in [\![1, 15]\!]$ of the target word in the final list or a cross ($\times$) if the word was not found at all.

Table 2 shows that much poorer results would be obtained if one kept only 15 prefixes at *each* step in the algorithm. This shows the importance of considering larger numbers of stored prefixes at intermediate steps.

Table 1. Results of the stack algorithm when f is the product of the probabilities: $f = \prod_i LAW(pr_i, I[i], \epsilon)$. Success rates are **81 %** for target found in the final list; **52 %** found in the top 3; **34 %** ranked first.

Tested word	N1	N2	N3	N4	N5	N6	N7	N8	N9	N10
bases	4	1	×	2	4	8	×	×	6	9
barbe	2	3	1	2	5	7	4	×	1	4
bague	1	1	×	1	1	1	6	1	1	1
atome	1	×	1	1	3	3	2	6	11	4
cache	15	7	×	×	12	7	×	×	11	×
cadre	15	×	×	4	×	15	×	×	×	×
maman	1	2	1	2	1	1	1	1	1	1
parle	1	2	1	1	2	10	5	5	2	1
pomme	5	1	8	3	1	2	1	1	2	9
neige	2	5	1	×	1	10	1	1	3	2

Table 2. Results of the stack algorithm when f is the product of the probabilities and only 15 prefixes are kept at each step in the algorithm. Success rates drop down to **50 %** for target found in the final list; **38 %** found in the top 3; **25 %** ranked first.

Tested word	N1	N2	N3	N4	N5	N6	N7	N8	N9	N10
bases	1	×	×	1	×	×	1	×	×	1
barbe	×	2	×	1	×	×	×	×	3	×
bague	×	1	×	×	×	×	2	×	1	×
atome	2	2	×	×	×	1	1	×	×	3
cache	×	×	9	10	11	10	11	×	×	×
cadre	×	6	×	×	×	4	×	×	3	×
maman	1	2	×	1	×	1	1	×	1	×
parle	7	1	×	×	1	1	×	1	1	2
pomme	5	2	5	×	1	2	5	3	×	1
neige	×	2	1	×	1	1	×	1	5	×

5.2 Other Choices for the Likelihood Function

For the stack algorithm with a fixed number of kept words at each step, in addition to the choice where f is the product of the probabilities:

$$f = \prod_i LAW(pr_i, I[i], \epsilon)$$

we have tested other formulas for the likelihood function: sum of the probabilities:

$$f = \sum_i LAW(pr_i, I[i], \epsilon)$$

and weighted sum

$$f = \sum_i (n - i) LAW(pr_i, I[i], \epsilon)$$

that gives more importance to the first letters. The choice of likelihood as a product of probabilities gives the best results among the tested functions (see Fig. 4 below), which is coherent with the theory.

5.3 Results Using the Threshold Variant

For the threshold version of the algorithm, taking likelihood f as the product of the probabilities is again the best choice. A lower threshold allows more accuracy,

Table 3. Results of the stack algorithm with threshold $T = 0.1$. Success rates are **89 %** for target found in the final list; **56 %** found in the top 3; **36 %** ranked first.

Tested word	N1	N2	N3	N4	N5	N6	N7	N8	N9	N10
bases	1	×	×	×	1	1	2	2	2	1
barbe	1	1	1	1	2	×	2	2	×	1
bague	6	1	1	7	1	5	1	1	3	1
atome	1	2	1	5	3	1	×	1	1	1
cache	4	17	11	4	11	37	18	21	4	20
cadre	30	11	29	18	26	56	13	3	3	8
maman	1	1	1	1	1	1	1	1	1	1
parle	2	3	1	×	3	4	2	3	×	4
pomme	5	4	4	1	×	1	5	1	2	5
neige	2	4	1	3	6	3	4	5	×	×

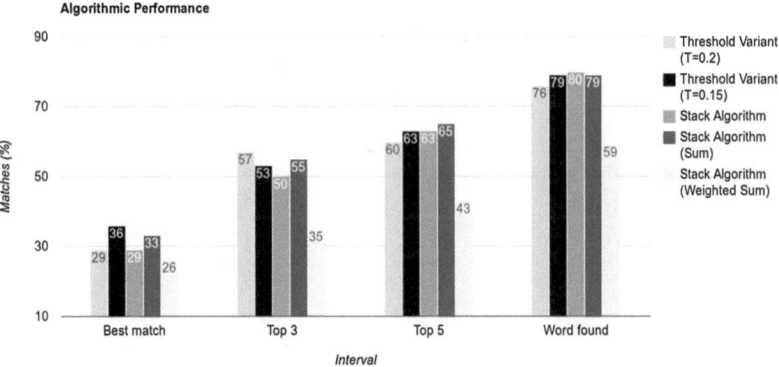

Fig. 4. Results of additional test runs. The threshold variant was tested once with a threshold of 0.15 and once with a threshold of 0.2. The likelihood variants were the product, sum and weighted sum of the probabilities.

in spite of a slightly longer execution time (which remains less than 15 min). Table 3 is presented similarly as above, except that the target rank may now be larger than 15.

5.4 Global Performance

Our results are summarized in Fig. 4. This chart shows how often the target word was found by the algorithm, how often it was among the best 5 matches, among the best 3 matches and how often it was the best match.

The results show that the variants perform similarly, except the weighted sum version which actually performs worse. On average, the target word is in the word list 8 times out of 10, in the best three matches more than 5 times out of 10, and is the best match about 3 times out of 10.

Interestingly, the tables show that some words are missed quite often, like *cache* or *cadre*. We found two plausible reasons for this:

- *Google* loads the result page after three ("cad") of four ("cadr") letters. Since we have assumed that two result page loadings cannot be distinguished, there remains few different packet sizes available;
- it turns out that those sizes are very common among all possible packet sizes (about 480 bytes which is the most probable packet length): too many words match the same sizes.

5.5 Implementation Issues

From our experience, the step that is always the most time-consuming is the first one that fetches the relevant file from the search engine. It is a good idea to cache the results in order to save time. Once a probability law is computed, it is stored so that it is not necessary to compute it again. This is particularly

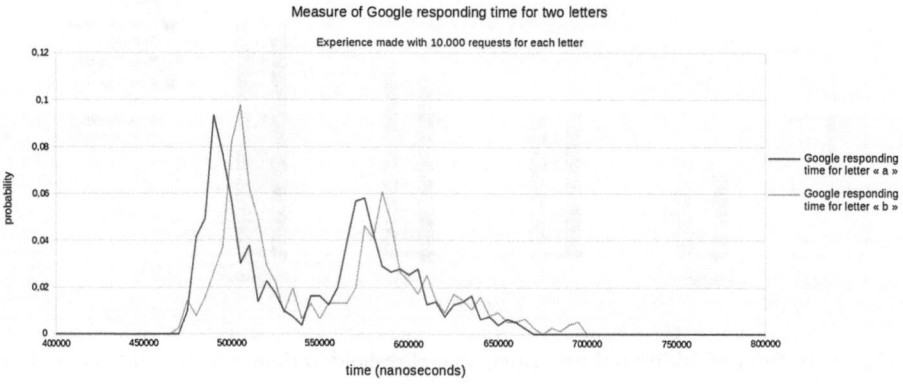

Fig. 5. Google response time for two different queries.

effective when several tests are performed; even on a single run, the duration may be divided by 2. Also, most of the time is wasted by waiting for the search engine to respond, using several *threads* can be more efficient.

Side-channel attacks can be used to work over Ethernet as well as protected Wifi networks. However, we noticed that *Google* often sends the important data in a packet containing two or more encrypted Application Data chunks. This is not a problem for an attack over Ethernet, since the different chunk sizes can be easily determined, but it is more of an issue over Wifi. Also, some constant *offset* is to be determined, that depends on the wireless access point configuration, which allows to convert the compressed suggestion data size to the actual captured packet size. This offset depends on the other data chunks in the intercepted packet, and it may therefore require some time to determine the actual suggestion data size for a packet captured over Wifi.

6   Conclusion

In this paper, the side-channel leakage of a major search engine, *Google*, has been analyzed. Knowledge of encrypted packet lengths can be used to deduce the user's search query, even if the packet sizes are randomized. Stack algorithms are presented to achieve this, based on multiple probabilities for each typed prefix and on natural language to limit the possibilities. These algorithms can be adapted to any other search engine that uses suggest boxes or similar features. Therefore, randomizing packet lengths is certainly not enough to mitigate side-channel leaks.

6.1   Perspectives

Some improvements and issues remain topics for future investigations.

Several words. In order to handle the use of the space key, it would be necessary to slightly alter the structure of the tree representing the dictionary. Every leaf (word) should be arrowed back to the root, where the arrow represents the whitespace character. It would actually not be a tree anymore, but rather a cyclic structure.

Use of backspaces. Our algorithm cannot find the search query if an user hits the backspace key because it would be searching for a word that would be too long. For example, for the word "mub←m", one would receive 5 packets related to the queries "m", "mu", "mub", "mu" and "mum". It is possible to add words like "mub←m" (considering this as a 5-letter word) but this increases the size of the 5-letter dictionary by $26^4 = 456976$ times the size of a 4-letter dictionary (even without considering that the backspace key may be used more than once).

Automatic downloads. Sometimes, *Google* is pretty sure about what the user is looking for and loads the corresponding page—for example, if one starts by hitting "f", Google will load the page with *Facebook*-oriented links.[4] This of course results in many packets sent by *Google* which can be easily detected.

Localization and customization. *Google*'s suggestions depend on the user's language defined in his/her *Google* homepage, and on the country of his/her ISP. They also depend on the browsing history and previous search history. This is the major problem for our algorithm since the latter relies on the fact that the victim and attacker get the same suggestions from *Google*. This would still be the case, however, if the victim uses the "Private Mode" implemented on most browsers—which here, ironically, causes a loss of privacy. Our algorithms could also be tested with other dictionaries, for example with a complete English dictionary and English search-terms, to see how it performs in this case. We don't expect the results to be much different.

Server's response time. We have only considered the lengths of the packets that are being sent. Another important side-channel information would be the time when the packets arrive to the client (or are intercepted by the attacker [11]). Figure 5 shows the estimated probability of time between the departure of the request and the arrival of *Google*'s answer for two different letters "a" and "b". The two curves seem shifted: *Google*'s computation time for letter "b" is longer than the one for letter "a", and this type of information could have been used in our algorithm. However, the delay between the two signals is very small compared to their deviations. Also, computing these curves is quite time-consuming—unlike packet lengths, it is not possible to compute the response times after having fetched only one file.

Multiple requests. One possible improvement of the attack would be to make *Google* send the suggestions several times, since this would reduce the uncertainty of the packet lengths. This could perhaps be achieved by re-sending the victim's encrypted request to *Google*, but it may not be easy to trick *Google* into thinking that the attacker is the victim.

6.2 How to Mitigate Side-Channel Leaks

Today, as we have shown, using a simple personal computer, it is possible to spy on anybody using a Wifi connection, even if this connection is made secure by other means. This is a serious threat to privacy over the Internet. Even though the randomization of packet lengths makes it harder to infer a search query, it is still possible to guess the target correctly in many cases. There have been numerous attempts to mitigate side-channel leaks in general [12,13], but it is generally considered that preventing *every* side-channel leak source is very difficult [14].

However, for the particular leak exploited in this paper, it would be easy to implement an efficient countermeasure by sending only packets of a given, fixed size (e.g., the size of the longest possible packet in response of a request). A similar procedure can be carried out for response times. For example, the server could always wait a fixed time before answering.

---

[4] This is known as *Google Instant*.

The cost of such a procedure can be criticized, but it would definitely make our present method useless. Nonetheless, we notice that such method can be limited to sensitive traffic (e.g., contextual to user interaction with the server). A simple way of achieving this would be to pad every packet to a fixed size M, and disable any compression feature. The remaining problem is to choose the correct value of M. A solution would be to choose the maximum packet length for M, but it is not always possible to determine this maximum. Whenever the initial packet length exceeds M, one could pad it to the closest multiple of M. Although this gives the attacker some information, it should not be enough to guess the search query.

References

1. A Face Is Exposed for AOL Searcher, New York Times article, 9 August 2006. http://select.nytimes.com/gst/abstract.html?res=F10612FC345B0C7A8CDDA10894DE404482. Accessed 27 July 2014
2. Making Search More Secure, 18 October 2011. http://googleblog.blogspot.fr/2011/10/making-search-more-secure.html. Accessed 27 July 2014
3. Post-PRISM, Google Confirms Quietly Moving To Make All Searches Secure, Except For Ad Clicks, 23 September 2013. http://searchengineland.com/post-prism-google-secure-searches-172487. Accessed 17 July 2014
4. Cantino, A.: Demasking Google Users With a Timing Attack (blog post). http://blog.andrewcantino.com/blog/2014/09/04/demasking-google-users-with-a-timing-attack/
5. Chen, S., Wang, R., Wang, X., Zhang, K.:Side-channel leaks in web applications: a reality today, a challenge tomorrow. In: Proceedings of the 2010 IEEE Symposium on Security and Privacy (SP 2010), pp. 191–206 (2010)
6. Liberatore, M., Levine, N.B.: Inferring the source of encrypted HTTP connections. In: Proceedings of the 13th ACM Conference on Computer and Communications Security (CCS 2006), pp. 255–263. ACM, New York (2006)
7. Herrmann, D., Wendolsky, R., Federrath, H.: Website fingerprinting: attacking popular privacy enhancing technologies with the multinomial Naïve-Bayes classifier. In: Proceedings of the 2009 ACM Workshop on Cloud Computing Security (CCSW 2009), pp. 31–42 (2009)
8. Mather, L., Oswald, E.: Pinpointing side-channel information leaks in web applications. J. Cryptogr. Eng. 2(3), 161–177 (2012). Also available in ICAR ePrint 2012:269
9. Sampreet Sharma, A., Bernard Menezes, M.: Implementing side-channel attacks on suggest boxes in web applications. In: Proceedings of the First International Conference on Security of Internet of Things, SecurIT 2012, Amritapuri, Kollam, pp. 57–62 (2012)
10. Fredkin, E.: Trie memory. Commun. ACM 3(9), 490–499 (1960)
11. Tey, C.M., Gupta, P., Gao, D., Zhang, Y.: Keystroke timing analysis of on-the-fly web apps. In: Jacobson, M., Locasto, M., Mohassel, P., Safavi-Naini, R. (eds.) ACNS 2013. LNCS, vol. 7954, pp. 405–413. Springer, Heidelberg (2013)
12. Nassar, M., Guilley, S., Danger, J.-L.: Formal analysis of the entropy/security trade-off in first-order masking countermeasures against side-channel attacks. In: Bernstein, D.J., Chatterjee, S. (eds.) INDOCRYPT 2011. LNCS, vol. 7107, pp. 22–39. Springer, Heidelberg (2011)

13. Backes, M., Doychev, G., Köpf, B.: Preventing side-channel leaks in web traffic: a formal approach. In: 20th Annual Network and Distributed System Security Symposium, NDSS 2013, San Diego, California, USA, 24–27 February 2013, 17 p. http://internetsociety.org/doc/preventing-side-channel-leaks-web-traffic-formal-approach
14. Dyer, K.P., Coull, S.E., Ristenpart, T., Shrimpton, T.: Peek-a-Boo, i still see you: why efficient traffic analysis countermeasures fail. In: Proceedings of the 2012 IEEE Symposium on Security and Privacy (SP 2012), San Francisco, California, USA, pp. 332–346 (2012)

Location–Aware RBAC Based on Spatial Feature Models and Realistic Positioning

Philipp Marcus$^{(\boxtimes)}$, Lorenz Schauer, and Claudia Linnhoff–Popien

Ludwig–Maximilians–Universität München, 80538 Munich, Germany
{philipp.marcus,lorenz.schauer,linnhoff}@ifi.lmu.de

Abstract. The location of a mobile user presents valuable information when deriving access control decisions. Hence, several location–aware extensions to role–based access control (RBAC) exist in literature. However, these approaches do not consider positioning errors. This leads to unexpected security breaches, when the user's ground truth differs from the reported location. Further, most approaches simply define a polygon as authorized zone and authorize when the reported position lies inside. To overcome these limitations, this paper presents a risk–optimal approach to RBAC. Position estimates are represented as probability distributions instead of points. Location constraints are assigned to RBAC elements and include cost functions for false positive and false negative decisions as well as feature models, which replace traditionally used polygons. Feature models describe for each location the likelihood that a specific feature can be observed. The evaluation shows that such risk–optimal RBAC outperforms risk–ignoring, polygon–based approaches. However, this risk–optimality is bought at the expense of a runtime highly increasing with the number of applied location constraints.

Keywords: Location–based access control · Risk · Positioning errors

1 Introduction

Controlling the access of users or any subject to critical resources is a fundamental and security relevant problem. Basically, if access to specific resources is granted erroneously, typically severe costs arise. The same holds for erroneously denying access. In order to tackle this problem, access control models like role–based access control (RBAC) have been developed [16]. Here, a user is assigned several roles, each allowing for a set of permissions. In the next step, the user starts a RBAC session and selects a subset of assigned roles, which makes the attached permissions available for the duration of this session. During an open RBAC session on a mobile device, e.g., a smartphone or tablet computer, access requests to use permissions can be issued from any possible location in original RBAC. However, such access requests must not be granted if the user's location lacks required features. For example, such a feature could be that the user resides on his company's site if the permission is related to sensitive information. Also, the permission to remotely control a physical machine via a tablet computer could be limited to specific locations. For example, such remote control might

© Springer International Publishing Switzerland 2015
J. Lopez et al. (Eds.): CRiSIS 2014, LNCS 8924, pp. 131–147, 2015.
DOI: 10.1007/978-3-319-17127-2_9

be only considered safe if the user has a chance to reach the machine's emergency switch in a predefined time span.

Therefore, many location–aware extensions to RBAC were proposed, which respect the user's location when deciding about access requests. Most approaches constrain the availability of roles or permissions in RBAC policies to users within predefined geographical polygons, i.e., authorized zones. However, in practice, the enforcement of these extensions is complicated by positioning errors observed with real positioning systems. To the best of our knowledge, all location–aware RBAC extensions do not account for occurring risk attended by positioning errors. Furthermore, only polygons are adhered for extending RBAC policies, which makes it hard to model scenarios like the mentioned emergency switch.

In order to solve these gaps, this paper presents a location–aware extension of RBAC, which considers risk attended by positioning errors and comprises a generalization of existing polygon–based approaches. Instead of polygons, our location constraints assign feature models and cost functions to RBAC elements. A feature model describes for each location x the probability that x shows the required feature, for example to be capable to reach the emergency switch or to be on a company's site. The cost values comprise both cost for false positives and false negatives. The former is assumed to occur if the constrained element is available for a RBAC session though the user's location does not show the required feature. The latter occurs in the opposite case. Position estimates are reported as probability distributions rather than simple points. This allows to derive the probability that the user's location shows a feature by integrating it over the feature model. This allows to derive both the risk, i.e., expected costs, of erroneously making the RBAC element available or unavailable respectively. Location constraints are enforced risk–based by taking the least risky choice.

The rest of this paper is structured as follows: Sect. 2 first discusses related work. Subsequently, Sect. 3 emphasizes the probabilistic nature of position estimates. Next, Sect. 4 presents the proposed RBAC extension in detail. Here, the basics of RBAC are revisited first in order to define the concept of location constraints based on feature models and cost values. A risk–based approach for enforcing location constraints on RBAC elements based on probabilistic position estimates is presented. Also, different ways to handle the sudden unavailability of RBAC elements in open sessions are identified. The effectiveness of the presented approach is evaluated in Sect. 5. Eventually, Sect. 6 concludes the paper.

2   Related Work

A detailed discussion of related work is given in this section. Discussed approaches stem from the research directions of spatio–temporal and risk–aware RBAC extensions, as well as risk–aware usage control.

Covington et al. introduced the concept of environmental roles, which are only active for predefined context states of the mobile user and need to be active in order to use certain permissions [5]. Hansen et al. constrain the permissions attached to a role based on the user's location [6]. Ray et al. constrain for each

RBAC session the allowed locations of users and objects [14]. During ongoing usage of the session, the user and objects are required to stay within the allowed locations. Chen et al. present ERBAC, a spatio–temporal RBAC model, which comes with different levels of restrictiveness and allows to constrain the availability of any RBAC element to specific spatio–temporal conditions [3]. Here, the availability of roles in the lifetime of an ongoing session depends on the spatio–temporal context. However, the semantic implications of reducing the set of initially active spatio–temporal roles is not considered. Furthermore, the dynamic assignment of permissions to roles complicates the construction and analysis of policies. Oleshchuck et al. [12] present GSRBAC, where permissions are also attached dynamically to roles based on the user's and the accessed resource's location. Again, implications of changed permission assignments in ongoing sessions are not discussed. Abdunabi et al. define a spatio–temporal RBAC model with trigger constraints, in order to control the availability of roles in ongoing sessions based on the user's location [1]. Trigger constraints are defined in order to react persistently on spatio–temporal state changes of users, even after resources have been accessed. These approaches and according formal analysis do not account for positioning errors that are unavoidable with real positioning systems in practice. Risk stemming from those errors is not considered.

To respect occurring uncertainty, several non RBAC related approaches for spatio–temporal access control have been developed. Ardagna et al. define location predicates, for example to constrain access to resources to specific areas [2]. Their approach is not RBAC specific and location predicates are evaluated probabilistically based on confidence values. Thresholds were introduced to require a minimum confidence for a positive evaluation of a location predicate. Shin et al. describe the user location as a probability density function and integrate it over predefined authorized areas [17]. The resulting probability is compared to predefined thresholds, when authorization decisions are derived. However, the derivation of threshold values is left open.

Also several related risk–based approaches have been developed up to now. Ni et al. derive the risk of access requests based on fuzzy inference and fuzzy sets defined on the domains of the subject's and the object's sensitivity score [11]. Krautsevich et al. define a general approach for risk–analysis on mutable attributes in usage control policies in order to decide about ongoing sessions [7]. Here, focus lies on bridging the time until a fresh attribute value is provided by predictions with Markov chains. Similarly, Marcus et al. proposed an extension of usage control policies with trajectory constraints [9]. Salim et al. derive costs for each access request from an underlying RBAC policy [15]. A user is granted an issued access request as long as his previously assigned budget is sufficiently high to pay its cost. Chen et al. define a risk–aware RBAC extension and assign risk values to each user's trustworthiness, degree of competence for each assigned role and the appropriateness of role–permission assignments [4]. For each access request, the involved risk values are combined to assess the overall risk. However, to the best of our knowledge, none of the existing approaches allows for location–aware RBAC while simultaneously respecting uncertainty of position estimates.

3   Characteristics of Imperfect Positioning Systems

All approaches to location–aware RBAC rely on positioning systems. In outdoor scenarios, GNSS based positioning systems like GPS are widely used. Indoor, where no line of sight to satellites exist, other techniques like, for example Wi–Fi fingerprinting are typically applied. Those approaches conduct measurements in order to derive a coordinate μ as the user's estimated position. However, environmental and physical influences pertain these processes, which causes that μ deviates from the user's real location [8]. The errors of GPS typically range from $9 - 11\,\mathrm{m}$ while the errors of Wi–Fi fingerprinting are about $1 - 2\,\mathrm{m}$ [10]. For each derived position estimate, it is uncertain where the real location actually lies. In order to model this uncertainty, a probability density function (pdf) $f_{(\mu,\Sigma)}(x)$ with the mean of μ and a scale parameter Σ can be derived by an error estimator to describe the proximity of the real location to the position estimate μ. Hence, a position estimate can be described as a tuple (μ, Σ). In case of Wi–Fi fingerprinting, those pdf can be modeled by Gaussians [10]. Here, the covariance matrix Σ can be derived from singularities of the conducted measurement. In the following, those pdf will be used to derive risk–optimal authorization decisions.

4   The Probabilistic RBAC Policy

This Section first revisits the classical RBAC Model and defines the proposed extension with location constraints. Next, the enforcement of applied location constraints is illustrated.

4.1   Revisiting the RBAC Model

Role-based access control (RBAC) comprises four models for designing access control policies and was originally proposed by Sandhu et al. [16]. Basically, RBAC policies represent access control policies based on the following elements:

- U representing the set of users known to the system.
- R representing the defined roles.
- P comprising the permissions to be controlled. In particular, this describes that a specific action can be performed on a given object or resource.

In order to formalize access rights, three relations are defined:

- $UA \subseteq U \times R$ represents user-role assignments
- $RP \subseteq R \times P$ encapsulates role-permission-assignments
- $RH \subseteq R \times R$ models a role hierarchy (only in RBAC_1 and RBAC_3)

In detail, UA assigns roles to users and RP assigns permissions to roles. Consequently, if a user u is assigned a given role $r \in R$, all permissions related to r are available to the user. The role hierarchy RH consists of tuples $(r, r') \in R \times R$, stating that role r' is superior to r. In such cases, a user with an assigned role r is granted all permissions assigned to r or superior roles of r.

Chen et al. transferred this mechanism to a graph-based approach [3]. Here, a concrete policy is represented as a directed acyclic graph $\mathcal{P} = (V, E)$, with vertices $V = U \cup R \cup P$ consisting of the union of all defined sets and the edges $E = UA \cup RP \cup RH$ consisting of all defined relations on vertices. A role r is *available* for user u if there exists an authorization–path (auth–path) $\langle u, \dots, r \rangle$ in $\mathcal{P}$. The availability of roles is directly implied by the RBAC policy $\mathcal{P}$ and the static relations UA and RP in detail. In order to work with permissions and to attend his tasks, a user u first needs to open an RBAC session s [16]. In detail, an RBAC session is defined as a subset of roles available to user u. The roles in this subset are selected when the session is opened and may only comprise roles which are *available* to the user. If an available role r is included in the session, r is said to be activated. Without any formal extensions to RBAC, the set of available roles does not change with time. Hence, a session in original RBAC stays valid until a user quits it manually.

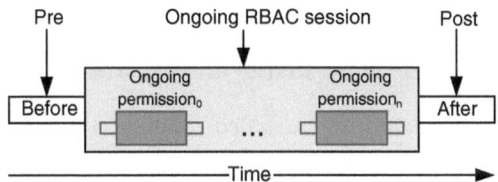

Fig. 1. Illustration of different phases of sessions (adapted from [13]).

A reference monitor for RBAC policies can be realized by usage control policies like UCON, originally proposed by Park et al. [13]. For a given ongoing session s, where permissions $p_0, \dots, p_n$ are currently used, this is depicted schematically in Fig. 1. When applied to RBAC, UCON basically divides the lifetime of each open session or used permission in three parts: pre–authorization, ongoing usage and post–authorization. Consequently, permissions are always used in the context of an ongoing session in the original RBAC.

4.2   Syntactic Definition of Location Constraints

This Section describes the syntactic extension of RBAC policies with location constraints. The approach is presented top–down: First, feature models for locations and the concept of cost functions are defined. Based on these building blocks, the formal definition of location constraints is given.

Feature Models for Locations. An element e of an RBAC policy, for example a role, can be considered *location sensitive*, if the user's current location provides a valid source to decide if e shall be available in his current session. In detail, the requirement that the user is at a certain location can be considered reasonable if the location has intrinsic features that naturally fit to the element e. For example, the activation of a role `employee` may only be reasonable if the user's location has the feature that it lies on the companies site. Furthermore, the operation of a physical machine via a mobile device in a factory may only be granted if the user's location has the feature that it allows to reach the machine's emergency switch in a given time. This may be required by legal safety and security restrictions. Often, it is not clear where to draw the borders of such areas that show a required feature. Thus, instead of defining according polygons for features, a Boolean random variable F_e is defined to describe the presence of a required feature F_e. In order to describe the probability that a required feature F_e is present at a given location x, a *feature model* is defined:

Definition 1 (Feature Model). *A feature model is defined as a conditional probability distribution $\mathbf{P}(F_e|X)$ that describes for each location $x \in X$ the probability that location x has the required feature F_e.*

Note, that probability distributions over a random variable F are denoted $\mathbf{P}(F)$. Single probabilities for $F = f$ are denoted $P(f)$. In the following, feature models are used as a generalization of the hitherto used polygons that describe authorized zones. This concept is illustrated by three distinct examples.

Example 1. In the first example, an office room was identified to possess the required features of a location sensitive role employee. In such cases, the model $\mathbf{P}(F_{\texttt{employee}}|X)$ represents a distribution over the office $\mathcal{L}$ (a closed polygon) with sharp bounds on its walls. Clearly, all points $\mathbf{x} \in \mathcal{L}$ show the feature of being within the according office contrary to points outside $\mathcal{L}$. This leads to the following definition of $P(F_{\texttt{employee}}|X)$:

$$P(f_{\texttt{employee}}|x) = \begin{cases} 1, \text{ iff } \mathbf{x} \in \mathcal{L} \\ 0, \text{ otherwise} \end{cases} \tag{1}$$

Note, this feature model is a generalization of approaches to location–based access control that use point in polygon tests to decide about authorizations.

When the required feature is only present at a given location x with a certain probability, the definition of polygons for existing approaches is a hard task.

Example 2. Assume a building, where a worker in role controller remotely controls a physical machine using his mobile device. Assume that legal constraints prescribe that during mobile usage of permissions assigned to role controller, the worker needs to be able to physically reach the machine's emergency switch within a time of t seconds. This property is modeled as the feature of locations for role controller. Consequently, given a mobility model for human movement, the probability of reaching the emergency switch can be modeled for each point on a building plan or the map in general. The according feature model shows a smooth decrease of $P(f_{\texttt{controller}}|x)$ with larger distances of x to the emergency switch and is thus called floating feature model in the following.

Floating models can be created in two steps. First, the specific point that a user has to reach within time needs to be identified on the building plan.

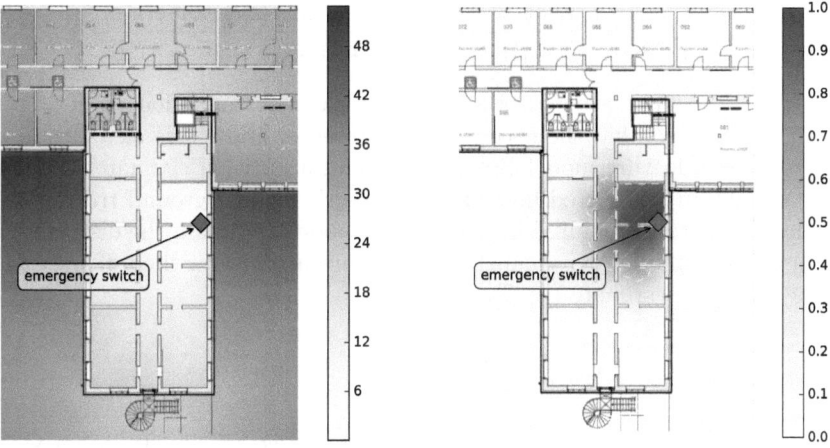

Fig. 2. Distances (m) to emergency switch. **Fig. 3.** Feature model with 50 % polygon.

For example, this point may represent the above–mentioned physical machine's emergency switch that a mobile user has to reach. Next, the distance to the specific point is computed for all other points on the map. This is illustrated in Fig. 2. In order to derive a feature model from the distance model, a minimum required velocity $v_{\min}$ is computed for each point by dividing the point's distance with the prescribed time span. Finally, the probability to reach the specific point in time can be obtained from the survival function of a cumulative distribution function for the human walking speeds. In our case, a Gaussian with a mean at $4 \frac{km}{h}$ and a standard deviation of $2 \frac{km}{h}$ is chosen. The feature model derived from the distance model of Fig. 2 with a time limit of 6 s is depicted in Fig. 3. Here, also a polygon is depicted that contains all points with a feature probability larger than 0.5. This polygon might have been chosen in classical point in polygon approaches to location–based access control to approximate the desired behavior. Clearly, such floating feature models do not respect that humans need to slow down when walking around corners nor a minimum distance to walls. However, it though represents a good approximation of the probability to reach the specific point in time.

At last, not only safety constraints can be adhered for deriving $\mathbf{P}(F_e|X)$ but also security considerations.

Example 3. Assume the site of a company with an office $\mathcal{L}$ protected by physical entrance control, e.g., locked doors with corresponding keys or RFID cards. The set of persons, which are able to enter a location x is a feature of each location. If a user's mobile device was stolen and used to activate a role r within $\mathcal{L}$, the theft also needs to possess that key card. Hence, a feature model can be defined that describes the Boolean feature, that the mobile device's current user stems from the role's assigned users $U' \subseteq U$. It is defined as the quotient of users U' assigned to r and all persons *Persons*, which may reside at point $\mathbf{x}$:

$$P(f_r|X = \mathbf{x}) = \frac{|\{u \in U \mid (u,r) \in UA \wedge \mathtt{has\_entrance}(u,\mathbf{x})\}|}{|\{p \in Persons \mid \mathtt{has\_entrance}(p,\mathbf{x})\}|} \qquad (2)$$

with $U' \subseteq U \subseteq Persons$. Here, the predicate $\mathtt{has\_entrance}$ denotes if a user or a real–world person has the necessary keys to enter and reside at a location x.

Based on a feature model $P(f_e|X = \mathbf{x})$ and a position estimate of a user u at time t, it can be derived how likely the user's current ground truth location satisfies the features required by the feature model. In detail, the distribution of $\mathbf{P}(F_e)$ is computed by marginalizing the feature model over the pdf $f_{(\mu,\Sigma)}(x)$ of user u's position estimate (μ, Σ):

$$P(f_e) = \int_X P(f_e|X = x) \cdot f_{(\mu,\Sigma)}(x)\,\mathrm{d}x \qquad (3)$$

Hence, Eq. (3) allows to derive the probability $P(f_e)$ that the user's current ground truth, i.e., real–world position showed the feature F_e at the moment his position estimate (μ, Σ) was taken.

Cost Values for RBAC Elements. Due to the probabilistic position estimates, a definitive proposition if the user's ground truth position satisfies the feature required by an element e is not possible. Only a probability can be derived that a user's ground truth location satisfies the feature at time t. However, in the following it is assumed that costs arise if an element e is made available though the user's location does not show the feature required by e. Thus, each location sensitive element e is assigned two cost functions c_{fp} and c_{fn} beneath its feature model. The cost c_{fn} describes the cost that arises if a user is not allowed by the policy to employ the location sensitive element e in his session though his ground truth location satisfies the required feature. Contrary, cost of c_{fp} arise if a user is allowed to employ the location sensitive element e in his session though his ground truth location does not show the required feature.

Extending RBAC with Location Constraints. Based on the concept of feature models and cost functions, location constraints can be defined for single elements of an RBAC policy. In the original RBAC model, a user u is granted all permissions that are reachable via an auth–path that only passes roles in u's open session s. In order to keep this semantic, location constraints must not be applied to RBAC elements e with $e \in RP$ or $e \in P$. Formally, a location constraint assigns a feature model and two cost values to an RBAC element:

Definition 2 (Location Constraint). *A Location constraint for an RBAC element $e \in U \cup UA \cup RH \cup R$ is defined as a 3-tuple $\left(\mathbf{P}(F_e|X), c_{fp}^e, c_{fn}^e\right)$, consisting of a feature model for a feature F and costs c_{fp} for false positives and c_{fn} for false negatives.*

A simple example of a location constrained RBAC policy is depicted in Fig. 4. Here, the assigned location constraints of the auth–path $\langle u, r_1, \ldots, r_n \rangle$ require

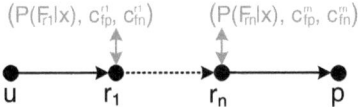

Fig. 4. Evaluation of the auth–path $\langle u, r_1, \ldots, r_n \rangle$. Assigned location constraints are associated to the according role by an arrow.

the features $F_{r_1}, \ldots, F_{r_n}$ to be **true** at the user's ground truth location. In order to finally decide if a given RBAC element e shall be available for a user, location constraints restrict the existence of auth–paths based on the user's current position estimate. This enforcement is presented in the next section.

4.3 Enforcement of Location Constraints

In this section, the enforcement of location constraints is presented. The authorization decisions are derived and enforced by a reference monitor based on the original RBAC policy and its assigned location constraints. The reference monitor is provided a stream of trustworthy position estimates of each user with an ongoing session by a trustworthy and tamper–proof location provider. The frequency of reported position estimates needs to be high in order to minimize time gaps of uncertainty about the user's position. However, the tamper–proof and high frequent measurement of position estimates is not subject of this paper.

Similar to original RBAC, each user first has to activate roles when starting a session s in a pre–authorization phase. Here, each role r can only be activated for s when there exists an auth–path $\langle u, \ldots, r \rangle$ in the original unconstrained RBAC policy $\mathcal{P} = (V, E)$. The location constraints are enforced in the next step by mapping the original session s to a constrained session s' with $s' \subseteq s$. That way, the original RBAC authorization semantic can be preserved, by substituting the original s by s' when searching for auth–paths. During ongoing usage of the session, this procedure is repeated by the reference monitor for each position estimate reported by the location provider. Consequently, a user u is only allowed to use a permission p in his ongoing session s if the roles in the according constrained session s' allow an auth–path $\langle u, \ldots, p \rangle$ such that all passed roles are contained in s'. This is illustrated by Algorithm 1. The next section finally presents the handling of location constraint violations by the procedures `handle_session_violation` and `handle_permission_violation`. The rest of this section describes the procedure `update_session_roles`. This procedure derives the constrained session s' by searching for an auth–path to each role $r \in s$. If an auth–path is found, r is also included in the constrained session s'. By enforcing the assigned location constraints, originally possible auth–paths can be deactivated, which can lead to the fact that s' is only a subset of s. The requesting user has a ground truth state, which means that each feature required by any of the auth–path's location constraints is either **true** or **false** at his ground truth location at the moment of the request. The likelihood that a single feature is **true** at a location x is described by its according feature model, as discussed above. When enforcing the location

Algorithm 1. Constraint enforcement in ongoing sessions.

Input: user u, session s, RBAC policy $\mathcal{P}$, location provider loc
Ensure: Enforcement of location constraints for s
   function ONGOING_SESSION_ENFORCEMENT(u,s,$\mathcal{P}$, loc)
      for each (μ, Σ) **reported_by** loc **do**
         $s' \leftarrow$ UPDATE_SESSION_ROLES(u, s, (μ, Σ), $\mathcal{P}$) $\triangleright$ Constrained session
         if $s \neq s'$ **then** $\triangleright$ React on session violations
            HANDLE_SESSION_VIOLATION(u, s, s', $\mathcal{P}$)
         end if
         for each ongoing permissions p **do**
            if $\exists \langle u, \ldots, p \rangle \in \mathcal{P}$. $\forall i \in \langle u, \ldots, p \rangle : i \in R \rightarrow i \in s'$ **then**
               continue $\triangleright$ There exists an auth–path in s'
            else
               HANDLE_PERMISSION_VIOLATION(u, s, s', $\mathcal{P}$)
            end if
         end for
      end for
   end function

---

constraints, each auth–path may happen to be deactivated. This may happen though some of the features required by the auth–path's location constraints are **true** at the user's ground truth location. In that case, the false negative cost of those location constraints are assumed to arise in the real world. Similarly, the opposite holds if the auth–path stays active though some of the features required by its location constraints are currently **false** at the user's ground truth location. In such cases, their according false positive cost will arise. Hence, the arising cost when activating or deactivating the auth–path depend on the user's ground truth state. In the optimal case, the user is in a ground truth state where either all features are **true** and the auth–path stays active or vice versa, as consequently no costs arise.

When operating the location constrained RBAC policy, such arising costs need to be minimized. Thus, all decisions about deactivating auth–paths have to be risk–optimal. Therefore, the expected cost of both deactivating the auth–path or leaving it active need to be examined. That decision with the least expected cost is finally chosen.

If the auth–path is assigned n location constraints, each required feature $F_1, \ldots, F_n$ is either **true** or **false** in ground truth. Hence, there exist 2^n possible ground truth states $\sigma_1, \ldots, \sigma_{2^n}$. Formally, each σ_i is a n–tuple assigning each feature $F_1, \ldots, F_n$ a Boolean value. Assume $\pi(\sigma_i)$ is the probability that a state σ_i reflects the user's current ground truth state. Further let $c_{fp}(\sigma_i)$ denote the sum of false positive cost c_{fp} of those location constraints assigned to the auth–path, whose required feature is **false** in σ_i. Similarly, $c_{fn}(\sigma_i)$ is the sum of false negative cost c_{fn} of those location constraints assigned to the auth–path, whose required feature is **true** in σ_i. This allows to derive the expected cost, i.e., risk, for both deactivating the auth–path or leaving it active:

$$\texttt{risk\_deactivate} = \frac{1}{2^n} \cdot \sum_{i=1}^{2^n} (\pi(\sigma_i) \cdot c_{fn}(\sigma_i)) \qquad (4)$$

$$\texttt{risk\_activate} = \frac{1}{2^n} \cdot \sum_{i=1}^{2^n} (\pi(\sigma_i) \cdot c_{fp}(\sigma_i)) \qquad (5)$$

In order to operate the location constrained RBAC policy risk–optimal, in each case that decision is chosen, that has the least expected cost:

$$\texttt{deactivate} \Leftrightarrow \texttt{risk\_deactivate} < \texttt{risk\_activate} \qquad (6)$$

In order to evaluate Eqs. (4) and (5), the likelihood $\pi(\sigma_i)$ that σ_i reflects the user's current ground truth state needs to be computed. Therefore, the state's joint feature model is derived first:

$$\forall x \in X : \mathrm{P}\left(\bigwedge_{j=1}^{n} F_j = \sigma_{ij} \Big| x\right) = \prod_{j=1}^{n} \mathrm{P}\left(F_j = \sigma_{ij} \Big| x\right) \qquad (7)$$

Here, the index j to a ground truth state σ_i references the Boolean value of feature F_j in this state. To clarify things, assume $\sigma_1 = (\texttt{true}, \texttt{false})$. The corresponding joint feature model $\mathrm{P}(F_1 = \texttt{true} \wedge F_2 = \texttt{false} \,|\, x)$ computes as $\mathrm{P}(F_1 = \texttt{true} | x) \cdot \mathrm{P}(F_2 = \texttt{false} | x)$ for all possible locations $x \in X$.

Finally, $\pi(\sigma_i)$ is obtained by marginalizing out the parameter X using the Gaussian pdf for the user's position estimate (μ, Σ):

$$\pi(\sigma_i) = \mathrm{P}\left(\bigwedge_{j=1}^{n} F_j = \sigma_{ij}\right) = \int_X \mathrm{P}\left(\bigwedge_{j=1}^{n} F_j = \sigma_{ij} | X = x\right) \cdot f_{(\mu, \Sigma)}(x) \, dx \qquad (8)$$

In order to derive the complete constrained session s', this methodology needs to be repeated for each role activated in the original session s. The final definition of the procedure $\texttt{update\_session\_roles}$ is presented in Algorithm 2.

4.4 Handling Location Constraint Violations

The enforcement of location constraints in an ongoing session produces constrained sessions with probably fewer available permissions, as seen above in Sect. 4.2. In detail, an ongoing session s is defined to be violated if not all roles from s are included in the according constrained session s'. Furthermore, if there is ongoing usage of a permission p in progress though no auth–path to p is allowed by s', the permission is considered violated. Both cases need to be handled by the reference monitor. Therefore, Algorithm 1 called the procedures $\texttt{handle\_session\_violation}$ and $\texttt{handle\_permission\_violation}$. This section shows possible realizations of these handlers and discusses their implication on the reference monitor's semantic.

Algorithm 2. Update algorithm for available session roles.

Input: user u, session s, position estimate (μ, Σ), RBAC policy $\mathcal{P}$
Output: location constrained session $s' \subset s$
  function UPDATE_SESSION_ROLES(u,s,(μ, Σ),$\mathcal{P}$)
    $s' \leftarrow \{\}$ ▷ Init result
    $s^* \leftarrow \{r' \in R | \exists r \in s : (r, r') \in RH\}$ ▷ Unfold sub–roles
    for each $r \in s^*$ **do**   ▷ For all roles of the session
      for each $\langle u, \ldots, r \rangle \in \mathcal{P}$ **do**   ▷ For all auth–paths to r
        $F_1, \ldots, F_n \leftarrow$ EXTRACT_REQUIRED_FEATURES($\langle u, \ldots, r \rangle$)
        $\sigma_1, \ldots, \sigma_{2^n} \leftarrow$ EXTRACT_GROUND_TRUTH_STATES($F_1, \ldots, F_n$)

        risk_deactivate $\leftarrow \frac{1}{2^n} \cdot \sum_{i=1}^{2^n} \left(\pi(\sigma_i) \cdot c_{fn}(\sigma_i) \right)$
        risk_activate $\leftarrow \frac{1}{2^n} \cdot \sum_{i=1}^{2^n} \left(\pi(\sigma_i) \cdot c_{fp}(\sigma_i) \right)$

        if risk_activate $\geq$ risk_deactivate **then**
          $s' \leftarrow s' \cup \{r\}$
        end if
      end for
    end for
  return s'
  end function

Both violation handlers can be realized by three basic reactions: *continue*, *pause* and *stop*. Thus, in case of session violations, sessions are either continued, paused (blocked from any user interaction) or stopped (terminated). The same holds for permission violations. When designing a reference monitor, appropriate implementations for both violation handlers need to be given. All possible combinations of these violation handlers span a 3×3 matrix, which is depicted in Fig. 5. Note, the reaction of handle_session_violation is abbreviated with h_s and similarly the reaction of handle_permission_violation is abbreviated with h_p. Let $\prec$ be a total ordering on the set of reactions with *continue* $\prec$ *pause* $\prec$ *stop*. Let $\sim$ denote similar restrictiveness of two reactions. These combinations form three distinct and semantically different categories:

1. The reaction h_s on the session is more restrictive than on the ongoing used permission h_p, i.e., $h_p \prec h_s$.

Session Permission	Continue	Pause	Stop
Continue	Model 1	Model 2	Model 3
Pause	Model 4	Model 5	Model 6
Stop	Model 7	Model 8	Model 9

Fig. 5. Models and categories (equal color) resulting from handler combinations.

2. The reaction h_s on the session and the reaction h_p on the ongoing used permission are both equally restrictive, i.e., $h_p \sim h_s$.
3. The reaction h_s on the session is less restrictive than h_p, which is applied to the ongoing used permission, i.e., $h_s \prec h_p$.

In order to clarify the different semantics, an example is given for each of the presented categories. From category 1, *Model 3* with $(h_s = stop, h_p = continue)$ is particularly useful, if the applied location constraints shall only be enforced when new ongoing permissions are started. For example, a permission to remotely start a physical machine in a factory could require the worker to stand next to the machine when he starts it, in order to check if it is equipped with enough raw material. Hence, new permissions must not be started after a constraint violation but ongoing permissions may be completed. In category 2, *Model 9* with $(h_s = stop, h_p = stop)$ is the most restrictive model. It is considered particularly useful, if the set of active roles in an ongoing session makes no sense anymore after the user changed to locations that lack required features.

For example, assume a role in a clinical environment for users, which are within a disinfected area and are considered hygienic. After leaving the disinfected area, the hygienic status of the user is unknown until he passes the procedure of disinfection again. Thus, a new session with an initial checking of the availability of selected roles needs to be started here. A special case is *Model 1*, which is the least restrictive within category 2 and neither the status of the session nor any ongoing used permission is affected by unjustified context. This annihilates the effect of any defined location constraints and hence behaves like original RBAC. Thus, sessions are only terminated by the user himself in that case. Within category 3, *Model 8* with $(h_s = pause, h_p = stop)$ is useful, if the result of a used permission is not trustworthy if one of the session's roles was temporarily unavailable due to location constraint violations. Finally, as shown by the discussed examples, the combination of violation handlers needs to be carefully selected by the policy designer as it is highly application specific.

5   Evaluation

The evaluation was conducted in the office environment depicted in Figs. 2 and 3 with feature models based on the underlying building plan. Two types of feature models were defined, bounded and floating feature models. Bounded feature models were inspired by Examples 1 and 3. They model a feature's occurrence with a probability of $p \in [0.5, 1.0]$ within the underlying room and 0 outside of it. Thus, the occurrence of a feature within the underlying room is the most likely case. Additionally, floating feature models were defined based on the idea of Example 2, where the user needs to reach a specific point within a predefined time span. Overall, 40 feature models with random specific points within the depicted rooms were created. The underlying time limits were chosen uniformly distributed from the interval $[3\,s, 15\,s]$. Additionally, 40 bounded feature models were created for the depicted rooms. Overall, 8000 possible location constrained auth–paths were simulated by randomly combining at least 2 feature models. In order to keep the simulated auth–paths satisfiable, in each case one of the rooms from Figs. 2 and 3 was chosen first. Next, a random number of feature models that are defined on that room or that have their specific point in that room were selected. For each simulated auth–path, the single location constraints were all assigned the same value of c_{fp}. Similarly, the value of c_{fn} was the same for each location constraint on that auth–path. The effectiveness of the approach was compared to classical approaches that use point in polygon tests. In order to obtain a polygon for each of the 8000 generated combinations of feature models, in each case a polygon was extracted. This polygon was extracted from the joint feature model where all features are **true**. The boundary of the polygon is the 50 % contour line such that the required features are **true** more likely than 50 % for each point within. Figure 3 shows such a polygon.

As underlying positioning system, SMARTPOS was chosen [10]. It is based on Wi–Fi fingerprinting and uses a kNN approach to estimate the user's position μ and an error estimate Gaussian with a covariance matrix Σ. A radio map of 816 Wi–Fi signal fingerprints was collected for the area depicted in Figs. 2 and 3 along with a large set of test samples to get position estimates. The cost of wrong auth–path (de)activations were recorded for the presented approach and the point in polygon based approaches and put in relation. The expected savings from running the presented approach are depicted in Fig. 6. Clearly, the benefit from running the risk–optimal approach rises with the cost stemming from false decisions. Consequently, the presented approach is especially useful for those policies that have location constraints with very different values for false positive and false negative costs. Also the runtime of both approaches was compared. In detail, the extraction of a 50 % polygon from a feature model was compared to the derivation of all ground truth states' joint feature models. The evaluation was conducted on a Intel Xeon X5650 CPU with 2.67 GHz and 8 GB RAM with Python 2.7.6 and Numpy 1.7.0. The results are shown in Fig. 7. Clearly, the risk–optimality and implied expected savings are at the expense of runtime, which increases exponentially with the number of location constraints on an auth–path. Thus, the risk–based approach is only practical for auth–paths

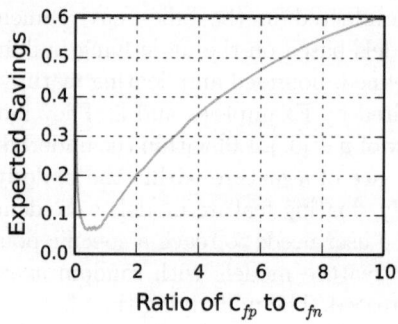

Fig. 6. Expected savings in percent.

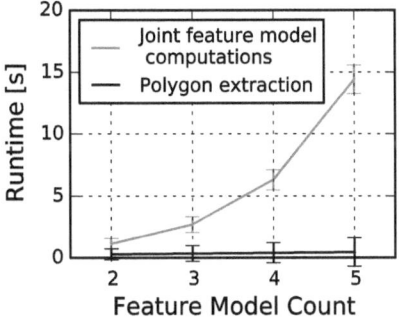

Fig. 7. Runtime for both approaches.

with a very limited number of assigned location constraints. However, most auth–paths in an RBAC policy have a common prefix due to the policy's tree structure. This allows to partially precompute joint feature models for such prefixes. For a final auth–path only the missing features need to be included.

6   Conclusion and Future Work

This paper has presented an approach for location–aware RBAC that restricts the set of available roles based on the user's location. This allows to keep the original authorization semantic of RBAC. The concept is realized by assigning location constraints to policy elements and enforcing them risk–optimal. Loca-tion constraints can be assigned to any RBAC element except permissions and permission assignments. They consist of three parts. A feature model and cost functions for false positives and false negatives. The feature model is highly spe-cific to the RBAC element that a constraint is assigned to. It describes for each location the probability that a feature that is required for enabling this RBAC element is present. For example, such features are the probability to reach an emergency switch within a predefined time span or the fact that a location is on the company's site. The cost functions describe monetary costs occurring from making the constrained element available though the user's location lacks the required feature or vice versa. Position estimates are reported as probability distributions and used to estimate the features that are present at the user's location by integrating it over the feature model. This allows to derive both the risk, i.e., expected cost, of erroneously making the RBAC element available or unavailable respectively. Location constraints are enforced risk–based by taking the least risky choice. However, existing approaches to location–aware RBAC do not account for uncertainty of position estimates and represent them as a point. Further, location constraints in literature are based on polygons to rep-resent authorized zones. Here, point in polygon tests decide about an element's availability instead of taking the least risky choice. The conducted evaluation showed that the presented approach can significantly reduce occurring cost from false authorization decisions. In detail, the expected savings compared to existing approaches were shown to highly depend on the ratio of false positive to false negative costs. This implies, that this approach is most effective if, for example, the false positive cost are high compared to the false negative cost. However, the evaluation also showed that such risk–optimal RBAC is only feasible when a limited number of location constraints is assigned to each auth–path. To conclude, the presented approach is risk–optimal and allows for improved expressiveness of location constraints compared to hitherto used polygons. Furthermore, positioning errors are respected, which is important if those errors are not negligible, like in many realistic scenarios. We argue that the presented approach helps to provide a more reliable and cost efficient foundation for integrating mobile devices in working environments, for example in manufacturing processes. Future work is seen in providing trustworthy location measurements. Also, the user's location demands a risk–optimal interpolation between two reported position estimates.

References

1. Abdunabi, R., Ray, I., France, R.B.: Specification and analysis of access control policies for mobile applications. In: SACMAT, pp. 173–184 (2013)
2. Ardagna, C.A., Cremonini, M., Damiani, E., di Vimercati, S.D.C., Samarati, P.: Supporting location-based conditions in access control policies. In: Proceedings of the 2006 ACM Symposium on Information, Computer and Communications Security, pp. 212–222. ACM (2006)
3. Chen, L., Crampton, J.: On spatio-temporal constraints and inheritance in role-based access control. In: Proceedings of the 2008 ACM Symposium on Information, Computer and Communications Security, pp. 205–216. ACM (2008)
4. Chen, L., Crampton, J.: Risk-aware role-based access control. In: Meadows, C., Fernandez-Gago, C. (eds.) STM 2011. LNCS, vol. 7170, pp. 140–156. Springer, Heidelberg (2012)
5. Covington, M.J., Long, W., Srinivasan, S., Dev, A.K., Ahamad, M., Abowd, G.D.: Securing context-aware applications using environment roles. In: Proceedings of the 6th ACM Symposium on Access control Models and Technologies, pp. 10–20. ACM (2001)
6. Hansen, F., Oleshchuk, V.: Spatial role-based access control model for wireless networks. In: 2003 IEEE 58th Vehicular Technology Conference, VTC 2003-Fall, vol. 3, pp. 2093–2097. IEEE (2003)
7. Krautsevich, L., Lazouski, A., Martinelli, F., Yautsiukhin, A.: Influence of attribute freshness on decision making in usage control. In: Cuellar, J., Lopez, J., Barthe, G., Pretschner, A. (eds.) STM 2010. LNCS, vol. 6710, pp. 35–50. Springer, Heidelberg (2011)
8. Küpper, A.: Location-Based Services: Fundamentals and Operation. Wiley, New York (2005)
9. Marcus, P., Kessel, M., Linnhoff-Popien, C.: Enabling trajectory constraints for usage control policies with backtracking particle filters. In: 3rd International Conference on Mobile Services, Resources, and Users, MOBILITY 2013, pp. 52–58 (2013)
10. Marcus, P., Kessel, M., Werner, M.: Dynamic nearest neighbors and online error estimation for smartpos. Int. J. Adv. Internet Technol. **6**(1 and 2), 1–11 (2013)

11. Ni, Q., Bertino, E., Lobo, J.: Risk-based access control systems built on fuzzy inferences. In: Proceedings of the 5th ACM Symposium on Information, Computer and Communication Security, pp. 250–260. ACM (2010)
12. Oleshchuk, V., et al.: Spatially-aware access control model: a step towards secure and energy-efficient mobile applications. J. Green Eng. 2(2), 125–138 (2012)
13. Park, J., Sandhu, R.: The UCON ABC usage control model. ACM Trans. Inform. Syst. Secur. (TISSEC) 7(1), 128–174 (2004)
14. Ray, I., Toahchoodee, M.: A spatio-temporal role-based access control model. In: Barker, S., Ahn, G.-J. (eds.) Data and Applications Security 2007. LNCS, vol. 4602, pp. 211–226. Springer, Heidelberg (2007)
15. Salim, F., Reid, J., Dawson, E., Dulleck, U.: An approach to access control under uncertainty. In: 2011 6th International Conference on Availability, Reliability and Security (ARES), pp. 1–8. IEEE (2011)
16. Sandhu, R.S., Coyne, E.J., Feinstein, H.L., Youman, C.E.: Role-based access control models. Computer 29(2), 38–47 (1996)
17. Shin, H., Atluri, V.: Spatiotemporal access control enforcement under uncertain location estimates. In: Gudes, E., Vaidya, J. (eds.) Data and Applications Security XXIII. LNCS, vol. 5645, pp. 159–174. Springer, Heidelberg (2009)

Inter-technology Conflict Analysis
for Communication Protection Policies

Cataldo Basile, Daniele Canavese, Antonio Lioy, and Fulvio Valenza[✉]

Dip. di Automatica E Informatica, Politecnico di Torino, Turin, Italy
{cataldo.basile,daniele.canavese,antonio.lioy,fulvio.valenza}@polito.it

Abstract. Usually network administrators implement a protection policy by refining a set of (abstract) communication security requirements into configuration settings for the security controls that will provide the required protection. The refinement consists in evaluating the available technologies that can enforce the policy at node and network level, selecting the most suitable ones, and possibly making fine adjustments, like aggregating several individual channels into a single tunnel. The refinement process is a sensitive task which can lead to incorrect or suboptimal implementations, that in turn affect the overall security, decrease the network throughput and increase the maintenance costs. In literature, several techniques exist that can be used to identify anomalies (i.e. potential incompatibilities and redundancies among policy implementations. However, these techniques usually focus only on a single security technology (e.g. IPsec) and overlook the effects of multiple overlapping protection techniques. This paper presents a novel classification of communication protection policy anomalies and a formal model which is able to detect anomalies among policy implementations relying on technologies that work at different network layers. The result of our analysis allows administrators to have a precise insight on the various alternative implementations, their relations and the possibility of resolving anomalies, thus increasing the overall security and performance of a network.

1   Introduction

Nowadays, computers have a pervasive presence in all our dailyactivities. The current technological trend is to reduce the human intervention and provide human beings with precise information that can be used for decision-making purposes. This is particularly important in areas where human lives, high economic costs and security in general are at stake. The final target is to lessen the human fallibility.

Protecting a networked IT infrastructure, guaranteeing user privacy, and securing communications are important facets of this technological evolution. For a human being is very difficult (if not actually impossible) to envision the whole configuration of large networked systems and implement it without errors and with an adequate amount of protection. As several studies have proven, the human factor is the main cause of misconfigurations [1,2]. To this purpose,

J. Lopez et al. (Eds.): CRiSIS 2014, LNCS 8924, pp. 148–163, 2015.
DOI: 10.1007/978-3-319-17127-2_10

a number of (semi-)automatic tools and techniques have been proposed. For instance, the policy-based network management paradigm proposes to define the security requirements by means of a set of business-level "statements" (the policy), that are later manually or semi-automatically refined into low-level configurations for the available security controls.

Communication protection policies are used to specify how to protect the network communications. Their correct deployment is crucial in several areas, such as protection of intellectual properties, and confidentiality of financial or corporate data (like credit card numbers). The specification of communication protection policies simply requires the definition of the communication end-points to protect (with minimal or no clues about the path in between), seldom the security properties to ensure (e.g. confidentiality and data integrity), and, seldom if ever, hints about the technology to adopt. Therefore, the refinement of communication protection policies is challenging since an administrator, or a tool mimicking his behaviour, must automatically infer and choose several technical details among several alternatives, such as the security protocol (e.g. SSL/TLS, SSH or S-FTP), the cipher-suite, the timeouts, and so on. To make the refinement easier to implement and manage, the transformation towards the low-level configurations is frequently split in several steps which make use of a series of intermediate representations of the policies that are enriched with new technical data at each step.

For instance, by adding to communication protection policies the type of protection (message or channel), the ISO/OSI layer where the protection must be implemented, the technology to use (e.g. IPsec VPN or TLS) and the security properties to enforce (such as header integrity, payload integrity, confidentiality), we obtain a middle-level policy representation. In this paper we will call this representation a *policy implementation*, or *PI*. Refining a set of PIs can lead to incompatibilities and redundancies, named *anomalies*, that cannot be detected at the upper layers, but are best noticed at the policy implementation level. Anomalies appear during the refinement due to several factors. First, the introduction of new technological parameters can produce overlapping or redundant PIs. Secondly, since the refinement is usually performed iteratively, one communication protection policy at the time, interactions between policy implementations are not known a-priori and can only be resolved a-posteriori.

In this paper, we propose a novel approach which is able to detect a number of anomalies between PIs taking into account the interactions between several technologies and security properties. Our model uses a set of FOL (first order logic) axioms which guarantee accurate results and performances. In literature a number of works on policy and configuration anomaly detection exists. Several notable works in this area are due to Al-Shaer, which proposed a model and a taxonomy of conflicts on low-level configurations for communication protections, with a particular focus on the IPsec protocol [3,4]. Another interesting work is by Li et al. [5]: it classifies the IPsec rules in access control lists and encryption lists. Most of the literature, however, focuses only on a single communication protection technology, thus lacking a way to classify and detect inter-technologies conflicts.

Our contribution to the state-of-the-art is three-fold:

- our model allows the detection of a number of anomalies arising from the interactions between various protocols (e.g. TLS and SSH), security properties and communication scenarios such as end-to-end connections, VPNs and remote access communications (see RFC-3457 [6]). We take into account both communication end-points (i.e. source and destination), but also tunnel terminators/gateways for a more accurate detection. To the best of our knowledge this is the first work that detects and classifies communication inter-technology policy anomalies;
- our model allows the detection of anomalies at different ISO/OSI layers, i.e. conflicts involving IP addresses, ports and URIs (e.g. for web services). Our approach internally represents every network device as a tree containing various "entities", able to establish or terminate secure communications, which live at different ISO/OSI levels. Our hierarchical view of networks and network nodes improves on existing works, which often only rely on a flat IP address-based representation of an IT infrastructure;
- we provides the administrators an effective reporting of the anomalies. Having built our model on a FOL family, we can use all its well-known equivalences and logical properties. For instance, we use an easy-to-read multi-graph representation to show the administrators the relationships between the anomalous implementations.

This paper is structured as follows. Section 2 provides an example which we use to introduce our model. Section 3 detail our mathematical model, the anomaly classification, and the axioms for detecting them. Section 4 describes our implementation using ontological techniques and the graphical notations for reporting the anomalies. Finally, Sects. 5 and 6 discuss the related works and the conclusions on our approach.

2 A Motivating Example

In this section we present an example which will be used to informally introduce the concepts of our model. We will use as a reference the simplified network scenario depicted in Fig. 1.

Figure 1 shows two subnets connected through an insecure area. The subnet C, on the left, consists of a number of administrative assistants have their own workstations and use their clients to connect to the subnet S, on the right, where several company servers are deployed. The server S_1 provides two services, a web service, where the administrative assistants in C can access a number of administrative functions, and the company database, containing the data about the employed, which the administrative assistants can query via a stand-alone client. Figure 2 presents the 'internals' of the S_1 server using a tree-like notation that emphasizes the different ISO/OSI levels involved. The node labeled 'S_1' aggregates all the lowest levels and plays the role of a placeholder for all the communications to and from S_1. The node 's_1^3', lying below, represents the network

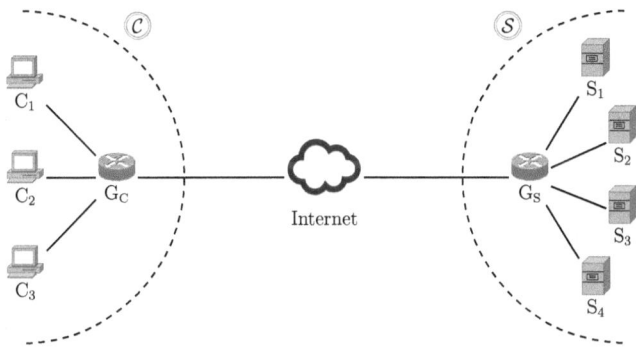

Fig. 1. A simplified network scenario.

layer (ISO/OSI level 3), where techniques are available to enforce network level channel protection (e.g. IPsec). This node forks in two branches, corresponding to two open ports, the port 3306 where the company database is waiting for requests, and the port 8080 where the administrative web service is available. These nodes are respectively labeled 's_{1a}^4' and 's_{1b}^4' and are both at the transport layer (ISO/OSI level 4), where channel techniques are available to enforce the traffic protection (e.g. TLS/SSL and SSH)[1]. Finally, we have the node labeled with 's_{1b}^7' at the application level (ISO/OSI level 7), where a message protection protocol can be chosen to secure the communication (e.g. WS-Security).

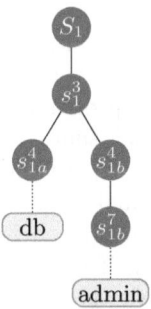

Fig. 2. Graphical representation of the S_1 node structure.

Let us consider the case where two high-level policies need to be refined and implemented. The policy p_1 states "users with the administrative assistant role must securely access the administration web service", and p_2 states "users with

---

[1] It is possible to debate about TLS and SSH being protocols that work at transport or session layer and if SSH is actually a general purpose channel protection protocol. We avoid to enter this discussion as both techniques, from our (practical) point of view, can be used to protect all the communications regarding a given port.

the administrative assistant role must securely access the company database". Even in this minimalistic network scenario, there are many different ways to enforce these policies. For instance, by just considering the administrative assistant working on the client C_1, there are the following alternative implementations for p_1:

- $i_{1,1}$ establishes a secure end-to-end channel between C_1 and s_1^3 at level 3 of the ISO/OSI stack with IPsec;
- $i_{1,2}$ creates a secure end-to-end channel between C_1 and s_{1b}^4 at level 4 with TLS;
- $i_{1,3}$ applies a message protection technique at level 7 to secure the messages exchanged between C_1 and s_{1b}^7 (e.g. by using WS-Security);
- $i_{1,4}$ uses a secure tunnel between G_C and G_S at layer 3 of the ISO/OSI stack, with IPsec in tunnel model, to protect the communications between C_1 and S_1;

For the policy p_2, instead, we have the following PIs:

- $i_{2,1}$ establishes a secure end-to-end channel between C_1 and s_1^3 at layer 3 of the ISO/OSI stack with IPsec;
- $i_{2,2}$ makes use of a secure end-to-end channel between C_1 and s_{1a} at level 4 with SSH;
- $i_{2,3}$ uses a secure tunnel between G_C and G_S at layer 3 of the ISO/OSI stack, with IPsec in tunnel model, to protect the communications between C_1 and S_1.

Furthermore, both p_1 and p_2 can be simultaneously enforced by establishing a single secure tunnel between G_C and G_S that protects the entire communications between the subnets C and S. We will name this policy implementation $i_{C,S}$.

These PIs present some peculiar properties. For instance, $i_{1,1}$ and $i_{2,1}$ require the enforcement of the same channel, that can be used to protect the communication towards both the services of S_1. In this case, $i_{1,1}$ and $i_{2,1}$ are *equivalent* implementations, the simplest anomaly type.

On the other hand, the implementation $i_{1,1}$ "protects more than" $i_{1,2}$, $i_{1,3}$ and $i_{2,2}$. Given the network stack, if the communications between two nodes are protected at layer 3, also all the layer 4 communications are protected. In this case, we have another type of anomaly, the *inclusion*. Inclusion anomalies have however a much broader spectrum. For example, we have also an inclusion if two PIs share the same end-points, but one implementation requires more security properties than the other (e.g. confidentiality and integrity instead of confidentiality only).

Another kind of anomaly we classified is the *affinity*, which indicates that two PIs share some common aspects, but none of the involved implementation includes the other. For instance, we have an affinity anomaly if two PIs have the two sources/destinations on the same node and/or if they impose 'disjoint' security properties (e.g., confidentiality only vs. data integrity only), like for $i_{1,2}$ and $i_{2,2}$. It is worth noting that affine PIs have an interesting property. There exists another "more general" PI that can substitute both the affine implementation, e.g., in the previous case $i_{1,1}$ can substitute both $i_{1,2}$ and $i_{2,2}$.

Another anomaly that we have identified is the *alternative* anomaly, that arises when two PIs have the same end-points but the in-between path is different. For instance, $i_{C,S}$ is an alternative to both $i_{1,1}$ and $i_{2,1}$[2].

In addition to the previously mentioned anomalies, involving PI pairs, we categorize another set of anomalies concerning only one policy implementation[3]:

- a PI is *inadequate* , if the secure communication does respects a set of minimum requirements defined by the administrators. For instance, if the minimum requirement is 'all the data transfers must be encrypted', the implementation $i_{1,4}$ is inadequate since the traffic inside the subnets C and S is sent in the clear;
- a PI is *filtered* if a secure communication is truncated by some filtering device[4];
- a PI is *irrelevant* if its removal does not alter the semantic of the network. For instance, a policy implementation with the same source and destination is irrelevant.

3   Policy Implementation Analysis and Resolution

In this section, we formally define our mathematical model. First, we give the definition of policy implementation, then we introduce our taxonomy of conflicts and finally we discuss the logical axioms needed to identify and resolve such anomalies.

3.1   Formal Definition of Policy Implementation

In our model, a policy implementation i is:

$$i = (s, d, t, c^h, c^p, c^c, G)$$

The symbols s and d respectively represent the PI source and destination. The symbol t specifies the adopted technology. In our analysis we will consider five technologies: IPsec, TLS, SSH, WS-Security and NULL. The NULL technology indicates that a communication should be created without any kind of protection. Our model is however extensible to other technologies, especially at application layer. The fields c^h, c^p and c^c are three Boolean values that indicate a required security property. They respectively denote the header integrity, payload integrity and confidentiality. If the chosen technology is NULL, obviously all

---

[2] To be more precise, from the security point of view, $i_{C,S}$ can be considered equivalent to $i_{1,1}$ and $i_{2,1}$ only if both the subnets are considered trusted.

[3] An well designed automatic refinement would never introduce these anomalies, but detecting them is nevertheless useful in case of manual refinement.

[4] Technically a filtered PI is an anomaly between a communication protection PI and a filtering PI, but in this paper we are only interested in communication protection policies.

these properties are false. The latest symbol $G = (g_1, \ldots, g_n)$ is an ordered list of gateway nodes. This information is particularly useful when analyzing site-to-site or remote access communications. In an end-to-end connection obviously $G = \varnothing$.

For an accurate detection, we need to precisely identify the layer in the ISO/OSI stack where a communication starts and terminates. To this purpose, we defined a hierarchical structure (a tree) that describes the points where the secure communications can be established for each network node (see Fig. 2). The root node represents the whole network node, while the other tree nodes model the available 'connection points' in the TCP/IP stack, that is, network, transport and application layers. These tree nodes may optionally be associated to IP addresses, ports and URIs.

We defined a set of relationships between the 'connection points', that are the network elements that play the role of source and destinations in a PI. Given two elements e_1 and e_2, we have:

– *equivalence* between e_1 and e_2, if they are exactly the same element. We denote this condition with $e_1 = e_2$;
– *dominance* of e_1 over e_2, if all the communications starting from/arriving to e_2 pass through e_1. We denote this condition with $e_1 \succ e_2$. This concept is useful when dealing with protocols working at different layers. For instance, an entity at layer 3 dominates all the transport and application nodes beneath it;
– *disjointness* between e_1 and e_2, if e_1 and e_2 belong to different network nodes. We denote this condition with $e_1 \perp e_2$. Note that if e_1 and e_2 are on the same device we will write $e_1 \not\perp e_2$ (that is they are not disjoint).

In a similar way to the network elements, we can define a number of relationships amongst the technologies. Given two technologies t_1 and t_2, we have:

– *equivalence* between t_1 and t_2, if they are exactly the same technology. We denote this condition with $t_1 = t_2$;
– *dominance* of t_1 over t_2, if the ISO/OSI layer of t_1 is strictly less than the layer of t_2. We denote this condition with $t_1 \succ t_2$. Obviously, NULL is dominated by all the other technologies;
– *disjointness* between t_1 and t_2, if t_1 and t_2 work at the same ISO/OSI layer and $t_1 \neq t_2$. We denote this condition with $t_1 \perp t_2$.

For the subset of technologies that we considered in this paper, the following relations hold:

$$\text{IPsec} \succ \text{TLS} \succ \text{WS-Security} \succ \text{NULL}$$
$$\text{IPsec} \succ \text{SSH} \succ \text{WS-Security} \succ \text{NULL}$$
$$\text{SSH} \perp \text{TLS}$$

Given two properties c_1^x and c_2^x (in the same field $x = \{h, p, c\}$), we have:

– *equivalence* between c_1^x and c_2^x, if they have the same value. We denote this condition with $c_1^x = c_2^x$;
– *dominance* of c_1^x over c_2^x, if $c_1^x = true$ and $c_2^x = false$. We denote this condition with $c_1^x \succ c_2^x$.

Finally, given two lists of gateway nodes G_1 and G_2, we have:

– *equivalence* between G_1 and G_2, if they have the same gateways in the same order. We denote this condition with $G_1 = G_2$;
– *disjointness* between G_1 and G_2, if they have at least one ordered couple of gateways not in common. For instance (gw_1, gw_2, gw_3) and (gw_1, gw_3, gw_2) are disjoint. We denote this condition with $G_1 \perp G_2$.

3.2 Algebraic Representation of Anomalies

Having now at our disposal a formal definition of a policy implementation, we can formalize, from an algebraic point of view, the anomalies that may occur between two PIs and the anomalies in the specification of a single PI.

Figure 3 presents the proposed taxonomy of the anomalies. In the following sections we will give both the axioms to detect such conflicts and a relative resolution strategy.

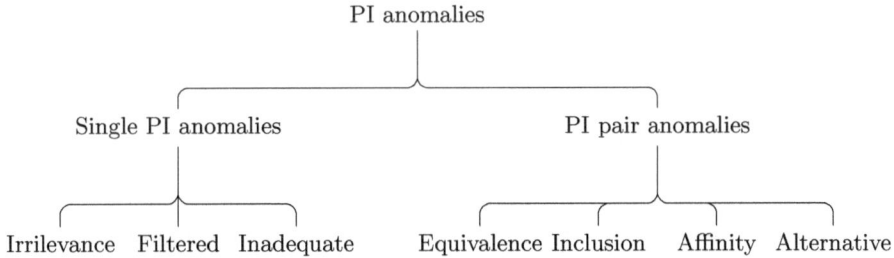

Fig. 3. The proposed taxonomy of anomalies.

Single PI Anomalies. A single PI anomaly occurs within a policy implementation itself. Given a policy implementation $i = (s, d, t, c^h, c^p, c^c, G)$, we have identified three kind of anomalies in this category.

A PI is *irrelevant* when the network behaviour remains unaltered if the PI is removed. These anomalies can be inferred using the axiom:

$$s \not\perp d$$

that identifies implementations such that the source and the destination lays on the same node, thus creating a sort of loop. The proposed resolution is to delete i.

A PI is *filtered* when there exists at least a filtering device in the network path that contains a filtering rule f that discards the traffic related to the policy implementation. Given an oracle-like function $\mathcal{F}(i)$, which returns true if the traffic related to i is discarded and false otherwise, we can identify this anomalies using the formula:

$$\mathcal{F}(i) = true$$

In practice, the output of this oracle-like function can be populated by means of a network reachability analysis [7]. This anomaly is the evidence of a number of severe errors in the policy definitions that can have dangerous repercussions on the security and connectivity of the network. In order to remove the anomaly, the administrator can choose to remove the PI or the filtering rule f.

A PI is *inadequate* when its security properties establish a security level lower than an acceptable threshold. Given an oracle-like function $\mathcal{C}(i)$ which returns true when the policy implementation i is considered protected and false otherwise, we can detect these anomalies with the trivial equation:

$$\mathcal{C}(i) = true$$

The oracle is a function that checks the security requirements defined a priori by the network administrators. For example an network administrator could define an oracle establishing that all the communications coming from and destined to the Internet must be confidential, while the internal communication could respect just the data integrity property.

The simplest way to implement the function $\mathcal{C}$ in practice is to define a triple $(\tilde{c}^h, \tilde{c}^p, \tilde{c}^c)$ defining the minimum security levels, so that:

$$\mathcal{C}(i) = \begin{cases} true & \text{if } c^h \succeq \tilde{c}^h \wedge c^p \succeq \tilde{c}^p \wedge c^c \succeq \tilde{c}^c \\ false & \text{otherwise} \end{cases}$$

To solve these anomalies the security properties of the policy implementation must be modified accordingly, for instance by setting to true the properties than are required to be true by the triple $(\tilde{c}^h, \tilde{c}^p, \tilde{c}^c)$.

PI Pair Anomalies. Given two PIs $i_1 = (s_1, d_1, t_1, c_1^h, c_1^p, c_1^c, G_1)$ and $i_2 = (s_2, d_2, t_2, c_2^h, c_2^p, c_2^c, G_2)$, our model allows the detection of a number of anomalies.

Two policy implementations i_1 and i_2 are *equivalent*, and we will write $i_1 = i_2$, if they have the same values for all their tuple fields, that is they are equivalent if:

$$s_1 = s_2 \wedge d_1 = d_2 \wedge t_1 = t_2 \wedge c_1^h = c_2^h \wedge c_1^p = c_2^p \wedge c_1^c = c_2^c \wedge G_1 = G_2$$

These anomalies are trivially resolved by removing one of the two PIs.

The policy implementation i_1 *includes* (or dominates) the policy implementation i_2, and we will write $i_1 \succ i_2$, if $G_1 = G_2$ and all the remaining fields of i_1 dominates or are equal to the respective i_2 field, but one that must be strictly dominant. For the sake of brevity, we report only one of the formulas able to detects this anomaly:

$$s_1 \succ s_2 \wedge d_1 \succeq d_2 \wedge t_1 \succeq t_2 \wedge c_1^h \succeq c_2^h \wedge c_1^p \succeq c_2^p \wedge c_1^c \succeq c_2^c \wedge G_1 = G_2$$

Since the protection requirements of i_1 are 'greater' than the i_2 ones, the latter can be safely removed without altering the network semantic. However, an administrator can also choose to keep both the PIs, by following a security in depth approach.

The policy implementation i_1 is *affine* with the policy implementation i_2, and we will write $i_1 \not\perp i_2$, if:

$$(s_1 \not\perp s_2 \wedge d_1 \not\perp d_2 \wedge t_1 \not\perp t_2 \wedge G_1 = G_2) \wedge (i_1 \not\succeq i_2 \wedge i_2 \not\succeq i_1)$$

In short, we have an affinity when the two PIs are incomparable (i.e. neither dominant nor equivalent), the sources and destinations are on the same network node, and use technologies at different ISO/OSI layers. In order to solve these anomalies, i_1 and i_2 can be replaced with the least upper bound policy, that is, a new policy implementation $i_3 = (s_3, d_3, t_3, c_3^h, c_3^p, c_3^c, G_3)$ with the following fields:

- s_3 is the least upper bound of s_1 and s_2 in the network node tree, that is, $s_3 \succeq s_1$ and $s_3 \succeq s_2$ (see Fig. 2);
- d_3 is the least upper bound of d_1 and d_2 in the network node tree, that is, $d_3 \succeq d_1$ and $d_3 \succeq d_2$;
- t_3 is the least upper bound technology between t_1 and t_2, that is, $t_3 \succeq t_1$ and $t_3 \succeq t_2$;
- $c_3^h = c_1^h \vee v_2^h$, $c_3^p = c_1^p \vee v_2^p$ and $c_3^c = c_1^c \vee v_2^c$;
- $G_3 = G_1 = G_2$.

The policy implementation i_1 is an *alternative* to the policy implementation i_2 if all the fields of i_1 are equal to the fields of i_2, but $G_1 \perp G_2$, that is:

$$s_1 = s_2 \wedge d_1 = d_2 \wedge t_1 = t_2 \wedge c_1^h = c_2^h \wedge c_1^p = c_2^p \wedge c_1^c = c_2^c \wedge G_1 \perp G_2$$

Two alternative PIs offers the same protection for the same end-points, but uses different communication paths, so that only one of them is really needed.

4   Implementation

In Sect. 3 we discussed our model and provided a set of FOL axioms which can be effectively used to detect the anomalies we identified. However, other equivalent representations are more usable and efficient, due to the availability of logical engines and other support tools.

We implemented the model presented in this paper as a set of Eclipse bundles in Java[5]. The plug-ins were developed during the PoSecCo FP7 project[6]. We tested our tool in two different scenarios:

---

[5] http://security.polito.it/posecco/sdss/.
[6] http://www.posecco.eu/.

- a small network with 18 nodes, 9 subnets, 5 gateways and 34 PIs;
- a medium-sized network with 37 nodes, 8 subnets, 7 gateways and 47 PIs.

We observed that, in the first case, the number of PI pair anomalies were 27: 9 inclusions, 4 alternatives and 14 affinities. While in the second case, are 52: 2 equivalences, 11 inclusions, 8 alternatives and 31 affinities. Taking into account that the number of conflicts varies mainly according to the network configuration chosen by the administrators. In both the cases the tool execution time was less than a second, proving that our model can be effectively used to analyse several kind of IT infrastructures.

In the following sections, we will discuss the implementation of our model using Horn clauses using the SWRL language and we will show a graph-based representation of the PI anomalies that can be helpful for the administrators to quickly identify such conflicts.

4.1   Anomaly Conditions as Horn Clauses

Horn clauses are axioms defined as a disjunction of literals (clauses) with at most one positive literal, that is:

$$\neg C_1 \vee \neg C_2 \vee \cdots \vee \neg C_n \vee A$$

They can also be expressed in a more natural way as a set of positive conditions implying an assertion, that is:

$$C_1 \wedge C_2 \wedge \cdots \wedge C_n \Rightarrow A$$

These clauses can be effectively used to represent all the axioms used in our model. Horn clauses are frequently encountered in model theory because they exhibit a simple and natural rule-like form. Horn clauses can be then easily translated in many different logic programming languages, such as Prolog, or generic programming language such as C or Java.

For instance, the Horn clause form of the equivalence anomaly is:

$$(s_1 = s_2) \wedge (d_1 = d_2) \wedge (t_1 = t_2) \wedge (c_1^h = c_2^h) \wedge$$
$$(c_1^p = c_2^p) \wedge (c_1^c = c_2^c) \wedge (G_1 = G_2) \Rightarrow (i_1 = i_2)$$

We implemented these axioms in an ontology, that naturally offers a hierarchical representation coupled with powerful inferential capabilities. We developed an ontology based on OWL 2 [8] and SWRL [9], which allows the specification of Horn-like rules that guarantee the computational soundness of the reasoning. In the ontology, the policy implementations and the network fields are represented as individuals. These individuals are interconnected together through a series of object property assertions that provide the semantic of the relationships between the various network entities such as the belonging of an IP address to a network node. By using a set of ad-hoc SWRL rules we are able to automatically infer the anomalies as a set of property assertions. For example, the snippet in Listing 1.1 contains the SWRL rule for identifying equivalent PIs, by imposing, if needed, the property **equivalence** between two individuals representing a couple of PIs.

Listing 1.1. SWRL rule for detecting equivalent PIs.

```
hasSource(?i1,?s1), hasSource(?i2,?s2), hasDestination(?i1,?d1),
hasDestination(?i2,?d2), hasTechnology(?i1,?t1), hasTechnology(?i2,?t2),
hasHeaderIntegrity(?i1,?h1), hasHeaderIntegrity(?i2,?h2),
hasPayloadIntegrity(?i1,?p1), hasPayloadIntegrity(?i2,?p2),
hasConfidentiality(?i1,?c1), hasConfidentiality(?i2,?c2),
hasGw(?i1,?g1), hasGw(?i2,?g2), SameAs(?s1,?s2), SameAs(?d1,?d2),
SameAs(?t1,?t2), SameAs(?h1,?h2), SameAs (?p1,?p2), SameAs(?c1,?c2),
SameAs(?g1,?g2) -> isequivalence(?i1,?i2)
```

4.2   Graph-Based Representation of Anomalies

In Sect. 2 we informally presented our hierarchical view of a network node (see also Fig. 2). By using such artifacts, we can depict a protected communication by the means of a multi-graph. The advantage of such graphical representation is that allows a network administrator to identify a series of anomalies in a more intuitive and natural way.

Our multi-graph representation includes a bush of network node trees which represent all the communication endpoints at network level and all the available gateways. Policy implementations are represented as paths that join together two vertices, that is, the source and the destination of the policy implementation. End-to-end communications are represented as a single edge path, on the other hand, tunnels require more edges to represent the communications to and from the gateways. To increase the graphical expressiveness, we also label each edge with the remaining policy implementation parameters, i.e. the technology and the security properties triple (with the trivial association f=false, and t=true).

With this graphical notation, PI pair anomalies are noticed by the presence of multiple paths between sources and destinations, while single PI anomalies can be noticed on the single edge.

We show here the graphical representation of two PI anomalies, namely an inclusion and an alternative conflicts taken from the simplified network scenario introduced in Sect. 2. Figure 4 shows the anomaly between $i_{1,1}$ and $i_{1,3}$. The first policy implementation $i_{1,1}$ is using a level 3 protection protocol without tunnels (e.g. IPsec via transport mode) while $i_{1,3}$ is another end-to-end connection but at application level (e.g. WS-Security). The multi-graph clearly shows that $i_{1,1}$ includes $i_{1,3}$, as there are two paths from the administrative assistant browser and the administrative web service and $i_{1,1}$ is at layer 3.

Figure 5 depicts the alternative anomaly between $i_{c,s}$ and $i_{2,1}$. We recall that an alternative anomaly is a state where two policy implementations connects the same two entities, but use different network paths. In this case we have an end-to-end connection offered by $i_{2,1}$ and a site-to-site (VPN) communication given by $i_{c,s}$.

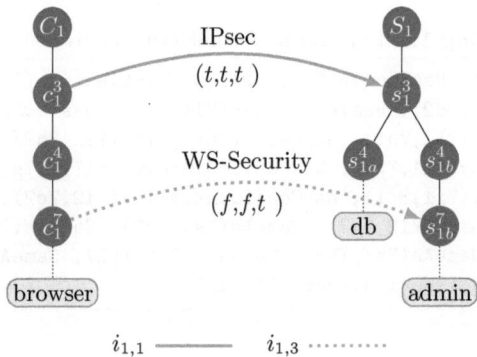

Fig. 4. Graphical representation of the anomaly $i_{1,1} \succ i_{1,3}$.

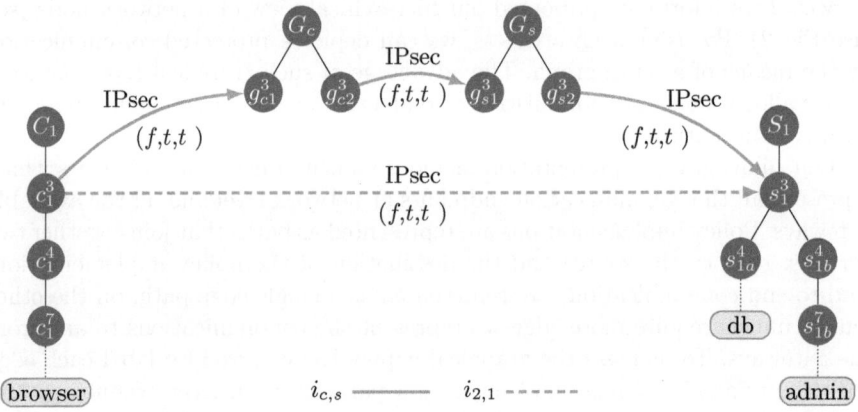

Fig. 5. Graphical representation of the anomaly $i_{c,s} \perp i_{2,1}$.

5 Related Works

Conflict analysis, detection and resolution in policy-based systems and security controls is a hot topic and the current literature offers several notable works that we will briefly discuss in the following lines.

One of the most prominent works in this area is due to Al-Shaer et al., which address the analysis of filtering configurations [10], and take into account the effect of IPsec rules on a network protection [4], by proposing a number of ad-hoc algorithms and axioms. The same authors also describe a classification system for conflicts between filtering and communication protection policies in [3]. Furthermore, a common idea, initially introduced by Zao in [11], is to combine conditions that belong to to different IPSec fields. This was the basis used also in [12], where Fu et al. described a number of conflicts between IPSec tunnels, through a simulation process that reports any violation of the security requirements. Another interesting paper is [5], due to Li et al., where the authors classified the IPSec rules in two classes: access control lists (ACL) and encryption lists (EL). All these works treat only a single technology (IPsec), ignoring the possible interaction with other data communication protocols. Our model instead is able not only to detect single-technology anomalies, but also errors that can arise when deploying a multi-technology policy set.

Network configuration/policy anomaly detection is not only restricted to communication protection technologies. In literature a rich collection of papers about filtering policy analysis is also available. Although these works are not directly related to the approach presented in this paper, they can be very useful as a general background on network conflict analysis. In the following paragraphs we present a brief selection of several relevant works in this field.

Basile et al. describe a geometric representation, detection and resolution of filtering configurations, based on the intersection of hyper-rectangles [13]. Authors extended the work performed by Al-Shaer by introducing the anomalies between more than two rules and by showing how to transform a policy representation in another form that preserves its semantic. Similarly, Hu et al. in [14] suggested to split the five-tuple decision spaces of packet filtering rules into disjoint hyper-rectangles, where the conflicts are resolved using a combination of automatic strategies.

A thoroughly different approach for detecting conflicts between a set of filtering configurations is proposed by Hu et al., who introduced an ontology-based anomaly management framework [15], and by Bandara et al., who use logic reasoning, thus obtaining excellent performances [16].

Alfaro et al. presented a collection of algorithms to remove a series of anomalies between packet filter configurations and NIDS in distributed systems [17]. This techniques were more recently implemented in the MIRAGE tool [18].

With respect to policy conflict schemas for filtering rules, some interesting works also exists. Thanasegaran et al. show how to transform the configuration rules in bit vectors in order to have a very efficient analysis [19], while Ferraresi et al. extend al-Shaer's work and provide an automatic algorithm to resolve the anomalies [20].

6 Conclusions and Future Work

In this paper we proposed a novel taxonomy of anomalies for communication protection policies and an algebraic model which is able to detect such anomalies. The proposed model can be used to detect incompatibilities and redundancies between policy implementations that use security technologies working at different ISO/OSI layers.

Our model has been implemented using Horn clauses and ontological techniques and it can be also easily represented as a multi-graph, thus providing the administrators with a more intuitive way to identify the anomalies. Indeed, the model can be used as a tool to assist administrators when implementing communication protection policies. Moreover, since the model provides a number of hints about conflict resolution for each of the identified anomalies, our tool can be used to support automatic policy refinement.

For the future, we plan to extend the expressivity and capabilities of our model by taking into account also the adopted/supported cipher-suites and the actual paths walked by packets/messages in the network. The extended model will be able to take into account several new problems, such as channel overlapping misconfigurations (for VPN tunnels), potential information leakage and non-enforceable policy implementations.

Acknowledgement. The research described in this paper is part of the SECURED project, co-funded by the European Commission under the ICT theme of FP7 (grant agreement no. 611458).

References

1. Wool, A.: Trends in firewall configuration errors: measuring the holes in swiss cheese. IEEE Internet Comput. **14**(4), 58–65 (2010)
2. Center for Strategic and International Studies: Securing cyberspace for the 44th presidency. Technical report, December 2008
3. Hamed, H., Al-Shaer, E.: Taxonomy of conflicts in network security policies. IEEE Commun. Mag. **44**(3), 134–141 (2006)
4. Hamed, H., Al-Shaer, E., Marrero, W.: Modeling and verification of IPsec and vpn security policies. In: 13th IEEE International Conference on Network Protocols, ICNP 2005, pp. 259–278. IEEE Computer Society, November 2005
5. Li, Z., Cui, X., Chen, L.: Analysis and classification of IPsec security policy conflicts. In: Japan-China Joint Workshop on Frontier of Computer Science and Technology, FCST 2006, pp. 83–88. IEEE Computer Society, November 2006
6. Kelly, S., Ramamoorthi, S.: Requirements for IPsec Remote Access Scenarios. RFC 3457, January 2003
7. Khakpour, A., Liu, A.X.: Quarnet: a tool for quantifying static network reachability. IEEE/ACM Trans. Netw. **21**(2), 551–565 (2009)
8. Group, W.O.W.: OWL 2 web ontology language document overview. Technical report, October 2009. http://www.w3.org/TR/2009/REC-owl2-overview-20091027/
9. W3C: SWRL: A Semantic Web Rule Language Combining OWL and RuleML. Technical report, World Wide Web Consortium, May 2004
10. Al-Shaer, E., Hamed, H., Boutaba, R., Hasan, M.: Conflict classification and analysis of distributed firewall policies. IEEE J. Sel. Areas Commun. **23**(10), 2069–2084 (2006)
11. Zao, J.: Semantic model for IPsec policy interaction. Technical report, Internet Draft, March 2000
12. Fu, Z., Wu, S.F., Huang, H., Loh, K., Gong, F., Baldine, I., Xu, C.: IPSec/VPN security policy: correctness, conflict detection, and resolution. In: Sloman, M., Lobo, J., Lupu, E.C. (eds.) POLICY 2001. LNCS, vol. 1995, p. 39. Springer, Heidelberg (2001)
13. Basile, C., Cappadonia, A., Lioy, A.: Network-level access control policy analysis and transformation. IEEE/ACM Trans. Netw. **20**(4), 985–998 (2012)
14. Hu, H., Ahn, G.J., Kulkarni, K.: Detecting and resolving firewall policy anomalies. IEEE Trans. Dependable Secure Comput. **9**(3), 318–331 (2012)

15. Hu, H., Ahn, G.J., Kulkarni, K.: Ontology-based policy anomaly management for autonomic computing. In: 7th International Conference on Collaborative Computing: Networking, Applications and Worksharing. CollaborateCom, IEEE Computer Society, pp. 487–494, October 2011

16. Bandara, A.K., Kakas, A.C., Lupu, E.C., Russo, A.: Using argumentation logic for firewall configuration management. In: Integrated Network Management-Workshops, 2009, IM 2009, pp. 180–187. IEEE Computer Society, June 2009

17. Alfaro, J.G., Boulahia-Cuppens, N., Cuppens, F.: Complete analysis of configuration rules to guarantee reliable network security policies. Int. J. Inf. Secur. **7**(2), 103–122 (2008)

18. Garcia-Alfaro, J., Cuppens, F., Cuppens-Boulahia, N., Preda, S.: MIRAGE: a management tool for the analysis and deployment of network security policies. In: Garcia-Alfaro, J., Navarro-Arribas, G., Cavalli, A., Leneutre, J. (eds.) DPM 2010 and SETOP 2010. LNCS, vol. 6514, pp. 203–215. Springer, Heidelberg (2011)

19. Thanasegaran, S., Yin, Y., Tateiwa, Y., Katayama, Y., Takahashi, N.: A topological approach to detect conflicts in firewall policies. In: IEEE International Symposium on Parallel & Distributed Processing, IPDPS 2009, pp. 1–7. IEEE Computer Society, May 2009

20. Ferraresi, S., Pesic, S., Trazza, L., Baiocchi, A.: Automatic conflict analysis and resolution of traffic filtering policy for firewall and security gateway. In: International Chamber of Commerce, ICC 2007, pp. 1304–1310. IEEE Computer Society, June 2007

Two-Level Automated Approach for Defending Against Obfuscated Zero-Day Attacks

Ratinder Kaur$^{(\boxtimes)}$ and Maninder Singh

Computer Science and Engineering Department, Thapar University,
Patiala 147004, India
{ratinder.kaur,msingh}@thapar.edu

Abstract. A zero-day attack is one that exploits a vulnerability for which no patch is readily available and the developer or vendor may or may not be aware. They are very expensive and powerful attack tools to defend against. Since the vulnerability is not known in advance, there is no reliable way to guard against zero-day attacks before they happen. Attackers take advantage of the unknown nature of zero-day exploits and use them in conjunction with highly sophisticated and targeted attacks to achieve stealthiness with respect to standard intrusion detection techniques. This paper presents a novel combination of anomaly, behavior and signature based techniques for detecting such zero-day attacks. The proposed approach detects obfuscated zero-day attacks with two-level evaluation, generates a new signature automatically and updates other sensors by using push technology via global hotfix feature.

Keywords: Zero-day attacks · Unknown attacks · Obfuscation · Signature generation · Push technology

1 Introduction

Today the Internet has become a pervasive threat vector for various types of organizations. As new technologies are developed and adopted to meet changing business requirements, sneaky sources lie in wait to exploit vulnerabilities exposed. In recent years, zero-day attacks have been dominating the headlines for political and monetary gains. They are being used as essential success vectors in various sophisticated and targeted attacks like Aurora, Advanced Persistent Threat (APT), Stuxnet, Duqu and Flame. Also, the number of such attacks reported each year increases immensely. According to Symantec's Internet Security Threat Report of 2013 [2] there is 42 % increase in targeted attacks in 2012, 31 % of all targeted attacks aimed at businesses and 14 zero-day vulnerabilities were discovered. Another security threat report by Sophos [20] reported that large tech companies like Apple, Facebook, Microsoft, Twitter and others were targeted with same zero-day Java vulnerability that attacks multiple customers. All such facts and figures look terrible and threatening.

A zero-day attack occur during the vulnerability window that exists in the time between when vulnerability is first exploited and when software developers

© Springer International Publishing Switzerland 2015
J. Lopez et al. (Eds.): CRiSIS 2014, LNCS 8924, pp. 164–179, 2015.
DOI: 10.1007/978-3-319-17127-2_11

start to develop a counter to that threat. It is difficult to measure the length of the vulnerability window, as attackers do not announce when the vulnerability was first discovered. Even developers may not want to distribute data for commercial or security reasons or they may not know if the vulnerability is being exploited when they fix it. So the vulnerability may not be recorded as a zero-day attack. The vulnerability window however, can be of several years long. According to an empirical study [1,12], a typical zero-day attack may last for 312 days on average and, after vulnerabilities are disclosed publicly, the volume of attacks exploiting them increases by up to 5 orders of magnitude.

In this paper a two-level automated approach for detecting zero-day attacks is proposed. This paper is an extension of our previous work with more detailed and optimized methodology [21]. It detects obfuscated zero-day attacks with two-level evaluation. At first level the system detects *unknown* by using Honeynet as an anomaly detector and at second level the system *confirms malicious* by analyzing behavior of unknown attack and at last generates new signatures automatically to update other IDS/IPS sensors via global hotfix. The contribution of this paper over our previous approach is three folds: (1) We have optimized our previous algorithms to efficiently extract zero-day attack candidate and to update other IDS/IPS sensors automatically. (2) We have observed an increase of 10 % in detection rate and 1 % decrease in false alarm rate. (3) We have evaluated our system with large datasets of real attacks from various malware repositories.

The remainder of the paper is organized as follows. In Sect. 2, related work is summarized. In Sect. 3, detailed working of the proposed technique is presented. Finally in Sect. 4, experimental evaluation is described with results and paper is concluded.

2 Related Work

To defend against zero-day attacks, the research community has proposed various techniques. These techniques are classified into: statistical-based, signature-based, behavior-based and other techniques [22].

2.1 Statistical-Based

- Supervised Learning [14] is a novel method of employing several data mining techniques to detect and classify zero-day malware based on the frequency of Windows API calls. A machine learning framework is developed using eight different classifiers, namely Nave Bayes (NB) Algorithm, k-Nearest Neighbor (kNN) Algorithm, Sequential Minimal Optimization (SMO) Algorithm with 4 different kernels (SMO-Normalized PolyKernel, SMO-PolyKernel, SMO-Puk, and SMO-Radial Basis Function (RBF)), Backpropagation Neural Networks Algorithm, and J48 decision tree. This system proves to be better than similar signature-free techniques that detect polymorphic malware and unknown malware based on analysis of Windows APIs.

- Contextual Anomaly Detection [15,18] is a contextual misuse and anomaly detection prototype to detect zero-day attacks. The contextual misuse detection utilizes similarity with attack context profiles, and the anomaly detection technique identifies new types of attacks using the One Class Nearest Neighbor (1-NN) algorithm.
- Combined Supervised and Unsupervised Learning [17] technique is presented for zero-day malware detection. It employs machine learning based framework to detect malware using layer 3 and layer 4 network traffic features. It utilizes supervised classification to detect known malware and unsupervised learning to detect new malware and known variants. A tree-based feature transformation is also introduced to overcome data imperfection issues and to detect the malware classes effectively.

2.2   Signature-Based

- SweetBait [6] is a distributed system that is a combination of network intrusion detection and prevention techniques. It employs different types of honeypot sensors, both high-interaction and low-interaction to recognize and capture suspicious traffic. SweetBait automatically generates signatures for random IP address space scanning worms without any prior knowledge. And for the non-scanning worms, Argos is used to do the job. A novel aspect of this signature generation approach is that a forensics shellcode is inserted, replacing malevolent shellcode, to gather useful information about the attack process.
- LISABETH [23] automatically generate signatures for polymorphic worms, Lisabeth uses invariant byte analysis of traffic content, as originally proposed in Polygraph [5] and refined by Hamsa [11]. Lisabeth leverages on the hypothesis that every worm has its invariant set and that an attacker must insert in all worm samples all the invariants bytes. Lisbeth and Hamsa systems are equally sensitive to the suspicious flows pool size but Lisabeth is lesser sensible to innocuous flow pool size than Hamsa. Lisabeth has shown significant improvement over Polygraph and Hamsa in terms of efficiency and noise-tolerance.
- In Honeycyber [3] a "Double-honeynet" is proposed as a new detection method to identify zero-day worms and to isolate the attack traffic from innocuous traffic. It uses unlimited Honeynet outbound connections to capture different payloads in every infection of the same worm. It uses Principal Component Analysis (PCA) to determine the most significant substrings that are shared between polymorphic worm instances to use them as signatures [4].
- ZASMIN [19] a Zero-day Attack Signature Management Infrastructure is an early detection system for novel network attack detection. This system provides early detection function and validation of attack at the moment the attacks start to spread on the network. To detect unknown network attacks, the system adopted new technologies. To filter malicious traffic it uses dispersion of destination IP address, TCP connection trial count, TCP connection success count and stealth scan trial count. Attack validation is done by call function and instruction spectrum analysis. And it generates signatures using content analysis.

- LESG [7] is a network-based automatic worm signature generator that generates length-based signatures for zero day polymorphic worms, which exploits buffer overflow vulnerabilities. The system generates vulnerability-driven signatures at network level without any host level analysis of worm execution or vulnerable programs.

2.3   Behavior-Based

- Network-Level Emulation [8,13] is a heuristic detection method to scan network traffic streams for the presence of previously unknown polymorphic shellcode. Their approach relies on a NIDS-embedded CPU emulator that executes every potential instruction sequence in the inspected traffic, aiming to identify the execution behavior of polymorphic shellcode. The proposed approach is robust to obfuscation techniques like self-modifications and non-self-contained polymorphic shellcodes.
- SGNET [9] is a distributed framework to collect rich information and download malware for zero-day attacks. It automatically generates approximations of the protocol behavior in form of Finite State Machines (FSMs). Whenever the network interaction falls outside the FSM knowledge (newly observed activity), SGNET takes advantage of a real host to continue the network interaction with the attacker. In that case, the honeypot acts as a proxy for the real host. This allows building samples of network conversation for the new activity that are then used to refine the current FSM knowledge.

2.4   Other Hybrid Techniques

- Hybrid Detection for Zero-day Polymorphic Shellcodes (HDPS) [10] is a hybrid detection approach. It uses an elaborate approach to detect NOP Sleds to be robust against polymorphism, metamorphism and other obfuscations. It employs a heuristic method to detect return address, and achieves high efficiency by incorporating Markov Model to detect executable codes. This method filters normal packets with accuracy and low overload. But this approach cannot block shellcodes in network packets and it is hard to obtain transition matrixes of Markov Model.
- Honeyfarm [16] is a hybrid scheme that combines anomaly and signature detection with honeypots. This system takes advantage of existing detection approaches to develop an effective defense against Internet worms. The system works on three levels. At first level signature based detection is used to filter known worm attacks. At second level an anomaly detector is set up to detect any deviation from the normal behavior. In the last level honeypots are deployed to detect zero day attacks. Low interaction honeypots are used to track attacker activities while high interaction honeypots help in analyzing new attacks and vulnerabilities. The controller is responsible to redirect suspicious traffic to respective honeypots which are deployed in honeyfarm.

2.5 Limitations of Existing Techniques

The following limitations of recent studies have been the prime motivation for our research.

- Statistical-based detection techniques cannot be used for instant detection and protection in real time. They are dependent on static attack profiles and requires manual adjustment of detection parameters.
- Signature-based techniques are widely used but, need improvement in generating good quality signatures. They suffer from one or more limitations of high false positives, false negatives, reduced sensitivity and specificity.
- Behavior-based techniques may detect a wide range of novel attacks but they are prone to evasion, computationally expensive and may not effectively capture the context in which the new attacks interact with the real victim machine.
- Other hybrid techniques combine heuristics and different intrusion detection techniques like signature-based, anomaly-based, etc. to detect zero-day attacks but they also suffer from high false positives, false negatives.

3 Proposed Technique

3.1 Architecture

An efficient and novel technique integrating the three main detection techniques (Anomaly, Behavior and Signature based) is proposed to minimize the impact of above identified challenges during zero-day attack detection. It does two-level evaluation to detect and confirm zero-day attack. Figure 1 shows the basic architecture of our proposed approach. It comprises of different components: Router, Port Mirroring Switch, Honeynet, Intrusion Detection and Prevention (IDS/IPS) Sensors, Zero-day Attack Detection (ZAD) System and Global IDS/IPS Hotfix Server. The router connects the entire setup to the Internet. Port mirroring switch passes network traffic simultaneously to both Honeynet and IDS/IPS sensors. Firstly, the network traffic is captured and filtered for known attacks. If the filtered traffic is found suspicious of containing some unknown attack it is evaluated for zero-day attack in the ZAD system and a new signature is generated and updated. Otherwise, if the traffic trace is found benign, whitelist in IDS/IPS sensors is updated.

Honeypots have been found to be effective against zero day threats therefore, Honeynet is used to identify the mechanism of a new attack and to collect evidence for attacker's activity. When a known attack hits Honeynet it is blocked and logged. When a new attack is encountered the network traffic associated with that attack is logged and is redirected to the high-interaction honeypots. The honeypots interact with the attacker and the entire communication is logged. The network logs and honeypot system interaction logs collectively addressed as "Honeynet Trace" or "Unknown Attack Trace" are kept for further analysis. At the same time the IDS/IPS sensor filters known attacks for the same traffic and stores rest of the filtered traffic in an online repository. Then the data

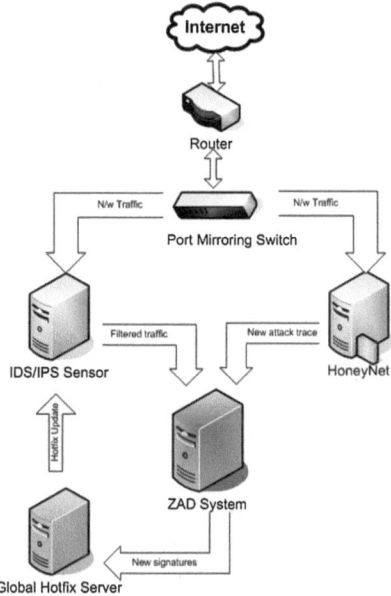

Fig. 1. Basic architecture of proposed approach

collected from both Honeynet and IDS/IPS sensor is compared and analyzed in ZAD. The ZAD system examines if similar unknown attack traces are found in IDS/IPS sensor's filtered traffic or not. If similar attack traces are found, then that is a candidate for zero-day attack undetected by an IDS/IPS sensor. Up to this level, this is assured that there is some malicious traffic which was missed by sensors. This could only happen when the IDS/IPS sensor does not have matching signature for the unknown malicious traffic in its database. After finding the candidate for zero-day attack it is necessary to do further analysis to confirm its malicious intent and to generate a new signature for it.

3.2 Evaluating Zero-Day Attack

The candidate for zero-day attack may result in false positive so it's essential to evaluate it. The evaluation process is used to confirm the malicious intentions of the candidate by analyzing system anomalies in which it is executed. This evaluation is done by ZAD-Analyzer in the ZAD system. Figure 2 depicts the internal process flow of ZAD-Analyzer. More details on each component is discussed in the following sections.

Compare and Extract Unit (CEU): CEU takes input from both Honeynet and IDS/IPS sensors to compare and extract the zero-day attack candidate. For comparison, it uses Rabin-Karp algorithm for string matching [24]. Rabin-Karp algorithm is an easy solution for string matching with linear complexity.

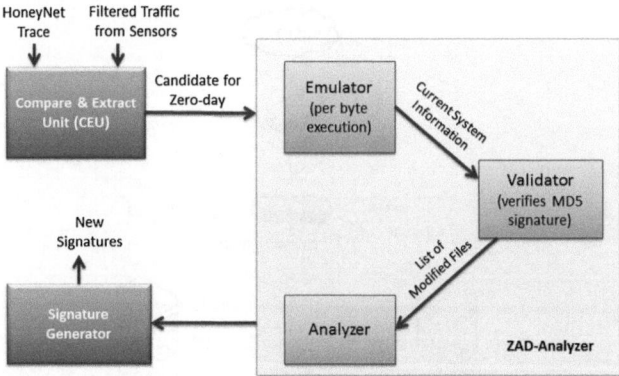

Fig. 2. ZAD-analyzer internal process flow [26]

Consider a new attack pattern captured by Honeynet, *Honeynet-Trace (HT)* of length m and filtered traffic stored by sensors, *Filtered-Traffic (FT)* of length n, where $m << n$. The general principle is that for every m byte of *FT*, the new hash value is calculated and this hash value is compared with the hash value of *HT*. For efficient string matching, the new hash value is computed by using the old hash value, the current byte of *FT*, and the byte of *FT* seen m byte before. The XOR operation $\oplus$ is a suitable function for this purpose. The hash value is calculated as:

$$hash \leftarrow hash \oplus FT[curpos] \oplus FT[curpos - m]$$

where *curpos* is the current position within the *FT*, and m is the length of *HT* to be searched. Using packet bytes directly leads to false positives. Therefore, the current byte is used as an index into a table containing randomly generated 32-bit values. The XOR is then calculated using the derived 32-bit values. Just XORing the 32-bit values is not sufficient to reduce false positives. Thus, along with XOR, Shift operation is also applied to 32-bit values and old hash values. To find all occurrences of *HT* in *FT* an Algorithm 1 is implemented.

Emulator: Figure 3 depicts the working of an emulator. The zero-day attack candidate (attack trace) is input to an emulator for per byte execution. The emulator is the right choice for analyzing decrypted and obfuscated code. Any type of obfuscated code is allowed to execute in its original form. The idea here is to let the code decrypt itself in the memory and do harm to the emulated system. After execution, the interesting part is to log all the changes made to the file system and registry.

The emulator executes attack trace by successively reading its instructions and performing equivalent operations in the emulated environment. After execution of the attack trace the system anomalies are analyzed. The system anomalies help to determine a system's status (whether or not malicious code is present) by comparing the system status information to a standard. For this, the abstract

Algorithm 1. Compare and Extract Algorithm

1: **procedure** *main*()
2:      Initialize DB drivers
3:      Start secure communication with database
4:      **for** iterate over *FT* **do**
5:          Fetch String *FT*[1..*n*] = get...string
6:          **for** iterate over *HT* **do**
7:              Fetch String *HT*[1..*m*] = get...honeynet string
8:              invoke *RabinKarp*(*FT*[1..*n*], *HT*[1..*m*])
9:          **end for**
10:      **end for**
11: **end procedure**
12: **procedure** RABINKARP(*stringFT*[1..*n*], *stringHT*[1..*m*])
13:      **for** *i* from 1 to *n* − *m* + 1 **do**
14:          **if** *hFT* = *hHT* **then**
15:              **if** *FT*[*i*..*i* + *m* − 1] = *HT* **then**
16:                  **return** New attack pattern is found in the filtered traffic at: *i*
17:              **end if**
18:          **end if**
19:          *hFT* := *hash*(*hFT*[*i* + 1..*i* + *m*])
20:      **end for**
21:      **return** No similar attack traces are found.
22: **end procedure**

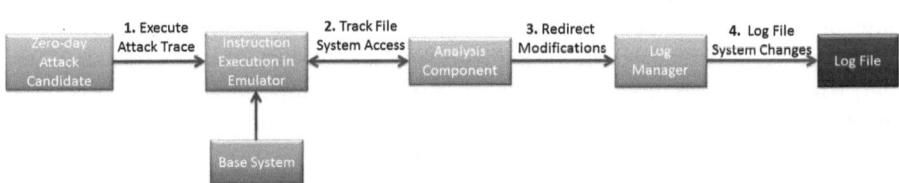

Fig. 3. Working of emulator

method of analyzing system anomalies is used that is validating checksums of critical files. The most critical files include the registry files (in Window's) and the file system (in both Window's and Unix). The file system is a vital storage component and any anomalous executions intended to damage it will likely be detected by monitoring the changes that attempt to alter or damage the file system. Our proposed approach may not be able to detect attacks that alters only runtime memory, while the majority of attacks which do result in changes to the file system will leave a proof of an malicious event. Thus, our analysis is based on the fact that it is not possible to compromise a system without altering a system file. A malicious code can only do one of three things: add, remove or modify files. It can remove system logs. It can add tools such sniffers or viruses for later use. And most important it can change the system in numerous ways like new accounts, modified passwords, tweaked registries, trojaned files etc. During execution of attack trace, the analysis component analyzes file system access in a stealthy manner and redirects all the modifications transparently to a log manager. The basic idea behind this is to keep the original base system image clean so that no reboot is required after every malicious code execution. The log manager generates a log file containing information about the file system changes during the execution of attack trace. This log file is then given to validator for further verification.

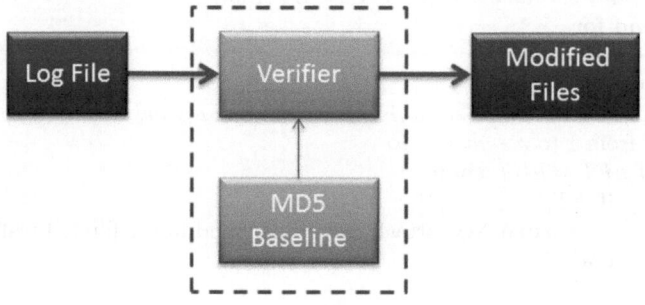

Fig. 4. Validator

Validator: In Fig. 4 the validator compares a log file to a MD5-baseline and results in list of modified files. The validator maintains a MD5-checksum database of the original base system files. After execution of an attack trace the file system gets corrupted and a log file containing file system changes is generated which is then sent to the validator. A critical component known as verifier, accurately recalculates MD5-checksum on logged files and compares them with the MD5-baseline. The MD5 algorithm takes an input of arbitrary length and produces a fixed-length fingerprint, hash, or checksum. As it is computationally infeasible to produce same fingerprint therefore, the MD5-checksum provides a mechanism to verify data integrity. So, when the data within a file is changed, its hash will also change. Such changes to the file system can be categorized into four cases as in Table 1. After comparing with the baseline a "List of Modified Files" is created for the analyzer.

Table 1. Enumeration of possible cases

File exists in:		Interpreted action
Log file	MD5-database	
X		Created
	X	Deleted
X	X'	Altered/Updated
X	X	Read/Accessed

Analyzer: The analyzer receives a "List of Modified Files" from the Validator. It then crosschecks the "List of Modified Files" with the "List of Critical Files" maintained. Critical files for e.g. in Windows can be registry files, startup files, system configuration files, system libraries, system binaries, password files, etc. In case of Linux, critical files are in directories like: /bin, /boot, /etc, /root, /sbin, /tmp, /usr/bin, /usr/etc, /usr/sbin, /var/log, /var/run, /var/spool, /var/tmp. If the critical files are modified, it proves that the candidate is a real zero-day attack. Thus, the system does two-level evaluation for detecting a zero-day attack. First-level (*Detects UnKnown*) where Honeynet flags a new suspicious event and IDS/IPS sensors ignores it. Second-level (*Confirms Malicious*) where MD5 baseline is used to confirm its malicious intentions. This two-level (*Detects Unknown Malicious*) evaluation decreases the false positives to nearly zero. After confirming a zero-day attack, ZAD-Analyzer commands the Signature Generator to generate a signature for the new attack. On the other hand, if no critical file is changed then the candidate is false positive and the Whitelist is updated.

3.3   Signature Generation (SG) and Hotfix Update

After evaluation zero-day attack packets are fed to the next module for signature generation. This module generates a common token-subsequence signature for a set of attack packets by applying the Longest Common Subsequence (LCSeq) algorithm. The algorithm compares two zero-day attack packets to get the longest common subsequence between them. Let two sequences be defined as follows: $X = (x_1, x_2...x_m)$ and $Y = (y_1, y_2...y_n)$. Let $LCSeq(X_i, Y_j)$ represent the set of longest common subsequence of prefixes X_i and Y_j. This set of sequences is given by the following.

$$LCSeq(X_i, Y_j) = \begin{cases} \Phi & \text{if } i = 0 \text{ or } j = 0 \\ LCSeq(X_{i-1}, Y_{j-1}) + 1 & \text{if } x_i = y_j \\ longest(LCSeq(X_i, Y_{j-1}), LCSeq(X_{i-1}, Y_j)) & \text{if } x_i \neq y_j \end{cases}$$

After the new attack signatures are generated by ZAD, they are sent to a server responsible for global IDS/IPS hotfix update. This hotfix signature update approach is quick and proactive which is necessary for containing zero-day attacks at the right time. Moreover, the hotfix can be applied to other sensors without stopping or restarting their service. The Global Hotfix Server uses push technology to initiate the transaction. The client sensors have to subscribe to the hotfix server for receiving updates. The hotfix server provides live-update whenever a new signature is generated. It collects the new signature in a file and sends out to the client sensors. The signature file is sent over HTTPS to client sensors. When a client sensor receives signature file, it calculates MD5 checksum. The result of the checksum is sent to the hotfix server. If the checksum doesn't match, the client discards the download and the server in response sends the same signature file again. In case, the update fails due to any network or installation error, the hotfix server retries to update client sensor for a given number of retries and exceeding the limit assumes that client is down and disables it. The

Algorithm 2. Hotfix Update Algorithm

```
 1: procedure server()
 2:     set MAX_RETRY_COUNT = 5
 3:     Initialize DB drivers
 4:     Start secure communication with database
 5:     for iterate over PUSH table do
 6:         set String update = get...update to be pushed
 7:         set current_update_date = get...current update date
 8:         for iterate over CLIENTS table do
 9:             set String clientInfo = get...string using IP and credentials
10:             set String last_update_date = get...the last update date
11:             if last_update_date < current_update_date then
12:                 Push update to clientInfo
13:                 invoke client
14:                 if SUCCESS then
15:                     update CLIENTS table.
16:                     Set last_update_date = current_update_date
17:                 else
18:                     Raise Alert "Update Failed".
19:                     Resend update
20:                     set RETRY_COUNT = RETRY_COUNT + 1
21:                     if RETRY_COUNT > MAX_RETRY_COUNT then
22:                         Disable Client node.
23:                     end if
24:                 end if
25:             end if
26:         end for
27:     end for
28: end procedure
29: procedure client()
30:     Receive update from server
31:     String new_md5sum = generate md5sum of update
32:     if new_md5sum = original_md5sum then
33:         update signature database and send SUCCESS to server
34:     else
35:         discard update and send DECLINE to server
36:     end if
37: end procedure
```

---

complete process is automatic that doesn't require and manual intervention. The best part of global update is that all the sensors remain updated and are in sync always. Algorithm 2 is optimized and depicts this scenario where new signatures are pushed to the various sensors. The Hotfix Update algorithm is optimized to decrease the delay between signature generation and update as a short update period leads to fast reaction time against new attacks. On evaluation it was observed that the optimized algorithm took less time to update IDS/IPS sensors as compared to our previous approach.

4   Experimental Results

All experiments run on an isolated network in the research lab. Honeynet comprises of Honeywall Roo-1.4 and high-interaction honeypots with the Linux Sebek client installed on them. For IDS/IPS sensors SNORT is used. We have also developed a prototype for ZAD System with Signature Generator for our experiment. It is implemented in Java using Eclipse as an IDE and Mysql as a database. Four standard metrics were used to evaluate the performance of our technique: True Positive Rate (TPR), False Positive Rate (FPR), Total Accuracy (ACC) and Receiver Operating Characteristic (ROC) curve. TPR is the percentage of correctly identified malicious code shown in Eq. 1. FPR is the percentage of wrongly identified benign code (Eq. 1). ACC is the percentage of absolutely correctly identified code, either positive or negative, divided by the entire number of instances as shown in Eq. 2. In ROC curve the TPR rate is plotted in function of the FPR for different points. The ROC curve shows a trade-off between true positive and false positive. In the equations below, True Negative (TN) is the number of correctly identified benign code and False Negative (FN) is the number of wrongly identified malicious code.

$$TPR = \frac{|TP|}{|TP| + |FN|}; \quad FPR = \frac{|FP|}{|FP| + |TN|} \tag{1}$$

$$ACC = \frac{|TP| + |TN|}{|TP| + |FP| + |TN| + |FN|} \tag{2}$$

The dataset comprises of 54,502 samples in total consisting of 40,112 malware samples (both obfuscated &non-obfuscated) and 14,390 benign samples. The dataset with obfuscated and unknown malware have been collected from various sources like Honeynet project, VX heavens [25] and other online malware repositories. The benign samples include: application software, system software, and many other user applications. The distribution of malware samples is represented in Table 2.

Table 2. Distribution of malware samples

Malware type	No. of samples	Not-obfuscated	Obfuscated
Virus	13,509	3,053	10,456
Worm	10,150	2,741	7,409
Rootkit	257	130	127
Backdoor	4,688	1,876	2,812
Exploit	1,206	262	944
Trojan	10,302	2,782	7,520

To compute the accuracy of the proposed approach both benign and malware samples were redirected towards Honeynet and IDS/IPS sensors simultaneously. Table 3 represents the recorded values of TPR, FPR, ACC and ROC for obfuscated and non-obfuscated zero-day malware.

Table 3. System detection accuracy

Malware type	Not-obfuscated				Obfuscated			
	TPR	FPR	ACC	ROC	TPR	FPR	ACC	ROC
Virus	0.993	0.021	0.992	0.982	0.987	0.022	0.99	0.98
Worm	0.996	0.018	0.986	0.991	0.976	0.0301	0.972	0.969
Rootkit	0.983	0.0233	0.971	0.981	0.967	0.032	0.961	0.957
Backdoor	0.972	0.0281	0.975	0.975	0971	0.031	0.972	0.970
Exploit	0.984	0.025	0.973	0.985	0.968	0.0323	0.972	0.972
Trojan	0.965	0.031	0.955	0.958	0.891	0.0331	0.903	0.893

Experiments were also conducted to measure the performance of each ZAD component. For each ZAD component, their average execution time was recorded under various attacks. The evaluation was performed on a system with a processor core i7, and 8GB of RAM. All components executed quickly to perform desired analysis. Figure 5 shows the experimental results. From the Fig. 5, it is clear that CEU took more time as it has to compare attack trace with entire online repository where filtered traffic is stored. The emulator takes slightly less time than the CEU to execute an attack trace, track file system accesses and send reports to the validator. On the other hand, the validator and analyzer took approx. similar time for comparison with a set baseline of md5-checksum and critical files respectively. However, the signature generation component requires more time to generate new signatures than to push hotfix updates to IDS/IPS sensors.

In another experiment, to check and verify hotfix updates, various unknown obfuscated attacks were launched and signature updates were observed. The experiment was conducted for 7 days and hotfix updates were recorded along the days. Figure 6 shows the actual updates, successful updates and failed updates for a week. Day 1, the experiment was started and total 10 updates were processed from which 8 were successful and 2 were declined by the client IDS/IPS sensors. The clients can decline the update if the update file is corrupted and the server couldn't resend the same update again. Day 2, there were 5 updates with no refused cases. On an average, minimum 2 updates were rejected a day and in worst case we recorded 3 rejections. From the results it is proved that new signatures were generated and updated efficiently with minimum misses to contain the zero-day attack in future.

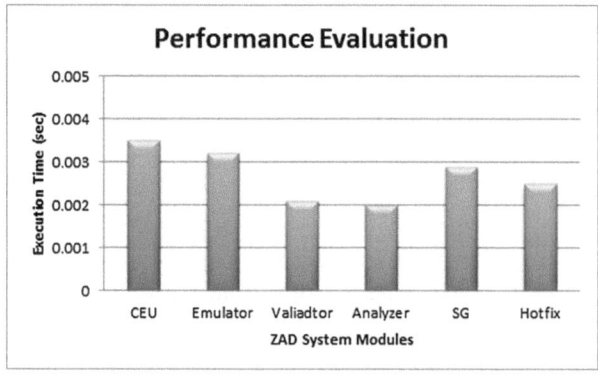

Fig. 5. Performance evaluation of ZAD components

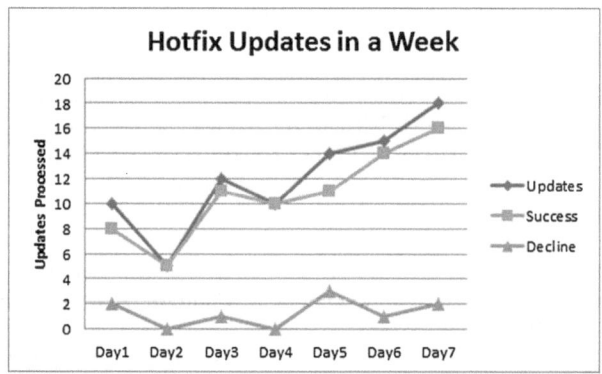

Fig. 6. Hotfix updates in a week

5 Conclusions

In this paper a two-level automated approach is proposed for detecting obfuscated zero-day attacks. This paper extends our previous work with more detailed and optimized methodology. It addresses the research problems with existing approaches and tries to provide a solution to the whole problem. The proposed approach provides an online detection mechanism against obfuscated zero-day attacks with automatic evaluation at two levels and automatically generating signatures with optimized global hotfix update. Experiments were conducted on real obfuscated zero-day malware, collected from various online malware repositories. The results were very promising achieving the best detection rate of nearly 99 % with 0.021 false positive rate and in the worst case, detection rate was 89 % with 0.033 false positive rate. Other results also showed that new signatures were generated and updated efficiently with least declines to contain the zero-day attack. The future work includes: (1) defining a system baseline to gather more information from other file system objects and attributes rather than from just one attribute i.e. md5-checksum. This detailed information can further help to categorize and provide more insight about the behavior of a zero-day malware. (2) To construct reliable signatures for obfuscated and polymorphic attacks. (3) To consider issues regarding anti-emulation techniques.

References

1. Bilge, L., Dumitras, T.: Before we knew it: an empirical study of zero-day attacks in the real world. In: Proceedings of ACM Conference on Computer and Communications Security, pp. 833–844. ACM Press, New York (2012)
2. Symantec's Internet Threat Report of 2013. https://scm.symantec.com/resources/istr18_en.pdf
3. Mohammed, M.M.Z.E., Chan, H.A., Ventura, N.: Honeycyber: automated signature generation for zero-day polymorphic worms. In: Proceedings of the IEEE Military Communications Conference (MILCOM 2008), pp. 1–6. IEEE Computer Society, Washington (2008)
4. Mohammed, M.M.Z.E., Chan, H.A., Ventura, N., Hashim, M., Amin, I., Bashier, E.: Detection of zero-day polymorphic worms using principal component analysis. In: Proceedings of the 6th IEEE International Conference on Networking and Services, pp. 277–281. IEEE Computer Society, Washington (2010)
5. Newsome, J., Karp, B., Song, D.: Polygraph: automatically generating signatures for polymorphic worms. In: Proceedings of the IEEE Symposium on Security and Privacy, pp. 226–241. IEEE Press, New York (2005)
6. Portokalidis, G., Bos, H.: SweetBait: zero-hour worm detection and containment using low-and high-interaction honeypots. J. Comput. Telecommun. Netw. 51(5), 1256–1274 (2007)
7. Wang, L., Li, Z., Chen, Y., Fu, Z., Li, X.: Thwarting zero-day polymorphic worms with network-level length-based signature generation. J. IEEE/ACM Trans. Netw. 18(1), 53–66 (2010)
8. Polychronakis, M., Anagnostakis, K.G., Markatos, E.P.: Network-level polymorphic shellcode detection using emulation. J. Comput. Virol. 2(4), 257–274 (2006)
9. Leita, C., Dacier, M.: SGNET: A Distributed Infrastructure to Handle Zero-day Exploits. Research report, EURECOM institute (2007)
10. Ting, C., Xiaosong, Z., Zhi, L.: A hybrid detection approach for zero-day polymorphic shellcodes. In: International Conference on E-Business and Information System Security, pp. 1–5. IEEE, Wuhan (2009)
11. Li, Z., Sanghi, M., Chen, Y., Kao M.Y., Chavez, B.: Hamsa: fast signature generation for zero-day polymorphic worms with provable attack resilience. In: Symposium on Security and Privacy, pp. 15–47. IEEE, Oakland (2006)
12. A 0-Day Attack Lasts On Average 10 Months. http://hackmageddon.com/2012/10/19/a-0-day-attack-lasts-on-average-10-months/
13. Polychronakis, M., Anagnostakis, K.G., Markatos, E.P.: Emulation-based detection of non-self-contained polymorphic shellcode. In: Kruegel, C., Lippmann, R., Clark, A. (eds.) RAID 2007. LNCS, vol. 4637, pp. 87–106. Springer, Heidelberg (2007)
14. Alazab, M., Venkatraman, S., Watters, P., Alazab, M.: Zero-day malware detection based on supervised learning algorithms of api call signatures. In: Proceedings of the 9th IEEE Australasian Data Mining Conference (AusDM 2011), Australia, pp. 171–182 (2011)

15. Aleroud, A., Karabtis G.: A contextual anomaly detection approach to discover zero-day attacks. In: IEEE International Conference on Cyber Security (CYBER-SECURITY 2012), pp. 40–15, Washington (2012)
16. Jain, P., Sardana, A., Defending against internet worms using honeyfarm. In: CUBE International Information Technology Conference (CUBE 2012), Pune, India, pp. 795–800. ACM Press, New York (2012)
17. Comar, P.M., Liu, L., Saha, S., Tan, P.N., Nucci A.: Combining supervised and unsupervised learning for zero-day malware detection. In: Proceedings of INFO-COM, pp. 2022–2030. IEEE Press, Turin (2013)
18. Aleroud, A., Karabatis G.: Toward zero-day attack identification using linear data transformation techniques. In: Proceedings of the 7th IEEE International Conference on Software Security and Reliability (SERE 2013), pp. 159–168. IEEE Press, MD (2013)
19. Kim, I., et al.: A case study of unknown attack detection against zero-day worm in the honeynet environment. In: Proceedings of the 11th IEEE International Conference on Advanced Communication Technology (ICACT 2009), pp. 1715–1720. IEEE Press, Ireland (2009)
20. Sophos Security Threat Report of 2014. http://www.sophos.com/en-us/media library/PDFs/other/sophos-security-threat-report-2014.pdf
21. Kaur, R., Singh, M.: Automatic evaluation and signature generation technique for thwarting zero-day attacks. In: Martínez Pérez, G., Thampi, S.M., Ko, R., Shu, L. (eds.) SNDS 2014. CCIS, vol. 420, pp. 298–309. Springer, Heidelberg (2014)
22. Kaur, R., Singh, M.: A survey on zero-day polymorphic worm detection techniques. J. IEEE Commun. Surv. Tutorials **99**, 1–30 (2014)
23. Cavallaro, L., Lanzi, A., Mayer, L., Monga, M.: Lisabeth: automated content-based signature generator for zero-day polymorphic worms. In: Proceedings of the 4th ACM International Workshop on Software Engineering for Secure Systems, pp. 41–48. ACM Press, Germany (2008)
24. Karp, R.M., Rabin, M.O.: Efficient randomized pattern-matching algorithms. J IBM J. Res. Dev. **31**(2), 249–260 (1987)
25. VX Heavens, VX Heavens Site. http://vxheaven.org/

Practical Attacks on Virtual Worlds

Graham Hili[(✉)], Sheila Cobourne, Keith Mayes,
and Konstantinos Markantonakis

Smart Card Centre, Information Security Group (SCC-ISG),
Royal Holloway, University of London, Egham, Surrey TW20 0EX, UK
{Graham.Hili.2009,Sheila.Cobourne.2008}@live.rhul.ac.uk
{Keith.Mayes,K.Markantonakis}@rhul.ac.uk

Abstract. Virtual Worlds (VWs) are immensely popular online environments, where users interact in real-time via digital beings (avatars). However, a number of security issues affect VWs, and they are vulnerable to a range of attacks on their infrastructure and communications channels. Their powerful architecture can also be used to mount attacks against live Real World servers, by using malicious VW objects. Researching these attacks in commercial VWs would not be acceptable, as it would be contrary to the terms of conditions which govern acceptable behaviour in a particular VW. So in this paper, attacks were conducted/analysed in a laboratory-based test bed VW implementation developed specifically for the research, with custom built attack and analysis tools: commercial VWs were used for data gathering only. Results of these experiments are presented, and appropriate countermeasures proposed which could reduce the likelihood of the attacks succeeding in live VWs.

1 Introduction

Massive multiplayer online Virtual Worlds (VWs) are immensely popular online environments, where users interact in real-time via digital beings known as avatars. Avatars interact with other virtual entities (e.g. avatars, objects, the VW itself) following rules determined by the VW developers. Different types of VW exist, such as game worlds, where the objective is to complete quests and enhance your avatar's skills and reputation (e.g. Blizzard's World of Warcraft (WOW) [12]), or civic worlds that mimic real life as closely as possible by including features such as commerce, democracy and education (e.g. Linden Research's Second Life (SL) [21]). There are security concerns about VWs, however. Not only do they face generic web-based security threats like the OWASP Top Ten [23], there are also specific issues directly related to the VW environment [14]. Additionally, the VW itself can be used as an attack platform, when malicious VW objects are created that interact with live Real World (RW) servers, a process which can lead to denial of service attacks (DDoS) on external RW resources. This paper presents some practical examples of attacks based on two popular VWs, SL and WOW, analysed and conducted in a laboratory-based

© Springer International Publishing Switzerland 2015
J. Lopez et al. (Eds.): CRiSIS 2014, LNCS 8924, pp. 180–195, 2015.
DOI: 10.1007/978-3-319-17127-2_12

test bed VW implementation developed specifically for the research. The objective of the research was to examine generic technical attack methods which could be used as a basis for further VW-specific attacks at a later stage. Conducting attacks using existing commercial VWs would be contrary to the terms of conditions which govern acceptable behaviour in the VW, so the only part of the research that was done in commercial VW Servers did not involve any attacks but solely gathered usage statistics. This paper analyses the results of attacks performed and proposes countermeasures that VW developers could adopt.

The paper is structured thus: background information about VWs and their security appears in Sect. 2. The VW attack testing framework is described in Sect. 3 and necessary attack/analysis tools are listed in Sect. 4. Attacks performed and results are detailed in Sects. 5, 6, 7 and 8. Analysis and countermeasures are shown in Sects. 9 and 10. The conclusion and potential future work follow in Sect. 11.

2   Virtual Worlds and Security

Typical Virtual World Architecture. Most commercial VWs use a *client-server* architecture, where a VW Client is downloaded onto the user's PC to interact with the VW Server [17]. The *VW Server* contains object-oriented components (modularised processes) which make up the VW itself. Core (essential) and secondary (non-essential) components run on one or more physical servers: redundantly replicating core components to different servers ensures high availability. A back-end database stores all the data needed for the VW to function, such as user credentials/inventory information, and VW rules of operation; the VW infrastructure can serve multiple connected clients. The *VW Client* software on the user's PC, connects to the VW Server and renders the VW into a graphical format for the user to interact with. As VW developers cannot control client software after it has been downloaded, it is regarded as untrusted.

Avatars and Objects. In VWs, avatars are encouraged to be inquisitive and more uninhibited than their RW controllers, to travel, complete quests and acquire new objects previously created by other avatars or the VW developers. Avatars will pick free, interesting and graphically appealing objects up and attach them to their inventory, as a prize or trophy. VW objects are simple to create. Each A VW object has a graphical user interface, behaviour, (needed for interactions) and properties (variables). Users can write and attach scripts to objects, and these scripts can be used to connect VW objects to external RW HTTP servers. The creator of a VW object can thus provide functionality, visual elements, real time streaming of data, or licensing on the object.

Security Issues in Virtual Worlds. Some VW security threats identified by ENISA [14] are: unauthorised monitoring/recording of avatar activities; harassment ('griefing') that hinders the activities of legitimate VW avatars; VW-specific denial of service, through scripted objects and malicious avatar actions; attacks through the VW Client; and cheating to gain unfair advantage with the VW. There are many motivations for attacking VWs. Alongside familiar malicious incentives such as financial gain and stealing credentials for later mis-use, VW-specific motivations, such as cheating and griefing aim to affect the VW experience for others.

Types of VW Attacks

Attacks on VW Client: This is often the easiest target to attack as it is completely under the control of the user. VW Client attacks vary from simple scripts to more sophisticated attacks such as debugging application machine code to circumvent security controls. Several VW Client attacks are suggested in [27], and the work in this paper uses some attack techniques from [18].

Attacks on VW Server: This targets the application level, e.g. by taking advantage of application vulnerabilities that exist on the server such as a potential vulnerable operating system accessible via an open SSH port.

Attacks on Communication Channels: Attack vectors here are different to the VW Server attack scenario, as actual bits of relevant packets at the lowest level of the communication protocol are targetted. Not all data transferred from the VW Client is encrypted [16], so man-in-the-middle attacks can tamper with this data and potentially give an attacker full control over the interface seen by the user, to lure them into insecure behaviour.

Attacks on the Real World from within the VW: VW objects that have scripts which communicate with external RW servers can be used maliciously in attacks, from DDoS to targetting a database attached to a web server.

The next section describes the testing framework used in our VW attacks.

3   VW Attack Testing Framework

Experiments were conducted in our own custom test environment because live attacks would not be acceptable to VW developers. The attack testing framework architecture was built using virtual machines (VMs), using VirtualBox [8], so that the framework could be deployed on a single machine. (VMs abstract the hardware layer of the framework, so it could be installed on multiple machines if required.) Our study did not focus on making these VMs efficient or more stable via the virtualisation software. Figure 1 illustrates the high level architecture of the testing framework.

There are two host VMs that represent the clients, *Client 1* and *Compromised Client.* Both clients have an operating system, (we used Windows XP) and the relevant VW Client. We used the Second Life (SL) Client since it was less restric-tive to install in such an environment and also considered vulnerable to attack. For our experiments one of the clients was deliberately compromised as if a malicious host had control over its host VM.

The *Malicious Host* was our main attack VM, with two network interfaces: one was connected directly to the client-compromised host and the other to the

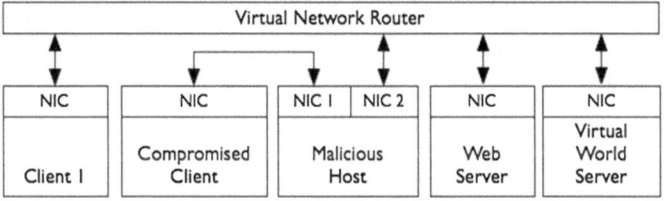

Fig. 1. Test environment framework

virtual router network. In this way we could conduct attacks such as man-in-the-middle attacks and easily monitor/modify in-coming and out-going packets via packet analysis. The malicious host also held our custom scripts and analytical applications used during the attacks.

A *Virtual Network Router* provided by VirtualBox created the interconnection between the hosts, communicating using TCP/IP standard. This also enabled measurements of bandwidth and traffic between VMs during our attacks.

The *Virtual World Server* host replicated the VW itself. We developed software that was intended to act as closely as possible to the real SL environment. We implemented this by primarily following an open VW standards approach (e.g. Aurora-SIM [1]). For functions where this was not possible we also reverse engineered protocols. We focused on communication aspects rather than the graphical interface, and we used the same inter process communication as in real systems: all the server components were built on sockets communication. Usually in real VWs each process is separated on a different server, whereas in our simulation model all the processes were running on a single VM (for convenience).

The *Web Server* was built on a Linux OS (backtrack-Linux upgraded to Kali-Linux [3]), a penetration testing specific Linux OS which has useful tools pre-installed such as Wireshark [13]. We ran two services; a web server (Apache v2) and a database server which was implemented with MySQL. This host was the VM targeted when conducting RW attacks from the VW. To make sure it followed normal standards we patched the operating system, web server and database to the latest releases.

In addition to developing a test framework architecture, we also created tools to conduct the attacks and analyse the results.

4   Tools Used for Attacks and Analysis

We developed the following attack and analysis tools for use in our testing.

AT1 - UDP Dissector: We used Wireshark with custom-built Lua plug-ins [4] to capture and dissect packets flowing between the VW Server/VW Client. The plug-ins initialised ports/Wireshark functions, analysed the packet's header, identified the communicating avatar, and tokenised/dissected packets.

AT2 - Packet Manipulator and Injector: Scapy [6] is a Python application used for scanning, probing and stress testing networks. Here it was used to craft packets sent between the VW Server and VW Client to find vulnerabilities.

AT3 - Binary Editor: 010 Editor [26] is a binary file editor which can be used on files such as executable code or image files. A template of the target file is created, and scripts can be used to run a series of commands together.

AT4 - Disassembler and Debugger: Two debuggers were used. OllyDbg [5] is an assembler level dynamic debugger tool that can analyse and modify a running process binary code in memory. Cheat Engine [2] identifies the position of certain value parameters in the process memory.

AT5 - Process Memory Editor: We built this tool using Python, which can directly manipulate the operating system memory and write back to the process memory, and Pymem, an external library for Python v2.5 and above.

AN1 - Protocol Analyser: Wireshark was used to put a particular network card into promiscuous mode to capture all the traffic, and we developed a Lua plug-in to look at the packet headers and speed up analysis.

AN2 - Object Script Parser: The VW scripting engine parses a piece of script when an object needs to use it. We analysed how the parser worked by consulting an open source project, Aurora-Sim [1], which claims that their server is based heavily on the SL Server. Consulting the source code of their scripting engine allowed us to develop our own engine in Python.

AN3 - Attacks Statistic Analyser: This was developed in Python and had two roles. Firstly it had to connect to the virtual network router and gather data such as bandwidth usage and type of packets being sent from each host during attacks. Secondly, it stored the data used for the customised attacks for subsequent analysis.

The next sections outline the attacks that were performed: Fig. 2 shows the various VW attack scenarios.

5   VW Client Attacks Performed

VW Client attacks used the test framework as shown in Fig. 1: the objective was to see how local attacks affected the client and/or if the attacks propagated to

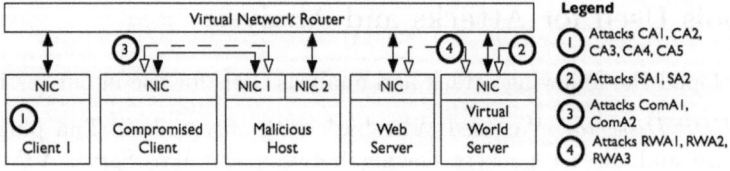

Fig. 2. Attack scenarios

the server. We also experimented on the WOW Client, which is protected by an anti-cheating agent (WOW's Warden [11]). To mount these attacks the malicious entity (User/3rd party) would need good technical programming/debugging skills along with administrative rights on the VW Client PC.

CA1 - Credential Retrieval from Client. We aimed to find if passwords were stored on the User's PC. We analysed the SL Client code [7] and found the 'remember me' feature stores credentials locally: the WOW client forces the user to input a password at every logon. During the WOW logon process, we used 'Watch 4 Folder' [9] to detect any folder/file changes and a System Registry Monitor [25] to check the OS registry.

Results: An MD5 hash of the SL password was stored on the PC, XORed with the MAC address of the primary network card and put in a password.dat file (Fig. 3). The WOW client did not store any credentials locally.

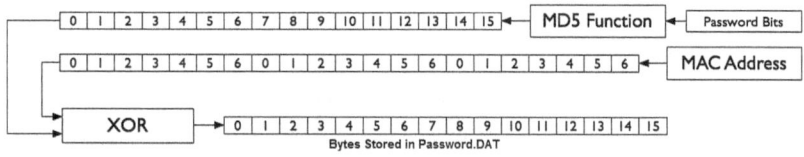

Fig. 3. Second life password storage

CA2 - Speed Attack via Manual Memory Manipulation. The objective here was to change the avatar's stored X,Y,Z coordinates to enable it to go directly to a location of our choice e.g. where treasures are situated. We used tool *AT4*: OllyDbug analysed the code flow of the client application, Cheat Engine provided a list of memory locations that had changed when we moved our avatar around corresponding to the avatar's X,Y,Z coordinates, and we modified these using 010 Editor. We tested both the SL and WOW clients, changing X and Y coordinates to locations at varying distances from the avatar's initial position, always ensuring target destinations were valid.

Results: Using the SL client, the avatar moved to every new location we specified, without any adverse reaction or security warning. With the more challenging WOW client, it was more difficult to find the memory addresses of the X,Y,Z coordinates, but we succeeded in manually manipulating their values. The avatar could be displaced by a small distance, but over a larger distances the WOW client disconnected us from the VW server, threw a generic error popup and closed gracefully. Either the client had detected manual movement of the avatar, or the Warden identified this as an impossible path between two end points. We identified that the Warden was intercepting the modified movements and blocking the client execution flow. The attack worked over small distances because the Warden needs to accept some tolerance to cater for network latency and high ping values when connecting client and server.

CA3 DLL Injection Attack. A DLL injection attack involves identifying a variable to target, then changing the relevant code to alter its value in memory. We chose to modify a 'health bar' variable to make our avatar invincible. We analysed the WOW client code, using tool *AT4*, and modified the relevant memory function without injecting new code using the *AT5* tool. We moved our avatar to a place where he would be attacked by a monster. To see the effect on the health variable. SL is not game focused, so there are no health bars during normal operation, but game mode environments exist where health bars can be used so we performed the DLL injection attack from there.

Results: In WOW, our avatar was attacked, the modified function was called, but the Warden detected an external event was trying to modify the internal data of the client and shut down the application. In SL, the attack was successful and the avatar's health increased instead of decreased when hit by an opponent.

CA4 UDP Dissection Attack. This attack aimed to intercept and compromise SL chat data using the UDP dissector *AT3*. (This attack was performed using only the SL Client.) Fig. 4 shows how packets were dissected and modified by the UDP Dissector.

Results: We captured a SL chat session between the compromised/uncompromised clients and identified the data passing over the UDP connection using *AN1*: the data was in clear text so we could easily manipulate it.

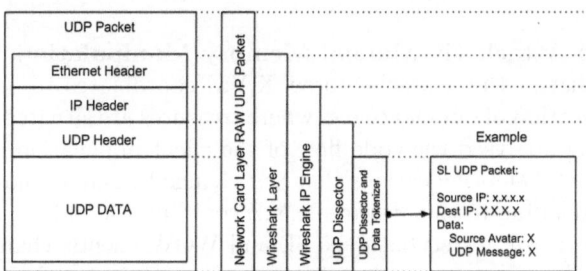

Fig. 4. UDP dissector

CA5 Duplication Attack. This attack modified the VW Client memory process area to alter the inventory and create duplicated objects which could be resold for financial gain. Using *AT4* we found that the client had a region in its process space which was being used to hold a cached copy of the VW Server inventory on the localhost. Firstly we changed an existing object in our inventory, using tool *AT3*. Tools *AT4/AT5* were used to modify parameters in the process space to duplicate the object in our inventory. We also attempted to clone an object completely.

Results: Modification of object parameters could be done easily in SL but in WOW all attempts to modify object parameters were detected by the Warden.

The new object was created successfully on the local SL Client but was not replicated on the VW server: its objectID showed up as an invalid object. This attack was only partially successful as the SL client could interact with the duplicated object but it was not fully functional.

The next section describes VW Server attacks.

6   VW Server Attacks

We performed generic web server attacks on the test VW Server: the malicious entity (an external third party) would need good network analysis skills.

SA1 Denial of Service. We targetted the Login Server in the VW application stack, by reducing some of the network resources in the VW Server VM using tool *AT2*, then creating a process that sent many packets on that network. We analysed the network traffic/processor workload using Microsoft's Process Explorer [24] and analysis tool *AN1*. With network traffic very high and the processor operating at around 95 per cent we then started sending malicious packets from the malicious host and simultaneously attempted to login via the VW Client.

Results: When a simulated denial of service attack was in place, the user login was rejected 9 times out of 10, which achieved the objective of the attack.

SA2 Malformed Packets Attack. We aimed to create an access violation on the VW Server by sending non-standard packets using tool *AT2*. Tool *AN1* analysed the whole stream to determine when the goal has been reached.

Results: Packets which were bigger than the actual packet frame (65535 bytes) were rejected by the server. If we manipulated the packet flags that handle TCP handshakes or FIN or RST packets, these were not always handled properly and often led to the VW Server crashing. Half open packets i.e. when the malicious host sends a SYN packet to the VW Server, but does not reply to the corresponding SYN-ACK, eventually caused the VW Server to exhaust its resources and suffer a denial of service outcome. As this was a test bed server implementation, this result may not necessarily be replicated in live environments.

The next section describes attacks on the communication channels.

7   Attacking Communication Channels

To attack communications channels, the malicious entity (here an external third party) needs good network protocol analysis skills and administrative privileges on the attacking VM to put the network card into promiscuous mode.

ComA1 Outbound Data. This attack accesses/modifies outbound packets from the VW Client to the VW Server. The two clients in our test framework were set to communicate with each other, and we intercepted their chat messages using the UDP dissector (*AT1*). Modifications were made using Scapy (*AT2*) and the packets were injected on the wire and sent to the server. The results were analysed using tool *AN1*.

Results: Some packets could be easily changed and modified, such as SL chat message packets sent over UDP, but on WOW again the security was much higher than SL. The data structure of WOW packets is not documented, and attempting to reverse engineer the protocol was difficult.

ComA2 Inbound Data. This MITM attack is intended to trick the client user into insecure actions e.g. divulging credit card details. We obtained genuine packets coming from the VW Server using tool *AT1*, then modified them using tool *AT2*, to change incoming chat messages from the server to the user. As this type of attack is difficult to capture on the server side, we did some experimentation to see if the VW client application could identify when packets were being manipulated.

Results: In WOW, the Warden disconnected the user immediately when packets were manipulated: one of the main roles of the Warden is to test data integrity from the server. On the SL client we could change parameters on the messages without the client noticing or sending any warnings to the user.

The next section shows how malicious VW objects can attack RW servers.

8   Attacks on RW Servers from Within the VW

Using malicious VW objects to attack RW servers from within the VW can have serious consequences. Attackers only need basic VW scripting/graphics skills, and could be users or malicious third parties: no access to other users' PCs is required. We introduced a malicious scripted object into our test VW. Our test web server (Apache v2) was configured to store logs of every request coming over port 80: once a request was received a small index.html page was returned to the request originator (the attacking object) and the logs were written (see Fig. 2 for set-up). Attack tool *AT2* and analysis tools *AN1*, *AN2* and AN3 were used in all these attacks.

RWA1 - Denial of Service of RW Server. In the test VW, we created a malicious VW object (an attractive shiny ball) that could be attached to an avatar. We gave it a malicious script (see Fig. 5) which sent HTTP requests to our test RW server once every 10 s, in an infinite loop, once the object had been attached to an avatar's inventory via a 'touch event'. As more avatars attach the object, the denial of service attack builds up.

To gather statistics on the potential effectiveness of this attack, a benign version of this VW object was introduced into the 'beginners' area' of the live SL environment, and was available for 24 h. The attach action initiated a single RW server request to the framework test server, recorded on log files in the relevant VM: this action did not present any threats to SL users or SL Servers.

Figure 6 shows the number of avatars who picked the object up and attached it their inventory (by hour, and cumulative). After 24 h, the VW object had been picked up approximately 500 times. The theoretical maximum number of HTTPS requests per hour that this one malicious object could generate without violating SL's current external HTTP request limit (i.e. 1 request per second) would be $500 \times 60 \times 60 = 1,800,000$.

Results: During this attack the originator of the request was recorded on the log files as the VW itself and not the user's client IP, therefore hiding the identity of the requesting avatar. No attack data was routed via the VW Client, which means that a powerful PC is not needed to conduct these attacks. The VW client could send requests to a RW server without RW server finding out the requestor's identity. Taking the object pickup statistics into account shows the potential for an effective DDoS attack.

RWA2 - Logic Bomb Attack on RW Server. In *RWA1* the malicious object contacts the RW server immediately once a touch event occurs, resulting in a gradual build up of RW server requests. This should be detected in good time by its system administrator so preventative actions can be taken. A more effective option would be to start attacking when a condition is met e.g. a predetermined number of objects has been picked up. This turns the *RWA1* attack into a logic bomb, and a large undetectable set of avatars with malicious objects can be created. A massive attack could be triggered at a time of the attacker's choosing. We tested this attack using three avatars, each picking up a malicious object with a script that specified the DDoS attack should commence on a particular date (see Fig. 7).

Results: The RW server suffered a DDoS attack on the date specified in the script: again requests appeared to originate from the VW. If multiple malicious

```
            ObjectInit(){
            Float Seconds = 10
            String URL = www.ourlocal.com
}
ObjectLoop(){
        ObjectTouch_Event(){
                if(TimeDelay(Seconds)){
                SendRequesttoServer(URL+index.html);
                }
        }
        ObjectDestroy_Event(){
        //Our Object will never be destroyed
        }
}
```

Fig. 5. Malicious code snippet - denial of service

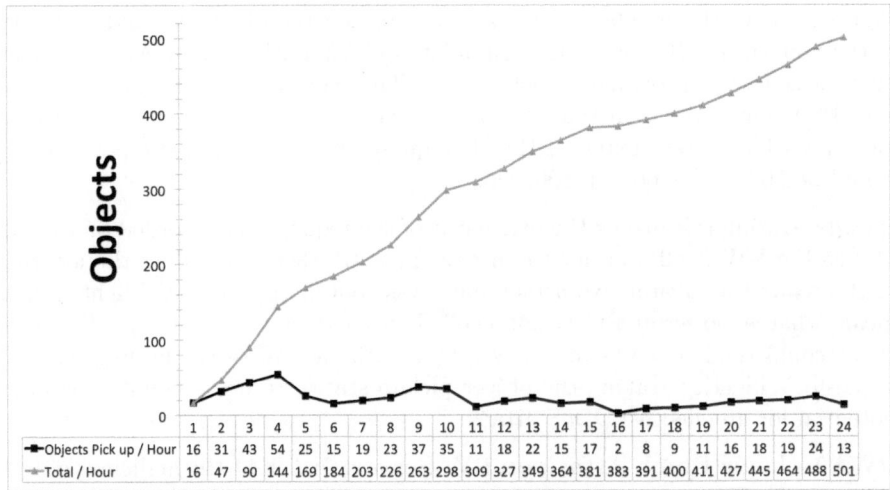

Fig. 6. VW object pickups

objects were picked up at the same rate observed in our data gathering exercise, an attacker could prepare/trigger an overwhelming DDoS attack.

RWA3 - Database Attack on RW Server. The objective of this attack was to find vulnerabilities to exploit in web applications. The script attached to the malicious object is shown in Fig. 8: when the object is touched it sends a specially crafted string to the RW server to try to find vulnerabilities and mount a SQL injection attack. Sensitive user data from several tables in the database could be acquired by tricking the SQL server with a fake request. In our test framework we used a standard installation/default install of mySQL with no extra protection, and the code on the target website also had no extra protection against SQL injection attacks, as our intention here was not to secure the web application/webserver components themselves.

Results: The attack was conducted successfully: we could see a dump of the Users table from the database we were attacking. Again the attack appears to originate from the VW Server IP address rather than that of the attacker.

Analysis of results and suggested countermeasures now follow.

9   Analysis

VW Client Attacks: The VW Client is a good entry point for an attacker, as it is downloaded onto a PC and the VW developers cannot control it. All the attacks conducted on the SL Client succeeded (although *CA5* produced a duplicated object that was not fully functional): there is no anti-cheating agent monitoring the correct operation of the SL Client. The WOW Client is protected by the

```
        ObjectInit()
{
        Float Seconds = 0.5
        String URL = www.ourlocal.com
}
ObjectLoop()
{
        ObjectDelay_Event(Seconds)
        {
                if(DateNow() >= 12/04/2017)
                {
                SendRequesttoServer(URL+index.html);
                }
        }
        ObjectDestroy_Event()
        {
        //Our Object will never be destroyed
        }
}
```

Fig. 7. Malicious code snippet - logic bomb

```
        ObjectInit()
{
        String URL = www.ourlocal.com
}
ObjectLoop()
{
        ObjectTouch_Event()
        {
        SendRequesttoServer(URL+searchuser.php?username=1%20or
%201%20=%201);
        }
        ObjectDestroy_Event()
        {
        //Our Object will never be destroyed
        }
}
```

Fig. 8. Malicious code snippet - database attack

Warden program, which detected and stopped each attack in its early stages, leading the WOW Client to close down gracefully each time. Security is high in WOW because preventing cheating is a priority for the developers, to safeguard their revenue stream.

VW Server Attacks: Our generic VW Server attacks were successful. Other VW Server subcomponents could have been attacked, such as object creation or message creation, which would be easier than targetting the global VW infrastructure. Using our test architecture meant these attacks could be studied in depth without risking expulsion from live VWs.

Communication Channel Attacks: These attacks intercepted and modified packets as required. *ComA1* modified outgoing packets, which could be used to attack potential victims in the VW, by exploiting the fact that if two VW clients are communicating their users are likely to have a relationship within the VW. As users are more trusting of avatars they already know in VWs, social engineering and phishing attacks can be made more effective. In *ComA2* there is a direct connection with the VW client, so attacks can change the user's VW experience and lure them into insecure behaviour.

Real World Attacks: There are well documented methods available to attack RW servers (e.g. create a VM on the Internet and use it to mount OWASP Top Ten [23] attacks) but the malicious object attacks presented in this paper have many advantages for an attacker. The VW developers provide the external HTTP requests facility, and an easy-to-learn scripting language, so creating malicious VW objects to harness the powerful resources of a VW in an attack does not require specialised technical skills. RW attacks from malicious objects do not identify the attacker as they appear to emanate from VW Servers. Multiple malicious objects could be created in the VW to launch a multi-step attack e.g. different objects attack different sub systems of a RW web server. The logic-bomb approach (*RWA2*) gives an attacker full control over when and how the attack is mounted, as malicious objects can be widely dispersed throughout the VW, behaving innocently until the trigger condition is met. An attacker can mount a range of attacks such as DDoS/SQL injection via an effective botnet-type operation. It can be seen from the statistics gathered in the live SL environment, the malicious object attack works because of innate user curiosity in VWs. There is no need for attackers to infect users' PCs with trojans/viruses, or for social engineering. Many VW users are unaware that harmful VW objects exist. RW attacks do not detract from a user's/avatar's VW immersive experience and might actually enhance it, if the malicious object is especially appealing. The avatar will not notice malicious activity until it affects the quality of service of the VW. There is no real incentive to change avatar behaviour (which is an economic externality - the cost of the attack does not fall on the avatar causing it). RW DDoS could almost be seen as a 'victimless' crime from the avatar's point of view. If the attacks were directed at assets such as VW credentials or virtual money then avatars might be persuaded to change their behaviour.

Effectiveness of the Testing Framework: The testing framework was developed using official SL documentation, and open source projects such as AuroraSim [1], and tried to mimic SL as much as possible. There were limitations due to the resources available on the host computer and from limited traffic generated by local (not public) testing. However, the experimental set-up worked well and allowed VW attacks to be performed effectively.

10   Countermeasures

VW Client Attacks *CA1-5* can be prevented by anti-cheating software: we saw in our testing that Blizzard's Warden anti-cheating software prevented all the attacks on the WOW Client. Third party anti-cheating products are available such as Punkbuster [15] which could be adopted by other VW developers to prevent unauthorised modifications to their VW Clients. However, there are serious privacy concerns here, as anti-cheating software often uses similar techniques to spyware. Also, a new VW infrastructure paradigm exists, where VW clients are being developed to work from the web browser (e.g. [19]). If VW clients were to be completely situated in the cloud, managed by the VW developer, they might then become accessible via minimalistic and security controlled VMs. VW Server Attacks *SA1, SA2* can be countered by good server side security. Encrypting communications between the VW Client and the VW Server would be effective here as well as preventing *ComA1, ComA2* communication channel attacks, but this may have an impact on the performance of the VW. Again, moving the VW Client to the cloud and using HTTPs to protect all communications between it and the VW server would provide a reasonable level of security against these attacks.

RW Attacks *RWA1, RWA2, RWA3* will not respond to traditional anti-botnet measures, but the following area should be explored:

– User authentication: The VW Developers' ultimate sanction against malicious parties under their terms and conditions of use is expulsion from the VW. However, this is not an effective deterrent, as a new VW identity is simple to set up, enabling attacks to be repeated. User authentication should be strengthened, by employing two-factor authentication mechanisms such as the WOW authenticator [10]) or phone based solutions [20].
– VW Security awareness: this is not a trivial task, given the more relaxed behaviour of avatars compared to their (more vigilant) RW controllers. There are basic security steps an individual can take in the RW (e.g. not clicking on links sent from unknown sources) which have no VW equivalents [22].
– Controlling external HTTP requests: this could be done in various ways. For example: removing the facility for HTTP requests in scripts, which may not be popular with legitimate avatars as it detracts from their VW experience; flexibly adjusting the throttling rate of external HTTP requests (in SL this is currently done on a per-object basis, at approximately 1 request per second); introducing a white list of registered, approved external sites [22]; applying a small monetary cost for each HTTP request or registration of external site.
– Securing VW objects is an open research problem, out of scope of this paper.

11   Conclusion and Future Work

This paper has analysed security issues that affect VWs, and as a result, designed and implemented a framework with associated tools for the experimental analysis of VW attacks. Several successful attacks were conducted, targetting the VW Client, VW Server and communications channels. Techniques using malicious objects to mount RW attacks were also shown, and statistics on the potential effectiveness of this approach were gathered from a live VW environment. The results of the practical experiments led to a number of suggested countermeasures. The logic bomb attack is particularly dangerous, as attackers can build up a large collection of malicious virtual objects without being detected, have full control over when an attack is initiated, and mount an overwhelming attack on a RW target. Further study of the VW client application may reveal vulnerabilities in open-source clients, and focussing on closed-source solutions and anti-cheating agents deployed by commercial VW developers may also be beneficial: cloud-based VW clients may present new attack vectors. An interesting attack study would be to try to compromise the anti-cheat agent by compromising the operating system (e.g. via a rootkit), and then propose protective measures, perhaps based on trusted platforms. Communication between client and server is also rapidly changing; VW users want access to their accounts from different devices, such as tablets and mobile phones. This communication model is likely to present a challenge and optimising transmissions over limited channels may result in new threats: mobile platforms are not generally renowned for their security and attack resistance. It is planned to offer the test framework described in this paper as an open source project for others to use and contribute to when analysing VW security.

References

1. Aurora-SIM: A new Vision of OpenSim (2014). http://aurora-sim.org
2. Cheat Engine (2014). http://www.cheatengine.org/
3. Kali linux (2014). http://www.kali.org/
4. LUA (2014). http://www.lua.org/
5. OllyDbg (2014). http://www.ollydbg.de/
6. Scapy (2014). http://www.secdev.org/projects/scapy/
7. Second Life source code (2014). http://wiki.http://secondlife.com/wiki/Get_source_and_compile
8. Virtual Box (2014). https://www.virtualbox.org/
9. Watch 4 Folder 2.3 (2014). http://leelusoft.blogspot.it/2011/10/watch-4-folder-23.html
10. Blizzard Entertainment Inc.: Battle.net authenticator (2014). https://www.eu.battle.net/support/en/article/battlenet-authenticator
11. Blizzard Entertainment Inc.: Warden (software) (2014). http://www.wowwiki.com/Warden_software
12. Blizzard Entertainment Inc.: World of Warcraft (2014). http://eu.battle.net/wow/en//
13. Combs, G.: Wireshark (2014). http://www.wireshark.org/
14. ENISA: Position Paper: Virtual Worlds, Real Money, November 2008. http://www.enisa.europa.eu/publications/archive/security-and-privacy-in-virtual-worlds-and-gaming
15. Even Balance Inc.: Punkbuster (2014). http://www.punkbuster.com/
16. Fernandes, S., Antonello, R., Moreira, J., Sadok, D., Kamienski, C.: Traffic analysis beyond this world: the case of second life. In: Proceedings of the 17th International Workshop on Network and Operating Systems Support for Digital Audio & Video (NOSSDAV) (2007)

17. Funkhouser, T.A.: Ring: a client-server system for multi-user virtual environments. In: Proceedings of the 1995 Symposium on Interactive 3D Graphics, I3D 1995, pp. 85–92. ACM, New York (1995)
18. Hoglund, G., McGraw, G.: Exploiting Online Games: Cheating Massively Distributed Systems. Addison-Wesley Professional, Reading (2007)
19. Katz, N., Cook, T., Smart, R.: Extending web browsers with a unity 3D-based virtual worlds viewer. IEEE Internet Comput. **15**(5), 15–21 (2011)
20. Kyrillidis, L., Hili, G., Cobourne, S., Mayes, K., Markantonakis, K.: Virtual world authentication using the smart card web server. In: Thampi, S.M., Atrey, P.K., Fan, C.-I., Perez, G.M. (eds.) SSCC 2013. CCIS, vol. 377, pp. 30–41. Springer, Heidelberg (2013)
21. Linden Research Inc.: Second Life (2014). http://secondlife.com/
22. Muttick, I.: Securing virtual worlds against real attacks -the challenges of online game development. Technical report, McAfee, Inc. (2008). https://www.info-point-security.com/open_downloads/2008/McAfee_wp_online_gaming_0808.pdf
23. OWASP: Top Ten Project (2013). https://www.owasp.org
24. Russinovich, M.: Process explorer (2014). http://technet.microsoft.com/en-gb/sysinternals/bb896653.aspx
25. Russinovich, M., Cogswell, B.: Process Monitor v3.1, March 2014. http://technet.microsoft.com/en-us/sysinternals/bb896645
26. Sweetscape Software Inc.: 010 Editor (2014). http://www.sweetscape.com/010editor/
27. Thumann, M.: Hacking SecondLife. In: Black Hat Briefings and Training (2008). https://www.blackhat.com/presentations/bh-europe-08/Thumann/Presentation/bh-eu-08-thumann.pdf

TabsGuard: A Hybrid Approach to Detect and Prevent Tabnabbing Attacks

Hana Fahim Hashemi[1]([⊠]), Mohammad Zulkernine[1],
and Komminist Weldemariam[1,2]

[1] School of Computing, Queen's University, Kingston, Canada
{hashemi,mzulker}@cs.queensu.ca
[2] IBM Research — Africa, Nairobi, Kenya
k.weldemariam@ke.ibm.com

Abstract. Phishing is one of the most prevalent types of modern attacks, costing significant financial losses to enterprises and users each day. Despite the emergence of various anti-phishing tools, not only there has been a dramatic increase in the number of phishing attacks but also more sophisticated forms of these attacks have come into existence. One of these forms of phishing attacks is the tabnabbing attack. Tabnabbing takes advantage of the user's trust and inattention to the open tabs in the browser and changes the appearance of an already open malicious page to the appearance of a trusted website. The existing tabnabbing detection and prevention techniques block scripts that are susceptible to perform malicious actions or violate the browser security policy. However, most of these techniques cannot effectively prevent the script-free variant of the tabnabbing attack. In this paper, we introduce `TabsGuard`, an approach that combines heuristics and a machine-learning technique to keep track of the major changes made to the layout of a webpage whenever a tab loses its focus. `TabsGuard` is developed as a browser extension and evaluated against the top 1,000 trusted websites from Alexa. The results of our evaluation convey a significant improvement over the existing techniques. Finally, `TabsGuard` can be deployed as an extension service as a viable means for protecting against tabnabbing attacks.

Keywords: Tabnabbing · Phishing · Detection · Heuristics · Browser extension

1 Introduction

According to the Anti-Phishing Working Group [1], "There were at least 115,565 unique phishing attacks worldwide in the second half of 2013. This is nearly a 60 % increase over the 72,758 seen in the first half of 2013." This places phishing attacks among the most prominent types of Internet attacks.

Typically, a phishing attack leverages social engineering techniques by sending a large number of luring emails containing a link (usually an obfuscated URL) that can potentially redirect users to an attacker-controlled website. These emails seem to be sent, for instance, from the user's bank or any popular website as the

© Springer International Publishing Switzerland 2015
J. Lopez et al. (Eds.): CRiSIS 2014, LNCS 8924, pp. 196–212, 2015.
DOI: 10.1007/978-3-319-17127-2_13

link mimics the look-and-feel of a trusted website. Upon a successful redirection, the attacker can automatically collect sensitive information (*e.g.*, bank account numbers, credit card numbers, and passwords) and use it for underground economy [2–5].

While still struggling with the destructive effects of typical phishing attacks, Web users were introduced to a new and more threatening form of phishing attack named `Tabnabbing` [6]. `Tabnabbing` takes over the inactive browser tabs by changing their title, favicon and appearance to those of a trusted website. The classical phishing attack relies on the deception of users with a similar URL and/or bogus resemblance to the original website whereas `tabnabbing` takes advantage of the user's inattention to the open tabs in the browser [7]. In this attack, a malicious but legitimate-looking webpage that is already open in one of the tabs reloads its contents to resemble a trusted website. The unsuspecting user most likely falls into the attackers' trap and inputs confidential information into the malicious webpage. The collected information is then sent to the attacker-controlled server and can be used for various types of abuses. Two variants of the tabnabbing attack have been identified to date. While one variant relies on scripts [6], the other launches an attack without the use of scripts and based on page refreshes that occur in predetermined time intervals [8]. The former can be combated by some of the existing script-blocking browser extensions (see [9–11] for examples). The latter, however, is more challenging to prevent, and the existing script-blocking techniques cannot guarantee full protection against it.

Attempting to address the above challenge, in this paper, we present a hybrid tabnabbing detection and prevention approach, named `TabsGuard`. `TabsGuard` combines heuristic-based metrics and machine-learning techniques. The metrics determine the degree of changes made to the tree representation of each webpage whenever a tab loses focus. We then leverage a machine-learning technique (specifically k-NN [12]) to analyze the occurred changes. In case the attack is detected on a browser, the user is informed with an alert message and blocked access to the website. `TabsGuard` is developed as a browser extension and integrated with Mozilla Firefox. We evaluated `TabsGuard` against Alexa's [13] top 1,000 websites. Our evaluation results show that `TabsGuard` enjoys 96.5 % accuracy. This is a noticeable improvement over one of the most popular existing techniques (`TabShots` [7]), which has reported only 78 % accuracy.

The rest of this paper is organized as follows. In Sect. 2, we provide background information on the tabnabbing attack. Section 3 introduces our proposed tabnabbing detection and prevention technique. The details of the dataset used and the experimental evaluation are discussed in Sect. 4. In Sect. 5, we review the existing phishing and tabnabbing detection solutions proposed thus far. Finally, we conclude in Sect. 6.

2 Tabnabbing Attack

As described earlier, tabnabbing is a complex form of phishing attack that takes over the inactive browser tabs. This section provides background information

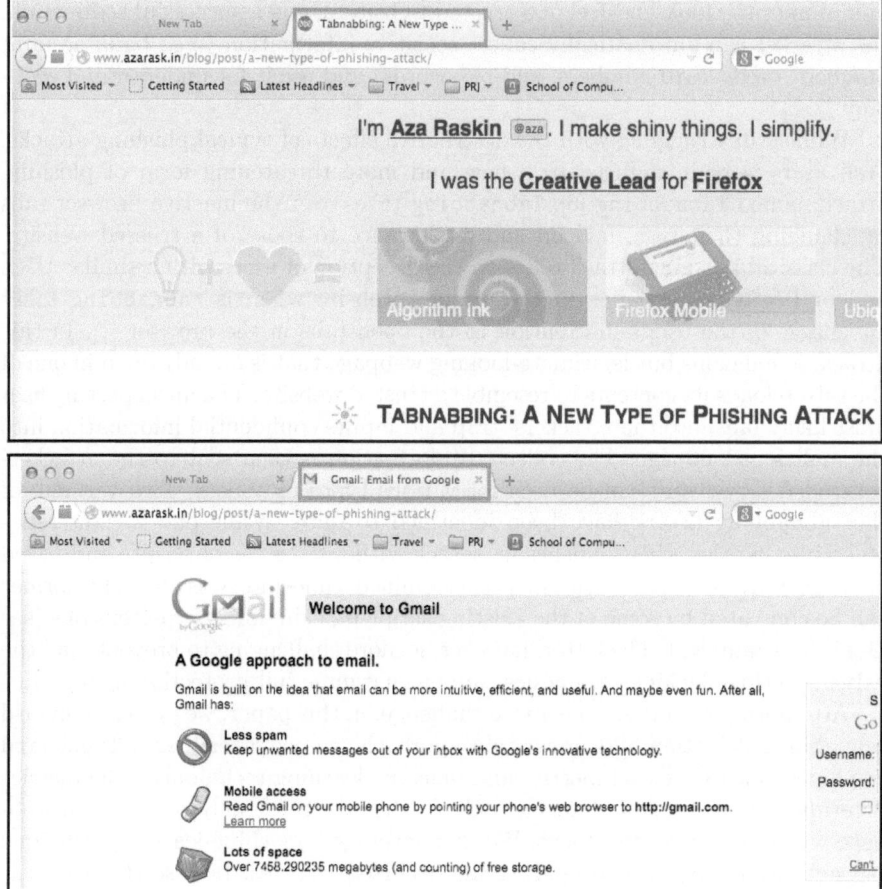

Fig. 1. Overview of the tabnabbing attack [6].

on the tabnabbing attack and its variants [6,8]. An overview of the tabnabbing attack is presented by Aza Raskin [6] (see also Fig. 1). The attack scenario assumes that the user has a number of open tabs in her browser. The steps for this scenario are as follows:

1. The user opens an already malicious page in a tab, navigates away from the tab after a short while, and moves to other open tabs.
2. The malicious page detects that the tab is out of focus. It reloads the title, favicon and contents of the page in the tab, replacing the title and favicon with those of a trusted website and the appearance of the page with one looking alike the appearance of the trusted website (in this case, the login page of Gmail).
3. The user moves back to the tab, views a trusted website's login page, assumes that she has been signed out, and enters her credentials into the login form.

4. The user's personal information is sent to the attacker-controlled server.
5. The malicious webpage redirects the user to the trusted website —of which the user has never been signed out— to make it seem like the login attempt was successful.

Some alterations have been made to the above attack scenario by Lokesh Singh [14]. In this alternative scenario [14], *iframes* are used for launching the tabnabbing attack. In addition, *timers* with predetermined values replace the tab switch events that trigger the attack. Using more complex attack methods, the tabnabbing attack could be developed into an even more threatening version. Some attacks make use of Cascading Style Sheets (CSS) history miner to access the user's full browsing history or find out which websites the user visits on a regular basis. Other types of the attack check whether the user is currently logged in to the target website and perform the attack when the user is actually logged in so as to make the attack more convincing. Cross-site scripting (XSS) vulnerabilities can also be utilized to force the attack to be launched by other websites.

There are two proof of concepts available for the tabnabbing attack. The first one [6] is based on the execution of JavaScript. Here, the state of a tab (*i.e.*, active or inactive) is identified by JavaScript `onblur` and `onfocus` events. The second one [8] does not rely on the execution of scripts and uses the meta-refresh HTML attribute. This attribute causes the automatic reloading of the page after a predefined time interval. Unlike the script-based variant of the attack, the script-free variant does not depend on user activity, but on the given time interval by which the attacker hopes the user has switched tabs and thus is not attentive to the tab under attack.

One popular solution to protect users from phishing and its variants is to enhance the capability of Web browsers with additional security features so that users can be warned whenever a phishing website is being accessed. Such browser security is often provided by a mechanism known as blacklisting, which is the most common technique to defend against phishing attacks [15]. In addition to this, there are many other types of techniques to combat phishing attacks (*e.g.*, whitelisting, webpage analysis, use of heuristics, machine-learning classifiers, and search engines). However, there are very few techniques specific to tabnabbing detection and prevention (see Sect. 5).

3   TabsGuard: Proposed Approach

According to the tabnabbing attack scenario, changes made to the title, favicon and contents of a webpage can best represent the changes made to the webpage under attack. Thus, an effective tabnabbing detection technique should be able to detect the degree of changes these three parameters go through when the tab is out of focus.

Figure 2 provides an overview of our proposed approach for tabnabbing detection and prevention. Our approach, given a page opened in a tab, fetches three parameters (*i.e.*, title, favicon and the HTML DOM tree of the page) at two times t_1 and t_2 and compares the data for each parameter at time t_1 with its corresponding parameter at time t_2; where t_1 is the time when the page is fully loaded and t_2 is when the user returns to that tab after at least one tab switch. This comparison is used to monitor the changes that the page goes through between timess t_1 and t_2.

As shown in Fig. 2, the design and implementation of `TabsGuard` consists of the following phases: (1) Fetching, (2) Parsing, (3) Metrics building, (4) Comparison, and (5) Analysis. Let us assume we have a webpage open in a browser tab. In phase 1, the extractor fetches the title and favicon of the page. Then, the parsing engine takes the HTML source code of the page, extracts pure HTML from the tags, and removes the text contents to get its DOM tree representation. It should be noted that DOM trees have traditionally been used to model the structural information of webpages. In our case, the HTML DOM tree represents the HTML layout of a webpage, defining its structure and the way it is accessed or manipulated.

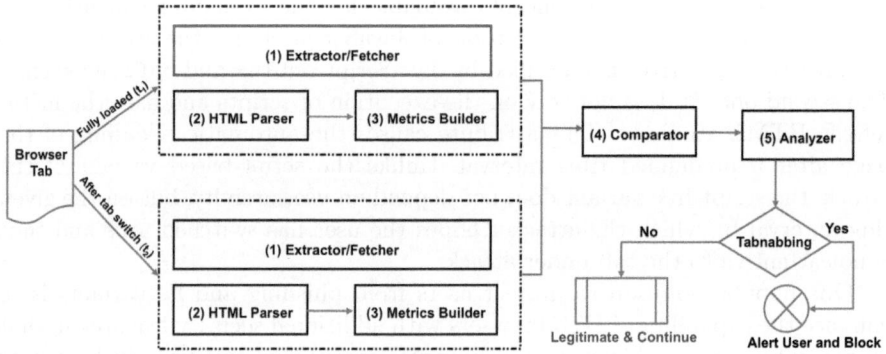

Fig. 2. Overview of TabsGuard's workflow. The numbers indicate the order of execution.

In phase 3, using the HTML content of the page, the metrics builder computes a number of heuristic metrics for comparing the DOM trees built at times t_1 and t_2. For this purpose, we studied a number of existing works [16, 17] used to detect layout/structural similarity between webpages and text documents. As presented by Ricca and Tonella [16, 17], there are three different ways to classify similar pages.

1. *Textual identity*: Two pages are considered identical if they have the exact same HTML code.
2. *Syntactical identity*: Syntax trees of the pages are compared, text content between HTML tags is removed, and pages with the exact same structure are considered identical.
3. *Syntactical similarity*: A similarity metric is computed based on the syntax trees of the pages, and pages with similar structure are classified.

The limitation of the first two classification approaches is that they look for exact matches. Syntactical similarity, on the other hand, can be used to define a similarity threshold according to which two pages are considered similar. In our comparison phase, we do not expect the webpage at time t_1 to have the exact same HTML source code or structure as the one at time t_2, but that the two webpages have similar structures. Thus, we define the following heuristic-based metrics for conducting the comparison with respect to syntactical similarity.

(H1) Common Paths (CP) [18]: We use CP for comparing the structure of two webpages by looking at the paths leading from the root node to the leaf nodes in the HTML DOM tree. A path consists of the concatenation of the names of the elements it passes from root to leaf. Each page can then be represented in terms of the set of paths it contains, *i.e.*, $p(P)$. Equation 1 illustrates the CP similarity measure, where P_1 is the page at time t_1 and P_2 is the page at time t_2. The closer a CP value to 1, the higher the degree of similarity between P_1 and P_2.

$$CP(P_1, P_2) = \frac{|p(P_1) \cap p(P_2)|}{max(|p(P_1)|, |p(P_2)|)} \qquad (1)$$

(H2) Cosine Similarity (CS) [19] and *Class names:* The cosine measure similarity is a similarity metric that has been used for detecting the similarity between text documents. We derive a vector of tags from the page at both times t_1 and t_2. For each tag that uses a class name, we append the class name to its corresponding tag name as well. Therefore, the page at times t_1 and t_2 is viewed as two vectors in a vector space, with each {tag-class} name having its own axis. Let P_1 be the page at time t_1 and P_2 be the page at time t_2. Cosine similarity is computed by dividing the dot product of P_1 and P_2 (the numerator in Eq. 2) by the product of their magnitudes (the denominator in Eq. 2). A CS value closer to 1 indicates more similarity between the two pages.

$$CS(P_1, P_2) = \frac{P_1.P_2}{|P_1||P_2|} = \frac{\sum_{i=1}^{n} P_{1_i} \times P_{2_i}}{\sqrt{\sum_{i=1}^{n}(P_{1_i})^2 \times \sum_{i=1}^{n}(P_{2_i})^2}} \qquad (2)$$

(H3) Tag Frequency Distribution Analysis (TFDA) [20,21]: TFDA is proposed with the assumption that tag frequencies reflect built-in characteristics of a webpage and are closely related to its structure. To calculate this metric, we compute the frequency of each HTML tag and incorporate them into Eq. 3, where F_{t_1} and F_{t_2} are the frequencies of tag t in pages P_1 and P_2, n is the total number of tags, w_t is the weight for the tth tag and $\sum_{t=1}^{n} w_t = 1$. TFDA values are then normalized to fall between 0 and 1. A TFDA value closer to 1 shows that P_2 resembles P_1 to a great extent.

$$TFDA(P_1, P_2) = \sum_{i=1}^{n}(F_{t_1} - F_{t_2})^2 \times w_t \qquad (3)$$

(H4) Input fields added to the page: Most of the time, a malicious page can be a threat to the user only if it requires user actions (in this case, user input).

Therefore, when comparing P_1 and P_2, we take the new input fields added to the page at time t_2 into account.

(H5) iframes in the page before and after tab switch: Tabnabbing attacks can also be launched using iframes. Hence, if a page consists of iframes at both times t_1 and t_2, we consider it a tabnabbing candidate.

The abovementioned metrics provide values for comparing the HTML DOM trees at times t_1 and t_2 (phase 4). This helps us detect any changes made to the HTML layout or the overall structure of the page during the time it was out of focus. The comparator then determines the percentage of similarity between the titles at times t_1 and t_2 using the algorithm of Longest Common Substring (LCS). Finally, we use base64 image encoding [22] to compare the resulting strings from the favicon of the page at times t_1 and t_2. We also check the favicon's URL at these two times to look for the changes made to the favicon after tab switch.

Once the comparison is completed, finally we analyze the changes (phase 5) using k-NN [12]. It should be noted that k-NN has been widely used for anomaly detection, *i.e.*, identifying cases or items that are unusual within seemingly homogeneous data and/or do not conform to an expected behavior [23]. In our case, an anomalous item, also known as an outlier, is an item that is considered unusual as it is distant or different from the normal distribution of data. To find the outliers in a dataset, a k-NN model can be used to score the input data. Outliers represent tabnabbing pages, and our aim is to find them in a given dataset. Thus, for each page in the dataset, if the score determined by the degree of changes is higher than the average outlier score, the page is detected as tabnabbing and an alert message is displayed to the user. To prevent the user from further proceeding into the tabnabbed website, the victim is redirected to a trusted domain and the page is added to a local blacklist on the user's browser.

4   Experimental Evaluation

In this section, first we provide an overview of the way `TabsGuard` is evaluated. Then, we explain the experiments and the results obtained. Finally, we analyze our results and compare them with those of `TabShots`.

4.1   Overview

We have implemented `TabsGuard` as a Mozilla Firefox (Version 29.0.1) extension. The toolsets we used for evaluating `TabsGuard` include: RapidMiner 5.3 [24] for facilitating the machine-learning process using k-NN and iMacros [25] for the automation of repetitive tasks on the browser during the data collection step. We also developed an in-house script to automatically create the dataset which is then fed to iMacros. In order to prevent from slowing down or crashing the browser, instead of once opening 1,000 tabs in the browser, we split the 1,000 websites into ten. Each list is given to the script as input in one separate run.

In our evaluation, we focused on addressing the following two points: (i) Using `TabsGuard` for correctly identifying tabnabbing pages as malicious; (ii) Using

TabsGuard for correctly identifying legitimate pages as benign. With respect to the first point, the detection of all tabnabbing pages is ensured by the way TabsGuard has been designed. As noted earlier, by definition, a tabnabbing attack changes the title, favicon and contents of a page either by the use of scripts (*i.e.*, the script-based variant) or by refreshing the page after a predetermined interval (*i.e.*, the script-free variant). TabsGuard guarantees zero false negatives, because our approach of keeping track of all major changes made to the title, favicon and HTML layout of a page cannot miss any tabnabbing attack of either variant. If among title, favicon and layout, one or two of the three do not change, the attack is still detected by TabsGuard, not as a tabnabbing attack, but as a classical phishing attack. The above claim is based on the evaluation of few tabnabbing pages we have at hand. Thus, since there is no single repository that maintains known tabnabbing websites, our claim is yet to be verified experimentally. With respect to the second point, we used the top 1,000 trusted websites from Alexa to evaluate the accuracy and performance of TabsGuard as a Firefox extension (see Sect. 4.2).

4.2   Experimental Analysis

When our in-house script is executed, first, each website is opened in a tab, and after being fully loaded, its title, favicon and HTML layout are recorded. After this step, a blank tab is opened to serve as a temporary location the browser is redirected to at the time of tab switches. For every website, the browser is redirected to its corresponding tab, switches location to the blank tab, and after staying on the blank tab for 60 s, again redirected to the former tab. At this point, the title, favicon and HTML layout of the page are recorded again, and the heuristic-based metrics are computed. Then, the script moves on to the next page and so on. When this is done for all the open tabs, the script execution is completed. This whole procedure is done once more for a tabnabbing attack we developed. Finally, a dataset consisting of the computed values of the five metrics for all 1,000 websites and the tabnabbing page is created. The complete dataset is then passed to an anomaly detection algorithm as input to determine the outlier score for each website, which is used for identifying the false positives.

As noted above, we set 60 s as the amount of waiting time required before switching back to each tab. The reason is that from the attacker's point of view, each page is reloaded with new contents either when the tab switch event is detected (in the script-based variant of the attack) or after a predetermined time interval (in the script-free variant of the attack). In the first case, reloading of the contents is done shortly after the user moves away from the tab. In the second case, page refresh should be done no later than 60 s after the user has switched tabs, because according to Nielsen [26], "The average page visit lasts a little less than a minute." Therefore, assuming that the user visits only one other page and then decides to return to the inactive tab, the interval is less than 60 s, meaning that the attacker has 60 s at most to reload the tab with a new appearance. Hence, in our detection scenario, we assume that the user returns to the tab after 60 s, and we measure the changes after the 60-second interval has elapsed.

Table 1. Comparison of TabsGuard and TabShots using top 20 Alexa sites.

Website	% of changed blocks by TabShots	% of changes by TabsGuard		
		$H1_2$	$H2_2$	$H3_2$
facebook.com	0.38	0.00	0.00	1E-07
google.com	0.00	0.00	0.00	0.00
youtube.com	4.05	0.00	0.00	0.00
yahoo.com	5.31	0.00	0.00	0.00
baidu.com	0.00	0.00	0.00	0.00
wikipedia.org	0.73	0.00	0.00	0.00
live.com	2.65	0.00	0.0015	6.2E-06
twitter.com	2.91	0.00	0.00	0.00
qq.com	6.00	0.00	0.00	0.00
amazon.com	2.57	0.00	0.00	0.00
blogspot.com	0.32	0.00	0.00	0.00
linkedin.com	0.26	0.00	0.00	0.00
taobao.com	0.49	0.00	0.00	2.59E-05
google.co.in	0.00	0.00	0.00	0.00
yahoo.co.jp	4.13	0.00	0.00	0.00
sina.com.cn	1.24	0.00	0.00	0.00
msn.com	23.22	0.00	0.01	0.00
google.com.hk	0.00	0.00	0.00	0.00
google.de	0.00	0.00	0.00	0.00
bing.com	0.00	0.00	0.00	0.00

k-NN is used to measure whether an item is distant from the other items in a dataset. As mentioned earlier, the outlier score of each item in the dataset is determined by the distance to its k-nearest neighbor. In RapidMiner, k-NN Global Anomaly Score serves as an operator to calculate the outlier score. The outlier score is the average of the distance to the nearest neighbors, and the higher the score the more anomalous the instance is. In our experiment, k, which is the number of neighbors to be considered, is set to 10. The five metrics introduced earlier are the attributes, and the label attribute is tabnabbing which is set to false for all Alexa sites and to true for the tabnabbing page in the dataset. For the 1,000 pages, the average outlier score obtained is 0.003 with the standard deviation of 0.045. We consider a page in the dataset an outlier if the score computed for it is greater than 0.003. This results in a 3.5 % false positive rate and 96.5 % accuracy for TabsGuard, which is a great improvement over the 78 % accuracy reported by TabShots. Now, if we define an outlier to be a page with a score greater than 0.048 (*i.e.*, 0.003+0.045) instead, we get 0.8 % false positive rate or 99.2 % accuracy. Websites recognized as outliers in our experiment are those that either use technologies such as AJAX to dynamically change the

Table 2. Comparison of TabsGuard and TabShots in worst-case scenarios.

Website	% of changed blocks by TabShots	% of changes by TabsGuard		
		$H1_2$	$H2_2$	$H3_2$
americanexpress.com	38.93	0.00	0.00	0.00
mlb.com	97.31	0.00	0.0009237	1.9E-06

contents of the page, or contain image slideshows, or both. Some examples of such websites are http://www.ebay.com, http://www.espn.go.com and http://www.uol.com.br.

4.3 Discussion

Table 1 shows the top 20 Alexa websites and their percentage of changed blocks. Column 2 shows the results of TabShots as reported in [7] and Columns 3-5 show the results obtained by TabsGuard. Since our metrics show similarity rate rather than the percentage of change, we normalized the values of $H1$, $H2$ and $H3$ accordingly. To avoid any confusion, we rename the normalized version of the metrics to $H1_2$ $H2_2$, and $H3_2$. Table 1 clearly shows that the mechanism we utilize for detecting changes in a page is superior to that of TabShots, because TabsGuard is able to detect very minor changes in legitimate websites. It should also be noted that TabShots measures the percentage of changed blocks (*i.e.,* 10×10 tiles in the screenshot of a webpage) whereas TabsGuard measures the changes across the whole webpage with respect to the tree structure of the page. This is a distinct advantage of TabsGuard over TabShots, because measuring the changes block by block might lead to missing some changes and this could result in more false negatives.

De Ryck et al. [7] have also given two examples of their worst-case scenario for the websites with changes between 5 % and 40 % and the websites with changes more than 40 %. These two examples are http://americanexpress.com and http://mlb.com with the reported results of 38.93 % and 97.31 % for the changed blocks, respectively. The high percentage of changed blocks for the former website is claimed to be due to the delayed loading of a background image. In our experiment, no such case has been observed with TabsGuard. The reason is that TabsGuard waits for each page to be fully loaded before it starts functioning. As shown in Table 2, we detect very small changes for these two websites.

Furthermore, we conducted an analysis on the proposed metrics to find out the individual impact of each metric on a page being tabnabbing or legitimate. Given Eq. 4, where $H1$ to $H5$ are our attributes and Y is the result indicating whether each page is legitimate or tabnabbing, we are interested in finding values for relevance coefficients a, b, c, d, and e.

$$Y = aH1 + bH2 + cH3 + dH4 + eH5 \qquad (4)$$

Using the Weight by Correlation operator in RapidMiner, we obtained the values shown in Table 3 for a, b, c, d, and e. This operator calculates the weight of attributes $H1$ to $H5$ with respect to the label attribute (tabnabbing) by computing the value of correlation for each attribute. The higher the weight of an attribute, the more relevant it is considered to result Y.

Table 3. Relevance values computed for the five proposed metrics.

Relevance coefficient	Value
a	0.668
b	0.980
c	0.995
d	1.00
e	0.00

As shown in Table 3, we can infer that $H4$ (*i.e.*, input fields added), $H3$ (*i.e.*, TFDA) and $H2$ (*i.e.*, Cosine similarity and class names) are the most relevant attributes to Y, whereas the relevance of $H1$ (*i.e.*, CP) is a little less. The zero value obtained for $H5$ conveys that the existence of iframes in the page before and after tab switch is not relevant to a webpage being tabnabbing. The reason is that nowadays, the majority of websites, especially the popular ones such as Google and Facebook use iframes for embedding advertisements or other non-malicious content within their HTML code.

5   Related Work

In this section, first we briefly describe phishing detection techniques and then we discuss the existing tabnabbing detection techniques in detail.

5.1   Phishing

Several anti-phishing solutions have been proposed in the literature. Some of these solutions focus on list-based (*i.e.*, blacklists [15,27] or whitelists [2]) to distinguish between phishing and legitimate websites. There are some approaches that leverage the combination of heuristics and machine-learning techniques [2,15,27] to check one or more characteristics of a website to detect phishing attacks. Other approaches leverage the properties of the webpage and utilize search engines or data mining tools to analyze suspicious pages according to certain properties derived from HTML code, URL and contents [4,28–30].

List-based techniques benefit from simplicity and efficiency. However, their major weakness is that they strongly rely on the completeness of the database in order to work properly. Heuristic-based techniques on the other hand do not suffer from this drawback and are able to detect zero-day phishing attacks. Nevertheless, heuristic-based techniques are more prone to result in a false alarm.

In addition, heuristic-based techniques enjoy shorter response times, but get less accurate results compared to blacklist-based techniques.

As part of the anti-phishing campaign, Mozilla also introduced *Mozilla Persona* [31] to protect users from being tricked into entering their personal information into fake login forms. This solution serves as an authentication system in which email addresses are used as identifiers to eliminate the necessity of multiple username/password submissions for signing into various accounts. Thus, it can reduce the risk of accidentally sending credentials to a malicious server.

Table 4. Overview of the existing tabnabbing detection solutions.

Techniques \ Criteria	Whitelist-Based	Blacklist-Based	Browser	Script-based Attack Prevention	Script-Free Attack Prevention	Technology in Use
NoScript [14]	X		Firefox	Yes	Detection only; Passive prevention	JavaScript
Controle de Scripts [15]			Firefox	No	No	JavaScript
YesScript [16]		X	Firefox	No	No	JavaScript
NotScripts [17]	X		Chrome; Opera	Yes	No	JavaScript; HTML5 storage caching
ScriptSafe [18]	X	X	Chrome	Not by default	No	JavaScript
Script Defender [19]	X		Chrome; Opera	Yes	No	JavaScript
Script Block [20]	X		Chrome	Yes	No	JavaScript
TabShots [4]			Chrome	Yes; Passive prevention	Yes; Passive prevention	Screenshot comparison; Threshold value
NoTabNab [21]			Firefox	Yes; Passive prevention	Yes; Passive prevention	HTML layout; Positions of the topmost elements
Signature-based Approach [22]				Yes	No, only checks script tags	Extracting text between script tags; Rule-based system
Our Work: TabsGuard			Firefox	Yes; Active prevention	Yes; Active prevention	HTML DOM; Heuristics and Machine-Learning techniques

5.2 Tabnabbing

We group the existing tabnabbing detection solutions into two. While the first group includes *script-blocking browser extensions* that block scripts which are susceptive to perform malicious actions or violate the browser security policy, the second group is specifically designed to detect or prevent tabnabbing attacks. Table 4 provides an overview of the existing anti-tabnabbing solutions as well as an overview of our proposed approach, TabsGuard, in the last row. In what follows, we discuss these solutions in detail.

Script-Blocking Browser Extensions. The following browser extensions provide protection against the script-based variant of tabnabbing — except for NoScript that provides a passive protection against the script-free variant of the attack as well. This protection is dependent on the default behavior of extensions towards preventing JavaScript code from execution on untrusted domains.

NoScript [9], `Controle de Scripts` [10], and `YesScript` [32] are Firefox-specific solutions. `NoScript` uses a whitelist-based approach, allowing JavaScript and other embedded content to be executed only by websites that the user trusts. Thus, the default behavior of NoScript is blocking all scripts that are not whitelisted, a behavior compromising the normal functioning of most websites. Additionally, being whitelist-based, it relies on the user's choice to allow scripts on a website, and therefore its tabnabbing protection mechanism is mainly manually provided. `Controle de Scripts` allows the user to control what JavaScript can do on the browser by adding extra settings to the browser preferences window, whereas `YesScript` lets the user make a blacklist of websites that are not allowed to run JavaScript. The main weakness of `YesScript` is its reliance on blacklists as blacklists always needs to be up-to-date.

`ScriptSafe` [33] and `ScriptBlock` [11] are both Chrome-specific solutions. `ScriptSafe` provides some of NoScript's functionalities and uses both blacklist-based and whitelist-based approaches. This extension does not prevent the script-based tabnabbing attack by default. In our understanding, this might be due to its dependability on blacklists. `ScriptBlock` [26] implements a whitelist-based approach to control JavaScript, iframes, and plugins.

Both `NotScripts` [34] and `Script Defender` [35] are implemented as extension services for Chrome and Opera browsers. `NotScripts` provides a high degree of NoScript-like control for Javascript, iframes, and plugins. Like NoScript, it implements a whitelist-based approach thereby leaving the decision to allow or block the scripts at the hands of the user. Moreover, it does not prevent inline scripts that are embedded in the HTML code of a webpage. On the other hand, `Script Defender`[1] allows JavaScript and other embedded content to be executed only on trusted domains that are whitelisted by the user. The default settings of `Script Defender` [24] block internal scripts and plugins. However, this extension allows external scripts, images, and iframes unless the preferences are changed by the user.

In general, there are some criticism on this group of anti-tabnabbing solutions. For instance, being the most popular browser extension to overcome tabnabbing attacks, `NoScript` cannot effectively prevent the script-free variant. NoScript blocks page refreshes on unfocused tabs and instead lets them automatically execute only when the tab gets in focus again. However, the reloading of the page happens any way, and it is likely that it still does not get noticed by inattentive users. Furthermore, among the browser extensions mentioned above, `NotScripts`, `ScriptSafe`, `Script Defender`, and `Script Block` for Chrome provide no protection against the script-free variant of the tabnabbing attack. Similarly, `YesScript` and `Controle de Scripts` provide no protection against either variant of the attack. The advantage of `TabsGuard` over this group of anti-tabnabbing solutions is that we do not rely on the user's decision to stop malicious scripts from running. Instead, we detect the pages that are potentially malicious with a very high probability and warn the user of the threat.

---

[1] This extension has recently been removed from Chrome and Opera repositories.

Tabnabbing Detection and Prevention Techniques. We found only three approaches for tabnabbing detection and prevention: TabShots [7], NoTabNab [36], and the approach proposed by Suri et al. [37].

TabShots is a Chrome extension that records the favicon and a screenshot of a webpage when it is visited for the first time and once after a tab switch. If the observed changes are higher than a predefined threshold value, a visual overlay appears on the page to warn the user about the possibility of the tabnabbing attack. TabShots has been evaluated against the top 1,000 Alexa sites, showing that 78 % of the websites go through less than 5 % changes, 19 % fall within 5 %-40 % changes, and 3 % go through more than 40 % changes. The main deficiency of Tabshots is relying on screenshots and image analysis to detect the changes made to a page. The reason is that in the websites that use dynamic refreshing of contents (Facebook, Linkedin and Twitter to name a few), small changes could be considered major, leading to a large number of false positives.

NoTabNab is a Firefox extension that records the favicon, title, and the positions of the topmost HTML elements of each webpage when the user navigates to the page for the first time. To detect tabnabbing attacks, NoTabNab computes the changes occurred in the layout of the page when the user navigates back to the inactive tab. However, the positioning of HTML elements of a page cannot be a determining factor for detecting tabnabbing, because it changes if the page is resized. In addition, since only the topmost elements are considered, changes cannot be detected if all page contents are placed in an iframe.

An approach to perceive tabnabbing attack is proposed by Suri et al. [37]. This approach leverages a signature-based technique for detecting tabnabbing attacks that are launched using iframes. For each webpage, the approach extracts the text content between script tags. The attack is then detected using a rule-based system which takes mouse clicks, onblur and onfocus events for iframes into account. The first limitation of this approach is that it is only designed for iframe-based tabnabbing attacks. Moreover, since only the contents of script tags are checked, the script-free variant of the attack cannot be detected using this approach. As for detecting the script-based variant of the attack, only inline scripts are considered, hence leaving out the external scripts undetected.

6 Conclusion

The Web has become an indispensable global platform as it glues together various services as a one stop shop (*e.g.,* daily communication, sharing, trading, and collaboration). Users of the Web often store and manage critical information that attracts attackers who misuse the Web and its infrastructure (*e.g.,* browsers) to exploit vulnerabilities for underground economy. Phishing is one of the most common types of contemporary attacks. While most of the existing anti-phishing techniques are still struggling with effectively detecting and preventing phishing, a new variant of phishing attack — named Tabnabbing — has benn identified. Tabnabbing is a more sophisticated way of tricking users by leveraging the facilities tabs offer to modern Web browsers.

This paper presented the `TabsGuard` browser extension mechanism. `Tabs Guard` combines the benefits of heuristic-based metrics and an anomaly detection technique to detect tabnabbing attacks. We evaluated `TabsGuard` against the top 1,000 Alexa websites and gained 96.5 % accuracy that is much higher than the 78 % accuracy obtained by `TabShots`.

As part of our future work, we plan to extend `TabsGuard` and the underlying implementation in a number of ways. We may incorporate more heuristic-based metrics into our tabnabbing detection approach to improve its accuracy. Moreover, regarding the shortage of tabnabbing pages, we plan to generate more tabnabbing pages to be able to build a training dataset and investigate and compare the effectiveness of different classification techniques for detecting tabnabbing attacks. Finally, we plan to extend `TabsGuard` to other Web browsers and make it available as a service for public use.

References

1. Anti-Phishing Working Group. Global Phishing Survey: Trends and Domain Name Use in 2H2013. http://docs.apwg.org/reports/APWG_GlobalPhishing Survey_2H2013.pdf
2. Belabed, A., Aïmeur, E., and Chikh, A.: A personalized whitelist approach for phishing webpage detection. In: Proceedings of the 2012 Seventh International Conference on Availability, Reliability and Security, ARES 2012, pp. 249–254. IEEE Computer Society, Washington, DC (2012)
3. Bin, S., Qiaoyan, W., and Xiaoying, L.: A DNS-based anti-phishing approach. In: Proceedings of the 2010 2nd International Conference on Networks Security, Wireless Communications and Trusted Computing - NSWCTC 2010, vol. 02, pp. 262–265. IEEE Computer Society, Washington (2010)
4. Dunlop, M., Groat, S., Shelly, D.: Goldphish: using images for content-based phishing analysis. In: Proceedings of the Fifth International Conference on Internet Monitoring and Protection, ICIMP 2010, pp. 123–128, May 2010
5. Maggi, F.: Are the Con Artists Back? A preliminary analysis of modern phone frauds. In: CIT, pp. 824–831. IEEE Computer Society (2010)
6. Tabnabbing: A New Type of Phishing Attack. http://www.azarask.in/blog/post/a-new-type-of-phishing-attack/
7. Ryck, P.D., Nikiforakis, N., Desmet, L., Joosen, w.: TabShots: Client-side detection of tabnabbing attacks. In: Proceedings of the 8th ACM SIGSAC Symposium on Information, Computer and Communications Security, ASIA CCS 2013, pp. 447–456. ACM, New York (2013)
8. Krebs on Security. Devious New Phishing Tactic Targets Tabs. http://avivraff.com/research/phish/article.php?1464682399
9. InformAction Open Source Software. Noscript. http://noscript.net/
10. Mozilla Foundation. Controle de Scripts. https://addons.mozilla.org/en-US/firefox/addon/controle-de-scripts/
11. Script Block. https://chrome.google.com/webstore/detail/scriptblock/hcdjknjpbnhdoabbngpmfekaecnpajba?hl=en
12. StatSoft. k-Nearest Neighbors. http://www.statsoft.com/textbook/k-nearest-neighbors
13. Alexa - Actionable Analytics for the Web. http://www.alexa.com/, May 2014

14. Learn How To Hack Best Online Ethical Hacking Website. Advanced Tabnabbing Tutorial. http://www.hackingloops.com/2012/04/advanced-tabnabbing-tutorial.html
15. Prakash, P., Kumar, M., Kompella, R.R., Gupta, M.: PhishNet: Predictive blacklisting to detect phishing attacks. In: Proceedings of the 29th Conference on Information Communications, INFOCOM 2010, pp. 346–350. IEEE Press, Piscataway (2010)
16. Ricca, F., Tonella, P.: Analysis and testing of web applications. In: Proceedings of the 23rd International Conference on Software Engineering, ICSE 2001, pp. 25–34, IEEE Computer Society Washington, DC (2001)
17. Tonella, P., Ricca, F.: Statistical testing of web applications. J. Softw. Maint. Evol. **16**(1–2), 103–127 (2004)
18. Gottron, T.: Clustering template based web documents. In: Macdonald, C., Ounis, I., Plachouras, V., Ruthven, I., White, R.W. (eds.) ECIR 2008. LNCS, vol. 4956, pp. 40–51. Springer, Heidelberg (2008)
19. Seeking Wisdom. TF-IDF and Cosine Similarity. http://janav.wordpress.com/2013/10/27/tf-idf-and-cosine-similarity/
20. Cruz, I., Borisov, S., Marks, M.A., Webb, T.R.: Measuring structural similarity among web documents: preliminary results. In: Hersch, R.D., André, J., Brown, H. (eds.) RIDT 1998 and EPub 1998. LNCS, vol. 1375, pp. 513–524. Springer, Heidelberg (1998)
21. Tombros, A., Ali, Z.: Factors affecting web page similarity. In: Fernández-Luna, J.M., Losada, D.E. (eds.) ECIR 2005. LNCS, vol. 3408, pp. 487–501. Springer, Heidelberg (2005)
22. IETF. The Base16, Base32, and Base64 Data Encodings. https://tools.ietf.org/html/rfc4648/
23. Oracle Data Mining Concepts. Anomaly Detection. http://docs.oracle.com/cd/B28359_01/datamine.111/b28129/anomalies.htm#DMCON006
24. RapidMiner. http://rapidminer.com/
25. Mozilla Firefox. iMacros for FireFox. https://addons.mozilla.org/en-US/firefox/addon/imacros-for-firefox/
26. Nielsen Norman Group. How Long Do Users Stay on Web Pages? http://www.nngroup.com/articles/how-long-do-users-stay-on-web-pages/
27. Gupta, G., Pieprzyk, J.: Socio-technological phishing prevention. Inf. Secur. Tech. Rep. **16**(2), 67–73 (2011)
28. Zhang, Y., Hong, J.I., Cranor, L.F.: CANTINA: A content-based approach to detecting phishing web sites. In: Proceedings of the 16th International Conference on World Wide Web, WWW 2007, pp. 639–648. ACM, New York (2007)
29. Ludl, C., McAllister, S., Kirda, E., Kruegel, C.: On the effectiveness of techniques to detect phishing sites. In: Hämmerli, B.M., Sommer, R. (eds.) DIMVA 2007. LNCS, vol. 4579, pp. 20–39. Springer, Heidelberg (2007)
30. Carine, G.: Webber, Maria de Ftima W. do Prado Lima, and Felipe S. Hepp. Testing Phishing Detection Criteria and Methods. In: Sambath, S., Zhu, E. (eds.) Frontiers in Computer Education. Advances in Intelligent and Soft Computing, vol. 133, pp. 853–858. Springer, Berlin Heidelberg (2012)
31. Mozilla Corporation. Mozilla Persona. https://login.persona.org/about
32. Mozilla Foundation. YesScript. https://addons.mozilla.org/en-US/firefox/addon/yesscript/
33. Chrome Web Store. ScriptSafe. https://chrome.google.com/webstore/detail/scriptsafe/oiigbmnaadbkfbmpbfijlflahbdbdgdf?hl=en

34. Chrome Web Store. NotScripts. https://chrome.google.com/webstore/detail/notscripts/odjhifogjcknibkahlpidmdajjpkkcfn?hl=en
35. Chrome Web Store. Script Defender. https://chrome.google.com/webstore/detail/scriptdefender/celgmkbkgakmkfboolifhbllkfiepcae?hl=en
36. Unlu, S.A., Bicakci, K.: NoTabNab: protection against the tabnabbing attack. In: eCrime Researchers Summit (eCrime), pp. 1–5 (2010)
37. Suri, R.K., Tomar, D.S., Sahu, D.R.: An approach to perceive tabnabbing attack. Int. J. Sci. Technol. Res. **1**, 447–456 (2012)

Towards a Full Support of Obligations in XACML

Donia El Kateb[1,2]($\boxtimes$), Yehia ElRakaiby[1], Tejeddine Mouelhi[1],
Iram Rubab[1,2], and Yves Le Traon[1,2]

[1] Security, Reliability and Trust, Interdisciplinary Research Center, SnT,
University of Luxembourg, Luxembourg, Luxembourg
{donia.elkateb,tejeddine.mouelhi,iram.rubab,yves.letraon}@uni.lu,
yehia.elrakaiby@gmail.com
[2] Laboratory of Advanced Software SYstems (LASSY), University of Luxembourg,
Luxembourg, Luxembourg

Abstract. Policy-based systems rely on the separation of concerns, by
implementing independently a software system and its associated security policy.

XACML (eXtensible Access Control Markup Language) proposes a
conceptual architecture and a policy language to reflect this ideal design
of policy-based systems.However, while rights are well-captured by authorizations, duties, also called obligations, are not well managed by XACML
architecture. The current version of XACML lacks (1) well-defined syntax to express obligations and (2) an unified model to handle decision
making w.r.t. obligation states and the history of obligations fulfillment/
violation. In this work, we propose an extension of XACML reference
model that integrates obligation states in the decision making process. We
have extended XACML language and architecture for a better obligations
support and have shown how obligations are managed in our proposed
extended XACML architecture: *OB-XACML*.

Keywords: Usage control · PEP · PDP · XACML

1 Introduction

Access control policies regulate users access to the sensitive resources in a given
system and they are commonly defined as a set of rules, specified according to an
access control model. Obligations [1] allow to extend the notion of access rights
with related duties. A complete security policy should encompass both rights and
duties, both access authorizations and obligations. XACML (eXtensible Access
Control Markup Language)[1] is a standardized policy specification language that
defines access control policies in an XML format and defines a standard way to
exchange access control requests/responses. Even though XACML supports several profiles to handle authorizations scenarios, its support for usage control is

---

[1] http://www.oasis-open.org/committees/xacml/.

© Springer International Publishing Switzerland 2015
J. Lopez et al. (Eds.): CRiSIS 2014, LNCS 8924, pp. 213–221, 2015.
DOI: 10.1007/978-3-319-17127-2_14

still in its infancy. Indeed, while access control is about a simple boolean decision-making (is the user authorized to access a service/resource?), obligations imply the notion of state. To the best of our knowledge, access control based on obligation states history is not yet handled by XACML architecture. To meet the challenges of reinforcing XACML standard to support obligations, going along the same line than Bertino [2], who pioneered the extension of XACML for usage control, we propose (1) Well-defined XML constructs that are compliant with XACML 3.0 to specify obligations. (2) *OB-XACML*: An underlying architecture that extends the current XACML architecture and that is able to take into consideration the history of obligations fulfillment/violation and obligation states at the level of the decision making process. *OB-XACML* introduces an interaction schema between the different key entities in XACML architecture to keep track of obligations fulfillment/violation related to the users in the system. To the best of our knowledge, our work is a first initiative that considers obligation states as a key element that must be considered at the evaluation time. This paper is organized as follows. Section 2 introduces obligations in XACML. Section 3 describes our extended architecture *OB-XACML*. Section 4 introduces the obligation syntax that supports OB-XACML and describes the different interactions between *OB-XACML* components. Section 5 presents the related work. Finally, Sect. 6 presents our conclusion and future work.

2   Obligations in XACML

XACML defines obligations as actions that have to be returned to the PEP with the PDP response[2]. XACML defines three PEP categories based on PDP decision and the ability of the PEP to handle obligations.

```
<Obligation ObligationId=''send-email'' FulfillOn=''Deny''>
<AttributeAssignment AttributeId=''email''>donia.kateb@uni.lu</AttributeAssignment>
</Obligation>
```

Listing 1.1. Obligation Example

In the reminder of this paper, we will only consider the *Deny-biased PEP*. In a *Deny-biased PEP* setting, the PEP decision is permit if the PDP decision is permit and all the obligations that are returned by the PDP are fulfilled. In all other cases, the PEP decision is deny. The reader may refer to [2] for more details about other PEPs categories. XACML 2.0[3] defines obligations as simple attributes assignment that are attached to the policy set or to the policy. In XACML 3.0[4], obligations can also be added to the rules additionally to the policies and policy sets. An obligation element contains the *obligation identifier* and the *FulfillOn* element which specifies the effect on which the obligation should be fulfilled by the PEP. For example, *FulfillOn* "Permit" specifies that the obligation should be enforced if the PEP decides to permit the request. The XML

---

[2] http://www.oasis-open.org/committees/xacml/.

[3] http://docs.oasis-open.org/xacml/2.0/accesscontrol-xacml-2.0-core-spec-os.pdf.

[4] http://www.oasis-open.org/committees/xacml/.

snippet in Listing 1.1 shows an example that illustrates that if the PDP decision is deny, the subject has to send an email to the address "donia.elkateb@uni.lu".

3   *OB-XACML* Architecture

In an XACML-based architecture, access control decisions are thus taken without taking into consideration obligations fulfillment or violation in previous accesses. In this work, we propose to introduce obligation information violations/fulfillment at the decision making time so that access control decisions are taken based on information related to obligation states or related to previous users obligations fulfillment/violation. Here are some motivating scenarios:

- A nurse has to send a report to the patient's treating doctor after each access to the patient's medical data. The report should describe some specific indicators about patient's health status. If the post-obligation of sending a report after the access is violated then the nurse should be prohibited from accessing patient's data in another access and some penalties measures have to be taken against her as a reaction to this non professional behavior.
- A user has the pre-obligation to sign a form before he accesses a web application. If the system keeps track of his fulfilled obligations then the user does not have to sign the form in every session. The system can thus record the fulfillment of the obligation in a first login and then the user can access the system in future sessions without the need to fulfill his pre-obligations.

To support such scenarios, we extend the current XACML architecture so that information inherent from subjects fulfillment/violation of their obligations is taken into consideration at the decision making time. To provide a decision making process that takes into consideration obligation states, we propose to store obligations states in the Policy Information Point (PIP) additionally to attributes values such as resource, subject, environment. Such information is retrieved dynamically at the decision making time and used for request evaluation. Our extension is shown in Fig. 1. The PDP sends to the PEP the access

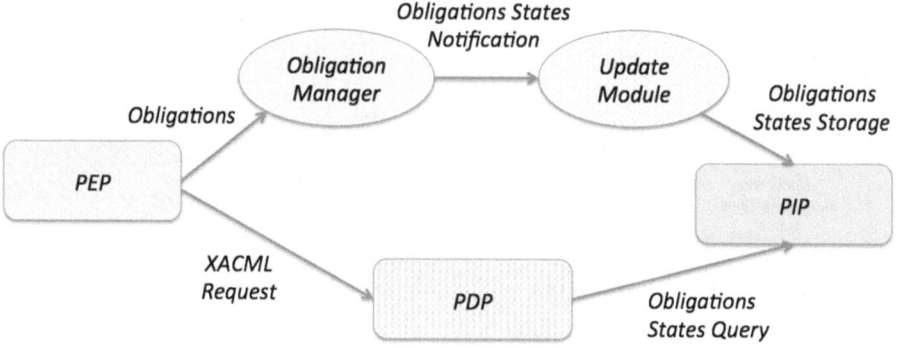

Fig. 1. OB-XACML workflow

decision and the obligations that have to be monitored by the PEP. Each obligation is handled by the obligation manager which tracks obligation states evolution by monitoring their execution in the system. An obligation life cycle can
been modeled as a state machine as illustrated in [3]. An obligation state can
be (1) Inactive when the fulfillment of the obligation is not needed, (2) Active
when the obligation fulfillment is required, (3) Fulfilled when the obligation
is satisfied, (4) Violated when the obligation is violated. (5) Fulfilled/violated
when the obligation is violated and later it has been fulfilled (6) An obligation
is inactive when it ends. The transition between the different states is driven by
contexts [4]. An activation context specifies the different conditions under which
the obligation has to be fulfilled whereas the violation context specifies the conditions under which the obligation becomes violated. For example the obligation
to send a report after an access to an administration system is handled as follows by the obligation manager: (1) The user has an access to the platform: The
obligation is in an *active* state.(2) The user sends the report to the platform: The
obligation is in a *fulfilled* state. (3) The user does not send the report within a
given time: The obligation is in a *violated* state. The user behavior at the system
level is monitored through aspects which capture the different users actions [5].
The update module receives information related to the changes in obligations
states and updates the PIP with obligation state attributes that are provided by
the obligation manager. We enrich XACML conditions to express access control
rules that are conditioned by obligations fulfillment/violation. These conditions
will be introduced in the next Section.To explain the processing of obligations in
OB-XACML, we took some illustrative examples from an Auction Management
System (AMS). AMS allows users to perform some bidding operations online
if they have enough money in their account before starting bidding operations.
We consider the following pre-obligations in the AMS system: (1) The user has

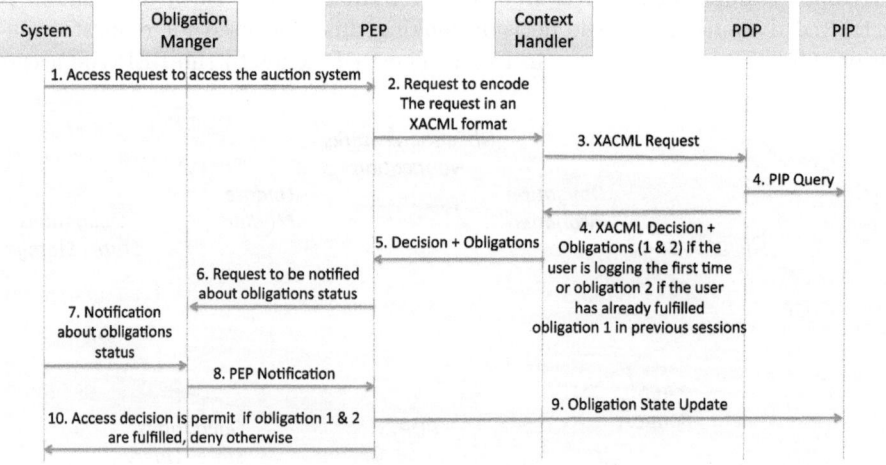

Fig. 2. Pre-obligations sequence diagram

Algorithm 1. - *PEP Obligation Management*

Input: PDP Decision, a set of obligations O, **Output:** PEP Decision
/*PDP decision is provided after all preobligations become in an inactive state*/
for all Preobligations $o_{pre} \in O$ **do**
   o_{pre}.state=active
end for
while o_{pre}.state $\neq$ inactive $\forall o \in O$ **do**
   /*The PEP is deny-based, all preobligations need to be fulfilled to permit the access if
   PDP decision is permit */
   if o_{pre}.state=violated **then**
      return Deny
   end if
   PIP update with $(o_{pre}.\text{id}, o_{pre}.\text{state}, o_{pre}.\text{subject}, o_{pre}.\text{update\_time})$
end while
if PDP Decision $\neq$ Deny **then**
   return Permit
else
   return Deny
end if
/*PDP decision is revoked if some ongoing obligations are violated*/
for all Ongoing obligations $o_{ongoing} \in O$ **do**
   $o_{ongoing}$.state=active
end for
while $o_{ongoing}$.state $\neq$ inactive $\forall o_{ongoing} \in O$ **do**
   if $o_{ongoing}$.state=violated **then**
      PDP Decision = Deny
   end if
   PIP update with $(o_{ongoing}.\text{id}, o_{ongoing}.\text{state}, o_{ongoing}.\text{subject}, o_{ongoing}.\text{update\_time})$
end while
/*Postobligations do not impact PEP decision*/
for all Postobligations $o_{post} \in O$ **do**
   o_{post}.state=active
end for
while o_{post}.state $\neq$ inactive $\forall o_{post} \in O$ **do**
   PIP update with $(o_{post}.\text{id}, o_{post}.\text{state}, o_{post}.\text{subject}, o_{post}.\text{update\_time})$
end while

---

to accept the usage terms of the auction before joining the auction system. (2) The user has to validate his payment for the session. Pre-obligation 1 has just to be fulfilled in the first login whereas the pre-obligation 2 has to be fulfilled in every session. Figure 2 illustrates message exchange to process the two pre-obligations in AMS. For a given access request, the PEP decision is taken under the assumption that our PEP is a deny-based PEP. Obligations O include pre-obligations o_{pre}, post-obligations o_{post} and/or ongoing obligations $o_{ongoing}$. The Algorithm 1 specifies how access control decision are handled by the PEP when the PEP receives an access decision with obligations.

4   *OB-XACML* Language and Proposed Architecture

This Section introduces the obligation syntax that supports *OB-XACML* and describes the different interactions between *OB-XACML* different components.

4.1   Obligations Syntax in *OB-XACML*

XACML defines obligations as simple attribute assignment. To specify obligations in XML, we have leveraged an existing formal obligation model [3] to identify the different elements of an obligation. In XACML 3.0, users are able to extend XACML syntax and to define their own categories, we added new identifiers to define obligation elements in XACML 3.0. To refer to the entity that is responsible of enforcing an obligation, we introduce a new Attribute identifier: the obligation-subject encoded as shown in Listing 1.2:

```
<Category=urn: oasis: names: tc: xacml:
    1.0:subject−category:obligation−subject>
```

Listing 1.2. Obligation Subject

Similarly, action and resource identifiers are added using *action-category: obligation-action* and *resource-category:obligation-object*. We distinguish between the obligations that have to be performed in each session by a given subject and those that have just to be performed by the first login using the identifier "each session" to specify obligations that have to be fulfilled in every access and "first login" to specify obligations that have just to be fulfilled in the first access.

4.2   Description of *OB-XACML* Components

Figure 3 illustrates the interactions between the different components in *OB-XACML*:

(a) AMS application: We consider an Auction Management System (AMS) which is a Java policy-based application which contains 122 classes and 797 methods.

(b) Obligation Manager: The obligation manager receives obligations from the PEP and maintains their states. It includes two mapping modules:

- A Mapper from abstract obligations to concrete obligations: This modules translates obligation parameters included in XACML obligations to parameters that are interpreted at the application level. For instance a required action in an obligation is translated to a method call that triggers some functionality at the business level logic, a role is mapped to a user, etc.
- An Obligation States Monitor: For obligations state monitoring, we define abstract rules that describe the impact of application parameters on obligation states. For example, the obligation to put a starting bid before joining an auction session evolves from an active state to a fulfilled one when the user validates the payment. This requirement is described by the rule $\Re_i$ that

describes the operations needed for the obligation "joining an auction" to transition from an active state to a fulfilled state:

$\Re_i$: State(Obl_1:joining an auction, active) $\mapsto$ State(Obl_1:joining an auction, fulfilled) *If* call method(Validate Bid.amount()) && Bid.amount(subject s) returns amount && amount > allowed_minimum_seuil)

To monitor the different parameters related to obligations state changes which are defined in our mapping rules, we use aspect oriented programming [5]. The obligation manager is a Java module that monitors a set of events. Each obligation is a Java class that extends an abstract class event.

(c) PIP attributes database: We implemented the PIP using a MySQL database that is updated with records describing obligation parameters whenever a change in an obligation state is reported using following form: (Obligation_ID, Obligation_Subject, Obligation_Object, Obligation_Action, Time, Obligation State). This database is queried by the PDP during access requests to fetch information related to the obligations status or related to obligations violation/-fulfillment.

(d) Update module component: The update module is triggered by aspects in each obligation state change and it updates the PIP with obligations state attributes.

(e) Extended PDP: To extend Sun's XACML implementation with a PDP that supports the new types and the new attributes that we have defined in this work, we have extended XACML standard factory[5] with our new factory.

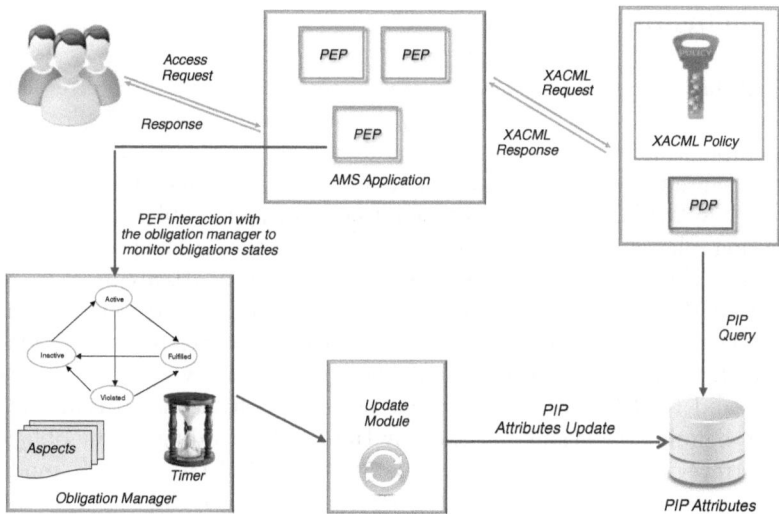

Fig. 3. *OB-XACML* Workflow

---

[5] http://sunxacml.sourceforge.net/guide.html.

(f) Timer: We use a Java timer to implement a timer that starts when the activation context starts, the violation context starts when the timer expires and the obligation is not fulfilled.

5   Related Work

In the last few years, several research initiatives have motivated the support of obligations in XACML at the level of XACML language and architecture. In [6], the authors have proposed a framework and a supporting language extending XACML to take into consideration UCON features. They have thus added some identifiers to XACML reference language to support mutability of attributes and identifiers to handle the different access phases, thus taking into consideration the continuity of access features in UCON model. The work presented in [7,8] follows the same direction and aims at enriching XACML model to take into consideration UCON features by adding the identifier in the condition element to distinguish between pre-obligations, ongoing and post-obligations. The element *AttrUpdates* is added to reason about attributes update and an XML retrieval policy has been introduced to specify where the attributes have to be retrieved for update. In [2], the authors have proposed a language and an underlying architecture to handle obligations. Obligations are commonly defined as application-specific and thus their handling is left to the platform that manages them. Their proposed obligation schema includes a list of event families that categorize events types interacting with an obligation. To the best of our knowledge, our XACML extend model is a first initiative that considers the user's history of obligation violation/fulfillment information at the decision making time.

6   Conclusion

The work that we are in presenting in this paper goes in a research direction that we are currently investigating, which spans over policy-based software architectures and particularly those that are based on XACML [9,10]. In this paper, we propose a syntax to support obligation polices in XACML and an extension of the standard XACML architecture to take into consideration obligations states and information related to their violation/fulfillment in the decision making process. The changes that we have introduced at the level of XACML architecture do not require to perform many modifications at the level of XACML reference model, which eases the adoption of *OB-XACML*. Our perspectives to extend this work are twofold: (1) At the level of XACML policy language, we plan to extend the language and to define a priority order between obligations so that the PEP is able to handle obligations returned by the PDP according to the obligations priority strategy stated in the policy. (2) At the level of *OB-XACML* model, we need to analyze the impact of messages exchange between the PEP and the PIP on the overall performance of real-life policy-based systems.

References

1. Zhang, X.: Formal model and analysis of usage control, Ph.D. dissertation (2006)
2. Li, N., Chen, H., Bertino, E.: On practical specification and enforcement of obligations. In: CODASPY, pp. 71–82 (2012)
3. Elrakaiby, Y., Cuppens, F., Cuppens-Boulahia, N.: Formal enforcement and management of obligation policies. Data Knowl. Eng. **71**(1), 127–147 (2012)
4. Elrakaiby, Y., Mouelhi, T., Traon, Y.L.: Testing obligation policy enforcement using mutation analysis. In: ICST, pp. 673–680 (2012)
5. Kiczales, G., Lamping, J., Mendhekar, A., Maeda, C., Lopes, C., Loingtier, J.-M., Irwin, J.: Aspect-oriented programming. In: Akşit, M., Matsuoka, S. (eds.) ECOOP 1997. LNCS, vol. 1241, pp. 220–242. Springer, Heidelberg (1997)
6. e-Ghazia, U., Masood, R., Shibli, M.A., Bilal, M.: Usage control model specification in XACML policy language. In: Cortesi, A., Chaki, N., Saeed, K., Wierzchoń, S. (eds.) CISIM 2012. LNCS, vol. 7564, pp. 68–79. Springer, Heidelberg (2012)
7. Maurizio Colombo, F.M., Lazouski, A., Mori, P.: A proposal on enhancing xacml with continuous usage control features. In: Desprez, F., Getov, V., Priol, T., Yahyapour, R. (eds.) Grids, P2P and Services Computing. Springer, USA (2010)
8. Lazouski, A., Martinelli, F., Mori, P.: A prototype for enforcing usage control policies based on XACML. In: Fischer-Hübner, S., Katsikas, S., Quirchmayr, G. (eds.) TrustBus 2012. LNCS, vol. 7449, pp. 79–92. Springer, Heidelberg (2012)
9. Kateb, D.E., Mouelhi, T., Traon, Y.L., Hwang, J., Xie, T.: Refactoring access control policies for performance improvement. In: ICPE, pp. 323–334 (2012)
10. Hwang, J., Xie, T., Kateb, D.E., Mouelhi, T., Traon, Y.L.: Selection of regression system tests for security policy evolution. In: ASE, pp. 266–269 (2012)

Managing Heterogeneous Access Control Models Cross-Organization

Samira Haguouche[(✉)] and Zahi Jarir

LISI Laboratory, Faculty of Sciences Semlalia, Cadi Ayyad University,
Marrakech, Morocco
{s.haguouche, jarir}@uca.ma

Abstract. Business process collaboration has gained a lot of attention due to the great need for integrating business process of different organizations. The most suitable issue to secure this collaboration is using access control model. However access control model diversity makes it more complex to collaborate cross-organization, especially when each organization refuses to change its security policies, prefers to preserve its access control model and needs to protect its information assets. To meet this problem we propose a flexible architecture based on Attribute Based Access Control (ABAC) model to ensure heterogeneity of access control cross-organization and on specified collaboration contract between these organizations. To validate our approach we have used web services technology, and we have implemented a prototype based on open source platforms WSO2.

Keywords: Access control · Collaborative system · Heterogeneous security policy · Web service · Heterogeneous access control · ABAC · XACML · WSO2

1 Introduction

Collaborative systems allow a group of collaborators to communicate, cooperate and share data. It may gather individuals from the same organization or among multiple organizations. In this paper, we are interested in cross organizational collaboration, more particularly, in the healthcare domain. For example, when a patient hospitalized in a general hospital needs a special treatment, physicians are forced to transfer him to a specialized hospital. In such a situation and to keep him moving, it is very critical that the medical staff of the two organizations collaborates in distance between them to ensure the proper treatment.

To exploit business process cross-organization, collaborative systems use web services technology as instance of Service Oriented Architecture SOA. This collaboration in most cases handles some sensitive or confidential information (sensitive medical data) or resources which should be secured. In this context, one of the most important issues of securing collaborative systems is using access control models.

This work is part of ongoing Moroccan-German project PMARS.

J. Lopez et al. (eds.): CRiSIS 2014, LNCS 8924, pp. 222–229, 2015.
DOI: 10.1007/978-3-319-17127-2_15

However several access control models exist [1]. This is why we have proposed in a previous work [2] the mandatory requirements for collaborative systems that are: dynamic change of policies, more fine-grained attribution of privilege, context-awareness and Ease of use. Based on these requirements, we have presented also a more fine-grained comparison between access control models presented in the literature. According to this study, we remark that the most suitable model for collaborative systems is ABAC because of its flexibility by supporting all others access control models concepts. In ABAC, identity, label, role, task... and every concept can be managed by attributes [3].

Each organization can define an access control policy and enforce it to control which subject can access to which object and in which context. So each organization adopts an appropriate model to control access to its information system. Consequently this implies heterogeneity in policy definitions as well as in enforcement mechanisms when organizations need to exchange assets via web services. In this case, each organization will force others organizations to use its security policy to have a permission to access to its shared resources via corresponding web services. Additionally a requester from the caller organization must also be controlled by the internal security policy when consuming an external web service to respect an established contract.

In the literature several research works have addressed the problem of managing heterogeneous access control model cross-organization by proposing a new access control model. These proposed approaches do not take into consideration the pre-existing access control model of each organization which is not always easy to change. This motivates us to propose a flexible approach that tackles heterogeneous access control model cross-organization management respecting the internal access control model of each concerned organization in the collaboration. This approach consists of an architecture based on Attribute Based Access Control (ABAC) model [3] and on a specified collaboration contract between these organizations.

The rest of the paper is organized as follows: Sect. 2 presents some of the research literature related to collaborative access control model cross-organization. Section 3 will propose and detail our approach to manage heterogeneity of access control models cross-organization. Next, Sect. 4 will describe implementation architecture to validate our architecture. Finally, Sect. 5 summarizes the work and highlights future work.

2 Related Work

An across organizational model OrBAC (Organization based access control) [4] is centered on the concept of organization. Each security policy is defined for and by an organization. Thus, the security policy specification is completely parameterized by the organization, so that it is possible to handle simultaneously several security policies associated with different organizations. OrBAC defines also the notion of role, view and activity which refer to subject, object and action respectively from the perspective of an organization. Using these concepts, a security policy that applies to a given organization is defined as a collection of permissions, prohibitions, obligations and recommendations within a context. Authors in [5] address access control within large-scale device collaboration systems. They propose a Multiple-Policy supported Attribute-Based Access

Control model with a centralized architecture. This model extends the traditional Attribute Based Access Control ABAC model by providing cross-domain authentication and authorization. They adopt a hierarchical structure to combine and enforce policies. These evoked works try to give a global architecture that ensures access control cross-organizations. But all of them require deep changing on existing systems, a situation that is difficult to achieve and is impractical in heterogeneous real systems.

Another interesting work presented in [6] have extended ABAC model to propose a centralized Attribute-Based Multi-policy Access Control model ABMAC that supports heterogeneous policies. In this paper, each policy is encapsulated in an independent Policy Decision Point (PDP) without changing its descriptions. At the same time, an abstract PDP that has the common characteristic of the policies is defined. Then, each PDP of heterogeneous policies implements that abstract PDP. Thus, Authorization decisions are made in centralized manner without changing policies descriptions. However, neither details about managing attributes nor their semantic heterogeneity are provided, giving that each model manipulates specific attributes.

Other works concerning Trust based Access Control are proposed. Trust in collaborative environments enables one party to access some other one's resources. Trust is established under conditions: based on the context and a third party [7] or based on the history of collaborations [8]. These works, also, propose models that do not take into account existing models neither their heterogeneity cross organization. Additionally, in sensitive domains, collaborating parties are responsible for any abusive actions. So trust cannot be established based on a trusted party or on the history of collaboration. In our case we use trust concept, but, it is conditioned by a legal contract, in view of information sensitivity in our target domains (healthcare domain).

3   Our Approach

In our approach we propose a solution that promotes collaboration, connects organizations' heterogeneous access control models without affecting the internal structure of the systems and protects the privacy of each organization. In this solution we consider that the management of access control for provided services is assumed by the consumer organization. Since responsibilities and qualifications of its staff are known only inside the organization. So, the organization consumes the service on behalf of its employees. The role of the provider organization is to check the identity of the issuing organization request, and to assign a set of privileges predefined in a contract, while keeping the identity of the original user transparent for the provider. Figure 1 depicts our proposed architecture. Its main components are detailed by the following subsections.

3.1   Collaboration Contract

When organizations decide to collaborate by exchanging confidential information and manipulating sensitive data, they need a legal authority to protect each one from abusive use. For instance, medical data in HealthCare domain are confidential, thus, any collaboration between institutions must be regulated and enforced by a legal authority. In this work we suppose that collaboration is ruled by a legal contract. In this

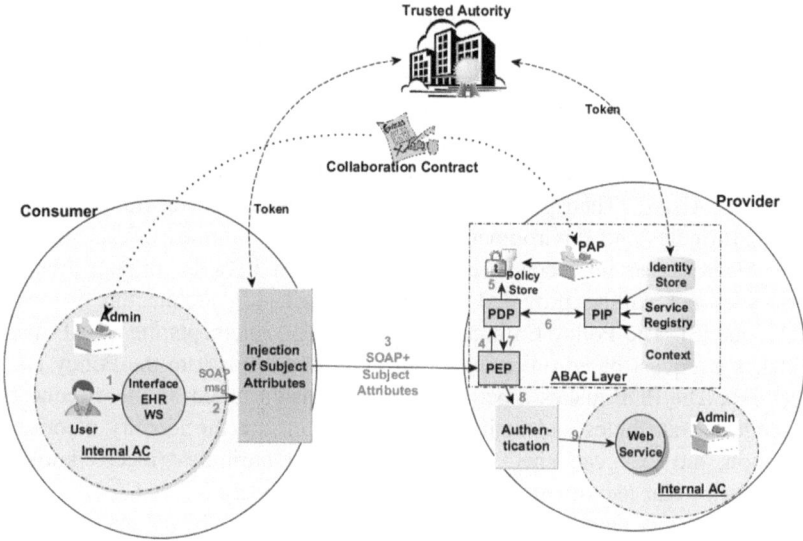

Fig. 1. Managing heterogeneous access control models cross-organization architecture

contract we define, for each organization, a set of access rules that are expressed as ABAC policy rules.

A policy rule in ABAC [3] is a Boolean function of subject, resource and environment attributes, if the function is evaluated as true, then the access to the resource is granted.

Rule: can_access (s, r, e) ⟵
    f(ATTR(s), ATTR(r), ATTR(e))

3.2 Consumer Side

According to the contract, and based on users' qualifications and responsibilities in the organization, the access control administrator assigns permissions to access to the interfaces of each provided web services. Eventually, the administrator defines new elements specific to the access control model (e.g. new role, new task…). Then when an authorized user requests an external service through an interface, consumer system prepares a SOAP message and injects required attributes (e.g. organization identity, user category…) as headers of the SOAP message. The injected attributes are those defined in the collaboration contract and are selected based on user's internal qualifications in the organization.

To prove its identity, consumer organization requests a token from a third party. The latter must be a trusted authority from the point of view of contracting organizations.

3.3 Provider Side

When the provider decides to share services with other organizations, the administrator creates an external user account and assigns it all permissions on resources he want to share. Eventually, the administrator can define new elements (e.g. new role, new task…) in terms of the adopted access control model. On the other hand, to insure access control for the provided service, we propose, in provider side, an ABAC layer that intercepts every incoming request and permit or deny access to internal access control model. A new contract involves definition of new rules in the ABAC component's policies. Policies are defined on XACML [9], an XML-based policy language that supports ABAC. Then policies define access rules based on Subject Attributes, Resource Attributes and Environment Attributes.

The ABAC layer intercepts every communication between organizations, then, authorizes or not calling provided service. Authorization architecture is based on ABAC's one [3]. The Policy Enforcement Point (PEP) intercepts the SOAP message, then makes a request based on received attributes and sends it to the Policy Decision Point (PDP). The PDP makes a permit or deny decision based on these request attributes, collected attributes and defined policies. To ensure the identity of originating organization, the PEP can check validity of subject attributes (received token) by referring back to an identity store or to the trusted authority.

If the request is authorized, it will be authenticated as being the external user. Thereafter, request will be handled as any other internal request. It means current user will access to all permitted resources.

4   Implementation

In this section we describe how we have implemented a prototype for our proposed architecture using WSO2 products [10] and Java as programming language. This section is divided into two sub-sections that expose respectively the implementation modules of an instance of our proposed architecture, and required configuration and installation needed to start the deployment.

4.1   Implementation Architecture

In our prototype we have used two instances of Identity Server to implement respectively the Trusted Security Token Service (STS) to issue security tokens, and the PDP, PIP and PAP as depicted in the Fig. 2. We have relied on WSO2 ESB to implement the PEP and on WSO2 Application Server to deploy the target web service.

To insure collaborative communication between these components, it is mandatory to configure WSO2 platforms before deploying, which is described in the following sub-section.

4.2   Platform Configuration

Deploying and Securing Web Service. We have created a simple bottom up web service that represents an interface for an E-Health Record (EHR) using eclipse IDE and Apache Axis2. This web service offers simplified primary functionalities (e.g. getMedicalHistory and getPersonalInfo) that we have deployed in WSO2 Application Server.

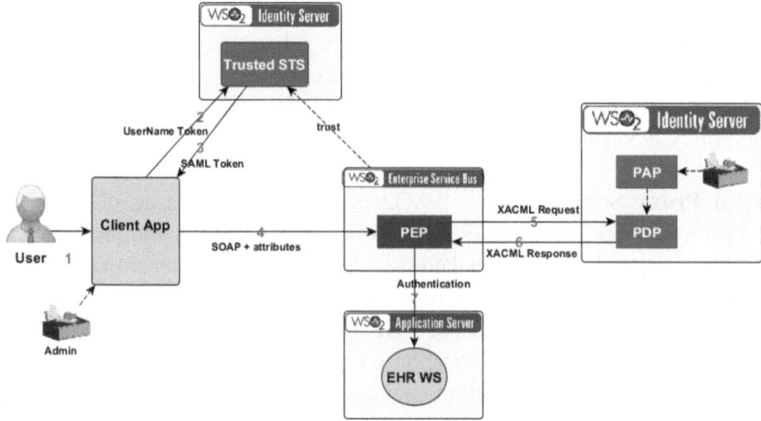

Fig. 2. Structure of the implemented architecture.

To consume this web service from external environment, we suggest creating an internal account, called "mediatorUser", having permission to access its operations according to internal access control model. This account creation is recommended specifically to more secure the resource consumption. Then we have secured this service using Username Token over HTTPS authentication policy that uses simple username/password token for authentication.

Editing Authorization Policy. Using Policy Editor in PAP of WSO2 Identity Server, we defined a XACML policy that contains the two following rules:

Surgeons from a specialist hospital can access to all medical history of the patient during a surgery, while administrative staff can only access to social information.

```
<Policy ...>   <Target>...
  <Rule Effect="Permit" RuleId="SurgeonRule">
    <Target><AnyOf><AllOf>
      <Match MatchId="urn:oasis:names:tc:xacml:1.0:function:string-
      equal">
        <AttributeValue...>https://192.168.1.2:9445/service s/EHR/get
        MedicalHistory</AttributeValue>
        <AttributeDesignator
        Category="urn:oasis:names:tc:xacml:3.0:attribute-
        category:resource" MustBePresent="true" ...>... </Target>
    <Condition>
      <Apply FunctionId="urn:oasis:names:tc:xacml:1.0:function:and">
        <Apply ...>
          <AttributeValue
          DataType=...>PatientReceived</AttributeValue>
          <AttributeDesignator
          Category="urn:oasis:names:tc:xacml:3.0:attribute-
          category:environment"  MustBePresent="true" ...> ...
        <Apply ...>
          <AttributeValue ...>SpeHospital/Surgeon</AttributeValue>
          <AttributeDesignator
          Category="urn:oasis:names:tc:xacml:3.0:attribute-
          category:subject" ...>...</Rule>
  <Rule Effect="Permit" RuleId="AdminRule">....</Rule>
  <Rule Effect="Deny" RuleId="DenyRule"></Rule>
</Policy>
```

This policy defines a third deny rule that will be applied if neither of the two rules is verified. So, we define a "permit-overrides" as a rule combining algorithm. Then we publish the policy in the PDP. We choose the Policy Combining Algorithm "permit-overrides". This means that if we define many policies, request will be authorized if at least one policy is verified.

Creating a Proxy Service. Using WSO2 ESB, playing the role of PEP, we have defined a proxy service for the EHR web service which handles the incoming requests before they are dispatched to the backend service. So we define an entitlement mediator and configure it to create an XACML request (based on Property mediator that retrieves SOAP headers), and to send it to the PDP which evaluates it against the XACML policy defined at the PDP. If PDP's response is positive, the message will be forwarded to the EHR service. If it isn't, a fault message will be sent back to the client application. Regarding authentication to PDP, we used Username Token over HTTPS.

Client Application. On consumer's side, we define a simple Java class with two methods: getMedicalHistory() and getPersonalInfo(). Then we consider two Java interfaces to simulate access control in the organization: Surgeons can access to SurgeonInterface that defines getMedicalHistory() method and administrative staff can access to AdminInterface that defines getPersonalInfo() method. Both interfaces are implemented by the class.

Configure STS and KeyStores. We used Java keytool to create a keystore for all parties. Then we exchanged certificates between communicating parties. In the Security Token Service (STS) component of the WSO2 Carbon, we defined relying party endpoint address (the proxy ESB) and its corresponding public certificate. Then we created a new user for client application. Then we secured the STS using Username Token over HTTPS authentication.

5   Conclusion

In this paper, we meet the problem of access control models heterogeneity in collaboration cross organizations. We focus on areas that exchange sensitive information where collaboration is guaranteed by an established legal contract. We rely on the ABAC model to manage heterogeneity of access control between organizations since it is more flexible, dynamic and fine-grained.

To avoid affecting internal access control models adopted by each collaborating organization, we propose a secure and collaborative architecture that preserves for each organization its resources. To validate our architecture, we have implemented a prototype based on SOA using WSO2 open source platform and experimented it using some scenarios inspired from healthcare domain. We are currently working on more complex functionality in such domain.

References

1. Tolone, W., Ahn, G., Pai, T., Hong, S.: Access control in collaborative systems. ACM Comput. Surv. (CSUR) **37**(1), 29–41 (2005)
2. Haguouche, S., Jarir, Z.: An architecture based on trust for collaborative access control models. In: Workshop on Security Policies in Cloud Environment. (PoliCE 2014) (2014)
3. Yuan, E., Tong, J.: Attributed based access control (ABAC) for Web services. In: IEEE International Conference on Web Services (ICWS 2005), p. 569. IEEE (2005)
4. Kalam, A.A., El Benferhat, S., Miège, A., Baida, R., El Cuppens, F., Saurel, C., Balbiani, P., Deswarte, Y., Trouessin, G.: Organization based access control. In: Proceedings of the 4th IEEE International Workshop on Policies for Distributed Systems and Networks (2003)
5. Liang, F., Guo, H., Yi, S., Ma, S.: A multiple-policy supported attribute-based access control architecture within large-scale device collaboration systems. J. Netw. **7**(3), 524–531 (2012)
6. Lang, B., Foster, I., Siebenlist, F., Ananthakrishnan, R., Freeman, T.: A flexible attribute based access control method for grid computing. J. Grid Comput. **7**, 169–180 (2008)
7. Bhatti, R., Bertino, E., Ghafoor, A.: A trust-based context-aware access control model for Web-services. In: 2004 Proceedings of the IEEE International Conference on Web Services, pp. 184–191. IEEE (2004)
8. Skopik, F., Truong, H., Dustdar, S.: VIeTE-enabling trust emergence in service-oriented collaborative environments. In: International Conference on Web Information Systems and Technologies (2009)
9. Standard, O.: eXtensible Access Control Markup Language (XACML) Version 3.0 (2013)
10. WSO2. http://wso2.com. Accessed 02 June 2014

ISER: A Platform for Security Interoperability of Multi-source Systems

Khalifa Toumi[1][✉], Fabien Autrel[2], Ana Cavalli[1], and Sammy Haddad[3]

[1] Telecom-SudParis, 9 Rue Charles Fourier, 91000 Evry, France
{Khalifa.Toumi,Ana.Cavalli}@telecom-sudparis.eu
[2] Telecom-Bretagne, 2 Rue de la Chataigneraie, 35576 Cesson Sevigne, France
fabien.autrel@telecom-bretagne.eu
[3] Oppida, 6 Avenue du Vieil Etang, 78180 Montigny-le-Bretonneux, France
sammy.haddad@oppida.fr

Abstract. Multi-source systems have become a crucial infrastructure for the organization of modern information systems. This distributed environment enables the different participants to collaborate, exchange data and interact among them in order to achieve a global goal. However, some security issues such as the malicious use of resources, disclosure of data or bad services can appear during this collaboration.

In this paper, a new platform is proposed that ensures secure interoperability between multi-source systems. It is based on the choice, the integration and the update of three existing tools in order to (1) provide a secure virtualization of guests system, (2) create, model and manage systems secure interoperability, (3) verify the security policies and (4) monitor the system behavior. A case study is presented to illustrate the application of the platform.

1 Introduction

Information Technology (IT) is present everywhere and it has become very easy and common to produce and exchange data between heterogeneous devices and systems. These networks and services are required to be more and more open and new technology is designed to facilitate the interoperation between these networks composed of heterogeneous, communicating devices. Guaranteeing that they interoperate securely has become a major concern for individuals, enterprises and governments. This has given rise to the need to constantly maintain and protect these networks and services to achieve the high level of trust necessary so that they become an asset and not an added risk for society.

The security interoperability challenges have been rapidly increased [1,3,4]. This produces a lack of a global interoperability platforms which limits the ability of people to work efficiently together.

The solution we present in this paper is an architecture and a platform, ISER, that is a combination of techniques and tools such that it allows the management of multilevel interoperability links. The proposed architecture can handle

---

The research work presented in this paper is supported by the French ISER project.

J. Lopez et al. (Eds.): CRiSIS 2014, LNCS 8924, pp. 230–238, 2015.
DOI: 10.1007/978-3-319-17127-2_16

the communication with different external systems with the ability to have a specific link configuration and communication policy for every link. The aim is to be able to precisely customize these links, both technically and in terms of policy, with respect to the two stakeholders of the connected systems. Another complementary objective is to ensure optimum security and communication efficiency. The ISER platform is based on the combination of three components: a secure OS PolyXene, a formal policy editor MotOrBAC and a monitoring tool MMT.

In summary, the contributions of this paper are the following:

– Design of an architecture for secure interoperability of multi-source systems.
– Design of modeling techniques for interoperable security policies.
– Design of a platform for ensuring the secure interoperability of multi-source systems.

The rest of the paper is structured as follows. In Sect. 2 the architecture of the platform is presented. In Sect. 3 the different tools composing the ISER platform are described. Next, in Sect. 4 a case study presenting how to use the platform is detailed and discussed. Finally, we conclude in Sect. 5.

2   Architecture of the Studied System

2.1   General Description

We describe in this section the architecture of the ISER framework. Figure 1 presents the platform architecture. We have N Information Systems (IS). Each one of them communicates with the external entities via our interoperability platform. Based on polyXene, our solution creates N Virtual Machines (VM) that are used as proxies for the external systems to interrogate the IS behind the platform. Besides another virtual machine, named *Interop*, is created to manage the interoperability of security policies. This instance is a specific running VM that collects and processes all the requests from the different proxies and accordingly to the interoperability security policies. The *Interop* instance hosts

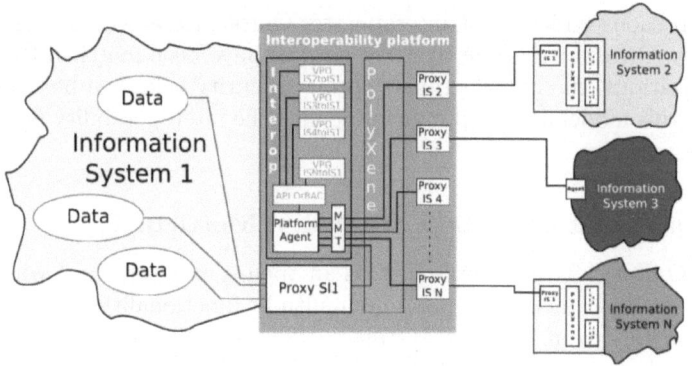

Fig. 1. Platform Architecture

the MotOrBAC and MMT tools, which are used, respectively, to process the formal requests and to monitor the requests processing.

The concept of the platform is as follows: to get data, an external IS has to make a request to the platform, corresponding thus to a pulling mode. Then once a data transfer is agreed, the home system behind the platform handles the connection, i.e. open the corresponding specific secured channel, and then pushes through that channel the data to the external system that made the request. Thus we have a pulling mode for the requests and a pushing mode for the data transfer.

3 Platform and Tools

3.1 The OrBAC Model

The Organisation Based Access Control model (OrBAC [2]) is well-suited for the expression of complex and dynamic security policies. The central concept is the organization concept. An organization represents an entity which defines and manages a security policy.

As in the RBAC model, the concept of role in the OrBAC model abstracts the notion of subject. The abstraction of concrete entities, i.e. subject, actions and objects, is more complete in the OrBAC model as actions are abstracted into activities and objects into views. The OrBAC model defines three rule types: permission, prohibition and obligation. The dynamic aspect of OrBAC policies lies in the context concept. A context is a condition associated with an abstract rule.

In our approach, we use the OrBAC model to define the security policies used in the information systems which interoperate.

3.2 The O2O Model

The O2O model tackles the problem of interoperability between organizations. It defines how two organizations A and B which use the OrBAC model to express their respective security policies can proceed to establish interoperability policies. The O2O model proposes an approach to define the interoperability policy by comparing the concepts associated with the abstract entities defined in the two organizations which must interoperate. Ontologies are used to implement this process. Once the relevant abstract entities have been matched between the two organizations, the interoperability policy security rules can be defined.

We use this model in our approach to define the interoperability policies from the OrBAC policies.

3.3 Management of the Security Policy: MotOrBAC

The MotOrBAC Tool. MotOrBAC is an open-source software[1] which implements the OrBAC model. It provides multiple functionalities such as policy specification based on the OrBAC model [2], potential and effective conflict detection, policy simulation and administration policy specification.

---

[1] http://motorbac.sourceforge.net.

Using MotOrBAC. In the context of interoperability between multiple systems exchanging sensible information, MotOrBAC can be used to specify both local policies and interoperability policies. For instance, in the example we consider in this article and accordingly to the O2O model, the two nations France and N1 which interoperate define several policies: the two local policies which define how the subjects access the system's resources and an interoperability policy which controls how local resources are accessed by subjects of the other nation, i.e. the O2O policy.

3.4   Monitoring of the Security Properties: MMT

Monitoring is one of the most effective techniques to test the conformance of an implementation with respect to its security policies. In the following, we present the different steps of our approach and the test architecture proposed for the case study.

Monitoring Process. The test architecture is based on the implementation of the multi-national information system. Figure 2 illustrates our test architecture.

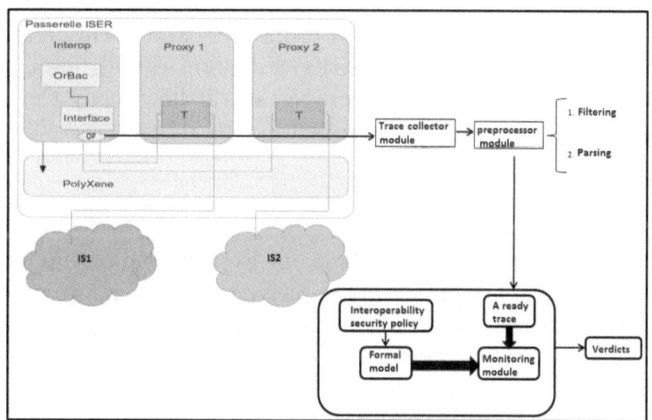

Fig. 2. Testing architecture

We designed a single Observation Point (OP) for testing the interoperability policy between IS2 and IS1 (IS1 and IS2 describe respectively intelligence systems of nations France and N1). The OP will be responsible for collecting messages exchanged between the proxy and the guest system, which implements the interoperability policy.

Trace Collector Module. This module is responsible for two tasks, the first one is to facilitate the integration of the observation points. The second one is to extract the exchanged messages to be grouped in a single file named initial trace. This trace will be sent to the preprocessor module to be processed.

The Preprocessor Module. This initial trace will be processed by a pre-processor module that performs the filtering and the parsing tasks.

The Monitoring Module. This module is composed by the monitoring tool to be used. For this work, we have chosen the MMT (Montimage Monitoring Tool[2]) tool.

1. Utility of MMT
MMT is a monitoring tool that allows capturing and analyzing network traffic. It can be used to verify network functional and security properties.

This tool is able to provide an overall verdict about the state of the inter-operability policy implementation. We have three possible cases, if one of the intermediate verdicts related to the policy is FAIL, the overall verdict will be FAIL, otherwise if one of the verdicts is INCONCLUSIF the final verdict will be INCONCLUSIF. Otherwise, the final verdict will be PASS.

2. Use and operation
The use of MMT requires the implementation of a new plug-in to analyze the traces and to verify the correct implementation of the security properties speci-fied in this environment. Therefore, all the communication are captured period-ically by the MMT tool. Then a filtration is performed to only store the needed information. Based on a list of required properties, MMT will be able to detect the compliance or not to these properties. Finally a HTML file is periodically designed to indicate (1) the checked properties (2) how many times they were respected and (3) details about the requests.

3.5   Polyxene

PolyXene is an operating system developed by Bertin Technologies for military or civil organizations with a high level of security requirements. It is an estimated EAL-5 + system on the basis of a security target whose perimeter is higher compared to other evaluated operating systems (Windows, Mac OS X ...) system.

The reason for the choice PolyXene[3] as a support for the gateway is that it can perform the various platform services in virtualized and confined environments.

4   Experimentation

This section presents the case study and the results of the application of the ISER platform. Figure 3 presents the architecture of our case study. It contains two nations France and N1. Each one of them is sharing some resources. Each organization will have an ISER gateway. This latter is responsible for managing, editing the interoperability security policy and validating the system security. In Fig. 3, we have two systems, each one of them has three roles, the ORO, ORT and DRM that are respectively the intelligence officer for an operational

---

[2] http://www.montimage.com.

[3] PolyXene is free within the community LDSN (Critical Software for Defence and National Security).

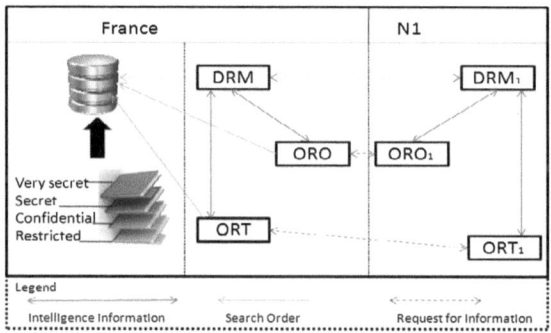

Fig. 3. Our case study

level, the intelligence officer for tactical level and the directorate of military intelligence. These entities may have the rights to manage (read and/or write an information), read (read an information), write (write an information), tag (add a label to the information) and tag_interop (add an interoperability label for shared data).

Besides, we have classified the different views into four sets inspired from the information classification of the European Commission and the OCCAR (Organisation for Joint Armament Cooperation) organizations [5]: IR_TS (very secret information), IR_S (secret information), IR_C (confidential information) and IR_R(Restricted information). Finally, France has defined four contexts that are: Default_ctx (a condition that is always enabled), false_ctx (a condition that is always disabled), after_adding_IR (a condition that will be activated after the addition of any information) and kneed_to_know (a condition that will be activated if some inputs are checked).

4.1   How to Use the ISER Platform

Figure 4 shows the different steps to use our framework. Firstly, the administrator of the security policy for France should prepare the local policy of his organization.

The France local security policy contains 8 rules, we give an example of some of these rules in the following:

A local rule 1: `permission(France, ORT, manage, IR_C, defaut_ctx)`

Description: An ORT has the right to manage intelligence information if the information has a lower security level than confidential.

Then, a derivation of an interoperability security policy based on the O2O model will be done automatically. This derivation will be based on the local policy and some mapping rules that are fixed after a negotiation process. As an example, a Virtual Private Organization (VPO) policy, called VPO_N1_France, will be created to control the access of N1 members to the France resources.

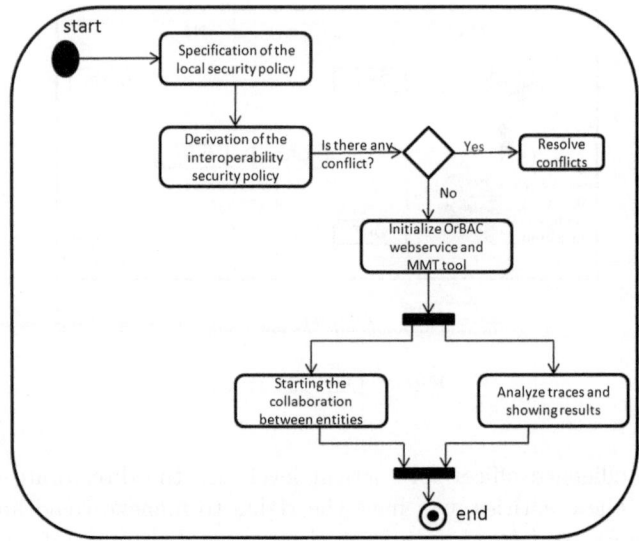

Fig. 4. How to use the ISER platform.

The mapping rules will permit to (1) assign an external user to a role, (2) minimize the available shared resources and (3) reduce the number of activities. Here are some examples of mapping rules:

`empower(VPO_N1_to_france, S, ORT) ←— empower(N1, S, ORT₁)`

Description: This rule means that any user S with the role ORT in nation N1 will be assigned to the same role ORT in the VPO_N1_to_france.

`use(VPO_N1_to_france, O, IR_C) ←— use(france, O,IR_C) and tag_interrop (O, true).`

Description: This rule means that a resource belonging to the IR_C view in the local policy will be assigned to the same view only if its interoperability tag is activated.

Based on these mapping rules, the local rule 1 will automatically be transformed to the following new interoperability rule:

`permission(VPO_N1_to_france, ORT, manage, IR_C, defaut_ctx).`

Description: An ORT in N1 has the right to manage the intelligence information of France if the security level of this information is lower than confidential and if the data can be shared.

The next step is to solve potential the conflicts. MOtOrBAC offers a methodology to help the administrator to solve conflicts. Then, the OrBAC engine should be initialized. It will receive the request and it will determinate the request response based on its interoperability policies. Before starting the communication, MMT tool has to be initialized. Then, the different entities will start the communication following the ISER protocol.

Security rules summary results

Id	Description		✓	✗
1	SECURITY RULE:		0	0
2	SECURITY RULE:	An officer has the right to read intelligence information if this information has a lower level of safety than the confidential level	17	13
3	SECURITY RULE:	An egnineer has the right to modify the information with a secret level label	10	0
4	SECURITY RULE:	A DRM has the right to read any type of data	0	0

Fig. 5. An example of a results file.

4.2 ISER Protocol

This section describes the communication protocol used between information and interoperability systems. This protocol is described in an XML format and relies on two programs: the interfaces of the interoperability system and the customers of the information systems.

The interoperability protocol is one of the central elements of the platform. We present here an outline of the protocol. An interoperability message between an information system and the system interoperability can be a request for an open access. The connection request is made specifying the information system of origin, the original label, the target information, the target label and finally the port of communication for the open system (for example, 22 for ssh). Accepting a connection is represented by the message *opened* specifying an IP destination address of the message. A connection can be interrupted by the *close* message.

During this communication, the MMT tool will be based on our new plugin to collect traces and analyze them in order to prepare some html files as outputs that describe the different properties, the number of times they have been respected and providing different details (time, actions and other details). MMT will be responsible for checking the correct implementation of the interoperability security policies and the detection of several security or functional vulnerabilities. Figure 5 shows an example of the results file.

5 Conclusion

This paper presents the architecture and the ISER platform designed to perform secure interoperability between multi-source systems. It also presents the results of the experiments performed on a case study. A number of major activities are included in the experiments: modeling, verification of rules and monitoring. The security rules are described using the OrBAC and O2O models. Several interoperability security rules are identified from the case study specification and then described as properties. Based on these properties, the validation of the implementation of the case study is carried out using the platform composed by the three tools: Motorbac, Polyxene and MMT.

Note that the main objectives specified in order to obtain a secure inter-operability have been achieved, i.e., the connection of systems with different technologies and the connection of systems with different security policies. The case study proposed for experimentation illustrates clearly all these issues.

References

1. Barnaghi, P., Cousin, P., Malo, P., Serrano, M., Viho, C.: Simpler iot word(s) of tomorrow, more interoperability challenges to cope today. In: 2013 European Research Cluster for the Internet of Things Book, Internet of Things Converging Technologies for Smart Environments and Integrated Ecosystems (2013)
2. Abou El Kalam, A., El Baida, R., Balbiani, P., Benferhat, S., Cuppens, F., Deswarte-and, Y., Miège, A., Saurel, C., Trouessin, G.: Organization based access control. In: IEEE 4th International Workshop on Policies for Distributed Systems and Networks (Policy 2003), Lake Come, Italy, 4–6 June 2003
3. Rezaei, R., Chiew, T.K., Lee, S.P.: A review on e-business interoperability frameworks. J. Syst. Softw. **93**, 199–216 (2014)
4. Walsh, B.: Report cites lack of interoperability as biggest barrier to robust it infrastructure[online]. clinical innovation + technology (2014). http://www.clinical-innovation.com/topics/interoperability/report-cites-lack-interoperability-biggest-barrier-robust-it-infrastructures
5. wikipedia. Classified information (2014). http://en.wikipedia.org/wiki/classified-information

Key Extraction Attack Using Statistical Analysis of Memory Dump Data

Yuto Nakano$^{(\boxtimes)}$, Anirban Basu, Shinsaku Kiyomoto, and Yutaka Miyake

KDDI R&D Laboratories Inc., 2-1-15 Ohara, Fujimino, Saitama 356-8502, Japan
{yuto,basu,kiyomoto,miyake}@kddilabs.jp

Abstract. During the execution of a program the keys for encryption algorithms are in the random access memory (RAM) of the machine. Technically, it is easy to extract the keys from a dumped image of the memory. However, not many examples of such key extractions exist, especially during program execution. In this paper, we present a key extraction technique and confirm its effectiveness by implementing the Process Peeping Tool (PPT) – an analysis tool – that can dump the memory during the execution of a target program and help the attacker deduce the encryption keys through statistical analysis of the memory contents. Utilising this tool, we evaluate the security of two sample programs, which are built on top of the well-known OpenSSL library. Our experiments show that we can extract both the private key of the RSA asymmetric cipher as well as the secret key of the AES block cipher.

Keywords: Memory dump · Key extraction · OpenSSL · RSA · AES

1 Introduction

The growth of various services on the Internet has given rise to a dramatic increase in the information that is exchanged over Internet protocols. Sensitive information in private e-mails, confidential documents, e-commerce and other financial transactions need to be guarded against eavesdropping. In order to protect the communication between two network hosts, the Secure Sockets Layer [4] and Transport Layer Security [3] (SSL/TLS) are commonly used. OpenSSL[1] is the one of most commonly used open source libraries for the SSL and TLS protocols. The core library offers implementations for various cryptographic algorithms and other utility functions. Recently, a critical bug, referred to as CVE-2014-0160, has been found in OpenSSL TLS Heartbeat extension [10], which makes for the attacker to recover cryptographic keys by reading 64 kilobytes of memory at a time [1,2].

Any unauthorised access to cryptographic keys constitutes a security breach. Tamper-proof devices and obfuscation cannot be used during program execution. It is well-known that the cryptographic keys are present in the random access

---

[1] See: https://www.openssl.org/.

© Springer International Publishing Switzerland 2015
J. Lopez et al. (Eds.): CRiSIS 2014, LNCS 8924, pp. 239–246, 2015.
DOI: 10.1007/978-3-319-17127-2_17

memory (RAM) during the execution of a program; a knowledge that an adversary can use to extract the keys from the RAM [7–9]. Protecting the keys or any other valuable information from unauthorised access during program execution is an important area of on-going research. Oblivious RAM schemes and related works [5,6] can protect the RAM access patterns of programs from unauthorised access. However, these schemes require trustworthy and secure CPUs for the protection, and cannot prevent attacks where the attacker can access the CPU and extract information such as operations, access to memory addresses of operations and values stored in those addresses.

In this paper, we present a new attack method that can extract a private key for RSA and a secret key for AES from dumped memory image. We have implemented a tool called the Process Peeping Tool (PPT) to demonstrate the attacks. PPT enables us to analyse the structure and behaviour of the target program by observing its memory use. It can also statistically analyse the data that is acquired from the RAM, thus enabling the attacker to determine cryptographic keys. We use PPT to extract cryptographic keys (both for RSA and for AES) from sample programs, which use the OpenSSL library. In the key recovery attack against RSA, we iterate through cycles of encryption and decryption. Assuming that the private key remains fixed during the execution of the program the key can be extracted by observing the memory accesses of the decryption function. In case of AES, we encrypt a random number with one fixed secret key. We demonstrate that the secret key can be extracted by observing the memory access patterns of the encryption process. The address of any shared libraries has to be public for the PPT to be able to analyse the program. Using a static library and deleting symbol information makes it harder for the attacker to obtain the keys. However, the keys can still be extracted once the attacker determines the functions that need to be observed. Although, adding dummy data and/or dummy operations also make the attack harder, these can be distinguished from the actual data since the dummy data and accesses do not affect the output of the program.

2   Aquiring Data from Memory

In this section, we introduce two methods which can extract data from memory.

2.1   Memory Dump

Memory dump is usually used for debugging programs especially to detect buffer overflows. It also can be used to attack programs. During the execution of the program, its data is temporally stored in RAM and any process with the same privilege as the user executing the program or a root privilege can access that region. If the program is an encryption/decryption program, the decryption key must be stored in RAM and it is possible for the adversary to dump the contents in the RAM and search for the key. On Linux systems, `dd` or `ptrace()` can be used to dump memory. We can also access the memory of a running process that runs with different privileges than the user, assuming root is not involved, by using Linux capabilities. By giving the user a capability for the particular program, the user will be able to execute it without the normally required privilege. However, setting capabilities to a program/process requires, initially, root privileges or an appropriate capability.

On operating systems which use virtual memory, part of or entire memory contents of a program are sometimes moved from main memory to secondary storage (i.e., the hard disk drive). If the adversary can access the region of a disk where the pages are stored, it is easy to read the content of memory. Another possibility that the memory content can be stored on the disk is core dump. When a process is unexpectedly stopped, the memory image of that process is saved as a core file in order for debugging. The adversary can access the core file and try to analyse the memory image.

2.2 `ptrace` System Call

The `ptrace()` system call enables one process (the "tracer") to observe, control the execution of another process (the "tracee"), examine and change the tracee's memory and registers. It is primarily used to implement breakpoint debugging and system call tracing. Other than `ptrace()` system call, there are several other system calls that may help the adversary to monitor the process and its access to memory, such as `ltrace()` for monitoring dynamic libraries and `strace()` for system calls.

There is a mode called `PTRACE_SINGLESTEP` in `ptrace`, which can load a program or can be attached to an existing program. The `PTRACE_SINGLESTEP` mode allows the attacker to execute the program step-by-step. We can also acquire the values stored in the CPU registers in each step such as program addresses, register values of operand and values in RAM pointed to by the registers by using a `PTRACE_PEEKDATA` mode.

3 Attack Scenarios and Key Extraction Attack

The private key of RSA and the secret key of AES are assumed to be of fixed values, or at least fixed during the execution of the program. Such a key can be hidden inside the program with some protection. However, when the program is initiated, the key must be loaded in the RAM in plaintext. If the attacker can dump the memory when the key is loaded in the RAM, it is possible to extract the secret key from the dumped image. We assume that the adversary has the access to the target program and memory dump data.

Attack Scenario 1. A service provider provides various services such as hosting, web application and file sharing. The clients connect to the server through secure channels established with SSL/TLS or any equivalent protocols. When the clients connect to the server, the secret keys have to be stored in the RAM. While the connection is active, the malicious operator can attach his attacking process on the server-side to the target and dump the related area in the memory without being detected by the clients; and thereby extract the secret key. Even when there is no malicious operator, the server may be compromised by malware, which acquires the root privilege and mounts similar attacks on the processes handling secure connections.

Attack Scenario 2. Several users share the same physical server (i.e., public cloud) on which they operate their own separate virtual machines (VMs). However, once the attacker can login as the administrative user, it is possible to attach the attacking process to the victims' VM processes and extract keys from memory dumps.

Attack Scenario 3. Last but not the least is the user-as-the-attacker scenario, where the aim of the user is to extract the secret keys or other valuable information from the target program by attaching the attacking process to the target process.

3.1   Attack Against RSA

The exponentiation of RSA decryption involves variable length arithmetic, it is expected that decryption process uses shift operations. The Chinese Remainder Theorem (CRT), which involves division operations, is often used for exponentiation operations of encryption and decryption. Therefore, shift and division operations deal the private key and we can recover the key by dumping and analysing memory region used by these operations.

Assume that both the public and private keys are fixed while the plaintext and the ciphertext keep changing. Every time the encryption or decryption functions are executed, the program's accesses to the key which is the fixed value, while its accesses to the plaintext or the ciphertext which are keep changing. Therefore, as the number of executions increase, the accesses to keys can be distinguished from other accesses by counting the number of accesses to each value. The procedure can be summarised as: (a) iterate encryption and decryption of random numbers with the fixed key, (b) dump values which are accessed by shift and division operations, and (c) output key candidate values which are accessed considerably more than other values. If the multiplication of two recovered values matches the modulo N, the key can be correctly recovered.

3.2   Attack Against AES

AES consists of four functions, and one of them is called AddRoundKey. The AddRoundKey takes two inputs – the round key and the internal state. Hence, we can recover the round keys and the secret key, by dumping and analysing memory region accessed by the AddRoundKey function. As one of the inputs of AddRoundKey is the fixed key while the other is the variable internal state, the key can be distinguished from the internal state by counting the number of accesses during the iteration of encryption. The procedure can be summarised as:

(a) iterate the encryption of random numbers with the fixed key (b) dump values which are accessed by AddRoundKey operations, and (c) output key candidate values which are accessed considerably more than other values.

We can also use Maartmann-Moe et al.'s idea [8], which uses the character of the key expansion, to confirm if the key is correctly recovered. As the round keys are derived from the secret key, we can apply the key expansion to the recovered candidate values and see if derived values appear on RAM.

4   Process Peeping Tool (PPT)

The core component of the PPT is the `ptrace()` system call, which enables one process (the "tracer") to observe, control the execution of another process (the "tracee"), examine and change the tracee's memory and registers. PPT can analyse the structure of the target program, including which shared libraries it uses and which functions are used in each library. It can also analyse memory addresses that the target process accesses and values that the target process uses. These addresses and values are recorded and statistically analysed. Dumped data can be used efficiently for the key extraction attack as, unlike existing memory dump tools, we can specify libraries and functions of interest.

One can attach the PPT process to the target program by specifying the target's process ID (PID). Once successfully attached to the target PID, the evaluator can browse inside the target as if the target and the analysing tool were respectively a file system directory structure and the shell. In the next step, the child process is executed with PTRACE_TRACEME. When the child process executes a function, the parent process receives SIGTRAP and pauses the child process. The parent process replaces, keeping a copy of the original values, the function's addresses with breakpoints in Procedure Linkage Table (PLT). Then the original operation is restored to execute a single step of the child process with PTRACE_SINGLESTEP, and the parent process obtains information on which libraries the child process accessed. After the single step, the parent process again takes over the control and continues the operation until it encounters the next breakpoint. The evaluator, therefore, can find out which libraries are used and which functions inside these libraries are called.

The evaluator can control how each function can be executed by setting its status. The available statuses are: **watch** – execute the function step-by-step recording its data; **watchdeeply** – in addition to *watch*, this status enables recording the behaviour of other functions called inside the target function; **through** – execute the function step-by-step without recording data; and **skip** – execute the function as usual.

When the function is under surveillance with "watch" status, the function is executed with a PTRACE_SINGLESTEP. When the single step of the child process is executed, the addresses and the values from the child task can be read by PTRACE_PEEKDATA. The addresses and values are recorded by PPT and used for static analysis. Any function with a "watch" status is skipped if that function is called by one with a "skip" status. In order for the "watch" status to work with a function, it should be ensured that its caller function has a status set to "through".

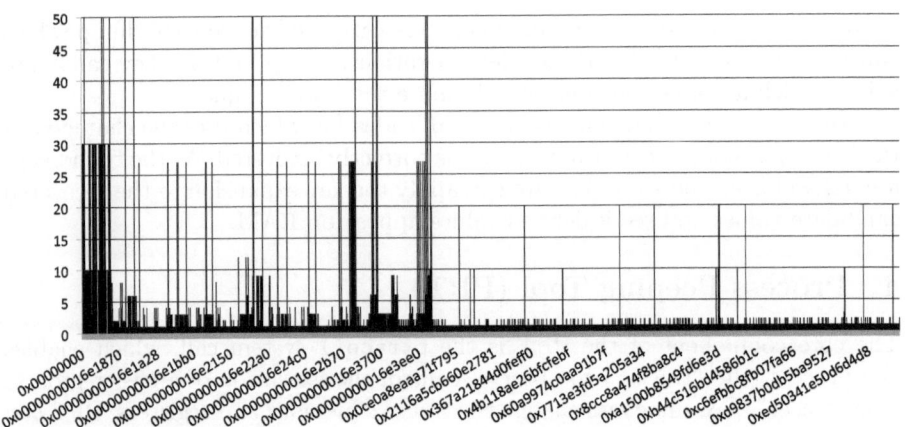

Fig. 1. Values referred from RAM when we iterate RSA encryption and decryption ten times

5   Key Extraction from Memory Dump

In this section we demonstrate how the Process Peeping Tool can help extract the private key and the secret key of RSA and AES respectively from two separate target sample programs. The attack procedure is summarised as follows:

1. analyse the structure of the target program including libraries and functions,
2. specify which library or function to monitor,
3. execute the target program while specified libraries and functions are executed step-by-step,
4. record addresses and values,
5. recover the key by statically analysing data acquired in step 4.

The experimental environment is following; CPU: Intel Core i7 4930 K, RAM: 24 GB, OS: Ubuntu 13.10 64-bit, Library: OpenSSL 0.9.8.

In case of RSA, PPT retrieves the private key and a lot of random numbers from RAM. We perform statistical analysis to distinguish the key from the random numbers. On the other hand, the key extraction of AES is simple and we do not need any additional analysis to separate the secret key from other values. Maartmann-Moe et al.'s attack [8] uses the facts that round keys are derived from the initial key and the round keys are stored on RAM right after the initial key. Therefore, their attack cannot be applied when the initial key and round keys are stored on the separate locations on RAM. On the other hand, our attack can recover the key even when the initial key and round keys are stored on the separate locations as we observe the values, which are accessed by the encryption functions.

Table 1. The watch list of functions for RSA decryption and AES encryption

Library	Function	Status
RSA		
rsaoOs_so	RSA_private_decrypt	through
libcrypto.so.0.9.8	BN_div	watch
libcrypto.so.0.9.8	BN_lshift	watch
libcrypto.so.0.9.8	BN_rshift	watch
AES		
aesopenssl	AES_encrypt	watchdeeply

5.1 RSA

We implemented a simple RSA encryption and decryption program using the OpenSSL library, which repeatedly encrypts random numbers and decrypts the generated ciphertexts. Both keys remain unchanged during the experiment. Table 1 summarises the list of the methods to be observed.

We initiate the sample program and start the encryption and decryption operations. Then, we initiate PPT and attach its process to the sample program. PPT can show the structure of the program, when it is successfully attached to the target. By executing the program while watching the specified functions in Table 1, we record the values and their frequencies in which they are referred to in the RAM. Figure 1 shows relations between the values and their frequencies. The x-axis shows the values and the y-axis shows the number of referred times. As it is unlikely that the private key is a sparse value, we can eliminate the sparse candidates, for instance 0x0000000000000001. These sparse values are mostly used for controlling the operations such as counters.

For the remaining candidates, we use number of referred times as a clue. In this example, we iterate encryption and decryption 10 times. Thus, the private key has to be used at least 10 times. Even when we do not know how many times encryption and decryption is iterated, the secret key can still be distinguished from other random numbers after sufficient number of iterations.

5.2 AES

We also implemented a simple AES encryption program, named aesopenssl, using the OpenSSL library. This sample program continuously encrypts random numbers with a fixed secret key. Table 1 shows the function to be observed.

We execute the program while observing the aesopenssl function, and apply the method similar to what we did for RSA to eliminate the non-key values. The secret key we used for the sample program is "THISISSECRETKEY!", which is 0x54, 0x48, 0x49, 0x53, 0x49, 0x53, 0x53, 0x45, 0x43, 0x52, 0x45, 0x54, 0x4b, 0x45, 0x59, 0x21 in ASCII. PPT recovered all these values, and it also recovered 0x0000000a, which is the number of rounds in AES-128, followed by the round key.

6 Conclusion

In this paper, we introduced a statistical key extraction attack on cryptographic keys using memory dump data, and confirmed the effectiveness of the attack by utilising our Process Peeping Tool. The tool can be attached to the target process and can trace the target's memory usage. We used RSA and AES as example cryptosystems in the target programs, which utilised the OpenSSL library implementations. Thus, it is possible to apply the same approach to other applications using OpenSSL library or similar cryptographic libraries. Although we only applied PPT to RSA and AES implemented in the OpenSSL library, it is possible to apply the same extraction mechanism to other, including non-cryptographic, algorithms or libraries. Although we execute the PPT with the root privilege, we can still apply our method obtaining memory dump data without the root privilege.

References

1. arstechnica.: Critical crypto bug in OpenSSL opens two-thirds of the web to eaves-dropping (2014). http://goo.gl/JUm3dq
2. Codenomicon Ltd.: The heartbleed bug (2014). http://heartbleed.com
3. Dierks, T., Rescorla, E.: The transport layer security (TLS) protocol version 1.2. RFC 5246 (2008)
4. Freier, A., Karlton, P., Kocher, P.: The secure sockets layer (SSL) protocol version 3.0. RFC 6101 (2011)
5. Goldreich, O.: Towards a theory of software protection and simulation by oblivious RAMs. In: Aho, A.V. (ed.) STOC, pp. 182–194. ACM (1987)
6. Goldreich, O., Ostrovsky, R.: Software protection and simulation on oblivious RAMs. J. ACM **43**(3), 431–473 (1996)
7. Halderman, J.A., Schoen, S.D., Heninger, N., Clarkson, W., Paul, W., Calandrino, J.A., Feldman, A.J., Appelbaum, J., Felten, E.W.: Lest we remember: cold-boot attacks on encryption keys. Commun. ACM **52**(5), 91–98 (2009)
8. Maartmann-Moe, C., Thorkildsen, S.E., Årnes, A.: The persistence of memory: forensic identification and extraction of cryptographic keys. Digit. Investig. **6**, S132–S140 (2009)
9. Müller, T., Spreitzenbarth, M.: FROST - forensic recovery of scrambled telephones. In: Jacobson, M., Locasto, M., Mohassel, P., Safavi-Naini, R. (eds.) ACNS 2013. LNCS, vol. 7954, pp. 373–388. Springer, Heidelberg (2013)
10. Seggelmann, R., Tuexen, M., Williams, M.: Transport layer security (TLS) and datagram transport layer security (DTLS) heartbeat extension. RFC6520 (2012)

How Robust is the Internet? – Insights from Graph Analysis

Annika Baumann and Benjamin Fabian[✉]

Institute of Information Systems, Humboldt-Universität zu Berlin,
Spandauer Str. 1, 10178 Berlin, Germany
{annika.baumann,bfabian}@wiwi.hu-berlin.de

Abstract. The importance of the Internet as todays communication and information medium cannot be underestimated. Reduced Internet reliability can lead to significant financial losses for businesses and economies. But how robust is the Internet with respect to failures, accidents, and malicious attacks? We will investigate this question from the perspective of graph analysis. First, we develop a graph model of the Internet at the level of Autonomous Systems based on empirical data. Then, a global assessment of Internet robustness is conducted with respect to several failure and attack modes. Our results indicate that even today the Internet could be very vulnerable to smart attack strategies.

1 Introduction

Cost efficient and fast worldwide communication is critically depending on the Internet; many innovative companies and services in the world rely on it to achieve their business goals. Therefore, reduced Internet reliability can lead to significant financial losses for businesses and economies. A study of an IT systems integrator estimated for example that network disruptions caused $1.7 billion financial losses for US companies in 2010 [1]. But how robust is the Internet with respect to failures, accidents and malicious attacks? Internet failures already happened in reality, caused by natural disasters, power failures [2], misconfiguration, or vicious attacks, and affected Internet connectivity [3–5].

Because of its size, structure, and dynamic nature, the Internet can be seen as a complex network. Several abstraction levels for representing the Internet in graph theory are possible: graphs of routers, points of presence, or Autonomous Systems (AS). An AS can be considered as an Internet domain, which is often under the control of a single organization such as an Internet service provider. Normally all entities assigned to one certain AS share a common routing policy, which is relevant for the traffic forwarding procedure. Because of rich data sources and a good research basis, we investigate Internet robustness at the AS level. Basing on empirical data we will develop a graph model of the Internet in order to conduct a global assessment of Internet robustness with the help of graph analysis.

J. Lopez et al. (Eds.): CRiSIS 2014, LNCS 8924, pp. 247–254, 2015.
DOI: 10.1007/978-3-319-17127-2_18

2   Literature Review

Several graph models have been used to imitate the Internet structure. Classical network modeling approaches include the Erdös and Renyi [6,7] graph model (ER) and the scale-free BA model developed by Barabsi and Albert [7]. Albert et al. [8] study attack and failure tolerance of the Internet at the AS-level using both models. They focus on the diameter as a global connectivity metric. In [9], the Internet is studied at the AS level with restrictions caused by its economically driven character (policy-driven routing). Reference [4] examines resilience of the Internet in case of router removal. In [10] the authors develop attack techniques that are based only on local information. Reference [11] also focuses on malicious attacks and develops a method for making the AS-level network more robust by interchanging edges of node pairs. In [5,12] resilience frameworks, metrics, and case studies are presented. Reference [13] investigates the k-fault tolerance of the Internet.

3   Data Collection and Preparation

Collection and preparation of the dataset are crucial steps when studying the Internet topology. All publicly available sources suffer from incomplete or inaccurate data. We used three different approaches to gather data on the Internet structure: BGP routing tables, traceroute, and the Internet Routing Registry (IRR) during the same time period (mid of 2012). In the case of BGP routing tables it was possible to utilize data from other sources such as Oregon Route-Views [14], RIPE-RIS [15], or from UCLA [16]. These projects integrate many data sources, namely BGP routing tables and updates, route servers as well as looking glasses. The Macroscopic Topology Project of CAIDA is based on Ark [17] and collects IPv4 address paths with the help of several monitors located around the world, resulting in an AS link dataset. For IRR data, we retrieved data files of all available 34 IRRs [18]. We only considered those AS paths that were changed not later than in 2012. Moreover, we demanded that any AS relationship is mentioned at least twice, by each of both participating ASs, for mutual verification. All of these individual datasets of CAIDA AS Rank, UCLA, Ark, and IRR were merged into one final graph, resulting in a single connected component consisting of 44,397 nodes and 199,073 edges.

4   Internet Graph Statistics

Any graph can be characterized by various metrics, which are helpful for understanding its topological structure and connectivity. Figure 1 presents an overview of selected relevant graph metrics and their respective values computed by our Python programs that are based on the NetworkX framework [19]. An average clustering coefficient of around 0.46 indicates that almost half of all the possible connections between neighboring nodes are actually realized in the network. The AS-level graph is therefore quite well connected with respect to the neighborhood of each node; for comparisons to other networks see [20].

Metric	Mean	Median
Average Clustering Coefficient	0.4554	0.3333
Average Node Degree	8.9679	2.0000
Assortativity Coefficient	-0.1847	–
Average Eccentricity (Diameter / Radius)	7.8302 (11 / 6)	8.0000
Average Neighbor Connectivity	312.08	302.3766
Average Neighbor Degree	703.2874	315.0000
Average Shortest Path Length	3.5585	3.5056
Average Node Betweenness Centrality	5.76296e-05	0.0000

Fig. 1. Graph metrics

The average node degree of 8.97 indicates that on average nine edges are connected to a node in the AS-level network. The assortativity coefficient of the graph is −0.1847. This value implies that nodes in the network prefer to connect to other nodes having a dissimilar degree. In general, graphs with an assortativity coefficient below zero are considered more vulnerable to attacks because a large amount of nodes concentrates around those nodes with a high degree. The average neighbor degree with a value of 703.29 is yet another sign of the well-connectedness of the Internet. On average, every node in the network has 703 possible next hops to send its data to the desired destination. This is also confirmed by average neighbor connectivity [21]. Average eccentricity for the whole AS-level graph is around 7.83, indicating the average length of the longest shortest path from each node in the network. The Internet diameter at the AS level is 11. The average shortest path length is 3.56. This means that every possible pair of nodes can reach each other on average within less than four hops, which indicates a small world character [22]. Average betweenness centrality calculates the number of shortest paths passing through a certain node, which roughly approximates the potential traffic flow through it. More than 24,000 nodes have a betweenness centrality of zero, i.e., there is no shortest path passing through that specific node. Nodes with a high degree usually also have large betweenness centrality because they are important for routing. These nodes usually form the center of the network and provide short routes through the entire network for other nodes.

To summarize, the Internet AS-level graph shows typical characteristics of so-called small world networks, in particular a high clustering coefficient as well as a small average shortest path length. Moreover, there are nodes with an extraordinarily high degree that represent central connection hubs.

5   Robustness Analysis

The robustness of the Internet topology can be analyzed by methods of graph theory. Our article will comprehend and update the findings of earlier robustness analyses based on more recent data. For this purpose, four different modes will be applied in order to examine the failure tolerance of the Internet. The first mode, random failure, is using the successive random deletion of nodes from the network. The second approach, the degree-based attack, involves the successive targeted deletion of nodes that are having the highest degree. This mode will simulate an organized attack that is disregarding any local links to select the next target node.

The third method, the mixed mode, is based on an approach proposed in [10]. At first, a certain node will be chosen at random and removed from the network. Then, its former neighbors will be investigated whereupon the neighbor node with the highest degree will be deleted next. This approach will model a targeted attack that is restricted by limited knowledge because the necessary global information on the optimal next node might not be easily available with enough precision. This could simulate the continuous spreading of a worm or a similar threat through the network, starting at a random point and then trying to most efficiently distribute itself through the network based on local information. The fourth mode, the so-called random path mode, is similar to the third approach. Again, in the beginning a random node is chosen in the network and attacked. This time, however, the next neighbor node to be removed will be selected at random, moving continuously through the network using a randomized path. If a selected node becomes isolated, the next node for removal is chosen globally at random. This method simulates a realistic, randomized spread of malicious software or another threat through the network. This variant also utilizes the connections between nodes but not as efficiently as the third approach. For all modes, the results for the removal of the first ten percent of nodes will be presented. This is sufficient to show the impact of each mode.

To characterize the decay of the network in case of failures and attacks, we apply special metrics from graph theory that are describing connectivity of the network as a whole. One important global metric is the size of the giant component, i.e., the current size of the single largest connected component in the entire graph. Figure 2 shows the degeneration of this giant component in case of failures, attacks, the mixed, and the random-path modes.

The fastest network destruction is the degree-based attack. Only around two percent of the nodes need to be removed from the network in order to reduce the giant component to 50 percent of its original size. After eight percent of the nodes are eliminated, the former giant component has become negligibly small.

In case of the random failure mode, the size of the giant component decreases much slower, approximately by the amount of nodes removed from the network. Therefore, this mode has almost no effect on the network's global communication ability. The Internet is highly resistant in case of random and uncorrelated failures. In general, the mixed approach is a lot more efficient than the random elimination of nodes and for a particular amount of removed nodes even slightly more efficient than the attack mode. One reason could be that in case of the mixed approach the path-based selection of nodes with a high degree splits the network faster into a number of smaller components. Nevertheless, after a certain

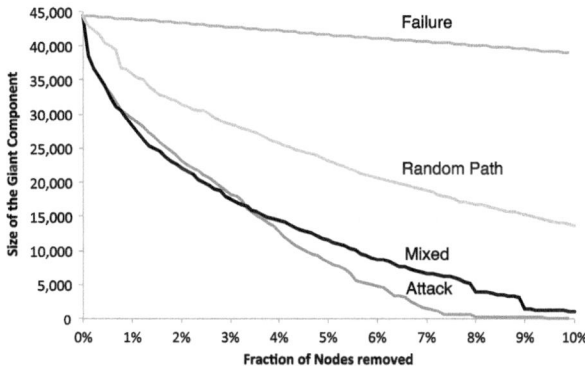

Fig. 2. Size of the giant component

threshold is reached, the degree-based attack is consistently more destructive. In terms of destructiveness, the random path approach lies somewhere between these two highly efficient modes and the almost insignificant random deletion of nodes; the decay of the network is, however, much stronger than in the purely random case. The path-based selection criterion might again cause a fast splitting of components in the network topology. This illustrates the vulnerability of the Internet if a threat spreads throughout the network at random but is still aware of connecting paths. A lot of nodes with a low degree, whose removal does not affect the communication ability of the Internet by much, could still play an important role as some kind of glue holding the network together.

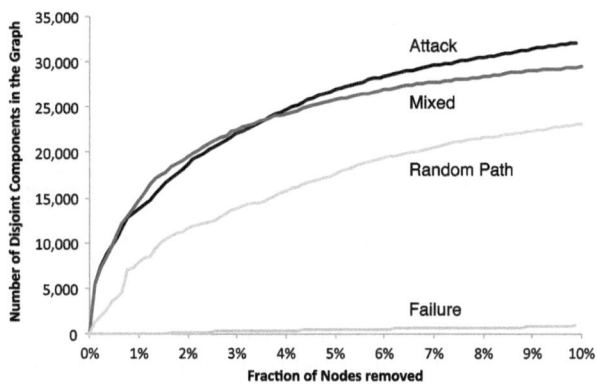

Fig. 3. Number of disjoint components

A similar result is provided by the metric of the total number of disjoint – but internally connected – components in the network (see Fig. 3). In case of the random removal of nodes, only around 900 disjoint components arise after ten percent of nodes are eliminated. In case of the most efficient degree-based attack modus, the number of connected components grows rapidly. After ten percent of the nodes are missing from the network, the number of disjoint components is greater than 32,000. With mixed mode, after eliminating ten percent of the nodes almost 30,000 components exist – this is only 6.3 percent less than in previous case. The random path deletion of nodes again takes the third place in terms of efficient network destruction. Compared with the purely random deletion, it is again a lot more efficient due to its path awareness. Around 23,000 disjoint components arise after ten percent of nodes have been removed. Therefore path-based elimination of nodes is highly efficient in both cases, based on random or targeted neighbor selection. Furthermore, both approaches could be easier to perform since they are based on local properties rather than on global ones.

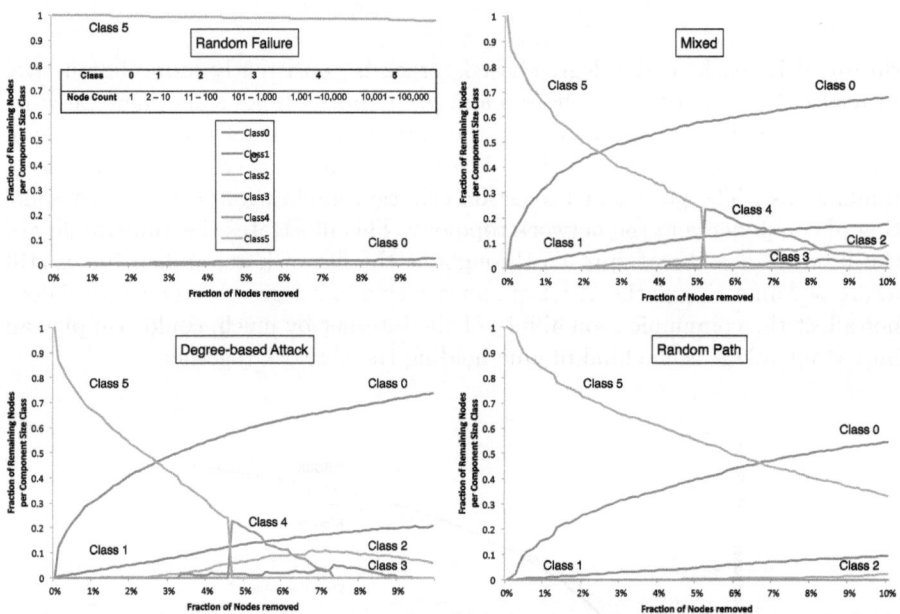

Fig. 4. Fraction of nodes per component size class

An even more detailed view on the network decay can be achieved by the distribution of the sizes of the connected components [23]. For this purpose, six distinct classes of component sizes are defined; each of them comprises components with certain amounts of nodes (Fig. 4). Before the decay of the network starts, there is only one single connected component, which is part of class 5. To demonstrate the decay of the network in even more detail, the metric is refined in such a way that it measures the fraction of current nodes per connected component size class. This is the relation of the number of current nodes contained in each component class, divided by the total number of current nodes, i.e., all original nodes in the undamaged network minus the nodes already removed from the network. In case of the random deletion of nodes, there is almost no difference between the undamaged graph and the version having ten percent of its nodes lost. Class 5 dominates and its size is only reduced by the deletion of nodes and a very small number of components in classes 0 and 1. The decay of the network is therefore only driven by the deletion of nodes itself but not by further effects.

However, a different picture of the decay of the network is obtained when the nodes with the highest degree in the network are removed first. With such a degree-based attack, the fraction of nodes for component size class 5 drops rapidly. On the other hand, the fraction of nodes for class 0 rises fast continuously. After removing ten percent of the nodes, class 0 accounts for 73 percent of all remaining nodes in the network. This means there are almost 29,500 fully isolated nodes in the network. It is evident that the decay of the network in case of a targeted attack takes place much faster than in case of a random removal of nodes. The decay of the network in case of the mixed approach is quite similar to the degree-based attack modus. The random path approach does not generate such a drastic collapse as in the two previous cases. Again the curve of class 5 drops continuously but not as fast as in the attack or mixed mode. Even with partial randomness this is still a highly efficient mode to destroy a network.

In summary, based on the total range of ten percent of node removal, the attack mode is the most efficient one. A disadvantage of this approach is the relatively high amount of information needed, which is based on the global graph and therefore not easy to obtain for any current Internet situation since most data sources are rather historical. If an initially faster but finally less destructive decay is adequate, the mixed approach is the better choice. But the major advantage of this mode lies in its strategy since no global information is necessary, which makes it easier to perform. By far not as efficient but still destructive is the random path method. This mode might be even easier to perform due to its randomness. It is sufficient to find any neighbor and then move along a randomly chosen path in the network.

6   Conclusion

Our results indicate that even today the Internet could be vulnerable to smart attack strategies, such as the degree-based attack, the mixed and even the random path attack mode. Our analysis is based on the abstraction level of ASs and on public data that is an incomplete snapshot. It is possible that valid links are not visible in our data, which would lead to somewhat better robustness results. In contrast, however, we would also like to further study the impact of economic relationships between ASs by considering policy-driven routing, and the very complex router level. Finally, we did not discuss practical IT security or fault tolerance of routing protocols. Our results motivate that further complementary studies are necessary, especially because the Internet has become a critical global infrastructure for businesses and everyday life.

References

1. CDW: Billions Lost due to IT Network Outages in 2010 (2011). http://www.eweek. com/c/a/Enterprise-Networking/Billions-Lost-Due-to-IT-Network-Outages-in-2010-Survey-559569/
2. Cerf, V.: Natural disasters and electric infrastructure. IEEE Internet Comput. **15**(6), 103–104 (2011)
3. Agapi, A., Birman, K., Broberg, R., Cotton, C., Kielmann, T., Millnert, M., Payne, R., Surton, R., van Renesse, R.: Routers for the cloud: can the Internet achieve 5-nines availability? IEEE Internet Comput. **15**(5), 72–77 (2011)
4. Wu, J., Zhang, Y., Morley Mao, Z., Shin, K.: Internet routing resilience to failures: analysis and implications. In: Proceedings of the 2007 ACM CoNEXT Conference, New York, NY, USA (2007)
5. Sterbenz, J., Hutchison, D., Cetinkaya, E., Jabbar, A., Rohrer, J., Schöller, M., Smith, P.: Resilience and survivability in communication networks: strategies, principles, and survey of disciplines. Comput. Netw. **54**(8), 1245–1265 (2010)
6. Erdös, P., Renyi, A.: On random graphs I. Publicationes Mathematicae (Debrecen) **6**, 290–297 (1959)
7. Newman, M.: The structure and function of complex networks. SIAM Rev. **45**(2), 167–256 (2003)
8. Barabasi, A., Albert, R.: Emergence of scaling in random networks. Science **286**(5439), 509–512 (1999)
9. Dolev, D., Jamin, S., Mokryn, O., Shavitt, Y.: Internet resiliency to attacks and failures under BGP policy routing. Comput. Netw. **50**(16), 3183–3196 (2006)
10. Xiao, S., Xiao, G., Cheng, T.: Tolerance of intentional attacks in complex communication networks. IEEE Commun. Mag. **46**(1), 146–152 (2008)
11. Schneider, C., Moreira, A., Andrade Jr., J., Havlin, S., Herrmann, H.: Mitigation of malicious attacks on networks. PNAS **108**(10), 3838–3841 (2011)
12. Smith, P., Hutchison, D., Sterbenz, J., Schöller, M., Fessi, A., Karaliopoulos, M., Lac, C., Plattner, B.: Network resilience: a systematic approach. IEEE Commun. Mag. **49**(7), 88–97 (2011)
13. Deng, W., Karaliopoulos, M., Mühlbauer, W., Zhu, P., Lu, X., Plattner, B.: k-fault tolerance of the Internet AS graph. Comput. Netw. **55**(10), 2492–2503 (2011)
14. Route Views (2014). http://www.routeviews.org/
15. RIPE RIS (2014). http://www.ripe.net/data-tools/stats/ris/
16. UCLA: Internet Topology Collection (2014). http://irl.cs.ucla.edu/topology/
17. CAIDA Ark (2014). http://www.caida.org/projects/ark/
18. Internet Routing Registry (2014). http://www.irr.net/
19. NetworkX (2014). http://networkx.github.io/
20. Newman, M.: Random graphs as models of networks. In: Bornholdt, S., Schuster, H.G. (eds.) Handbook of Graphs and Networks, pp. 35–68. Wiley-VCH, Berlin (2003)
21. Mahadevan, P., Krioukov, D., Fomenkov, M., Huffaker, B., Dimitropoulos, X., claffy, k., Vahdat, A.: The Internet AS-level topology: three data sources and one definitive metric. ACM SIGCOMM Comput. Commun. Rev. 30, 17–26 (2006)
22. Watts, D., Strogatz, S.: Collective dynamics of 'Small-World' networks. Nature **392**, 440–442 (1998)
23. Magoni, D.: Tearing down the Internet. IEEE J. Sel. Areas Commun. **21**(6), 949–960 (2003)

Regularity Based Decentralized Social Networks

Zhe Wang$^{(\boxtimes)}$ and Naftaly H. Minsky

Rutgers University, New Brunswick, USA
{zhewang,minsky}@cs.rutgers.edu

Abstract. Centralized online social networks (OSNs) have drawbacks, chief among which are the risks posed to the security and privacy of the information maintained by them; and the loss of control over the information contributed by their members. The attempts to create decentralized OSNs (DOSNs) enable each member of an OSN keeps its own data under its control, instead of surrendering it to a central place; providing its own access-control policy. However, they are unable to subject the membership of a DOSN, and the interaction between its members, to any global policy. We adopt the decentralization, complementing it with a means for scalably specifying and enforcing regularities over the membership of a community, and over the interaction between its members.

1 Introduction

An *online social network* (OSN) is a *community* of people that interact with each other, which operates subject to some *laws* that regulate the membership and the manner in which its members interact with each other. Such laws are easy to implement in traditional OSNs (Facebook, etc.). Because they mediate all interactions between their members, and maintain the information supplied by the members of the community.

However, this convenient way of implementing OSNs has several drawbacks. Chief among them are the risks posed to the security and privacy of the information maintained by them and the loss of control over the information contributed by individual members. Security may not be of much concern to the millions of users of Facebook or Twitter. But they are, or should be, of serious concern to other types of OSNs, that exchanges more sensitive information—such as medical and financial information; or internal information of an enterprise.

There are several attempts to create decentralized OSNs (DOSNs); such as LotusNet [1], Safebook [2], PeerSoN [3]. The essential idea of these attempts is that each member should keep its own data under its control, instead of store it to a central place, providing its own access-control policies. However, it's not sufficient as they cannot establish *regularities* over the membership, and the interaction between its members. A set of enforced global law is essential for an OSN, and makes it into a social community.

We designed a model of OSNs with ways to scalably specify and enforce regularities over the membership and interaction between the distributed members.

© Springer International Publishing Switzerland 2015
J. Lopez et al. (Eds.): CRiSIS 2014, LNCS 8924, pp. 255–262, 2015.
DOI: 10.1007/978-3-319-17127-2_19

The rest of this paper is organized as follows. Section 2 introduces an example of OSNs for which security is critical and would thus benefit from decentralization. Section 3 introduces examples of law that are essential for an OSN— particularly for the types of OSNs for which security tends to be critical, but cannot be established under DOSN. Section 4 introduces our model of decentralized OSN. Section 5 is an implemented case study that demonstrates how this model can be used for a concrete application. And we conclude in Sect. 6.

2 OSN in an Enterprise—Case Study

Consider a large and geographically distributed enterprise that provides an OSN for its employees, which distinguishes between groups of employees. The groups may overlap, as an employee could belong to several groups. Let the members have a profile, which is a set of attributes visible to the whole OSN and can be indexed and searched. The members can publish *posts* and build *following* relationships with each other.

There are two types of security needed. First, the information exchanged between the employees can carry sensitive information about the business of company. It is important for this information not to be exposed to the outside. Second, there is need of preventing information exchanged within a certain group from being accessible to anybody else, or other groups.

3 Some of Regularities Imposed over an OSN

We show here the type of *regularities* that an OSN may need to establish. All the regularities discussed here can be easily achieved in centralized OSNs, but cannot be established under the DOSNs' architecture.

3.1 Global Access Control (AC) Policies

DOSNs enable each member to apply its own AC policy to its own data, which are maintained in its own database. The problem is that, unlike in Facebook or Twitter, a member of an enterprise may not have the complete authority over the data it maintains. It could really belong to the enterprise, which thus has the ultimate authority about how they should be distributed. The enterprise may relegate to individual members the right to apply their own AC policies, *provided* that these policies conform to the global policy of an enterprise.

3.2 Associative Sending via Gossip Protocol

By *associative sending*, we mean the ability to send a message, to a subset of the members of the OSN, having constraint on the profile of receivers. We will describe below how both of these capabilities can be provided via *gossip protocol*.

Now a member wants to send a message to all members whose profile satisfies a condition. It starts gossiping, by sending the query to its acquaintances.

Any member that gets the query continues gossiping it; and one should be able to read the message only if it is in the target of this associative sending.

Unfortunately, this mechanism cannot be implemented under DOSN without seriously undermining the security and privacy of members. For example: (1) the basic protocol of gossip could be violated via some members of DOSN. They withhold the message instead of forwarding it; they may violate the frequency or forwarding limit to overwhelm the network; and they may even manipulate the content or source of the message. (2) when a message is sent via gossip, one needs to distinguish between the targets of the message and its carriers. A carrier gets the message and is supposed to gossip it to others, but it is not itself in the target of this message, so it should not read this message. But since it got this message there is no way under DOSN to prevent it from reading the message, and thus learning not only the profile of sender, but also the kind of members that the sender wants to communicate with, judging from the search condition. This is a massive violation of privacy, because every member would see most messages issued by other members.

3.3   Profile Search

Although all published versions of DOSN provide *identity search*, none of them supports *profile search*, despite its obvious importance in OSNs. This is, in part, due their concern about the negative effect that such search would have on privacy [4]. Indeed, simpler and most efficient way to provide for such a search is by creating a central database of the profiles of all members. But this would seriously undermine the privacy of the members of the OSN.

3.4   Membership Control

Control over membership is critical to many OSNs. Such control may have several complementary aspects. First, one may require that to be a member of an OSN, one needs to authenticate itself via a certificate. One may think that this policy can be established under the DOSN architecture by having every member of the DOSN require everyone to authenticate itself in a specified manner. But DOSN has no way for ensuring that all its members behave in this way. Second, one may require that to be a member of an OSN, one needs to garner the support of several current members of it. Third, it is often important to establish some procedure for removing members from a given OSN. This can be done in many ways. For example, consider an OSN that has a member that plays the role of a *manager*. Now, let the manager be given the power to remove any current member of the OSN, simply by sending it a message *remove*. Then it should lose its ability to interact with other members of the OSN.

3.5   Constraints on What Members Can Do

Sometimes we want to impose constraints on what members can do. Constraints may depend on the profile of members, or on the history of their interaction with others. As shown before, only a member that plays the role of manager can send the *remove* message to others. And any member that gets such a message must cease all communication with others. The type of messages that members are allowed to send, or the type of posts that they are allowed to issue, depend on their roles in the OSN.

4   A Model of Decentralized OSN—OSC

We introduce here a model of decentralized OSNs that differs from the current approach employed under the DOSN architecture, in that it enables the enforcement of law over it. We call a specific OSN under this model an *online social community* (OSC). The model employs our previous work—the Law-Governed Interaction (LGI) middleware. LGI is a middleware that can govern the interaction (via message exchange) between distributed *actors*, by enforcing an explicitly specified law about such interaction. A detailed presentation of LGI, and a tutorial of it, can be found in its manual [5]—which describes the release of an experimental implementation of the main parts of LGI.

Now, a community C under the OSC model is broadly defined as a 4-tuple $\langle M, \mathcal{L}, T, S \rangle$, where M is the set of members; $\mathcal{L}$ is the set of law that governs this

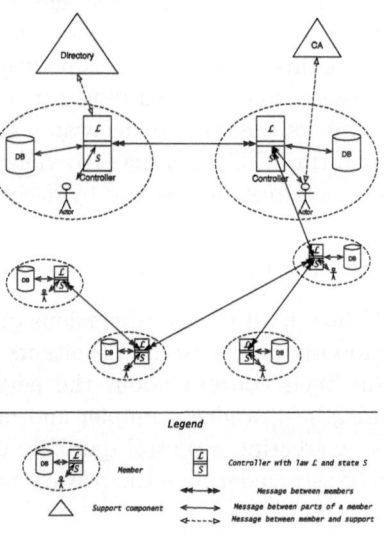

Fig. 1. The Anatomy of an OSC Community

community; T is a set of generic LGI controllers that serve as the middleware that enforces law $\mathcal{L}$; and S is a set of components that support the operations of C, and is specific to it—this set may be empty.

4.1   The Anatomy of a Community Under OSC

We describe here the anatomy of a community C under this model by elaborating on its various components, and on the relations between them. This anatomy is depicted schematically in Fig. 1.

The Set M of Members. An individual member m of a community C is a triple $\langle user, mediator, database \rangle$, where *user* is usually a human, operating via some computer; *mediator* is an LGI-controller that mediates all interactions between this member and the rest of the community—subject to law $\mathcal{L}C$ (which we denote by $\mathcal{L}_C$); and *database*, which is an optional part of the member, maintains information associated with this member.

The Law $\mathcal{L}_C$ of Community. It is the law that endows an OSC-community with its overall structure and behavior. And the fact that the law can be any well formed LGI law endows this model with great deal generality regarding the law that can be enforced over a community.

The set T of LGI Controllers. Every user can create its own controller, using the LGI middleware. But if malicious corruption of controllers by their users is of concern, then it is better for them to adopt controllers maintained by a trusted *controller service* (CoS). In particular, the CoS may be managed by the organization in the context of which the community is to operate. Alternatively, the CoS may be managed by a reputed and trusted organization. For more about the security and trustworthiness of controllers, please see [5].

The Support S. An OSC-community may require services of various components that are not themselves members of this community. For example: (a) a certification authority (CA) used for the authentication the various members of the community; (b) a *naming service* that provides unique names of community members; (c) an index service for searching. It is worth pointing out that this set of support components may be empty for some communities.

4.2   The Launching of an OSC-Community

A specific OSC-community, C is launched by constructing its *foundation*—described below—and then having individual members join it. The construction of the foundation of a community C consists of the following steps: (a) defining law $\mathcal{L}_C$ under which this community is to operate; (b) implementing the required support components; and (c) selecting, or constructing, a *controller-service* (CoS) for the use of this community.

Once the foundation of C is constructed, anybody can attempt to join it as a member, via adopting an LGI-controller, and loading law $\mathcal{L}_C$ into it. It should be pointed out that such an attempt to join a given community C may fail, if the conditions for joining imposed by law $\mathcal{L}_C$ are not satisfied.

4.3   The Operation of a Community

Consider a member x sending a message m to another member y. The message first arrives at the controller of x, that operates under law $\mathcal{L}_C$. These controllers would then carry out the ruling of law $\mathcal{L}_C$, which can mandate the execution of any number of the following kind of actions: (a) change its own state in some way; (b) send the message m, or some other message, to the controller of the original target of y; and (c) send some other messages to the controllers of some other members, or to some of the support components of the community. Among other things, this means that members of a community interact with each other via their controllers, and the controllers communicate with each other.

The ruling of a law for a given event that occurs at a controller depends on the state of this controller, which may be different for different members. This difference can come from the role of the user in the organization. Or the state may change dynamically in response to some interactive activity of the community. For example, the manager of the community may be allowed by the law of community to transfer its managerial baton to some other member, which would then be able to send *revoke* messages. In other words, *the members of a community C may not be equal under its law $\mathcal{L}_C$.*

5 Implementation of OSN in an Enterprise

In this section, we describe the implementation of the OSC community, introduced in Sect. 2. It has been implemented in the scale of two hundred users as a proof of concept. The law $\mathcal{C}$ of the Community is used for regulating every aspects of the operations and behaviors of the community. We split it into several parts according to their functionalities. Due to lack of space, we only discuss the detailed law of some functionalities of the communities.

5.1 Member Profile and Membership Control

To join the community, a member needs to adopt a controller under law $\mathcal{C}$. Rule $\mathcal{R}1$ allows a user to join the community by presenting a certificate to prove that it is an employee. Once certificate is verified by the controller, the set of attributes in its profile will be inserted into the user's control state. Rule $\mathcal{R}2$ allows the user to join the group t_i by providing a group certificate (Fig. 2).

```
R1.  UPON adopted(X,cert(issuer(ca),subj(X),attr(A))) :-
            do(+A).
R2.  UPON certified(X,cert(issuer(ca),subj(X),attr(t_i))) :-
            do(+t_i); do(+filter(group(t_i))).
R3.  UPON sent(X,addProfile(Attribute(Value)),X) :-
            if ( ¬ (Attribute in controlledAttributes) ) then do(+Attribute(Value)).
R4.  UPON sent(X,updateProfile(Attribute(Value)),X) :-
            if ( ¬ (Attribute in controlledAttributes) ) then do(-Attribute); do(+Attribute(Value)).
R5.  UPON sent(X,addFilter(Attribute(Value)),X) :-
            do(+filter(Attribute(value))).
R6.  UPON sent(X,#revoke#,Y) :-
            if(role(manager)@CS) then do(Forward);
            else do(Deliver(X,notAllow,X)).
R7.  UPON arrived(X,#revoke#,Y) :-
            update(certificateBlacklist); inform(certificateBlacklist); do(Quit).
```

Fig. 2. Law $\mathcal{C}$: Member's Profile and Membership Control

User can directly add attributes into its profile via Rule $\mathcal{R}3$ and update them via Rule $\mathcal{R}4$. Rule $\mathcal{R}5$ shows how a user sets up its subscription filter. When user adds the filter content into control state. Its controller will only allow the members who have the required attributes to subscribe to it. The following operations will be described in Sect. 5.2.

Finally, rule $\mathcal{R}6$ shows that only the manager role can remove a member from the community. Non-managers are not allowed to use the type *revoke* when sending messages. When the *revoke* message arrives at the member's controller, according to Rule $\mathcal{R}7$, the controller will directly terminate the connection to the actor. The member has no way to control or avoid that.

```
R8.  UPON sent(X,publish(P),X) :- group(t_i)@CS
             if (typeof(P) == #management# and ¬ role(manager)@CS) then return;
             updateProfile(lastTenPosts(P)); updateDB(P);
             if(subList[group(t_i)] = []) then return;
             else forEach(subscriber in subList[group(t_i)])
             do(Forward(X,P,subscriber)).
R9.  UPON arrived(X,P,Y) :-
             do(Deliver); do(inform(X,P,Y)).
R10.
     UPON sent(X,requestSubscribe(profile),Y) :-
             do(Forward).
R11.
     UPON arrived(X,requestSubscribe(profile),Y) :- group(t_i)@CS
             if(filter(Attribute(Value))@CS and Attribute(Value)@profile) then do(Forward(Y,subscribeNotAllowed,X));
             else do(updateSublist[group(t_i)]); do(Forward(Y,subscribeAllowed,X)).
```

Fig. 3. Law $\mathcal{C}$: Communication

5.2 Communication

Members can publish *posts* and build subscription relationships with each other. The control over communication has two complementary parts: global control and local control. The global control is imposed on every member of the community, but can be sensitive to the state of members, while the local control is discretionary to each member (Fig. 3).

The global control is imposed on both publishing and subscription. The control over publishing is on what types of posts a member can publish. For example, only the managerial staff can publish posts with type *management*. The control on the subscription regulates who can subscribe to whom, and to which types of posts. An example is that only the members from a same group can talk to each other. Sometimes, a member does not want to be subscribed by certain members, it can block the subscription requests from them. That's what we call *Local Access Control*. To achieve this, a member adds a filter *filter(X)* in its profile, then its cannot be subscribed by the member who has attribute X in profile.

In Rule $\mathcal{R}8$, when the user wants to publish a post to its subscribers, the controller will read local subscriber list and push the post to each of them. When the subscriber receives the post or message, according to the Rule $\mathcal{R}9$, controller will show the post to the user.

By Rule $\mathcal{R}10$, any user can send a subscription request to any user. The controller will attach its profile to the request. In Rule $\mathcal{R}11$, when the request arrives at the user, the controller will check whether there is an access control filter in its control state. If not, it will add the request user to the subscriber list. If there are filters, it will examine whether this user satisfies by checking the required attributes of the profile. If the requester satisfies, the controller will add it to the subscriber list and send back the result to the request user.

5.3 Search

The method we are using for search is gossip protocol. Rule $\mathcal{R}12$ initiates the search request. Rule $\mathcal{R}13$ describe the whole forward procedure of gossip search. When controller receives a search query, it first check whether this user satisfies the search. If it is, it will send back the hit message. Then the controller will check whether the Time To Live is reduced to zero. When it is not, it will send the

```
R12.
      UPON sent(X,search(M),Y) :-
              if(X=Y) then do(Forward).
R13.
      UPON arrived(X,search(M,C,TTL),Y) :-
              if(M@CS) then do(Forward(Y,hit,X))
              if(TTL > 0) then if(subList=[]) then return
              else if(fanout < subList.length) then subSubList = randomPick(subList,fanout);
              do(Forward(Y,search(M,C,TTL-1),subSubList))
              else do(Forward(Y,search(M,C,TTL-1),subList))
              if(C@CS) then do(Deliver).
```

Fig. 4. Law $\mathcal{C}$: Search

search query to its subscriber. If the user is qualified to see the search message, the controller will display the message (Fig. 4).

A main feature of our search method is the enforcement of the law can make sure the user on the search topology will not see the search query unless it is qualified for that search. Therefore, the sender will not need worry about the leak of the secret, while making the best use of the whole network.

6 Conclusion

This paper addresses the risks to privacy and security posed by centralized online social networks (OSNs). These risks, which are the consequence of centralization, should be of serious concerns to many OSNs. Several recent attempts have been made to decentralize OSNs, by letting each member keep maintaining its own data. But this DOSN approach to decentralization is not able to establish any kind of regularity over the social network, which is necessary for both real life social community, as well as for OSNs. We have introduced a decentralized architecture of OSNs, called *online social community*, which is able to establish law concerning both the membership of OSC and the manner in which its members interact. The preliminary testing and experiments of our implementation show that our method is feasible and promising.

References

1. Aiello, L.M., Ruffo, G.: LotusNet: Tunable privacy for distributed online social network services. Comput. Commun. **35**(1), 75–88 (2010)
2. Cutillo, L.A., Molva, R., Strufe, T.: Safebook: Feasibility of transitive cooperation for privacy on a decentralized social network. In: WOWMOM, 1–6. IEEE (2009)
3. Bodriagov, O., Buchegger, S.: P2p social networks with broadcast encryption protected privacy, QC 20120126 (2011)
4. Datta, A., Buchegger, S., Vu, L.H., Strufe, T., Rzadca, K.: Decentralized online social networks. In: Furht, B. (ed.) Handb. Soc.Netw. Technol., pp. 349–378. Springer, NewYork (2010)
5. Minsky, N.H.: Law Governed Interaction (LGI): A Distributed Coordination and Control Mechanism (An Introduction, and a Reference Manual), February 2006. http://www.moses.rutgers.edu/

Online Privacy: Risks, Challenges, and New Trends

Esma Aïmeur[(⊠)]

Département d'informatique et de recherche opérationnelle,
Faculté des arts et des sciences, Université de Montréal, Montréal, Canada
aimeur@iro.umontreal.ca

1 Summary

Being on the Internet implies constantly sharing information, personal or not. Nowadays, preserving privacy is not an easy feat: technology is growing too fast, leaving legislation far behind and the level of security awareness is insufficient. Websites and Internet services are collecting personal data with or without the knowledge or consent of users. Not only does new technology readily provide an abundance of methods for organizations to gather and store information, people are also willingly sharing data with increasing frequency, exposing their intimate lives on social media websites. Online data brokers, search engines, data aggregators, geolocation services and many other actors on the web are monetizing our online presence for their own various purposes. Similarly, current technologies including digital devices such as smartphones, tablets, cloud computing/ SaaS, big data, BYOD are posing serious problems for individuals and businesses alike. Data loss is now a common event and the consequences are exceedingly damaging. Although there are means at our disposal to limit or at least acknowledge how and what we're sharing, most do not avail themselves of these tools and so the current situation remains unacceptable. Many privacy enhancing technologies (PETs) have been available for some time, but are not effective enough to prevent re-identification and identity theft.

In this tutorial, we propose how to address various issues inherent to Internet data collection and voluntary information disclosure – the Achilles' heel of privacy. We emphasize the problems and challenges facing privacy nowadays and conclude with some recommendations and best practices.

2 Goals

The goals of this tutorial are: (i) present the different facets of online privacy; (ii) review the various risks and technologies for preserving privacy (iii) provide recommendations and best practices.

3 Outline

Online Privacy. We introduce the ten principles of privacy and present various problems that make it difficult to preserve privacy.

© Springer International Publishing Switzerland 2015
J. Lopez et al. (Eds.): CRiSIS 2014, LNCS 8924, pp. 263–266, 2015.
DOI: 10.1007/978-3-319-17127-2_20

Information Sought. There are diverse types of information that can be obtained: Identifying information (name, age, gender, address, phone number, mother's maiden name, social insurance/security number, personal identification number (PIN), income, occupation, marital status, place of residence, etc.); Buying patterns (stores visited on a regular basis, accounts, assets, liabilities, etc.); Navigation habits (websites visited, frequency of visits, pseudonyms used on forums, acquaintances on the net, etc.); Lifestyle (hobbies, social networks, travel behaviour, vacation periods, etc.); Sensitive data such as employment, medical or criminal records; or Biological information (blood group, genetic code, fingerprints).

Internet Data Collection Techniques

Social Media. By their very nature, those websites aggregate, classify and collect various data about our preferences (*Likes, Shares, Re-tweets,* etc.), our opinions, and what we follow. As they try to mimic our day-to-day life, social networks can provide better insight about how we shop, how we judge products and services and how we share our preferences to marketers and companies.

Online Data Brokers. There are websites such as Abika.com or USSearch.com that, for a fee (sometimes for free), let anyone search for a name in order to retrieve all personal information about him or her available in a multitude of public records. Possible data include the person's name, address, date of birth, marital status, age of children, list of relatives, mortgage information, bankruptcy history and even sensitive information such as Social Security numbers, voting records or court records.

Search Engines. Search tools such as 123people.com, Whozat.com, Pipl.com, Peekyou.com, PeopleSearch.net, Peoplefinder.com, AnyWho, Yasni.com, are also good sources of information for administrators. They are free real-time people search tools that look into nearly every corner of the web to provide and gather information. There are also social network aggregator web sites such as Lifehacker.com, Spokeo. com, Spoke.com and Intelius.com, which collect data from various, online and offline sources (phone directories, social networks, etc.) and have large databases which they may unknowingly sell to malicious people.

Geolocation. Most of today's mobile phones are equipped with a Global Positioning System (GPS) chip, allowing people to know where they are located at any instant. Not only does the GPS user have access to his location, so do applications residing on the device. This is now known as geolocation. Aside from the well-known map functionality made possible by this technology, there are many interesting applications such as FourSquare. They are used to indicate your location to friends and, conversely, see their location. Similarly, Twitter has the option of attaching the user's location to its tweets.

Background Check. As we're adding content each and every day on social network, writing in blogs, and commenting on websites, we are often unaware on how much of that information is freely available for anybody to see. This provides a tremendous source of information for future employers and background check firms. Since a company wants to minimize hiring risks, it will certainly refrain from hiring someone having tasteless pictures of him wandering online or expressing dangerous opinions whenever she or he gets the chance.

Online Conversations. Online conversation is clearly one of the main uses of the Internet: the rise of many webchat applications over the past few years (Facebook Chat, Google Chat, etc.) is a clear sign. IRC, even though we hear less and less about it, is still very active (approximately 400 000 simultaneously connected users on the top 100 servers at the time of writing) is still one of the most popular decentralized platforms. Since its creation, the use of SSL (secure socket layer) was slowly introduced for client-to-server connections, increasing the difficulty to eavesdrop in on a conversation.

Mobile Phones and Applications. Two main operating systems are now shaping the mobile market: Android, pushed by Google, and Apple iOS. Emerging from those two platforms are hundreds of thousands applications, or "apps", available from Google Play or Apple's AppStore. As some applications are tightly coupled with the users' personal data, some can go as far as requiring full access to the SMS information or the users' own address book. Most mobile platforms use two-way synchronization in order to keep the users' information up-to-date. This requires a considerable amount of trust from the user base, since the information shared can be very intimate and diverse: contacts, emails, passwords, credit card number, browser history, WIFI hotspots, WPA keys etc. The mobile-to-computer experience is narrowing the gap, allowing users to share all the information collected from one browser to another.

Big Data. Big data analytics offers powerful opportunities to access insights from new and existing data sets. It is driving data collection to become ubiquitous and permanent. Our digital traces can be used for different purposes including new ways of discriminating.

Privacy Enhanced Technologies (PETs). In order to ensure privacy and anonymity online, some technologies have been made available to the public.

PETs for Anonymization. For anonymous Communication Techniques, various technologies such as *Hordes, Crowds, Anonymizer1*, and private authentication protocols for mobile scenarios, have been proposed to keep users anonymous. Tor is a well known circuit-based low-latency anonymous communication service that addresses perfect forward secrecy, congestion control, directory servers, integrity checking, configurable exit policies, and has a practical design for location-hidden services via rendezvous points. Some ISPs and servers won't allow Tor for the time being.

PETs for Identity Management. There are several approaches in this area. In particular, Liberty Alliance's *federated approach7, OpenID8 authentication* (a decentralized approach), *Identity Metasystem Architecture* and *Generic Bootstrapping Architecture (GBA)* (focused telecommunication). More specifically, there are credential systems that allow authentication (and authorization) without identification by providing only the Personally Identifiable Information (PII) necessary for the transaction or a proof of entitlement.

PETs for Data Processing. In the field of data mining, various methods have been proposed to minimize access to users' privacy: *additive data perturbation; multiplicative data perturbation; data anonymization; secure multi-party computation; privacy preserving multivariate statistical analysis; probabilistic automata; privacy preserving formal methods; sampling-based methods; k anonymization classification; privacy in graph data; and statistical disclosure control.*

Re-identification. Despite all the tools cited above, it is possible to re-identify people—that is, to determine the exact identity of a person by gathering various pieces of information disseminated across the web. Different techniques exist such as: *Linkage, Inference, Homogeneity, Graphs and Machine Learning.*

This process has recently gained popularity following the emergence of personal databases on the Internet. As a consequence, there is no absolute protection, even with Privacy Enhancing Technologies.

Identity Theft. According to the definition given by the OCDE, "identity theft occurs when a party acquires, transfers, possesses, or uses personal information of a natural or legal person in an unauthorized manner, with the intent to commit, or in connection with, fraud or other crimes". People must understand that identity theft not only affects people using their credit card or debit card, it also includes people who use their name, their Social Insurance/Security, Number, online passwords and even their address.

The Right to Erasure. Another hot topic is the right to permanently remove our online presence and how the different services (search engines, social networks, etc.) should behave. Currently, it is very handy to sanitize our online presence as many services are keeping an artificial presence, Facebook being the main culprit here. Since anybody is able to tag any picture (even if the tag isn't linked to a precise profile, it can be used by facial recognition software), a bad picture can therefore be easily be retrieved.

Recommendations. To minimize harm we provide recommendations and best practices for each of the following aspects: technology, social behaviour, ethics, legislation etc. We conclude with the new challenges that face privacy nowadays.

Data Anonymization

Josep Domingo-Ferrer[✉] and Jordi Soria-Comas

Universitat Rovira i Virgili, Tarragona, Catalonia
josep.domingo@urv.cat

1 Summary

Database privacy means different things depending on the context. Here we deal with protecting the privacy of data subjects/respondents by anonymizing their data records: the scenario is a data collector who wants to release useful information while preserving the privacy of data subjects/respondents. We consider the various types of data releases, analyze their privacy implications and review the statistical disclosure control techniques in use.

2 Goals and Audience

The goals of this tutorial are: (i) present the different facets of database privacy; (ii) review the various types of data releases: microdata, tabular data, and queryable databases; (iii) describe the privacy models and techniques being used for each type of data release.

The intended audience consists of academics and practitioners working in information systems, data mining, data science or open data release. For more details and references to the literature on the contents outlined here, see [1].

3 Outline

Respondent privacy has been mainly pursued by statisticians and some computer scientists working in statistical disclosure control (SDC), also known as statistical disclosure limitation (SDL) or inference control.

Two types of disclosure are addressed by SDC. On the one hand, *attribute disclosure* occurs when the value of a confidential attribute of an individual can be determined more accurately with access to the released data than without. On the other hand *identity disclosure* occurs when a record in the anonymized data set can be linked with a respondent's identity. In general, attribute disclosure does not imply identity disclosure, and conversely.

Tabular Data Protection. There are several types of tables. *Frequency tables* display the count of respondents (in $\mathbb{N}$) at the crossing of the categorical attributes; *e.g.* number of patients per disease and municipality. *Magnitude tables* display information on a numerical attribute (in $\mathbb{R}$) at the crossing of the categorical

© Springer International Publishing Switzerland 2015
J. Lopez et al. (Eds.): CRiSIS 2014, LNCS 8924, pp. 267–271, 2015.
DOI: 10.1007/978-3-319-17127-2_21

attributes; *e.g.* average age of patients per disease and municipality. *Linked tables:* two tables are linked if they share some of the crossed categorical attributes, *e.g.* "Disease" × "Town" and "Disease" × "Gender".

Whatever the type of the table, marginal row and column totals must be preserved. Even if tables display aggregate information, disclosure attacks are possible:

– *External attack.* E.g., let a released frequency table "Ethnicity" × "Town" contain a single respondent for ethnicity E_i and town T_j. Then if a magnitude table is released with the average blood pressure for each ethnicity and each town, the exact blood pressure of the only respondent with ethnicity E_i in town T_j is publicly disclosed.
– *Internal attack.* If there are only two respondents for ethnicity E_i and town T_j, the blood pressure of each of them is disclosed to the other.
– *Dominance attack.* If one (or few) respondents dominate the contributions to a cell in a magnitude table, the dominant respondent(s) can upper-bound the contributions of the rest.

SDC principles for table protection can be classified into:

– *Non-perturbative.* They do not modify the values in the cells, but they may suppress or recode them. Best known methods: *cell suppression (CS)*, *recoding of categorical attributes*.
– *Perturbative.* They modify the values in the cells. Best known methods: *controlled rounding (CR)* and the recent *controlled tabular adjustment (CTA)*.

Cell Suppression. In this approach, *sensitive cells* are identified in a table, using a so-called *sensitivity rule*. Then the values of sensitive cells are suppressed (primary suppressions). After that, additional cells are suppressed (secondary suppressions) to prevent recovery of primary suppressions from row and/or column marginals. Examples of sensitivity rules for primary suppressions are (n, k)-dominance, the pq-rule and the $p\%$-rule. As to secondary suppressions, usually one attempts to minimize either the number of secondary suppressions or their pooled magnitude (complex optimization problems). Optimization methods are heuristic, based on mixed linear integer programming or networks flows (the latter for 2-D tables only). Implementations are available in the τ-Argus package.

Controlled Rounding and Controlled Tabular Adjustment. CR rounds values in the table to multiples of a rounding base (marginals may have to be rounded as well). CTA modifies the values in the table to prevent inference of sensitive cell values within a prescribed protection interval. CTA attempts to find the *closest* table to the original one that protects all sensitive cells. CTA optimization is typically based on mixed linear integer programming and entails less information loss than CS.

Queryable Database Protection. There are two main SDC principles for queryable database protection:

- *Query perturbation.* Perturbation (noise addition) can be applied to the micro-data records on which queries are computed (*input perturbation*) or to the query result after computing it on the original data (*output perturbation*).
- *Query restriction.* The database refuses to answer certain queries.

Differential Privacy for Output Perturbation. A randomized query function F gives ε-differential privacy if, for all data sets D_1, D_2 such that one can be obtained from the other by modifying a single record, and all $S \subset Range(F)$, it holds that

$$\Pr(F(D_1) \in S) \leq \exp(\varepsilon) \times \Pr(F(D_2) \in S).$$

Query Restriction. This is the right approach if the user does require deter-ministically correct answers and these answers have to be exact (*i.e.* a number). Exact answers may be very disclosive, so it may be necessary to refuse answering certain queries at some stage. A common criterion to decide whether a query can be answered is *query set size control*: the answer to a query is refused if this query together with the previously answered ones isolates too small a set of records. The main problem of query restriction are: (i) the computational burden to keep track of previous queries; (ii) collusion attacks can circumvent the query limit.

Tracker Attacks. Query set size control is justified by the existence of trackers, pointed out already in 1979 by Denning *et al.* A tracker is a sequence of queries to an on-line statistical database whose answers disclose the attribute values for a small subgroup of individual target records or even a single record.

Microdata Protection. A *microdata* file **X** with s respondents and t attributes is an $s \times t$ matrix where X_{ij} is the value of attribute j for respondent i. Attributes can be numerical (*e.g.* age, blood pressure) or categorical (*e.g.* gender, job). Depending on their disclosure potential, attributes can be classified as:

- *Identifiers.* Attributes that *unambiguously* identify the respondent (*e.g.* pass-port no., social security no., name-surname, etc.).
- *Quasi-identifiers or key attributes.* They identify the respondent with some ambiguity, but their combination may lead to unambiguous identification (*e.g.* address, gender, age, telephone no., etc.).
- *Confidential outcome attributes.* They contain sensitive respondent informa-tion (*e.g.* salary, religion, diagnosis, etc.).
- *Non-confidential outcome attributes.* Other attributes which contain non-sensitive respondent info.

Identifiers are of course suppressed in anonymized data sets. Disclosure risk comes from quasi-identifiers (QIs), but these cannot be suppressed because they often have high analytical value. Indeed, QIs can be used to link anonymized records to external non-anonymous databases (with identifiers) that contain the same or similar QIs; this leads to *re-identification*. Hence, anonymization proce-dures must deal with QIs.

There are two principles used in microdata protection, data *masking* and data *synthesis*:

- Masking generates a modified version $\mathbf{X}'$ of the original microdata set $\mathbf{X}$, and it can be *perturbative masking* ($\mathbf{X}'$ of the original microdata set $\mathbf{X}$) or *non-perturbative masking* ($\mathbf{X}'$ is obtained from $\mathbf{X}$ by partial suppressions or reduction of detail, yet the data in $\mathbf{X}'$ are still true).
- Synthesis is about generating synthetic (*i.e.* artificial) data $\mathbf{X}'$ that preserve some preselected properties of the original data $\mathbf{X}$.

Perturbative Masking. There are several principles for perturbative masking:

- *Noise addition.* This principle is only applicable to numerical microdata. The most popular method consists of adding to each record in the data set a noise vector drawn from a $N(0, \alpha\Sigma)$, with Σ being the covariance matrix of the original data. Means and correlations of original data can be preserved in the masked data by choosing the appropriate α. Additional linear transformations of the masked data can be made to ensure that the sample covariance matrix of the masked attributes is an unbiased estimator for Σ.
- *Microaggregation.* Microaggregation partitions records in a data set into groups containing each at least k records; then the average record of each group is published. Groups are formed by the criterion of maximum within-group similarity: the more similar the records in a group, the less information loss is incurred when replacing them by the average record. There exist microaggregation methods for numerical and also categorical microdata.
- *Data swapping.* Values of attributes are exchanged among individual records, so that low-order frequency counts or marginals are maintained. Although swapping was proposed for categorical attributes, its *rank swapping* variant is also applicable to numerical attributes.
- *Post-randomization.* The PRAM method works on categorical attributes: each value of a confidential attribute is stochastically changed to a different value according to a prescribed Markov matrix.

Non-perturbative Masking. Principles used for non-perturbative masking include:

- *Sampling.* Instead of publishing the original data file, only a sample of it is published. A low sampling fraction may suffice to anonymize categorical data (probability that a sample unique is also a population unique is low). For continuous data, sampling alone does not suffice.
- *Generalization.* This principle is also known as coarsening or global recoding. For a categorical attribute, several categories are combined to form new (less specific) categories; for a numerical attribute, numerical values are replaced by intervals (discretization).
- *Top/bottom coding.* Values above, resp. below, a certain threshold are lumped into a single top, resp. bottom, category.
- *Local suppression.* Certain values of individual attributes are suppressed in order to increase the set of records agreeing on a combination of quasi-identifier attributes. This principle can be combined with generalization.

k-Anonymity, Generalization and Microaggregation. A data set is said to satisfy *k*-anonymity if each combination of values of the quasi-identifier attributes in it is shared by at least *k* records. The principles originally proposed to attain *k*-anonymity were generalization and local suppression on the quasi-identifiers. Later, microaggregation was shown to also be a valid approach.

Synthetic Microdata Generation. Rubin proposed this principle, which consists of randomly generating data in such a way that some statistics or relationships of the original data are preserved. The advantage of synthetic data is that no respondent re-identification seems possible, because data are artificial. There are downsides, too. If a synthetic record matches by chance a respondent's attributes, re-identification is likely and the respondent will find little comfort in the data being synthetic. Data utility of synthetic microdata is limited to the statistics and relationships preselected at the outset: analyses on random subdomains are no longer preserved. Partially synthetic or hybrid data are more flexible.

Reference

1. Hundepool, A., Domingo-Ferrer, J., Franconi, L., Giessing, S., Schulte Nordholt, E., Spicer, K., de Wolf, P.-P.: Statistical Disclosure Control. Wiley, New York (2012)

Security of the Android Operating System

Yury Zhauniarovich[(✉)]

University of Trento, 38100 Trento, Italy
yury.zhauniarovich@unitn.it

1 Summary

Modern smartphones become an everyday part of our life. Checking emails,
browsing the Internet, photographing, navigation are successfully carried out
with the help of smartphones. Obviously, this happens because mobile phones
have been provided with the useful functions.

In the smartphone domain, the Android OS is by far the most popular platform being installed on about 79 % of all new mobile devices [3]. Those figures clearly show the pervasiveness of Android, mostly justified by its openness.
Being a part of the Open Handset Alliance initiative, Google released most of the
Android code under open source licences. Thus, we have an ability to explore this
operating system, change platform components and build customized images of
the Android OS. Moreover, the third-party applications can be easily developed
and tested on this platform without publishing them in an application market.
Hence, it is not surprisingly why this platform is so popular nowadays.

Unfortunately, the information about the intrinsics of this operating system is sparse and scattered around different resources. This does not concern
Android application programming during the last several years lots of books and
web resources appeared describing the process and best practices how to develop
Android apps. Moreover, the official documentation about app programming is
quite complete and can be treated as a credible source of information on that
topic. On the contrary, the official documentation about the system programming is poor and gives you good insights about how to download the Android
sources and build them. Additional information only partially covers the topics and does not provide you with the whole picture. The situation in case of
security is even more dismal.

In this tutorial we try to close the gap. We consider the layered structure of
the operating system and examine the main security mechanisms implemented
in Android. In particular, we inspect the sandboxing mechanism implemented at
the Linux Kernel level. We will consider how the kernel enforces the isolation of
applications and operating system components exploiting standard Linux facilities (process separation and Discretionary Access Control over network sockets
and filesystem). Further, we plan to consider the security mechanisms implemented at other layers. In particular, we give an understanding how the security
is designed at the Android Middleware level. On this level an IPC Reference
Monitor mediates all the communications between processes and controls how
applications access the components of the system and other apps. In Android,

© Springer International Publishing Switzerland 2015
J. Lopez et al. (Eds.): CRiSIS 2014, LNCS 8924, pp. 272–274, 2015.
DOI: 10.1007/978-3-319-17127-2_22

IPC Reference Monitor follows Mandatory Access Control (MAC) access control type and is based on permission system. The implementation details of the permission system is also planned to be considered in the tutorial.

Other notable part of the tutorial is dedicated to the limitations in the Android operating system and the state-of-the-art research approaches that close this gap. In particular, we plan to consider such systems as CRêPE [1], MOSES [6], FSquaDRA [5], etc.

2   Potential Audience

- Android security researchers
- Researchers working in the field of mobile and desktop operating systems
- Industry researchers and engineers interested in the deep understanding of the security procurement in the Android operating system
- Researchers, faculty and graduate students who explore the limitations of the Android operating system and its ecosystem
- Android application developers.

3   Expected Prerequisite Knowledge

- Basic knowledge of the Linux operating system and its security mechanisms
- Basic knowledge of Java/C/C++
- Experience in Android app development is a plus.

4   Outline

1. Introduction
2. Android Stack
3. Android Security
    - Linux Kernel Level
    - Native Userspace Level
    - Application Framework Level
    - Application Level
4. Android Security Extensions: Open Problems and Solutions
5. Conclusions and Questions.

References

1. Conti, M., Crispo, B., Fernandes, E., Zhauniarovich, Y.: CRêPE: a system for enforcing fine-grained context-related policies on android. IEEE Trans. Inf. Forensics Secur. **7**(5), 1426–1438 (2012)
2. Fernandes, E.: Instant Android Systems Development How-to. Packt Publishing Ltd, Birmingham (2013)

3. Gartner: Gartner Says Smartphone Sales Grew 46.5 Percent in Second Quarter of 2013 and Exceeded Feature Phone Sales for First Time. http://www.gartner.com/newsroom/id/2573415
4. Zhauniarovich, Y.: Android Security (and Not) Internals. Web (2014). http://zhauniarovich.com/files/asani/asani.pdf
5. Zhauniarovich, Y., Gadyatskaya, O., Crispo, B., La Spina, F., Moser, E.: FSquaDRA: fast detection of repackaged applications. In: Atluri, V., Pernul, P. (eds.) DBSec 2014. LNCS, vol. 8566, pp. 131–146. Springer, Heidelberg (2014)
6. Zhauniarovich, Y., Russello, G., Conti, M., Crispo, B., Fernandes, E.: MOSES: supporting and enforcing security profiles on smartphones. IEEE Trans. Dependable Secure Comput. **11**(3), 211–223 (2014)

Author Index